MARK MILLAR
WRITER

DAVE JOHNSON & KILIAN PLUNKETT
PENCILLERS

ANDREW ROBINSON & WALDEN WONG
INKERS

PAUL MOUNTS **COLORIST**
KEN LOPEZ **LETTERER**
DAVE JOHNSON **COVER PAINTER**

SUPERMAN CREATED BY
JERRY SIEGEL & JOE SHUSTER

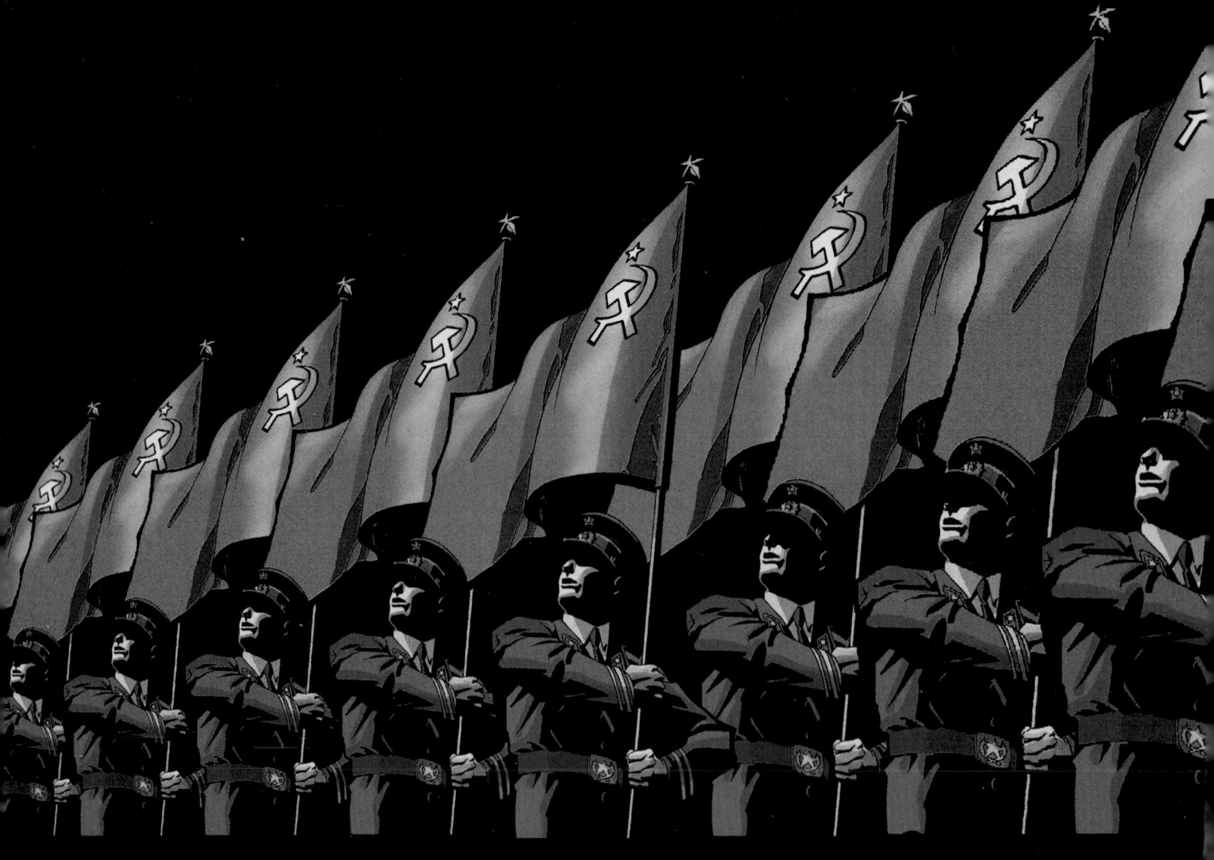

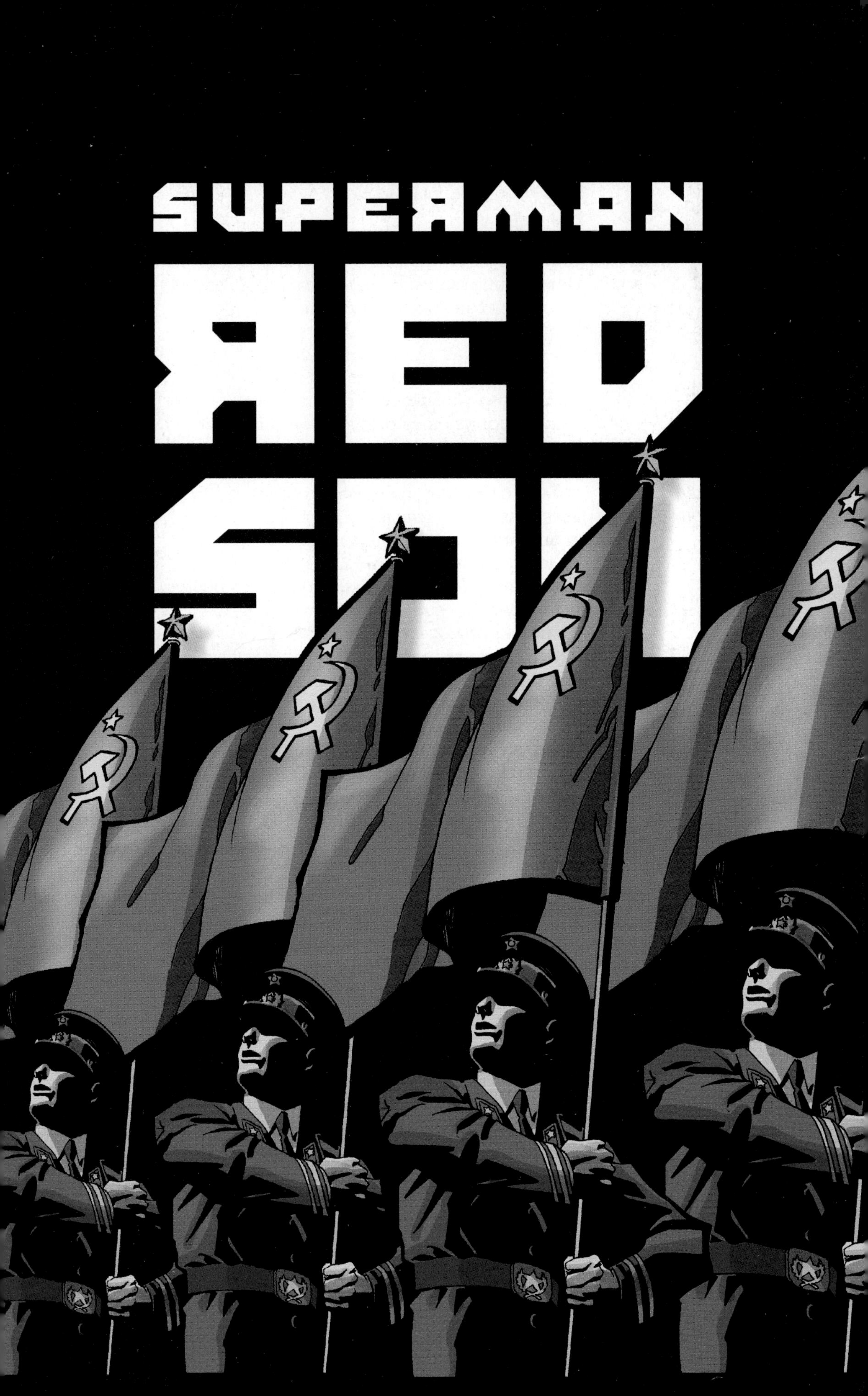
SUPERMAN
RED SON

MIKE McAVENNIE & TOM PALMER JR. EDITORS – ORIGINAL SERIES
MAUREEN McTIGUE ASSISTANT EDITOR – ORIGINAL SERIES
ANTON KAWASAKI EDITOR
ROBBIN BROSTERMAN DESIGN DIRECTOR – BOOKS
BOB HARRAS VP – EDITOR-IN-CHIEF
DIANE NELSON PRESIDENT
DAN DIDIO AND **JIM LEE** CO-PUBLISHERS
GEOFF JOHNS CHIEF CREATIVE OFFICER
JOHN ROOD EXECUTIVE VP – SALES, MARKETING AND BUSINESS DEVELOPMENT
AMY GENKINS SENIOR VP – BUSINESS AND LEGAL AFFAIRS
NAIRI GARDINER SENIOR VP – FINANCE
JEFF BOISON VP – PUBLISHING OPERATIONS
MARK CHIARELLO VP – ART DIRECTION AND DESIGN
JOHN CUNNINGHAM VP – MARKETING
TERRI CUNNINGHAM VP – TALENT RELATIONS AND SERVICES
ALISON GILL SENIOR VP – MANUFACTURING AND OPERATIONS
HANK KANALZ SENIOR VP – DIGITAL
JAY KOGAN VP – BUSINESS AND LEGAL AFFAIRS, PUBLISHING
JACK MAHAN VP – BUSINESS AFFAIRS, TALENT
NICK NAPOLITANO VP – MANUFACTURING ADMINISTRATION
SUE POHJA VP – BOOK SALES
COURTNEY SIMMONS SENIOR VP – PUBLICITY
BOB WAYNE SENIOR VP – SALES

SUPERMAN: RED SON

Published by DC Comics, 1700 Broadway, New York, New York, 10019.
Cover, introduction and compilation Copyright © 2004 DC Comics. All Rights Reserved.
Originally published in single magazine form in SUPERMAN: RED SON #1-3.
Copyright © 2003 DC Comics. All Rights Reserved. All characters, the distinctive
likenesses thereof and related elements featured in this publication are trademarks of DC Comics.
The stories, characters and incidents featured in this publication are entirely fictional.
DC Comics does not read or accept unsolicited submissions of ideas, stories or artwork.

DC Comics, 1700 Broadway, New York, NY 10019
A Warner Bros. Entertainment Company
Printed by RR Donnelley, Salem, VA, USA. 1/11/13. Eleventh Printing.
ISBN: 978-1-4012-0191-3
Cover painting by Dave Johnson
Logo design by Steve Cook

Library of Congress Cataloging-in-Publication Data

Millar, Mark.
Superman. Red son / Mark Millar, Dave Johnson, Kilian Plunkett , Andrew Robinson, Walden Wong.
p. cm.
"Originally published in single magazine form in Superman: Red Son #1-3."
ISBN 978-1-4012-0191-3
1. Graphic novels. I. Johnson, Dave, 1966- II. Plunkett, Kilian. III. Robinson, Andrew (Andrew C.) IV. Wong, Walden. V.
Title. VI. Title: Red son.
PN6728.S9M567 2012
741.5'973–dc23
2012040581

Mom, apple pie, Chevrolet, and SUPERMAN.

INTRODUCTION BY TOM DeSANTO

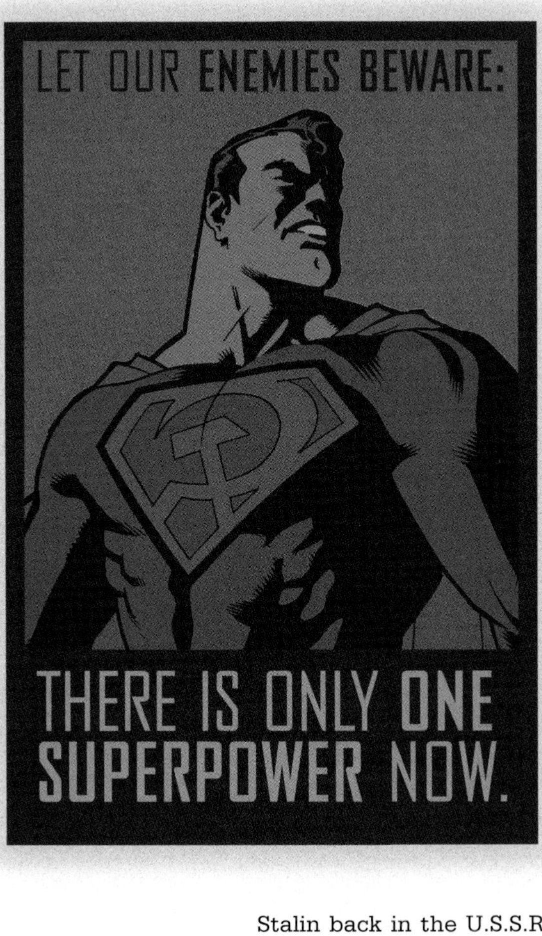
LET OUR ENEMIES BEWARE:
THERE IS ONLY ONE SUPERPOWER NOW.

With all due respect to Mickey Mouse, there is perhaps no greater American icon than the Man of Steel. When Mark Millar first told me the premise of RED SON — of taking the American icon of Superman and putting him in the ultimate what-if scenario — I was shocked. Imagine Superman wasn't red, white, and blue ...imagine Superman was red... Communist red? Instead of baby Kal-El landing in the loving arms of Ma and Pa Kent in the good ol' U.S. of A., he lands in the loving arms of Josef Stalin back in the U.S.S.R. No longer Superman American icon, but Superman Soviet comrade — needless to say, the premise is more than intriguing. In the hands of a lesser writer the story would have fallen into cookie cutter, black and white, America good, Soviets bad, feel-good propaganda. Thank God Mark Millar is not a lesser writer. And thank God his favorite color seems to be gray.

All that morally questionable gray is captured in what seems to be 1950s Technicolor glory. Fortunately the artistic palette of Dave Johnson's and Kilian Plunkett's pencils, Andrew Robinson's and Walden Wong's inks, and Paul Mount's colors combine to create a Kafkaesque, Max Fleischer cartoon that collides with the best of propaganda art. It is not like you are reading a graphic novel but watching a movie. This book is everything I love about comics — a great morality tale with art that leaps off the page and into your mind's eye.

Even if you have never read a comic before, you can pick up RED SON and follow the story and enjoy a great ride. But don't be fooled; it is much more than that. RED SON is a sharp social commentary on capitalism vs. communism and current American foreign policy. Not bad for a funny book. If you are a comic fan, then you will notice the detail to the Superman mythology. Having read the book three times, I find such an attention to detail that I am still discovering something new in the words or art that I somehow had missed before. All the elements that make Superman great are there: Lex Luthor, Lois Lane (oops, I mean Lois *Luthor*), Jimmy Olsen, even Batman, Wonder Woman, and the greatest Green Lantern of them all, Hal Jordan. All of them the same, yet different — all reinvented. Even though the traditional "S" on his chest has been replaced by the hammer and sickle, one thing is still the same — Superman believes he is doing the right thing. He has the best of intentions, but we all know what the road to hell is paved with. Yet Superman still wants to

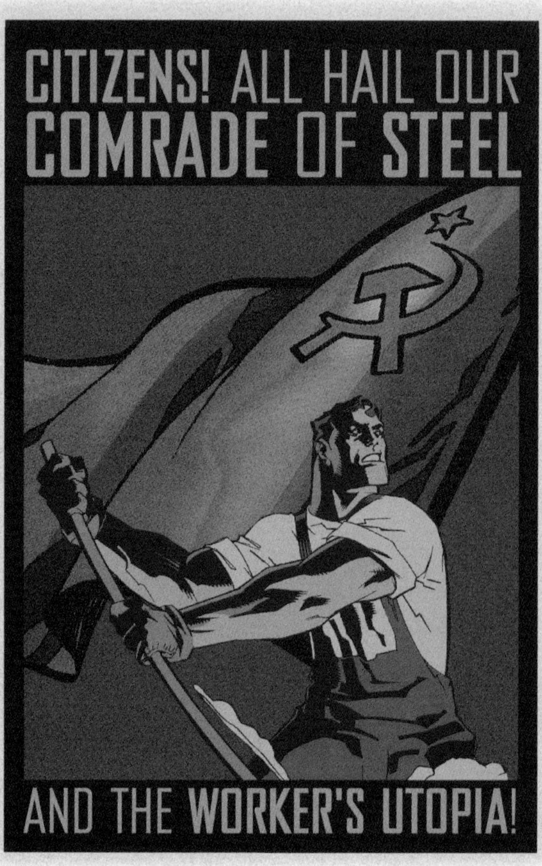
CITIZENS! ALL HAIL OUR
COMRADE OF STEEL
AND THE WORKER'S UTOPIA!

make the world safe, except this time he is willing to force us to see that his way is the best way.

Ben Franklin once wrote, "Those who would sacrifice their freedom for safety will find they inherit neither." That line, written over two hundred years ago, may have more meaning now than ever before. Good writing challenges the way you think. Great writing *changes* the way you think. RED SON is great writing. Mark actually started writing RED SON around 1995, and we all know it is a much different world than those days. Millar was able to gaze into his Orwellian crystal ball and see Superman as the poster child for Big Brother. The all X-ray vision seeing, all super-hearing listening, all-knowing, all-powerful Big Brother. All-encompassing security, like a baby in a super blanket — just one thing...don't think for yourself and don't challenge the system. Free will or freedom in exchange for absolute security — I don't think Ben Franklin would have liked that idea. Just remember Superman is watching you. But who's watching the watchmen? Mark Millar is, that's who.

CRIME DOESN'T EXIST. ACCIDENTS NEVER HAPPEN. ALL DUE TO
PRESIDENT SUPERMAN!

Be good,

Tom DeSanto

OCTOBER 9, 2003

A self-described pop culture junkie and longtime comic book fan, Tom DeSanto is a writer/producer who has worked on various films such as Apt Pupil, X-Men *and* X2: X-Men United, *among other projects. He currently lives in Los Angeles.*

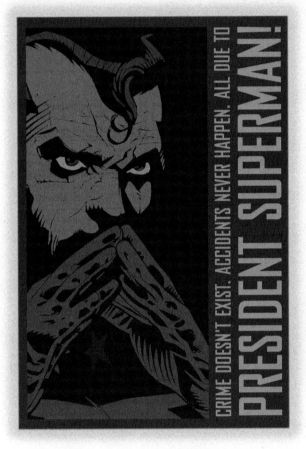

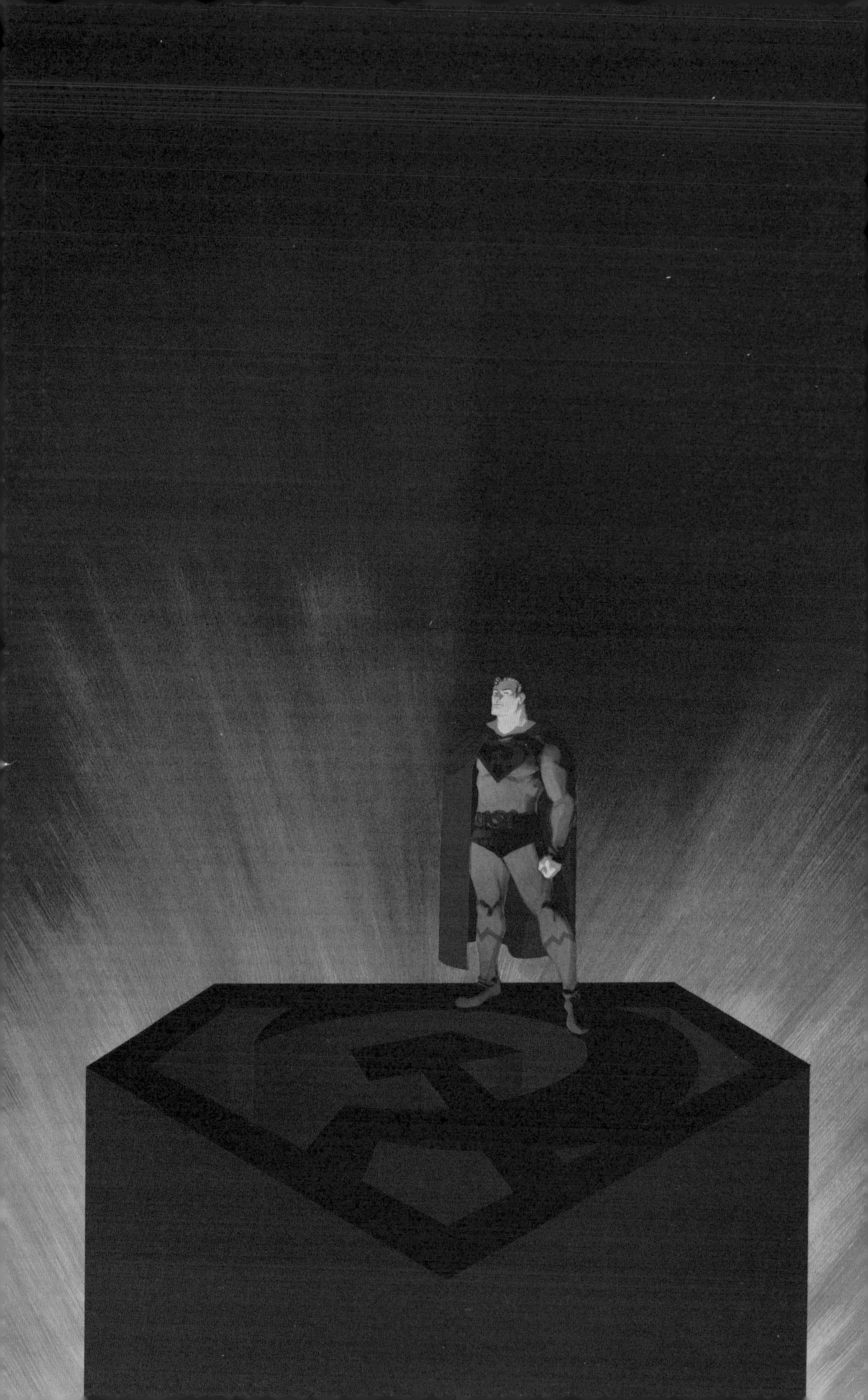

SUPERMAN RED SON

RED SON RISING

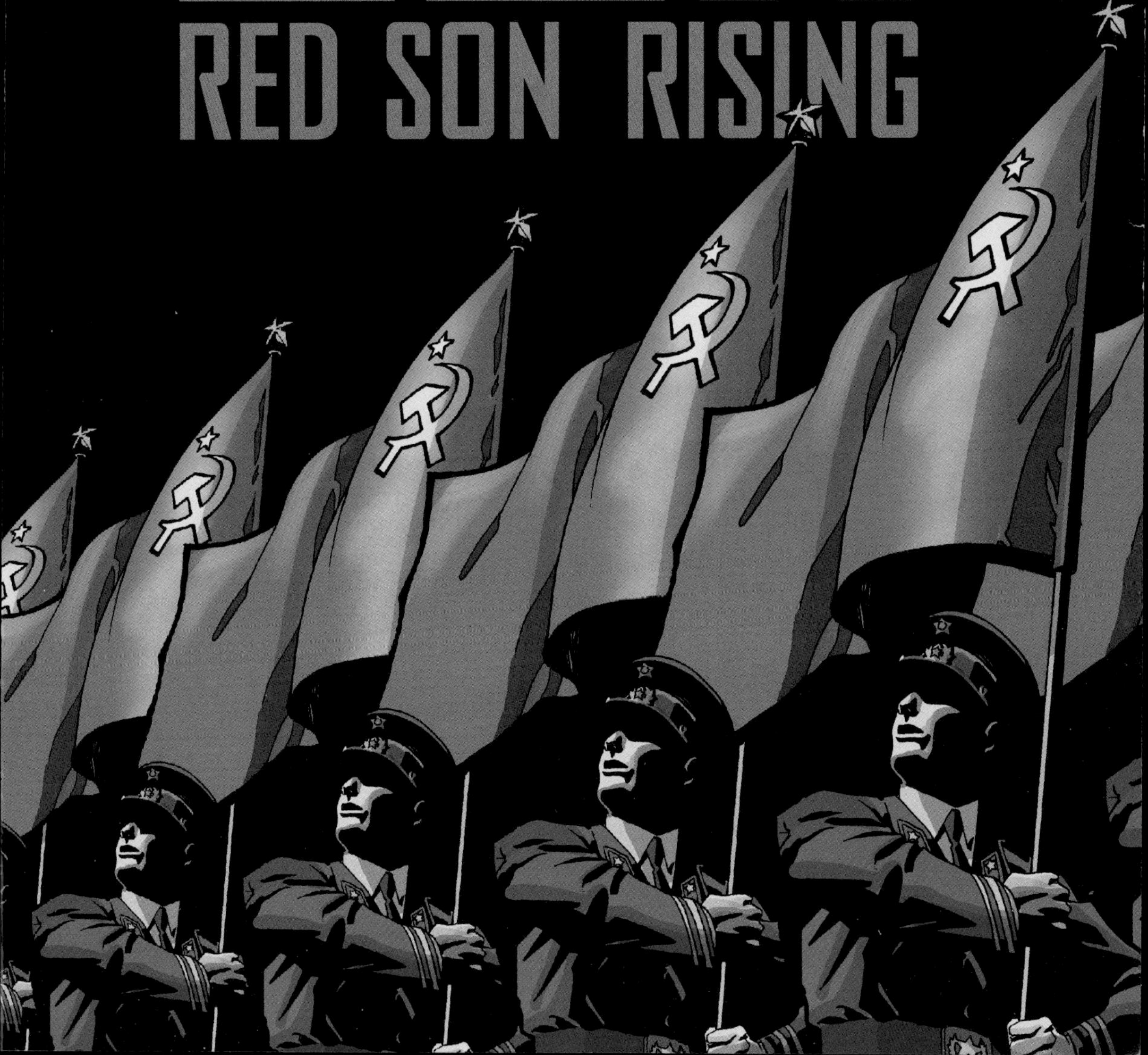

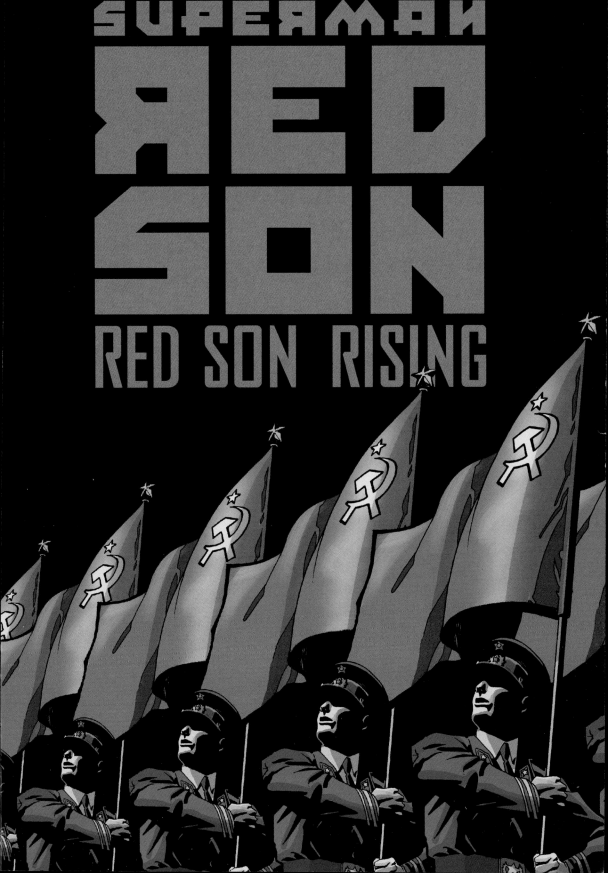

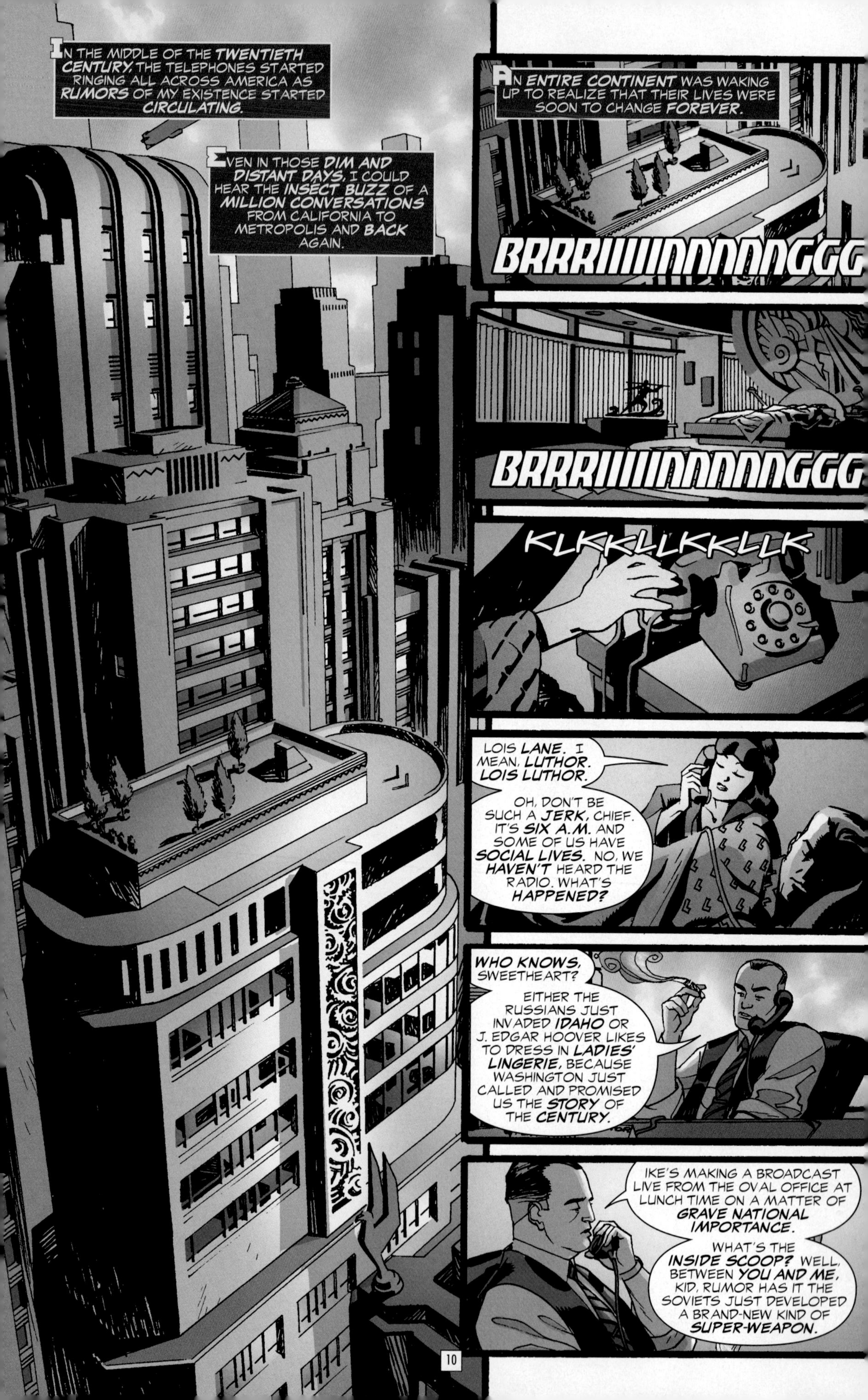

IN THE MIDDLE OF THE TWENTIETH CENTURY, THE TELEPHONES STARTED RINGING ALL ACROSS AMERICA AS RUMORS OF MY EXISTENCE STARTED CIRCULATING.
EVEN IN THOSE DIM AND DISTANT DAYS, I COULD HEAR THE INSECT BUZZ OF A MILLION CONVERSATIONS FROM CALIFORNIA TO METROPOLIS AND BACK AGAIN.
AN ENTIRE CONTINENT WAS WAKING UP TO REALIZE THAT THEIR LIVES WERE SOON TO CHANGE FOREVER.
BRRRIIIIINNNNNGGG
BRRRIIIIINNNNNGGG
KLKKLLKKLLK
LOIS LANE. I MEAN, LUTHOR. LOIS LUTHOR.
OH, DON'T BE SUCH A JERK, CHIEF. IT'S SIX A.M. AND SOME OF US HAVE SOCIAL LIVES. NO, WE HAVEN'T HEARD THE RADIO. WHAT'S HAPPENED?
WHO KNOWS, SWEETHEART?
EITHER THE RUSSIANS JUST INVADED IDAHO OR J. EDGAR HOOVER LIKES TO DRESS IN LADIES' LINGERIE, BECAUSE WASHINGTON JUST CALLED AND PROMISED US THE STORY OF THE CENTURY.
IKE'S MAKING A BROADCAST LIVE FROM THE OVAL OFFICE AT LUNCH TIME ON A MATTER OF GRAVE NATIONAL IMPORTANCE.
WHAT'S THE INSIDE SCOOP? WELL, BETWEEN YOU AND ME, KID, RUMOR HAS IT THE SOVIETS JUST DEVELOPED A BRAND-NEW KIND OF SUPER-WEAPON.

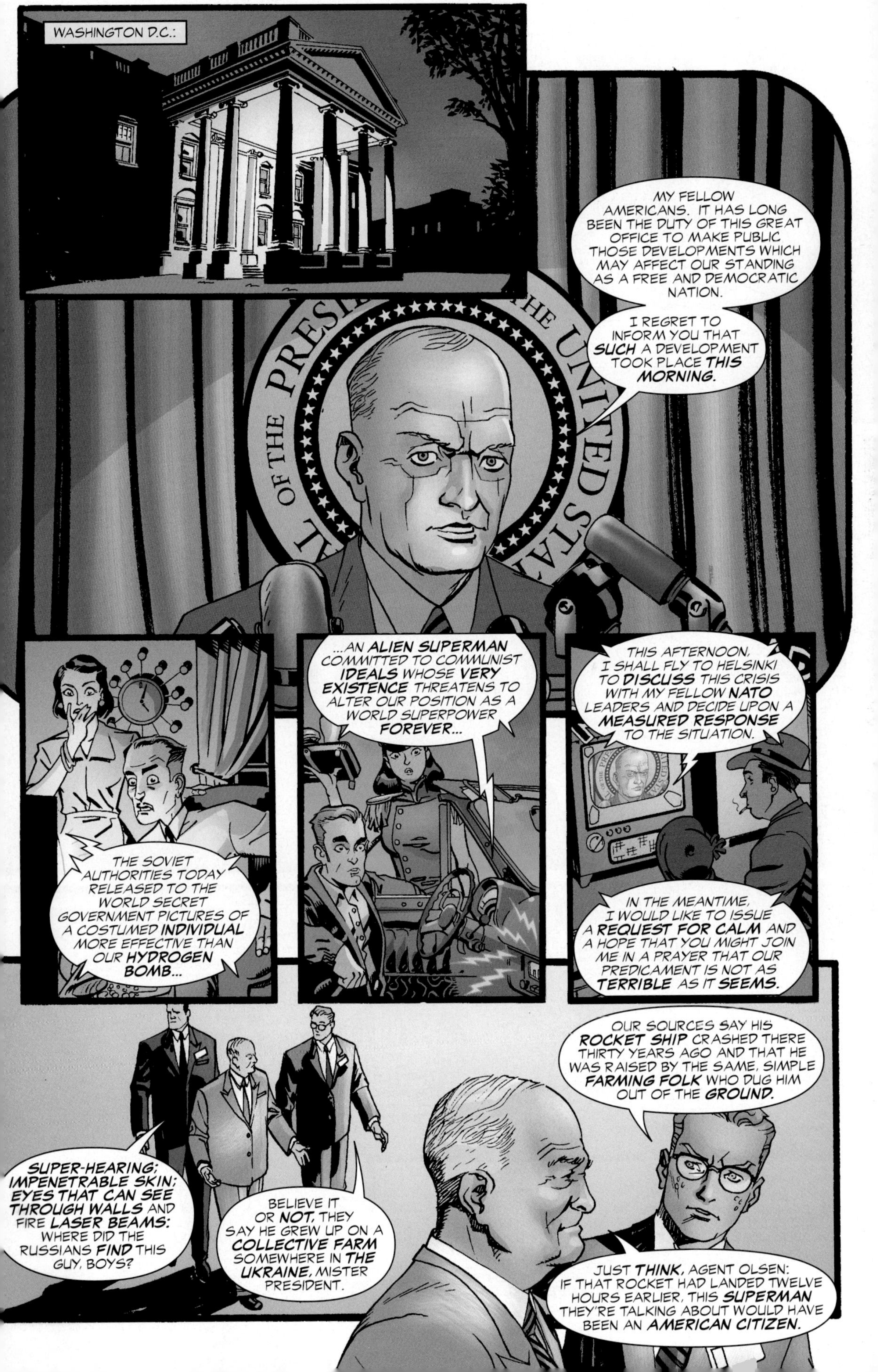
WASHINGTON D.C.:
MY FELLOW AMERICANS. IT HAS LONG BEEN THE DUTY OF THIS GREAT OFFICE TO MAKE PUBLIC THOSE DEVELOPMENTS WHICH MAY AFFECT OUR STANDING AS A FREE AND DEMOCRATIC NATION.
I REGRET TO INFORM YOU THAT SUCH A DEVELOPMENT TOOK PLACE THIS MORNING.
THE SOVIET AUTHORITIES TODAY RELEASED TO THE WORLD SECRET GOVERNMENT PICTURES OF A COSTUMED INDIVIDUAL MORE EFFECTIVE THAN OUR HYDROGEN BOMB...
...AN ALIEN SUPERMAN COMMITTED TO COMMUNIST IDEALS WHOSE VERY EXISTENCE THREATENS TO ALTER OUR POSITION AS A WORLD SUPERPOWER FOREVER...
THIS AFTERNOON, I SHALL FLY TO HELSINKI TO DISCUSS THIS CRISIS WITH MY FELLOW NATO LEADERS AND DECIDE UPON A MEASURED RESPONSE TO THE SITUATION.
IN THE MEANTIME, I WOULD LIKE TO ISSUE A REQUEST FOR CALM AND A HOPE THAT YOU MIGHT JOIN ME IN A PRAYER THAT OUR PREDICAMENT IS NOT AS TERRIBLE AS IT SEEMS.
SUPER-HEARING; IMPENETRABLE SKIN; EYES THAT CAN SEE THROUGH WALLS AND FIRE LASER BEAMS: WHERE DID THE RUSSIANS FIND THIS GUY, BOYS?
BELIEVE IT OR NOT, THEY SAY HE GREW UP ON A COLLECTIVE FARM SOMEWHERE IN THE UKRAINE, MISTER PRESIDENT.
OUR SOURCES SAY HIS ROCKET SHIP CRASHED THERE THIRTY YEARS AGO AND THAT HE WAS RAISED BY THE SAME, SIMPLE FARMING FOLK WHO DUG HIM OUT OF THE GROUND.
JUST THINK, AGENT OLSEN: IF THAT ROCKET HAD LANDED TWELVE HOURS EARLIER, THIS SUPERMAN THEY'RE TALKING ABOUT WOULD HAVE BEEN AN AMERICAN CITIZEN.

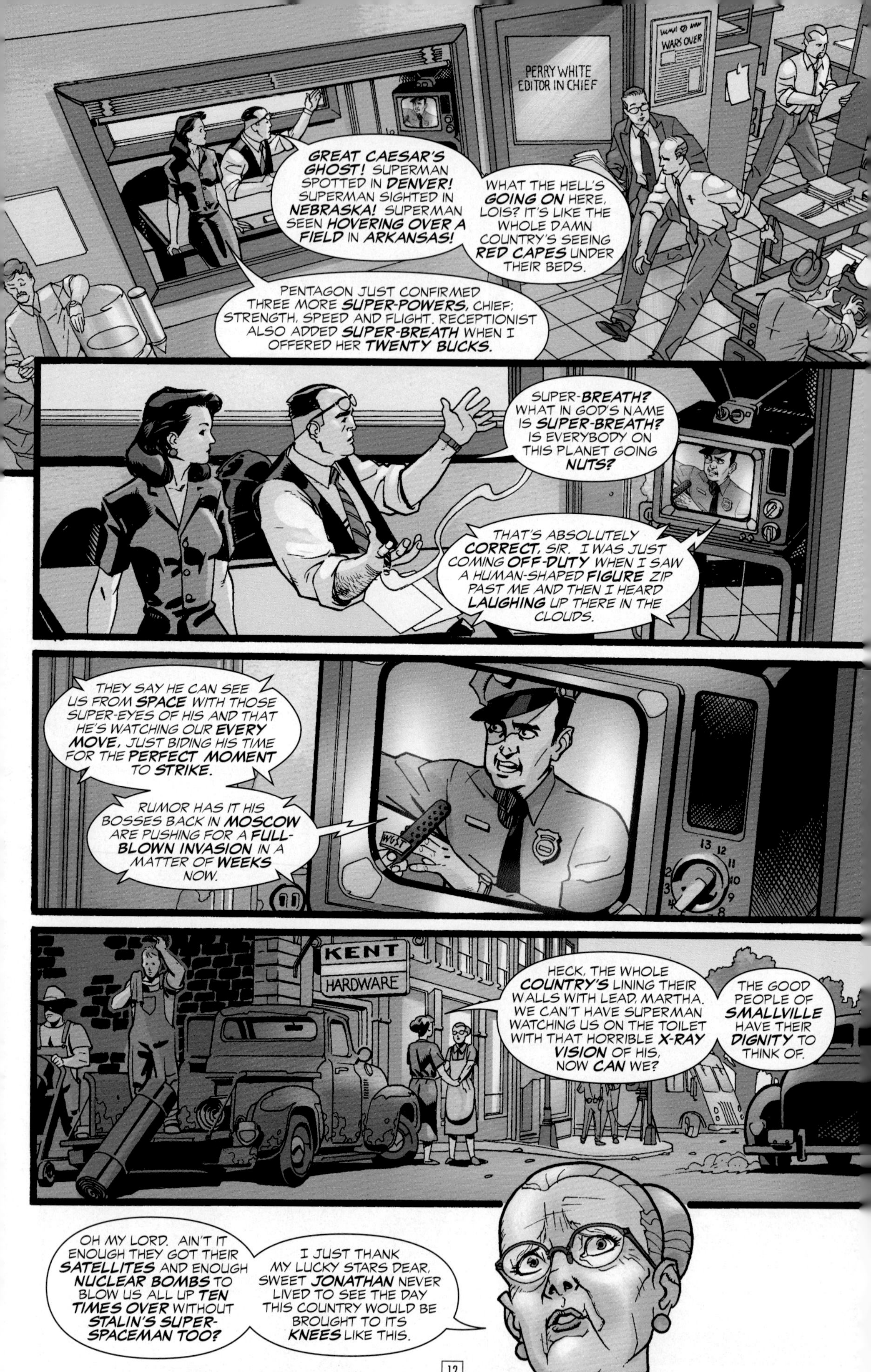
PERRY WHITE EDITOR IN CHIEF
WARS OVER
GREAT CAESAR'S GHOST! SUPERMAN SPOTTED IN DENVER! SUPERMAN SIGHTED IN NEBRASKA! SUPERMAN SEEN HOVERING OVER A FIELD IN ARKANSAS!
WHAT THE HELL'S GOING ON HERE, LOIS? IT'S LIKE THE WHOLE DAMN COUNTRY'S SEEING RED CAPES UNDER THEIR BEDS.
PENTAGON JUST CONFIRMED THREE MORE SUPER-POWERS, CHIEF; STRENGTH, SPEED AND FLIGHT. RECEPTIONIST ALSO ADDED SUPER-BREATH WHEN I OFFERED HER TWENTY BUCKS.
SUPER-BREATH? WHAT IN GOD'S NAME IS SUPER-BREATH? IS EVERYBODY ON THIS PLANET GOING NUTS?
THAT'S ABSOLUTELY CORRECT, SIR. I WAS JUST COMING OFF-DUTY WHEN I SAW A HUMAN-SHAPED FIGURE ZIP PAST ME AND THEN I HEARD LAUGHING UP THERE IN THE CLOUDS.
THEY SAY HE CAN SEE US FROM SPACE WITH THOSE SUPER-EYES OF HIS AND THAT HE'S WATCHING OUR EVERY MOVE, JUST BIDING HIS TIME FOR THE PERFECT MOMENT TO STRIKE.
RUMOR HAS IT HIS BOSSES BACK IN MOSCOW ARE PUSHING FOR A FULL-BLOWN INVASION IN A MATTER OF WEEKS NOW.
KENT
HARDWARE
HECK, THE WHOLE COUNTRY'S LINING THEIR WALLS WITH LEAD, MARTHA. WE CAN'T HAVE SUPERMAN WATCHING US ON THE TOILET WITH THAT HORRIBLE X-RAY VISION OF HIS, NOW CAN WE?
THE GOOD PEOPLE OF SMALLVILLE HAVE THEIR DIGNITY TO THINK OF.
OH MY LORD. AIN'T IT ENOUGH THEY GOT THEIR SATELLITES AND ENOUGH NUCLEAR BOMBS TO BLOW US ALL UP TEN TIMES OVER WITHOUT STALIN'S SUPER-SPACEMAN TOO?
I JUST THANK MY LUCKY STARS DEAR, SWEET JONATHAN NEVER LIVED TO SEE THE DAY THIS COUNTRY WOULD BE BROUGHT TO ITS KNEES LIKE THIS.

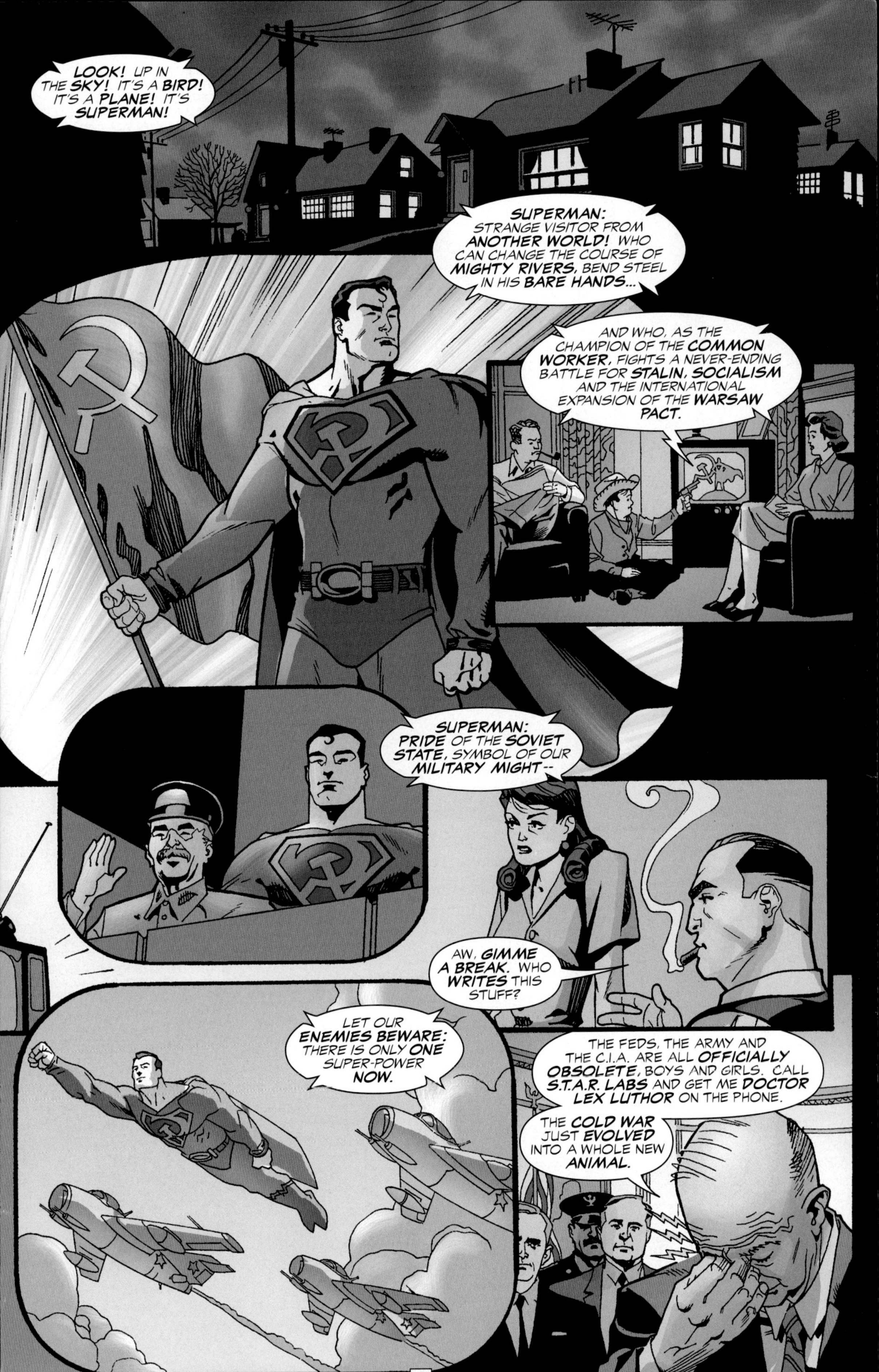
LOOK! UP IN THE SKY! IT'S A BIRD! IT'S A PLANE! IT'S SUPERMAN!
SUPERMAN: STRANGE VISITOR FROM ANOTHER WORLD! WHO CAN CHANGE THE COURSE OF MIGHTY RIVERS, BEND STEEL IN HIS BARE HANDS...
AND WHO, AS THE CHAMPION OF THE COMMON WORKER, FIGHTS A NEVER-ENDING BATTLE FOR STALIN, SOCIALISM AND THE INTERNATIONAL EXPANSION OF THE WARSAW PACT.
SUPERMAN: PRIDE OF THE SOVIET STATE, SYMBOL OF OUR MILITARY MIGHT--
AW, GIMME A BREAK. WHO WRITES THIS STUFF?
LET OUR ENEMIES BEWARE: THERE IS ONLY ONE SUPER-POWER NOW.
THE FEDS, THE ARMY AND THE C.I.A. ARE ALL OFFICIALLY OBSOLETE, BOYS AND GIRLS. CALL S.T.A.R. LABS AND GET ME DOCTOR LEX LUTHOR ON THE PHONE.
THE COLD WAR JUST EVOLVED INTO A WHOLE NEW ANIMAL.

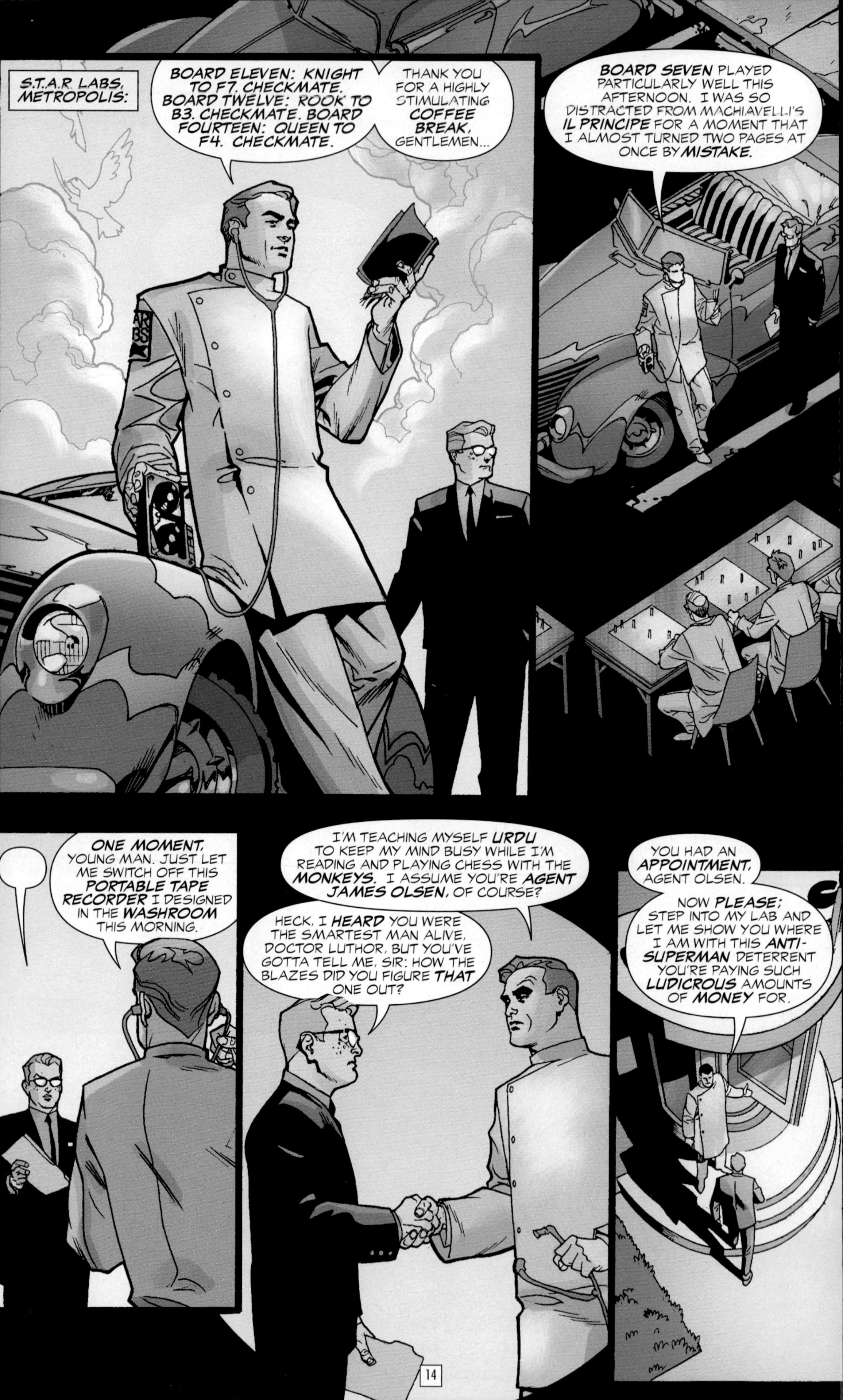
S.T.A.R. LABS, METROPOLIS:
BOARD ELEVEN: KNIGHT TO F7. CHECKMATE. BOARD TWELVE: ROOK TO B3. CHECKMATE. BOARD FOURTEEN: QUEEN TO F4. CHECKMATE.
THANK YOU FOR A HIGHLY STIMULATING COFFEE BREAK, GENTLEMEN...
BOARD SEVEN PLAYED PARTICULARLY WELL THIS AFTERNOON. I WAS SO DISTRACTED FROM MACHIAVELLI'S IL PRINCIPE FOR A MOMENT THAT I ALMOST TURNED TWO PAGES AT ONCE BY MISTAKE.
ONE MOMENT, YOUNG MAN. JUST LET ME SWITCH OFF THIS PORTABLE TAPE RECORDER I DESIGNED IN THE WASHROOM THIS MORNING.
I'M TEACHING MYSELF URDU TO KEEP MY MIND BUSY WHILE I'M READING AND PLAYING CHESS WITH THE MONKEYS. I ASSUME YOU'RE AGENT JAMES OLSEN, OF COURSE?
HECK, I HEARD YOU WERE THE SMARTEST MAN ALIVE, DOCTOR LUTHOR, BUT YOU'VE GOTTA TELL ME, SIR: HOW THE BLAZES DID YOU FIGURE THAT ONE OUT?
YOU HAD AN APPOINTMENT, AGENT OLSEN.
NOW PLEASE: STEP INTO MY LAB AND LET ME SHOW YOU WHERE I AM WITH THIS ANTI-SUPERMAN DETERRENT YOU'RE PAYING SUCH LUDICROUS AMOUNTS OF MONEY FOR.

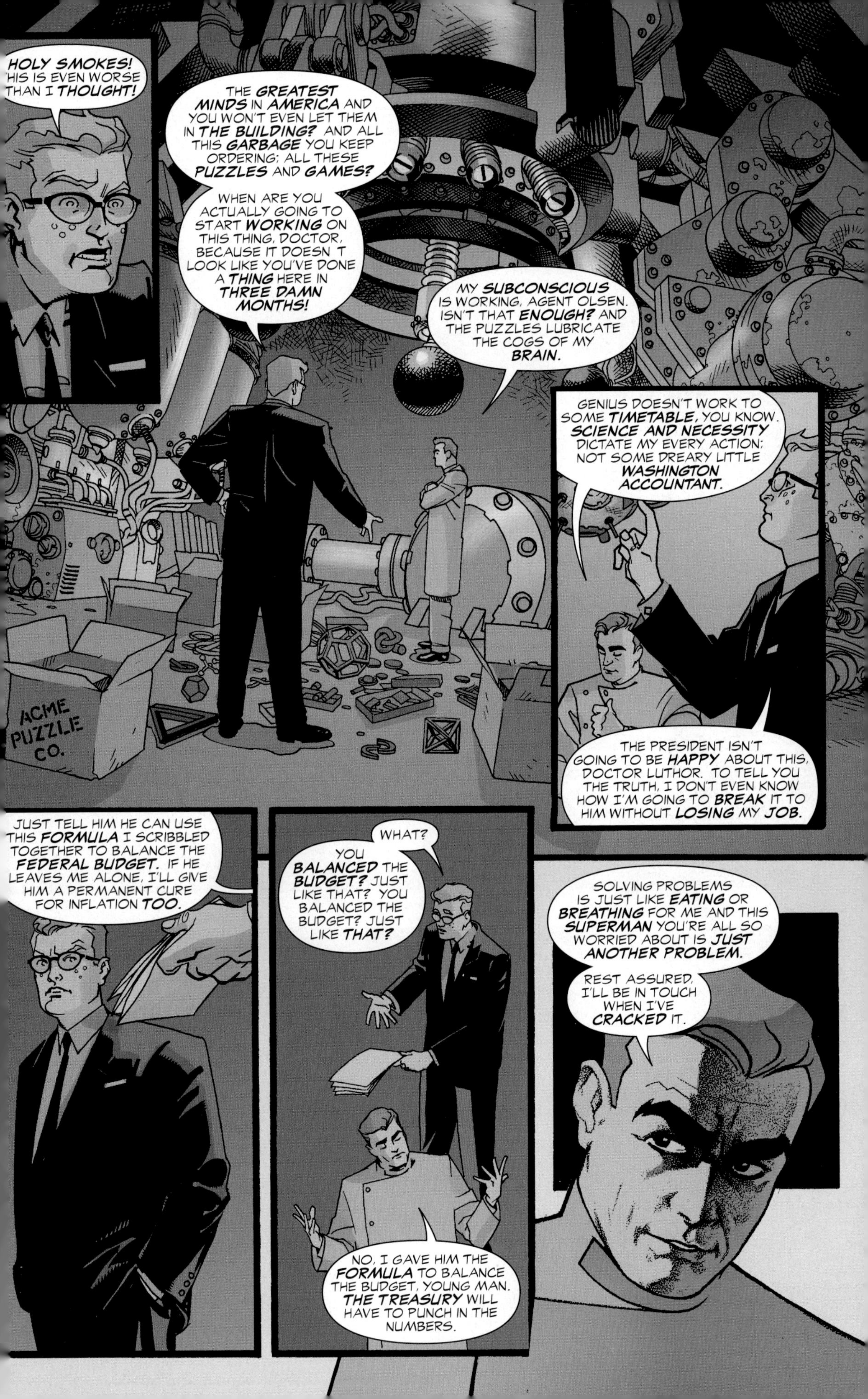
HOLY SMOKES! THIS IS EVEN WORSE THAN I THOUGHT!
THE GREATEST MINDS IN AMERICA AND YOU WON'T EVEN LET THEM IN THE BUILDING? AND ALL THIS GARBAGE YOU KEEP ORDERING; ALL THESE PUZZLES AND GAMES?
WHEN ARE YOU ACTUALLY GOING TO START WORKING ON THIS THING, DOCTOR, BECAUSE IT DOESN T LOOK LIKE YOU'VE DONE A THING HERE IN THREE DAMN MONTHS!
MY SUBCONSCIOUS IS WORKING, AGENT OLSEN. ISN'T THAT ENOUGH? AND THE PUZZLES LUBRICATE THE COGS OF MY BRAIN.
ACME PUZZLE CO.
GENIUS DOESN'T WORK TO SOME TIMETABLE, YOU KNOW. SCIENCE AND NECESSITY DICTATE MY EVERY ACTION; NOT SOME DREARY LITTLE WASHINGTON ACCOUNTANT.
THE PRESIDENT ISN'T GOING TO BE HAPPY ABOUT THIS, DOCTOR LUTHOR. TO TELL YOU THE TRUTH, I DON'T EVEN KNOW HOW I'M GOING TO BREAK IT TO HIM WITHOUT LOSING MY JOB.
JUST TELL HIM HE CAN USE THIS FORMULA I SCRIBBLED TOGETHER TO BALANCE THE FEDERAL BUDGET. IF HE LEAVES ME ALONE, I'LL GIVE HIM A PERMANENT CURE FOR INFLATION TOO.
WHAT?
YOU BALANCED THE BUDGET? JUST LIKE THAT? YOU BALANCED THE BUDGET? JUST LIKE THAT?
NO, I GAVE HIM THE FORMULA TO BALANCE THE BUDGET, YOUNG MAN. THE TREASURY WILL HAVE TO PUNCH IN THE NUMBERS.
SOLVING PROBLEMS IS JUST LIKE EATING OR BREATHING FOR ME AND THIS SUPERMAN YOU'RE ALL SO WORRIED ABOUT IS JUST ANOTHER PROBLEM.
REST ASSURED, I'LL BE IN TOUCH WHEN I'VE CRACKED IT.

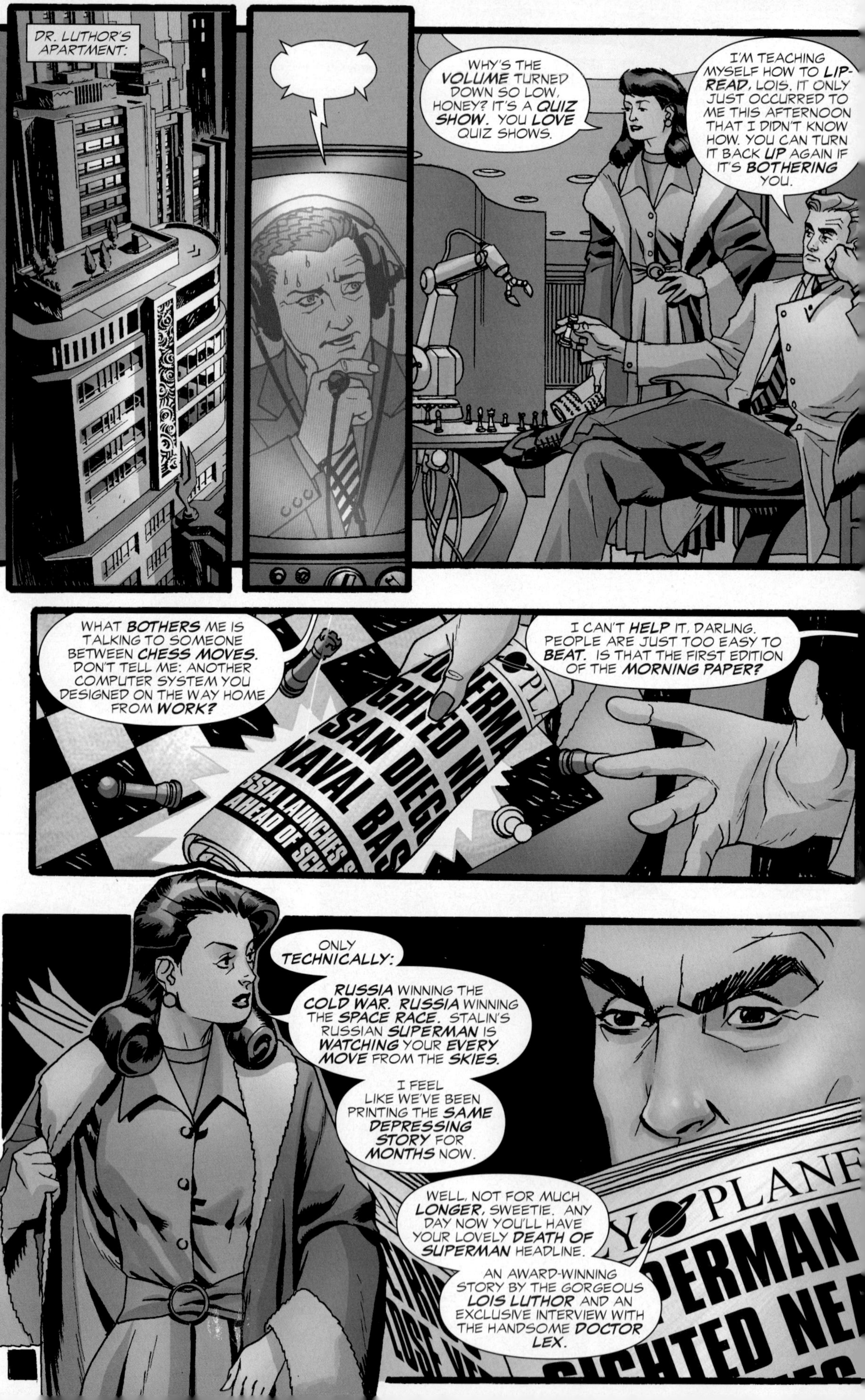
DR. LUTHOR'S APARTMENT:
WHY'S THE VOLUME TURNED DOWN SO LOW, HONEY? IT'S A QUIZ SHOW. YOU LOVE QUIZ SHOWS.
I'M TEACHING MYSELF HOW TO LIP-READ, LOIS. IT ONLY JUST OCCURRED TO ME THIS AFTERNOON THAT I DIDN'T KNOW HOW. YOU CAN TURN IT BACK UP AGAIN IF IT'S BOTHERING YOU.
WHAT BOTHERS ME IS TALKING TO SOMEONE BETWEEN CHESS MOVES. DON'T TELL ME: ANOTHER COMPUTER SYSTEM YOU DESIGNED ON THE WAY HOME FROM WORK?
I CAN'T HELP IT, DARLING. PEOPLE ARE JUST TOO EASY TO BEAT. IS THAT THE FIRST EDITION OF THE MORNING PAPER?
ONLY TECHNICALLY:
RUSSIA WINNING THE COLD WAR. RUSSIA WINNING THE SPACE RACE. STALIN'S RUSSIAN SUPERMAN IS WATCHING YOUR EVERY MOVE FROM THE SKIES.
I FEEL LIKE WE'VE BEEN PRINTING THE SAME DEPRESSING STORY FOR MONTHS NOW.
WELL, NOT FOR MUCH LONGER, SWEETIE. ANY DAY NOW YOU'LL HAVE YOUR LOVELY DEATH OF SUPERMAN HEADLINE.
AN AWARD-WINNING STORY BY THE GORGEOUS LOIS LUTHOR AND AN EXCLUSIVE INTERVIEW WITH THE HANDSOME DOCTOR LEX.

Angry clashes betw
police at Metrop

DAILY PLANET. **SPUTNIK.** METROPOLIS. SUPERMAN. **SPACE RACE.** SPUTNIK. GLOBE. **SPUTNIK.** GLOBE. **SPUTNIK.** GLOBE. **METROPOLIS...**

SUPERMAN SIGHTED NEAR SAN DIEGO NAVAL BASE

GOOD GRIEF! HOW COULD I HAVE BEEN SUCH AN **IDIOT?**

WHAT **IS** IT, LEX? WHAT'S **WRONG?**

THIS IS **LEX LUTHOR.** S.T.A.R. LABS CLEARANCE CODE **ONE-THREE-FIVE-ZERO-BRAVO.** I WANT TO SPEAK TO THE PRESIDENT AND I DON'T **CARE** IF HE'S IN A MEETING.

THIS IS INDESCRIBABLY MORE IMPORTANT, YOUNG LADY.

WHAT'S **GOING ON,** LEX? WHAT'S **HAPPENED?** HAVE YOU FIGURED OUT A WAY TO BEAT **SUPERMAN** OR SOMETHING?

I'M **SORRY,** DARLING, BUT I'M AFRAID THAT IS **OFFICIAL GOVERNMENT** INFORMATION ON A **NEED-TO-KNOW CAPACITY** NOW.

IKE? **LEX** HERE, SIR. I NEED A **HUNDRED TECHNICIANS, TEN MILLION DOLLARS** AND PERMISSION TO CRASH A SOVIET SATELLITE IN A **HIGHLY POPULATED AREA.**

OF **COURSE** YOU CAN THINK FOR A MINUTE...

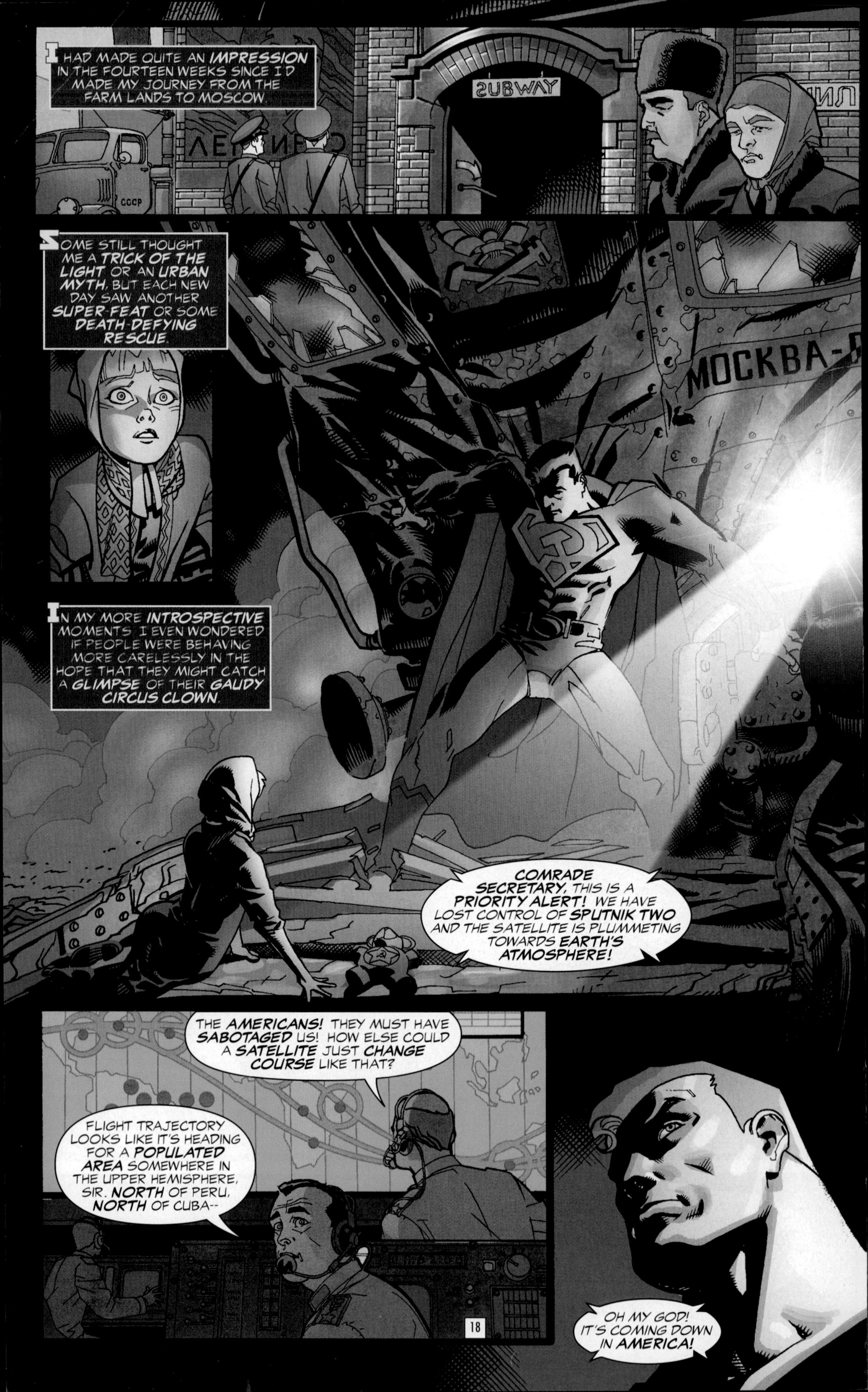
I HAD MADE QUITE AN IMPRESSION IN THE FOURTEEN WEEKS SINCE I'D MADE MY JOURNEY FROM THE FARM LANDS TO MOSCOW.
SUBWAY
CCCP
SOME STILL THOUGHT ME A TRICK OF THE LIGHT OR AN URBAN MYTH, BUT EACH NEW DAY SAW ANOTHER SUPER-FEAT OR SOME DEATH-DEFYING RESCUE.
MOCKBA-
IN MY MORE INTROSPECTIVE MOMENTS, I EVEN WONDERED IF PEOPLE WERE BEHAVING MORE CARELESSLY IN THE HOPE THAT THEY MIGHT CATCH A GLIMPSE OF THEIR GAUDY CIRCUS CLOWN.
COMRADE SECRETARY, THIS IS A PRIORITY ALERT! WE HAVE LOST CONTROL OF SPUTNIK TWO AND THE SATELLITE IS PLUMMETING TOWARDS EARTH'S ATMOSPHERE!
THE AMERICANS! THEY MUST HAVE SABOTAGED US! HOW ELSE COULD A SATELLITE JUST CHANGE COURSE LIKE THAT?
FLIGHT TRAJECTORY LOOKS LIKE IT'S HEADING FOR A POPULATED AREA SOMEWHERE IN THE UPPER HEMISPHERE, SIR. NORTH OF PERU, NORTH OF CUBA--
OH MY GOD! IT'S COMING DOWN IN AMERICA!

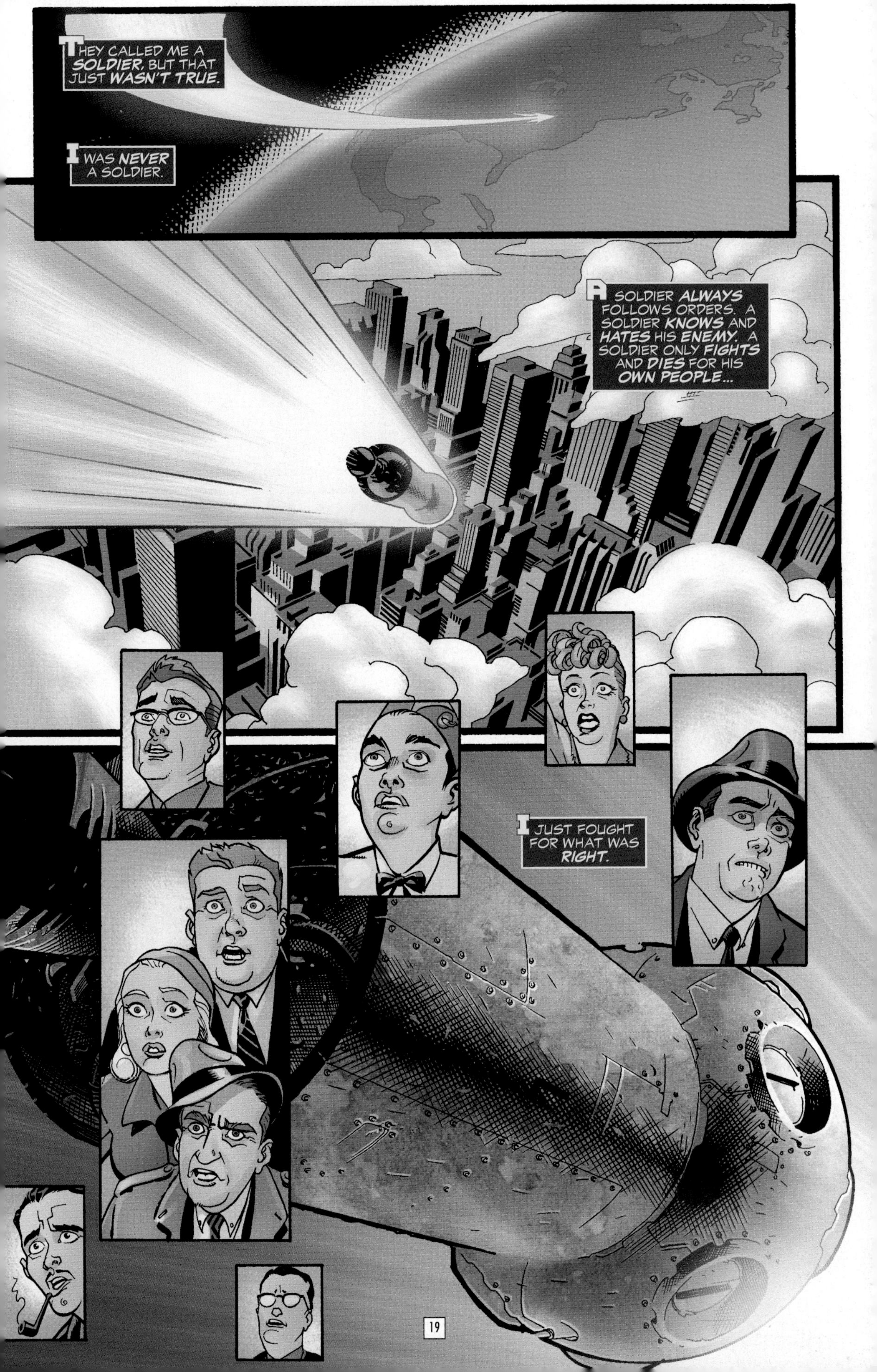
THEY CALLED ME A SOLDIER, BUT THAT JUST WASN'T TRUE.
I WAS NEVER A SOLDIER.
A SOLDIER ALWAYS FOLLOWS ORDERS. A SOLDIER KNOWS AND HATES HIS ENEMY. A SOLDIER ONLY FIGHTS AND DIES FOR HIS OWN PEOPLE...
I JUST FOUGHT FOR WHAT WAS RIGHT.

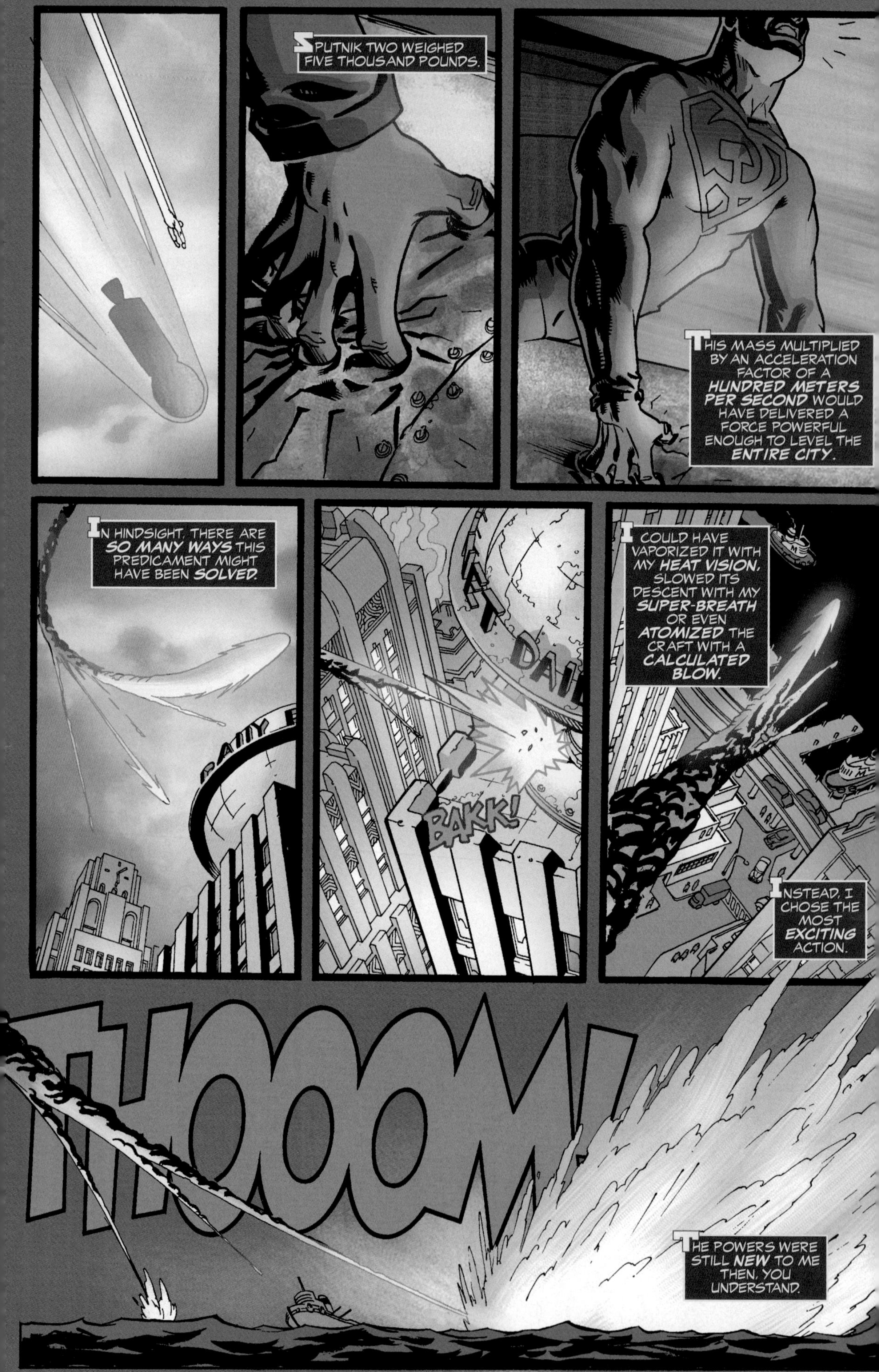
SPUTNIK TWO WEIGHED FIVE THOUSAND POUNDS.
THIS MASS MULTIPLIED BY AN ACCELERATION FACTOR OF A HUNDRED METERS PER SECOND WOULD HAVE DELIVERED A FORCE POWERFUL ENOUGH TO LEVEL THE ENTIRE CITY.
IN HINDSIGHT, THERE ARE SO MANY WAYS THIS PREDICAMENT MIGHT HAVE BEEN SOLVED.
BAKK!
I COULD HAVE VAPORIZED IT WITH MY HEAT VISION, SLOWED ITS DESCENT WITH MY SUPER-BREATH OR EVEN ATOMIZED THE CRAFT WITH A CALCULATED BLOW.
INSTEAD, I CHOSE THE MOST EXCITING ACTION.
THOOOM
THE POWERS WERE STILL NEW TO ME THEN, YOU UNDERSTAND.

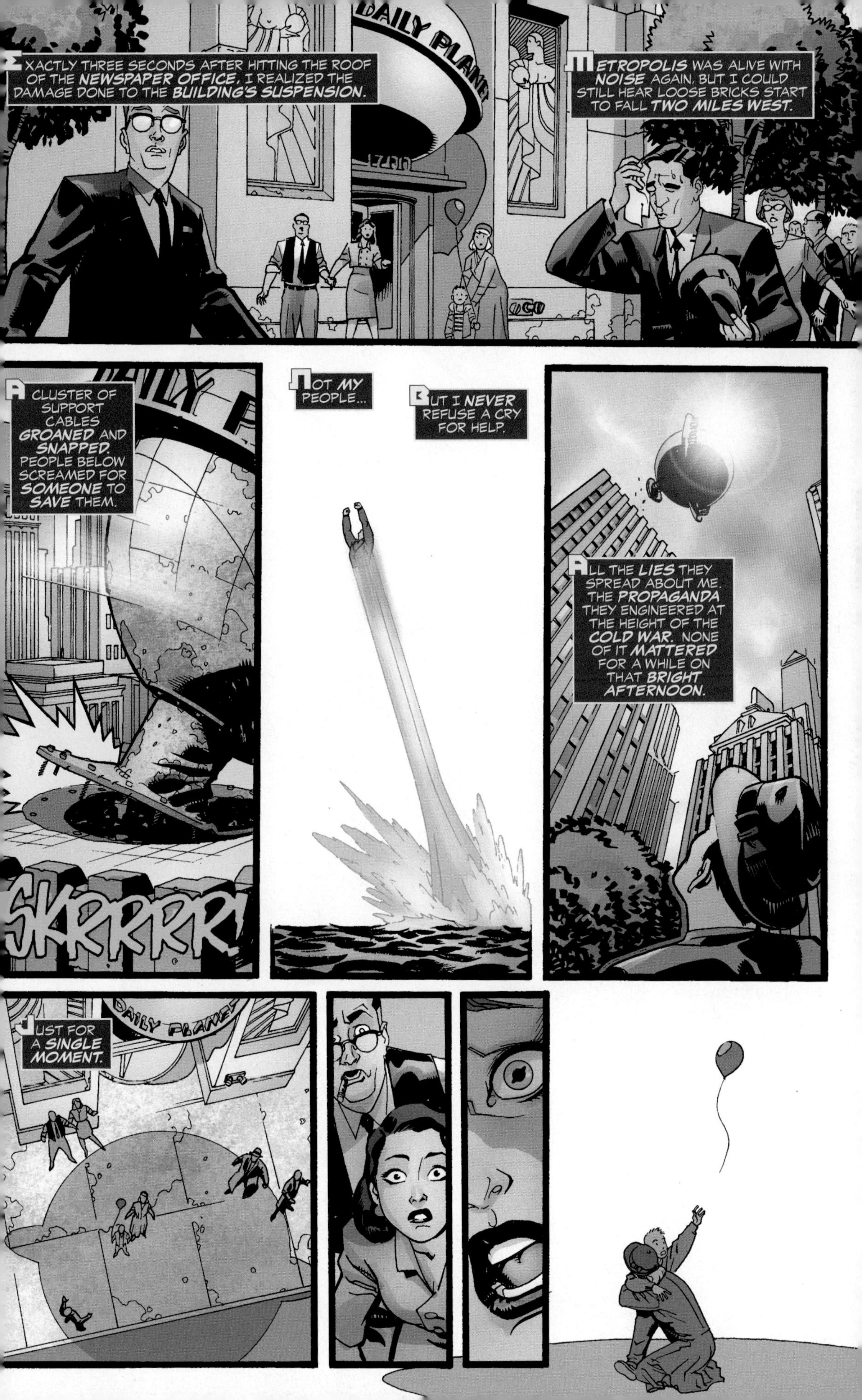
EXACTLY THREE SECONDS AFTER HITTING THE ROOF OF THE NEWSPAPER OFFICE, I REALIZED THE DAMAGE DONE TO THE BUILDING'S SUSPENSION.
METROPOLIS WAS ALIVE WITH NOISE AGAIN, BUT I COULD STILL HEAR LOOSE BRICKS START TO FALL TWO MILES WEST.
A CLUSTER OF SUPPORT CABLES GROANED AND SNAPPED. PEOPLE BELOW SCREAMED FOR SOMEONE TO SAVE THEM.
SKRRRR
NOT MY PEOPLE...
BUT I NEVER REFUSE A CRY FOR HELP.
ALL THE LIES THEY SPREAD ABOUT ME. THE PROPAGANDA THEY ENGINEERED AT THE HEIGHT OF THE COLD WAR. NONE OF IT MATTERED FOR A WHILE ON THAT BRIGHT AFTERNOON.
JUST FOR A SINGLE MOMENT.

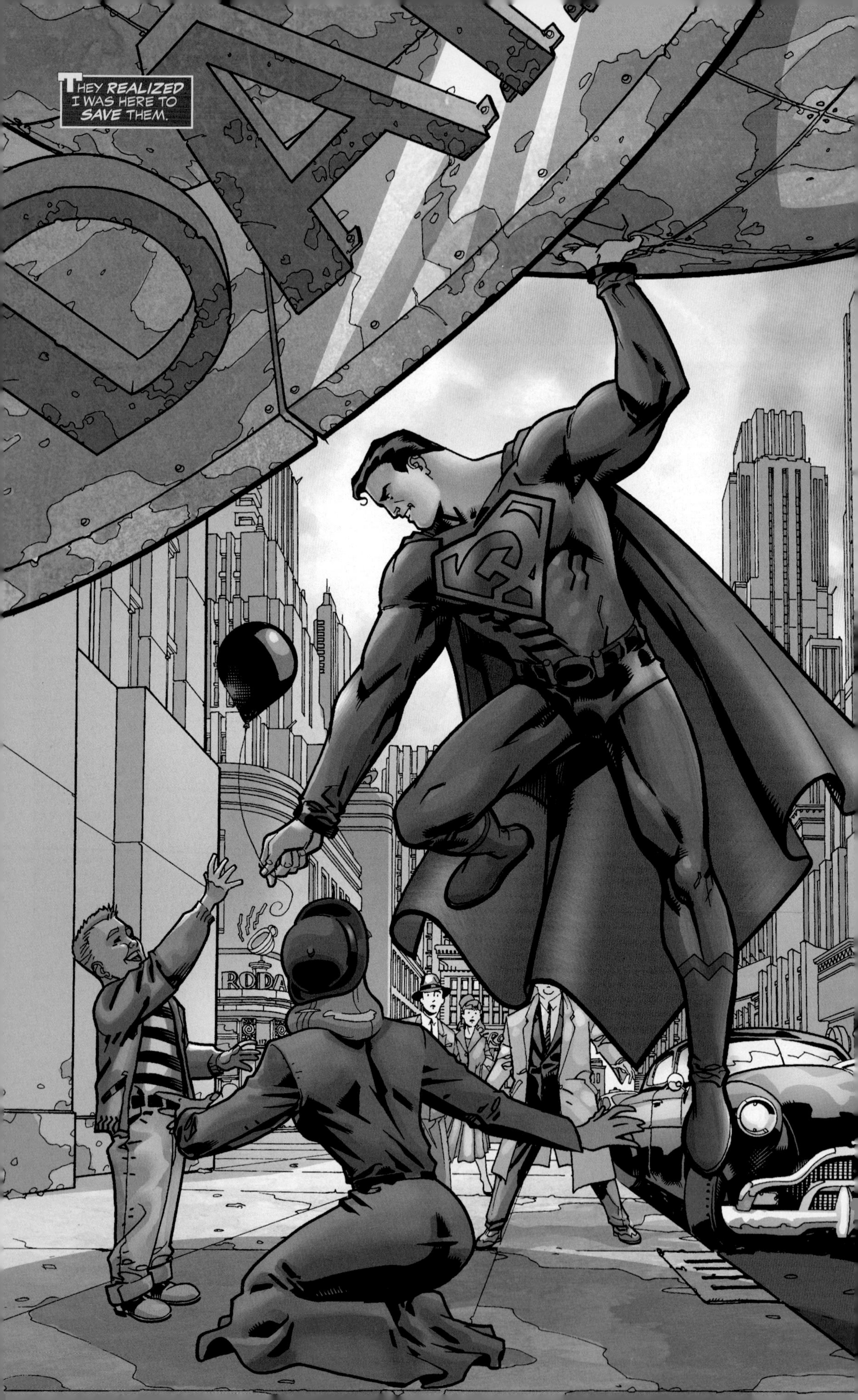
THEY REALIZED I WAS HERE TO SAVE THEM.
RODA

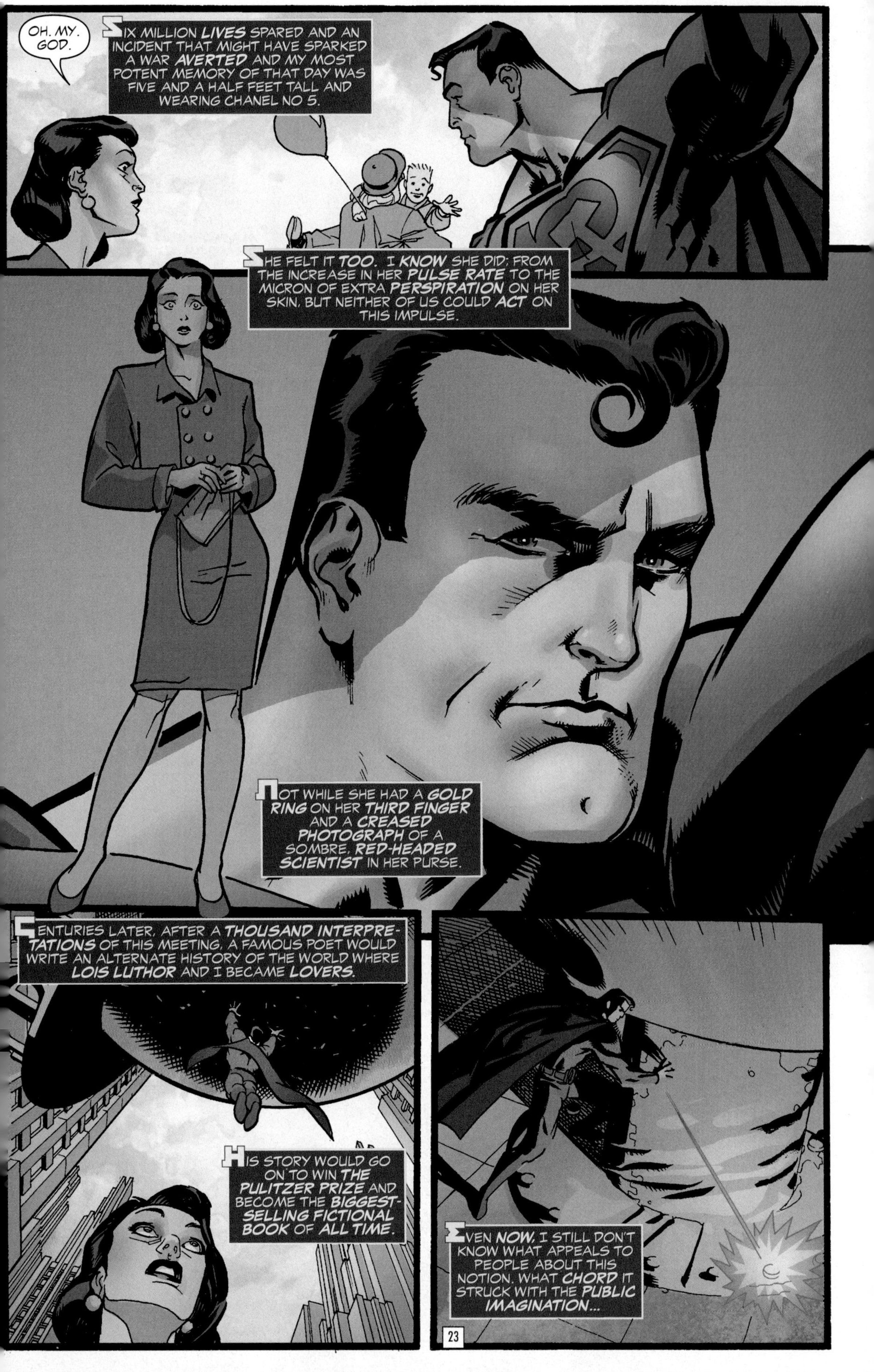

OH. MY. GOD.
SIX MILLION LIVES SPARED AND AN INCIDENT THAT MIGHT HAVE SPARKED A WAR AVERTED AND MY MOST POTENT MEMORY OF THAT DAY WAS FIVE AND A HALF FEET TALL AND WEARING CHANEL NO 5.
SHE FELT IT TOO. I KNOW SHE DID; FROM THE INCREASE IN HER PULSE RATE TO THE MICRON OF EXTRA PERSPIRATION ON HER SKIN, BUT NEITHER OF US COULD ACT ON THIS IMPULSE.
NOT WHILE SHE HAD A GOLD RING ON HER THIRD FINGER AND A CREASED PHOTOGRAPH OF A SOMBRE, RED-HEADED SCIENTIST IN HER PURSE.
CENTURIES LATER, AFTER A THOUSAND INTERPRETATIONS OF THIS MEETING, A FAMOUS POET WOULD WRITE AN ALTERNATE HISTORY OF THE WORLD WHERE LOIS LUTHOR AND I BECAME LOVERS.
HIS STORY WOULD GO ON TO WIN THE PULITZER PRIZE AND BECOME THE BIGGEST-SELLING FICTIONAL BOOK OF ALL TIME.
EVEN NOW, I STILL DON'T KNOW WHAT APPEALS TO PEOPLE ABOUT THIS NOTION, WHAT CHORD IT STRUCK WITH THE PUBLIC IMAGINATION...

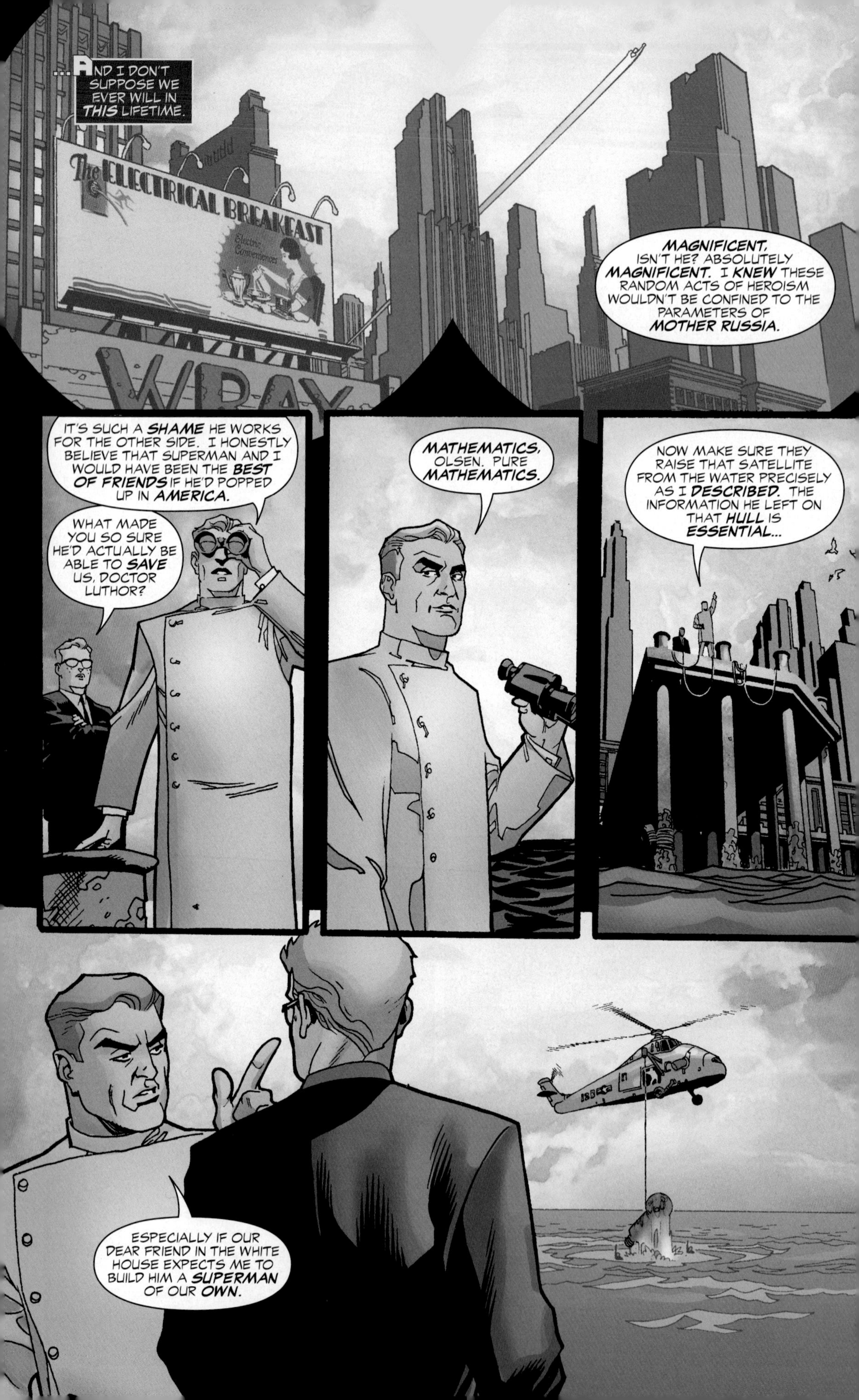
...AND I DON'T SUPPOSE WE EVER WILL IN THIS LIFETIME.
The ELECTRICAL BREAKFAST
WRAY
MAGNIFICENT, ISN'T HE? ABSOLUTELY MAGNIFICENT. I KNEW THESE RANDOM ACTS OF HEROISM WOULDN'T BE CONFINED TO THE PARAMETERS OF MOTHER RUSSIA.
IT'S SUCH A SHAME HE WORKS FOR THE OTHER SIDE. I HONESTLY BELIEVE THAT SUPERMAN AND I WOULD HAVE BEEN THE BEST OF FRIENDS IF HE'D POPPED UP IN AMERICA.
WHAT MADE YOU SO SURE HE'D ACTUALLY BE ABLE TO SAVE US, DOCTOR LUTHOR?
MATHEMATICS, OLSEN. PURE MATHEMATICS.
NOW MAKE SURE THEY RAISE THAT SATELLITE FROM THE WATER PRECISELY AS I DESCRIBED. THE INFORMATION HE LEFT ON THAT HULL IS ESSENTIAL...
ESPECIALLY IF OUR DEAR FRIEND IN THE WHITE HOUSE EXPECTS ME TO BUILD HIM A SUPERMAN OF OUR OWN.

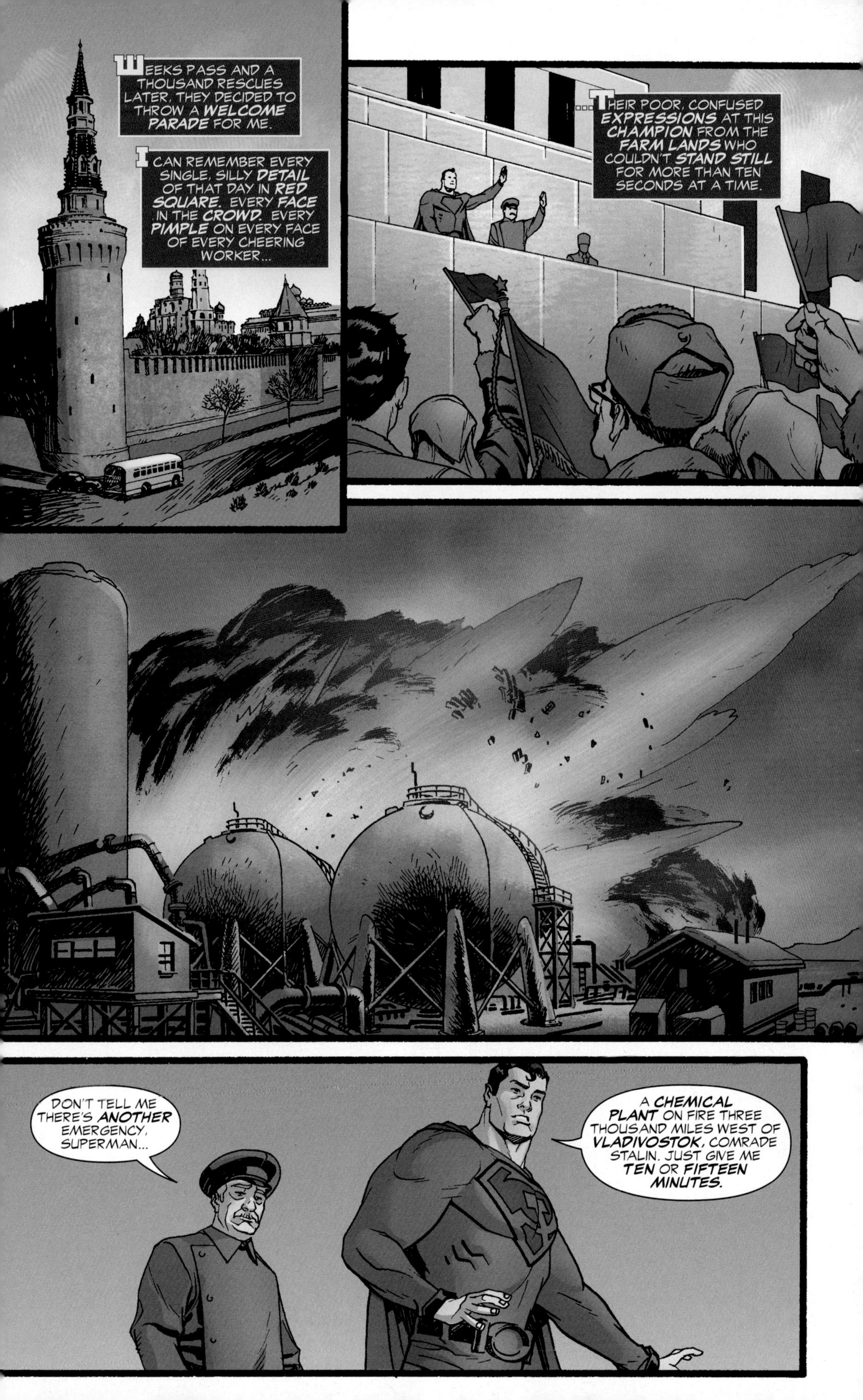
WEEKS PASS AND A THOUSAND RESCUES LATER, THEY DECIDED TO THROW A WELCOME PARADE FOR ME.
I CAN REMEMBER EVERY SINGLE, SILLY DETAIL OF THAT DAY IN RED SQUARE. EVERY FACE IN THE CROWD. EVERY PIMPLE ON EVERY FACE OF EVERY CHEERING WORKER...
...THEIR POOR, CONFUSED EXPRESSIONS AT THIS CHAMPION FROM THE FARM LANDS WHO COULDN'T STAND STILL FOR MORE THAN TEN SECONDS AT A TIME.
DON'T TELL ME THERE'S ANOTHER EMERGENCY, SUPERMAN...
A CHEMICAL PLANT ON FIRE THREE THOUSAND MILES WEST OF VLADIVOSTOK, COMRADE STALIN. JUST GIVE ME TEN OR FIFTEEN MINUTES.

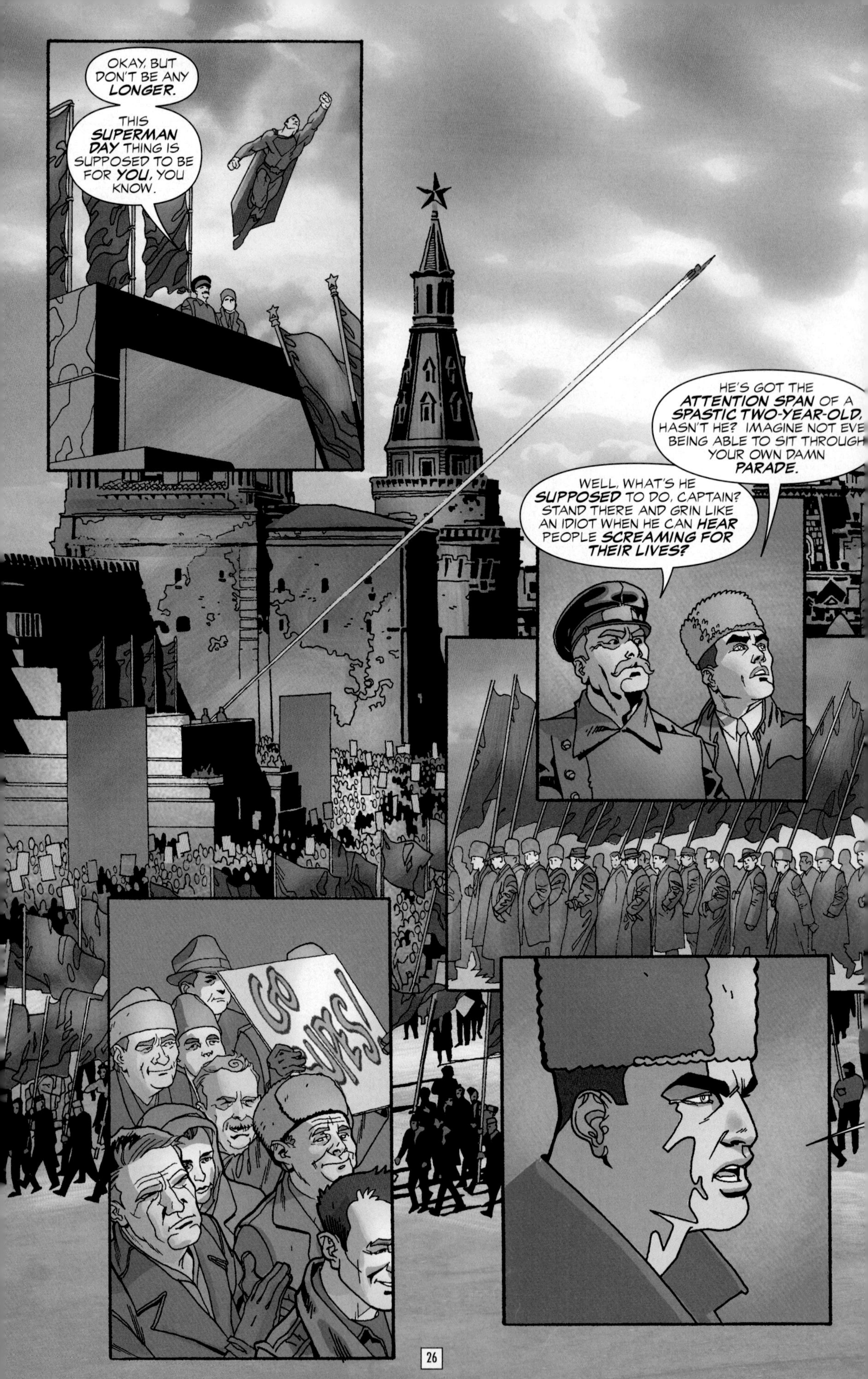
OKAY, BUT DON'T BE ANY LONGER.
THIS SUPERMAN DAY THING IS SUPPOSED TO BE FOR YOU, YOU KNOW.
HE'S GOT THE ATTENTION SPAN OF A SPASTIC TWO-YEAR-OLD, HASN'T HE? IMAGINE NOT EVE BEING ABLE TO SIT THROUGH YOUR OWN DAMN PARADE.
WELL, WHAT'S HE SUPPOSED TO DO, CAPTAIN? STAND THERE AND GRIN LIKE AN IDIOT WHEN HE CAN HEAR PEOPLE SCREAMING FOR THEIR LIVES?

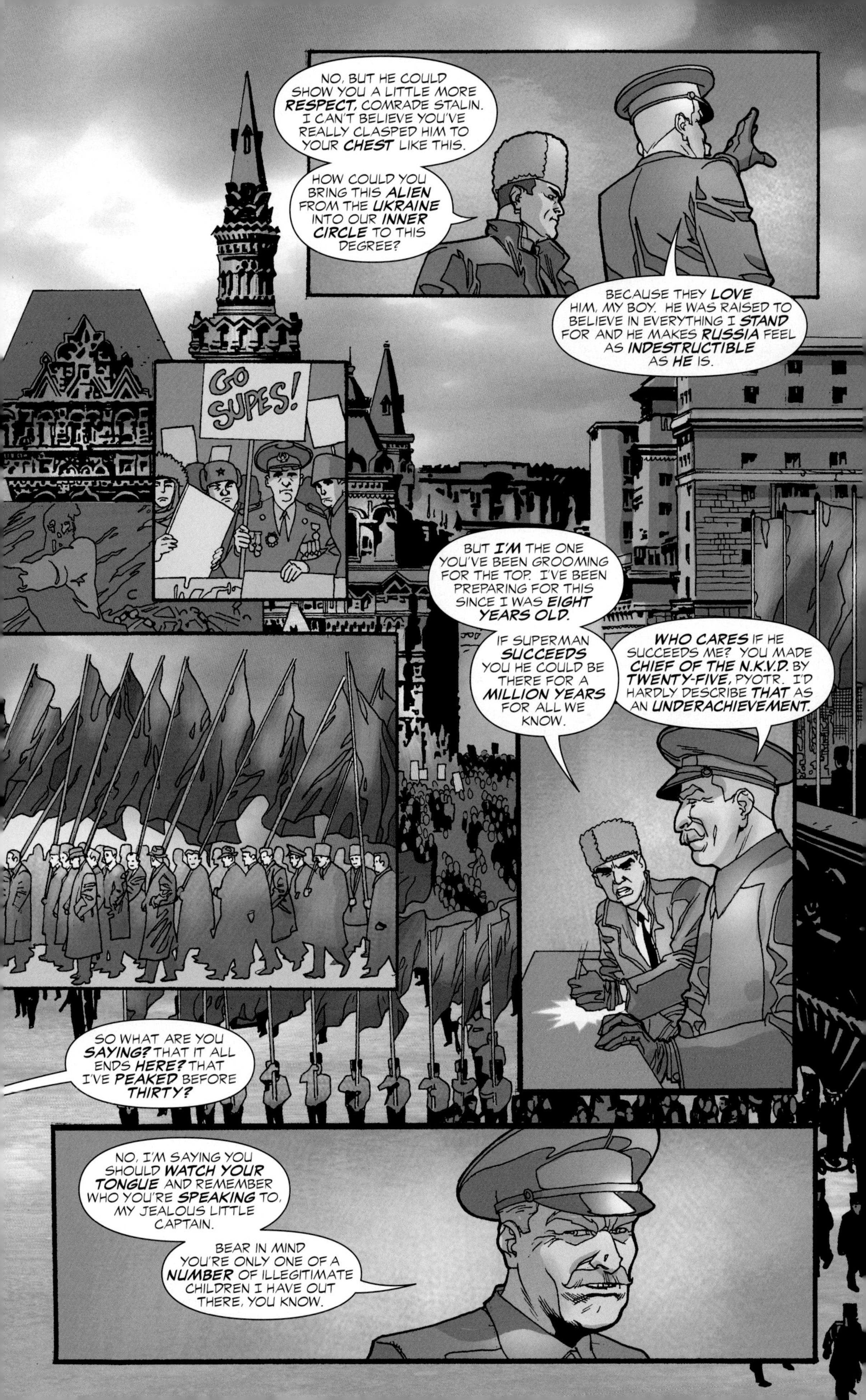
NO, BUT HE COULD SHOW YOU A LITTLE MORE RESPECT, COMRADE STALIN. I CAN'T BELIEVE YOU'VE REALLY CLASPED HIM TO YOUR CHEST LIKE THIS.
HOW COULD YOU BRING THIS ALIEN FROM THE UKRAINE INTO OUR INNER CIRCLE TO THIS DEGREE?
BECAUSE THEY LOVE HIM, MY BOY. HE WAS RAISED TO BELIEVE IN EVERYTHING I STAND FOR AND HE MAKES RUSSIA FEEL AS INDESTRUCTIBLE AS HE IS.
GO SUPES!
BUT I'M THE ONE YOU'VE BEEN GROOMING FOR THE TOP. I'VE BEEN PREPARING FOR THIS SINCE I WAS EIGHT YEARS OLD.
IF SUPERMAN SUCCEEDS YOU HE COULD BE THERE FOR A MILLION YEARS FOR ALL WE KNOW.
WHO CARES IF HE SUCCEEDS ME? YOU MADE CHIEF OF THE N.K.V.D. BY TWENTY-FIVE, PYOTR. I'D HARDLY DESCRIBE THAT AS AN UNDERACHIEVEMENT.
SO WHAT ARE YOU SAYING? THAT IT ALL ENDS HERE? THAT I'VE PEAKED BEFORE THIRTY?
NO, I'M SAYING YOU SHOULD WATCH YOUR TONGUE AND REMEMBER WHO YOU'RE SPEAKING TO, MY JEALOUS LITTLE CAPTAIN.
BEAR IN MIND YOU'RE ONLY ONE OF A NUMBER OF ILLEGITIMATE CHILDREN I HAVE OUT THERE, YOU KNOW.

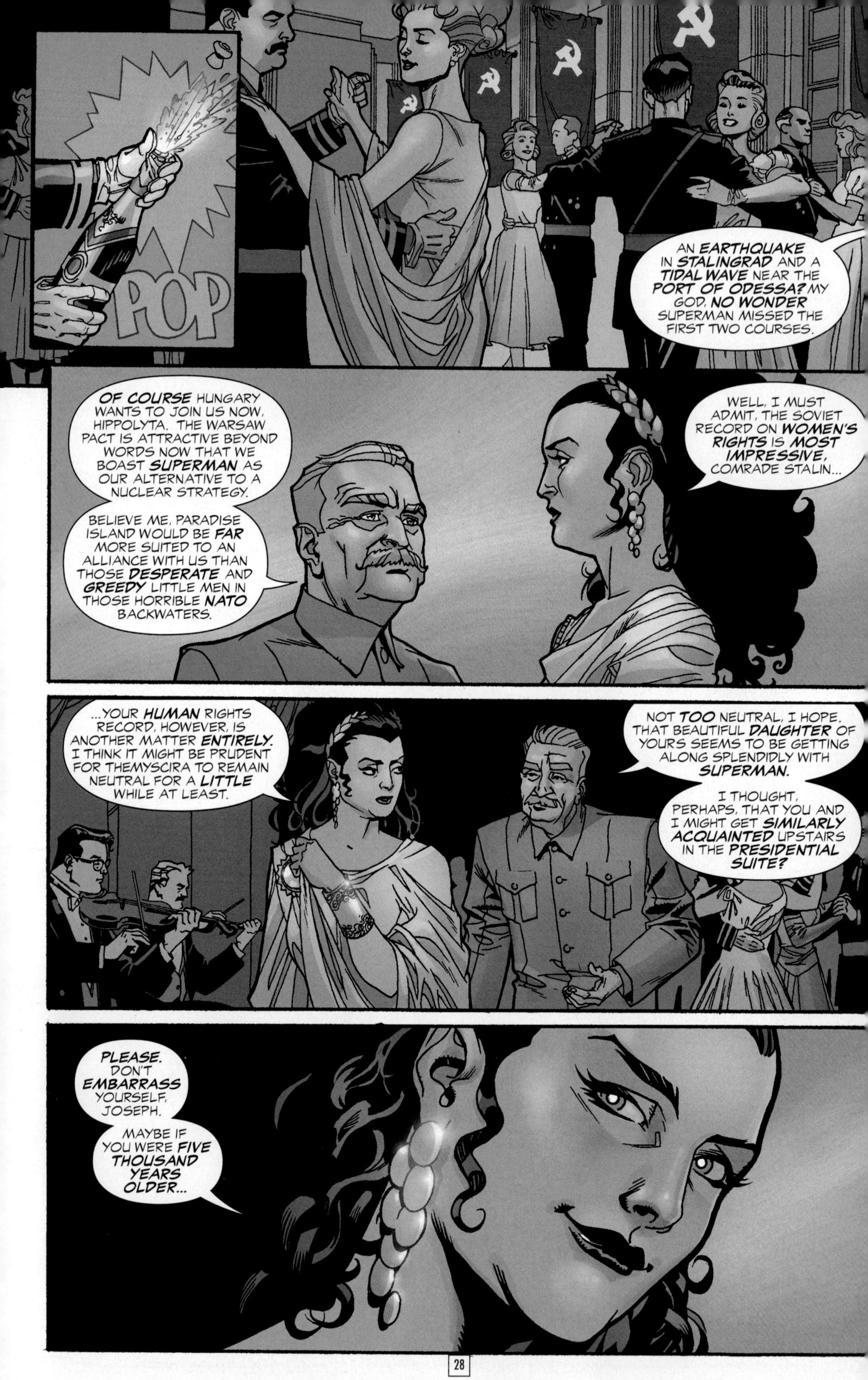
POP
AN EARTHQUAKE IN STALINGRAD AND A TIDAL WAVE NEAR THE PORT OF ODESSA? MY GOD. NO WONDER SUPERMAN MISSED THE FIRST TWO COURSES.
OF COURSE HUNGARY WANTS TO JOIN US NOW, HIPPOLYTA. THE WARSAW PACT IS ATTRACTIVE BEYOND WORDS NOW THAT WE BOAST SUPERMAN AS OUR ALTERNATIVE TO A NUCLEAR STRATEGY.
BELIEVE ME, PARADISE ISLAND WOULD BE FAR MORE SUITED TO AN ALLIANCE WITH US THAN THOSE DESPERATE AND GREEDY LITTLE MEN IN THOSE HORRIBLE NATO BACKWATERS.
WELL, I MUST ADMIT, THE SOVIET RECORD ON WOMEN'S RIGHTS IS MOST IMPRESSIVE, COMRADE STALIN...
...YOUR HUMAN RIGHTS RECORD, HOWEVER, IS ANOTHER MATTER ENTIRELY. I THINK IT MIGHT BE PRUDENT FOR THEMYSCIRA TO REMAIN NEUTRAL FOR A LITTLE WHILE AT LEAST.
NOT TOO NEUTRAL, I HOPE. THAT BEAUTIFUL DAUGHTER OF YOURS SEEMS TO BE GETTING ALONG SPLENDIDLY WITH SUPERMAN.
I THOUGHT, PERHAPS, THAT YOU AND I MIGHT GET SIMILARLY ACQUAINTED UPSTAIRS IN THE PRESIDENTIAL SUITE?
PLEASE. DON'T EMBARRASS YOURSELF, JOSEPH.
MAYBE IF YOU WERE FIVE THOUSAND YEARS OLDER...

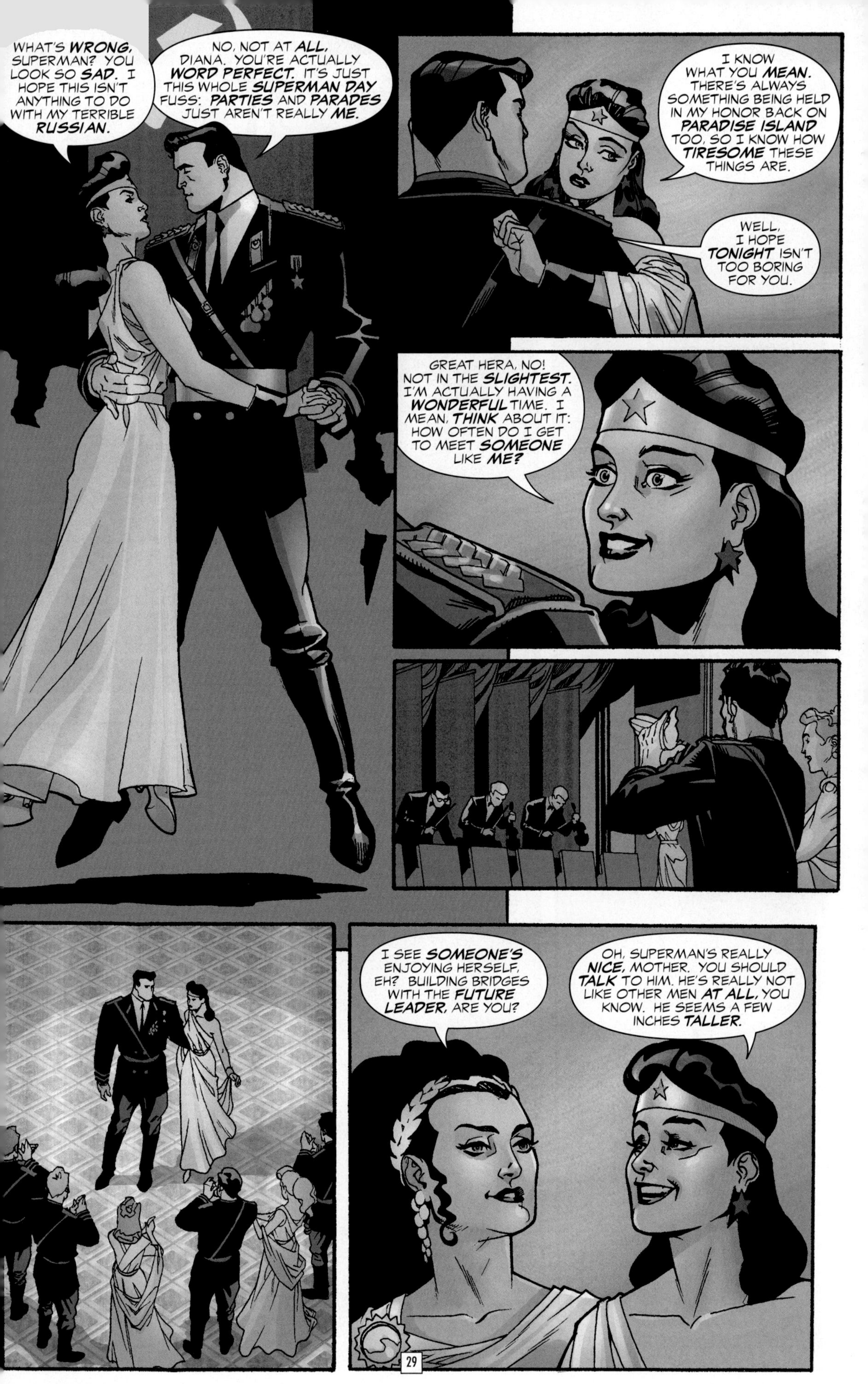
WHAT'S WRONG, SUPERMAN? YOU LOOK SO SAD. I HOPE THIS ISN'T ANYTHING TO DO WITH MY TERRIBLE RUSSIAN.
NO, NOT AT ALL, DIANA. YOU'RE ACTUALLY WORD PERFECT. IT'S JUST THIS WHOLE SUPERMAN DAY FUSS: PARTIES AND PARADES JUST AREN'T REALLY ME.
I KNOW WHAT YOU MEAN. THERE'S ALWAYS SOMETHING BEING HELD IN MY HONOR BACK ON PARADISE ISLAND TOO, SO I KNOW HOW TIRESOME THESE THINGS ARE.
WELL, I HOPE TONIGHT ISN'T TOO BORING FOR YOU.
GREAT HERA, NO! NOT IN THE SLIGHTEST. I'M ACTUALLY HAVING A WONDERFUL TIME. I MEAN, THINK ABOUT IT: HOW OFTEN DO I GET TO MEET SOMEONE LIKE ME?
I SEE SOMEONE'S ENJOYING HERSELF, EH? BUILDING BRIDGES WITH THE FUTURE LEADER, ARE YOU?
OH, SUPERMAN'S REALLY NICE, MOTHER. YOU SHOULD TALK TO HIM. HE'S REALLY NOT LIKE OTHER MEN AT ALL, YOU KNOW. HE SEEMS A FEW INCHES TALLER.

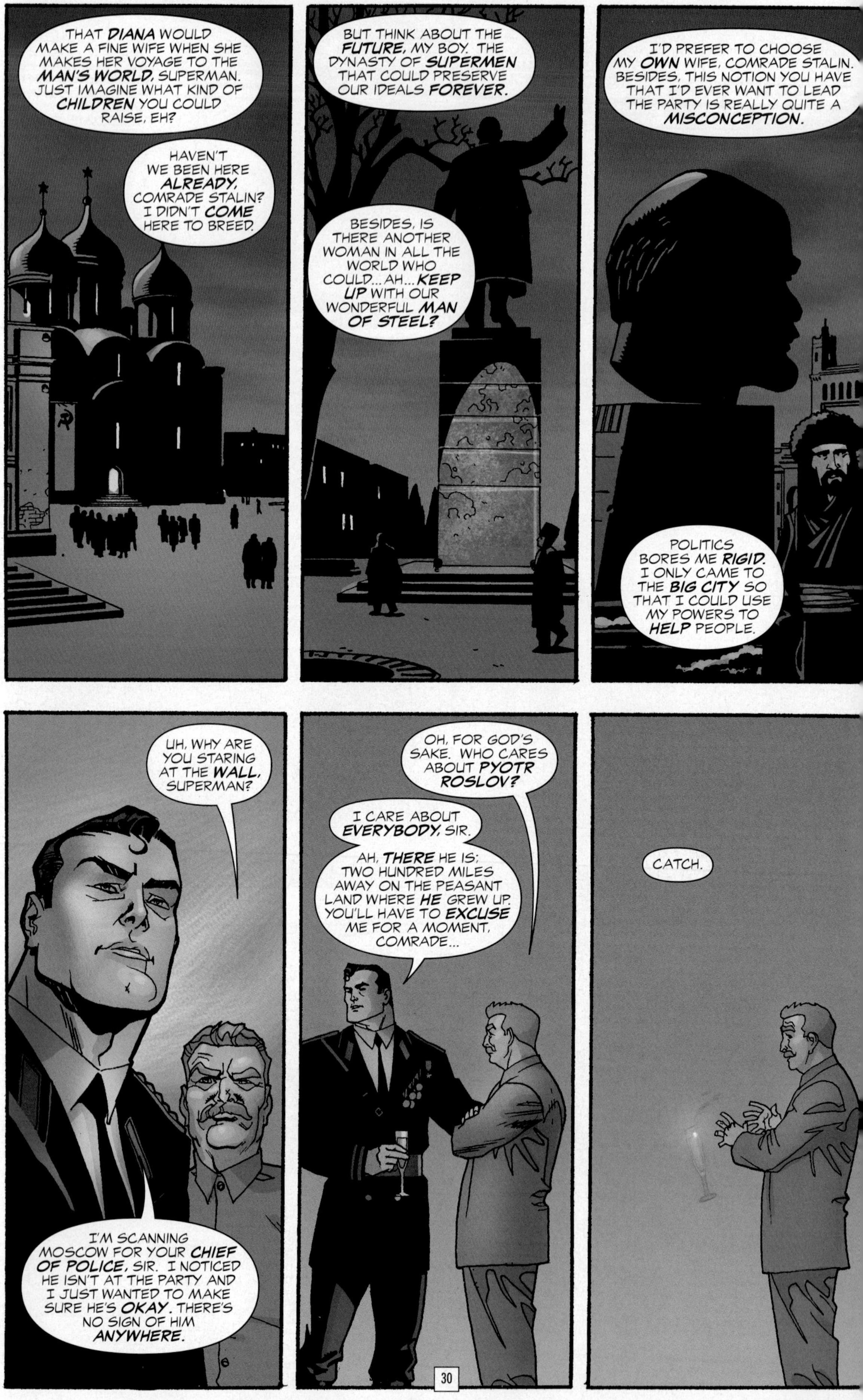
THAT DIANA WOULD MAKE A FINE WIFE WHEN SHE MAKES HER VOYAGE TO THE MAN'S WORLD, SUPERMAN. JUST IMAGINE WHAT KIND OF CHILDREN YOU COULD RAISE, EH?
HAVEN'T WE BEEN HERE ALREADY, COMRADE STALIN? I DIDN'T COME HERE TO BREED.
BUT THINK ABOUT THE FUTURE, MY BOY. THE DYNASTY OF SUPERMEN THAT COULD PRESERVE OUR IDEALS FOREVER.
BESIDES, IS THERE ANOTHER WOMAN IN ALL THE WORLD WHO COULD... AH... KEEP UP WITH OUR WONDERFUL MAN OF STEEL?
I'D PREFER TO CHOOSE MY OWN WIFE, COMRADE STALIN. BESIDES, THIS NOTION YOU HAVE THAT I'D EVER WANT TO LEAD THE PARTY IS REALLY QUITE A MISCONCEPTION.
POLITICS BORES ME RIGID. I ONLY CAME TO THE BIG CITY SO THAT I COULD USE MY POWERS TO HELP PEOPLE.
UH, WHY ARE YOU STARING AT THE WALL, SUPERMAN?
I'M SCANNING MOSCOW FOR YOUR CHIEF OF POLICE, SIR. I NOTICED HE ISN'T AT THE PARTY AND I JUST WANTED TO MAKE SURE HE'S OKAY. THERE'S NO SIGN OF HIM ANYWHERE.
OH, FOR GOD'S SAKE. WHO CARES ABOUT PYOTR ROSLOV?
I CARE ABOUT EVERYBODY, SIR.
AH, THERE HE IS; TWO HUNDRED MILES AWAY ON THE PEASANT LAND WHERE HE GREW UP. YOU'LL HAVE TO EXCUSE ME FOR A MOMENT, COMRADE...
CATCH.

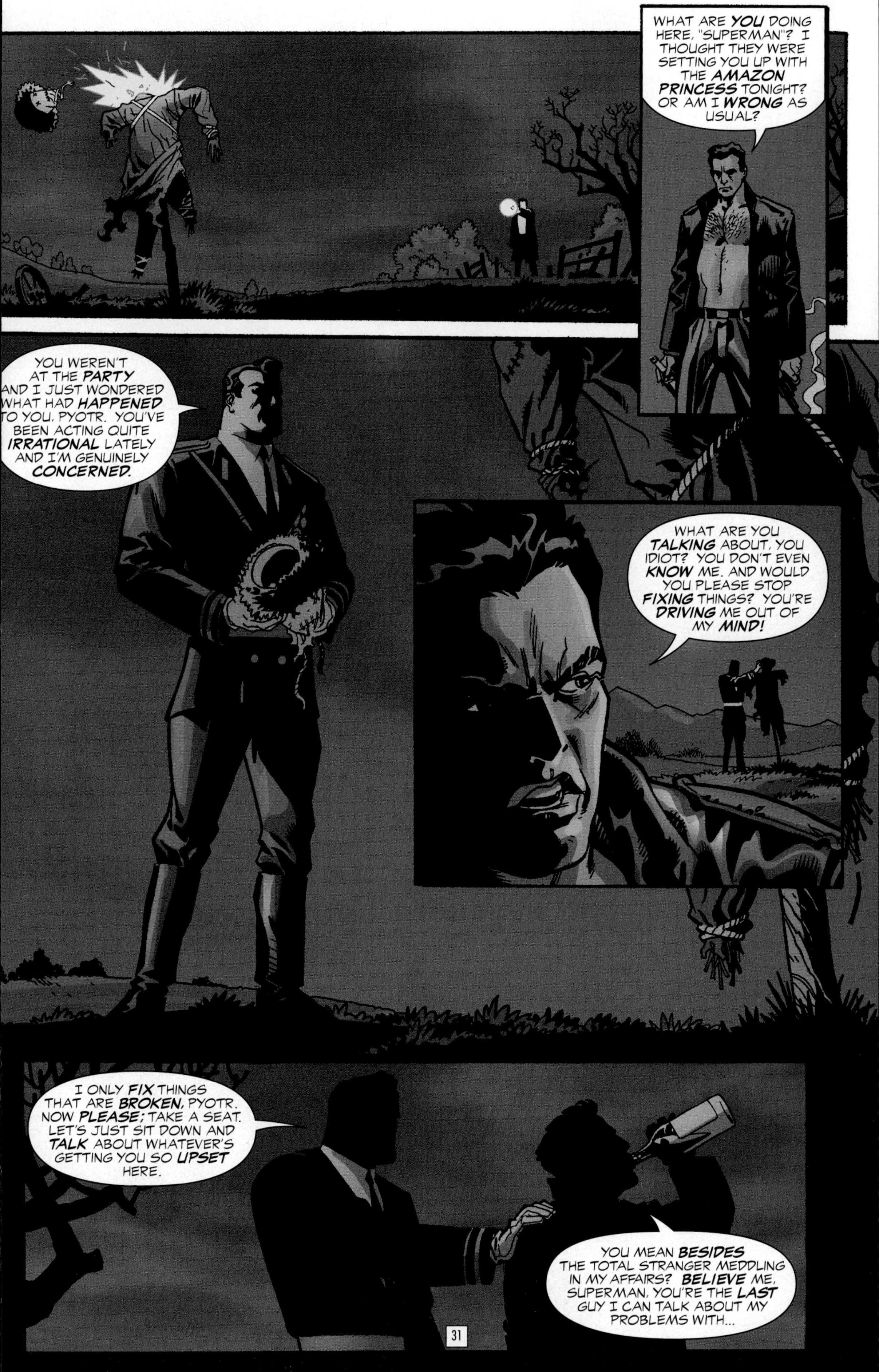
WHAT ARE YOU DOING HERE, "SUPERMAN"? I THOUGHT THEY WERE SETTING YOU UP WITH THE AMAZON PRINCESS TONIGHT? OR AM I WRONG AS USUAL?
YOU WEREN'T AT THE PARTY AND I JUST WONDERED WHAT HAD HAPPENED TO YOU, PYOTR. YOU'VE BEEN ACTING QUITE IRRATIONAL LATELY AND I'M GENUINELY CONCERNED.
WHAT ARE YOU TALKING ABOUT, YOU IDIOT? YOU DON'T EVEN KNOW ME. AND WOULD YOU PLEASE STOP FIXING THINGS? YOU'RE DRIVING ME OUT OF MY MIND!
I ONLY FIX THINGS THAT ARE BROKEN, PYOTR. NOW PLEASE; TAKE A SEAT. LET'S JUST SIT DOWN AND TALK ABOUT WHATEVER'S GETTING YOU SO UPSET HERE.
YOU MEAN BESIDES THE TOTAL STRANGER MEDDLING IN MY AFFAIRS? BELIEVE ME, SUPERMAN, YOU'RE THE LAST GUY I CAN TALK ABOUT MY PROBLEMS WITH...

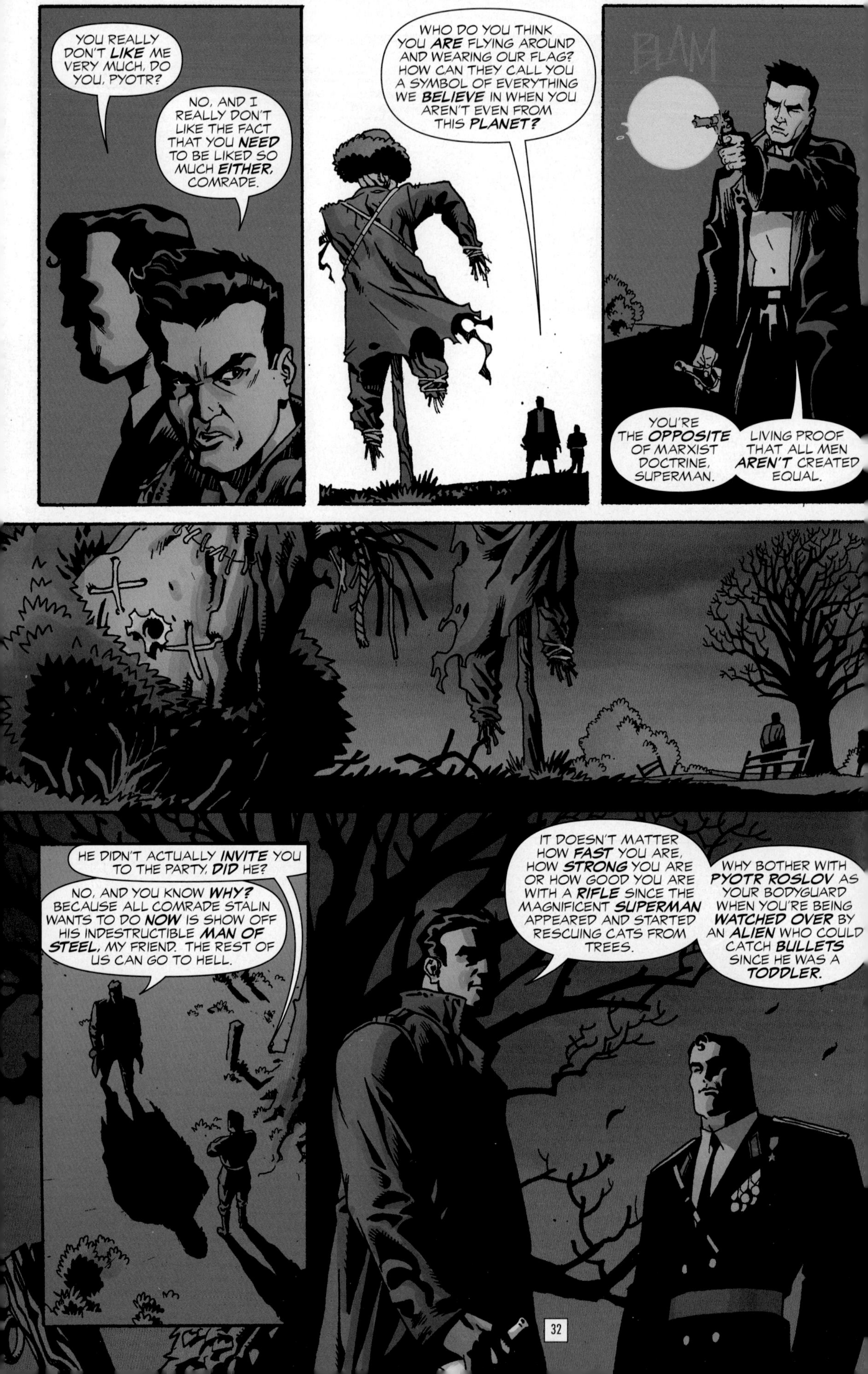
YOU REALLY DON'T LIKE ME VERY MUCH, DO YOU, PYOTR?
NO, AND I REALLY DON'T LIKE THE FACT THAT YOU NEED TO BE LIKED SO MUCH EITHER, COMRADE.
WHO DO YOU THINK YOU ARE FLYING AROUND AND WEARING OUR FLAG? HOW CAN THEY CALL YOU A SYMBOL OF EVERYTHING WE BELIEVE IN WHEN YOU AREN'T EVEN FROM THIS PLANET?
BLAM
YOU'RE THE OPPOSITE OF MARXIST DOCTRINE, SUPERMAN.
LIVING PROOF THAT ALL MEN AREN'T CREATED EQUAL.
HE DIDN'T ACTUALLY INVITE YOU TO THE PARTY, DID HE?
NO, AND YOU KNOW WHY? BECAUSE ALL COMRADE STALIN WANTS TO DO NOW IS SHOW OFF HIS INDESTRUCTIBLE MAN OF STEEL, MY FRIEND. THE REST OF US CAN GO TO HELL.
IT DOESN'T MATTER HOW FAST YOU ARE, HOW STRONG YOU ARE OR HOW GOOD YOU ARE WITH A RIFLE SINCE THE MAGNIFICENT SUPERMAN APPEARED AND STARTED RESCUING CATS FROM TREES.
WHY BOTHER WITH PYOTR ROSLOV AS YOUR BODYGUARD WHEN YOU'RE BEING WATCHED OVER BY AN ALIEN WHO COULD CATCH BULLETS SINCE HE WAS A TODDLER.

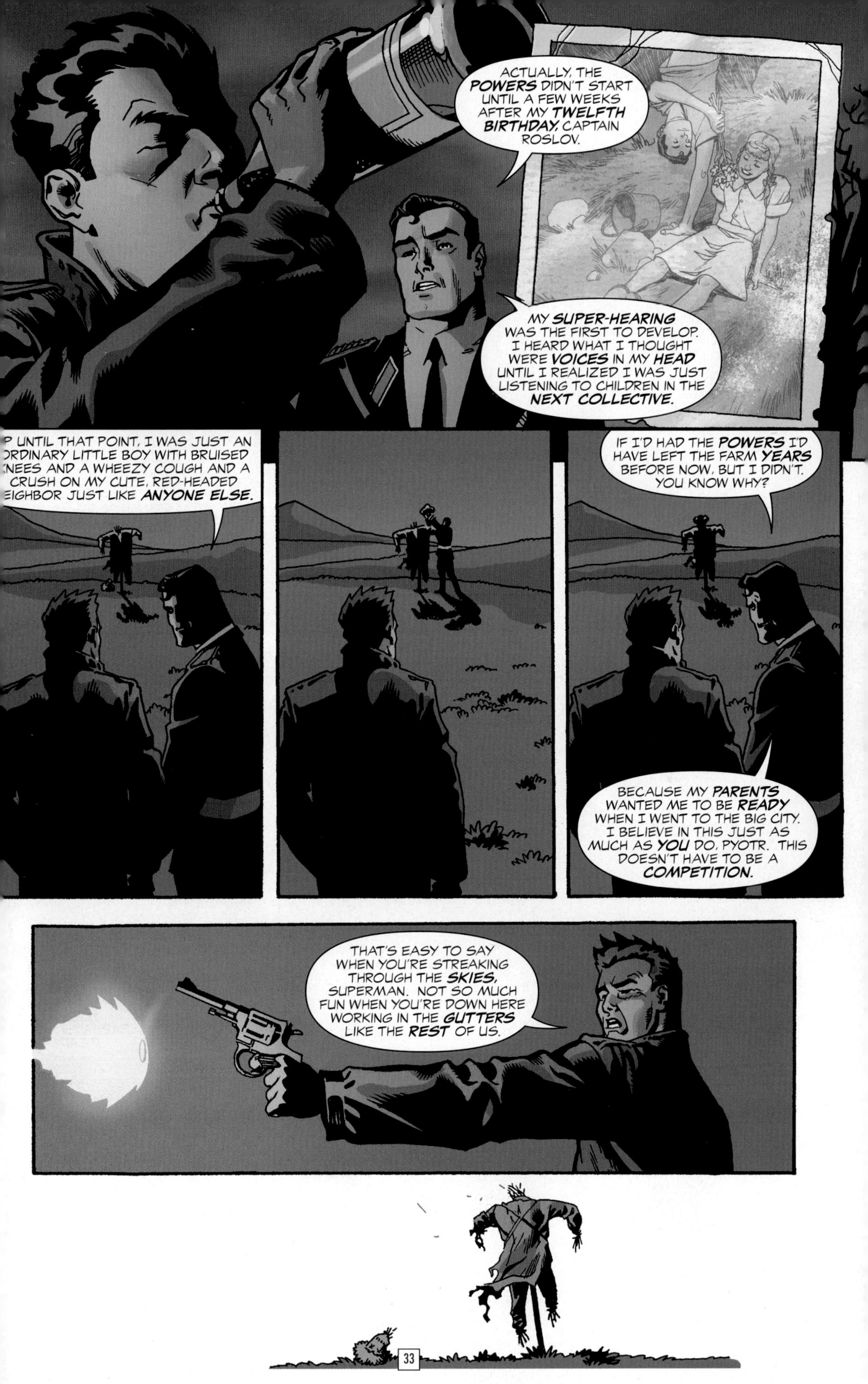
ACTUALLY, THE POWERS DIDN'T START UNTIL A FEW WEEKS AFTER MY TWELFTH BIRTHDAY, CAPTAIN ROSLOV.
MY SUPER-HEARING WAS THE FIRST TO DEVELOP. I HEARD WHAT I THOUGHT WERE VOICES IN MY HEAD UNTIL I REALIZED I WAS JUST LISTENING TO CHILDREN IN THE NEXT COLLECTIVE.
P UNTIL THAT POINT, I WAS JUST AN ORDINARY LITTLE BOY WITH BRUISED KNEES AND A WHEEZY COUGH AND A CRUSH ON MY CUTE, RED-HEADED EIGHBOR JUST LIKE ANYONE ELSE.
IF I'D HAD THE POWERS I'D HAVE LEFT THE FARM YEARS BEFORE NOW, BUT I DIDN'T. YOU KNOW WHY?
BECAUSE MY PARENTS WANTED ME TO BE READY WHEN I WENT TO THE BIG CITY. I BELIEVE IN THIS JUST AS MUCH AS YOU DO, PYOTR. THIS DOESN'T HAVE TO BE A COMPETITION.
THAT'S EASY TO SAY WHEN YOU'RE STREAKING THROUGH THE SKIES, SUPERMAN. NOT SO MUCH FUN WHEN YOU'RE DOWN HERE WORKING IN THE GUTTERS LIKE THE REST OF US.

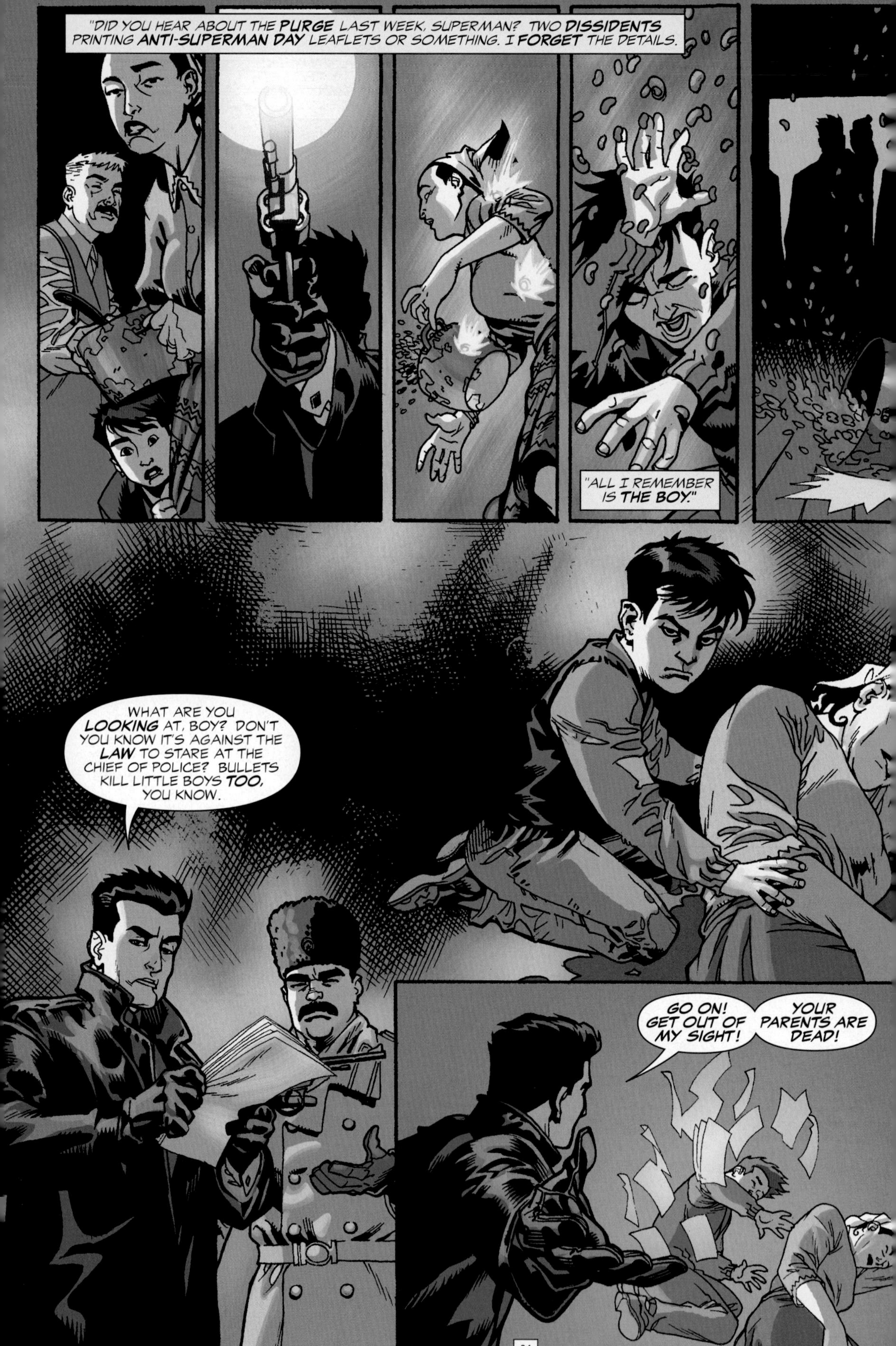
"DID YOU HEAR ABOUT THE PURGE LAST WEEK, SUPERMAN? TWO DISSIDENTS PRINTING ANTI-SUPERMAN DAY LEAFLETS OR SOMETHING. I FORGET THE DETAILS.
"ALL I REMEMBER IS THE BOY."
WHAT ARE YOU LOOKING AT, BOY? DON'T YOU KNOW IT'S AGAINST THE LAW TO STARE AT THE CHIEF OF POLICE? BULLETS KILL LITTLE BOYS TOO, YOU KNOW.
GO ON! GET OUT OF MY SIGHT!
YOUR PARENTS ARE DEAD!

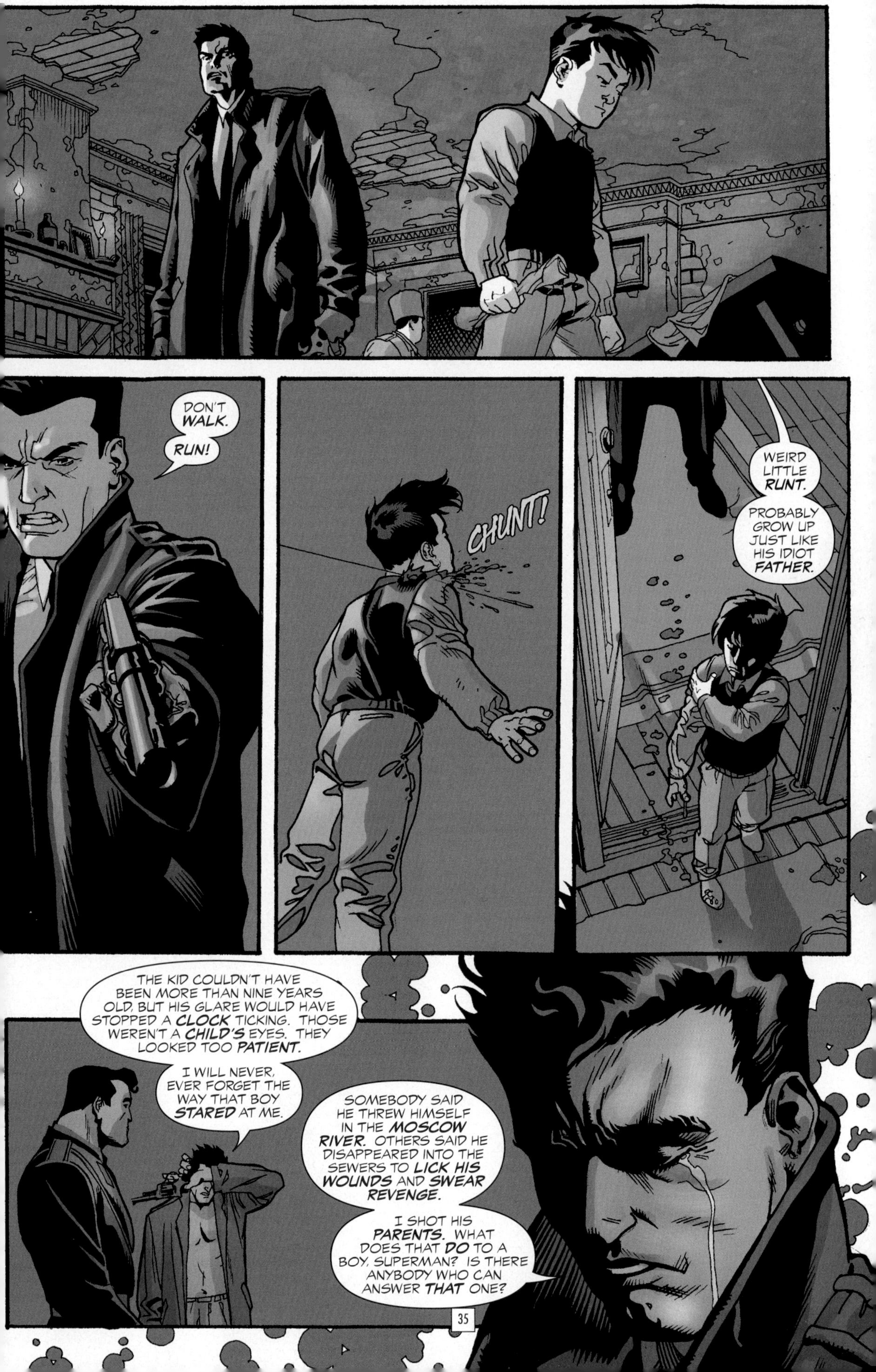
DON'T WALK.
RUN!
CHUNT!
WEIRD LITTLE RUNT.
PROBABLY GROW UP JUST LIKE HIS IDIOT FATHER.
THE KID COULDN'T HAVE BEEN MORE THAN NINE YEARS OLD, BUT HIS GLARE WOULD HAVE STOPPED A CLOCK TICKING. THOSE WEREN'T A CHILD'S EYES. THEY LOOKED TOO PATIENT.
I WILL NEVER, EVER FORGET THE WAY THAT BOY STARED AT ME.
SOMEBODY SAID HE THREW HIMSELF IN THE MOSCOW RIVER. OTHERS SAID HE DISAPPEARED INTO THE SEWERS TO LICK HIS WOUNDS AND SWEAR REVENGE.
I SHOT HIS PARENTS. WHAT DOES THAT DO TO A BOY, SUPERMAN? IS THERE ANYBODY WHO CAN ANSWER THAT ONE?

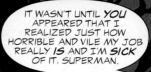

IT WASN'T UNTIL *YOU* APPEARED THAT I REALIZED JUST HOW HORRIBLE AND VILE MY JOB REALLY *IS* AND I'M *SICK* OF IT, SUPERMAN.

SICK OF *WORKING* IN A *SYSTEM* WHERE, NO MATTER HOW *HARD* I TRY, I'M NEVER GOING TO MAKE IT TO THE *TOP* OF THE *PARTY* NOW THAT *YOU'RE* HERE.

SICK OF GETTING MY *HANDS* DIRTY FOR A MAN WHO WON'T EVEN ADMIT I'M HIS OWN *FLESH AND BLOOD.*

CLICK

CHUNT

NO!

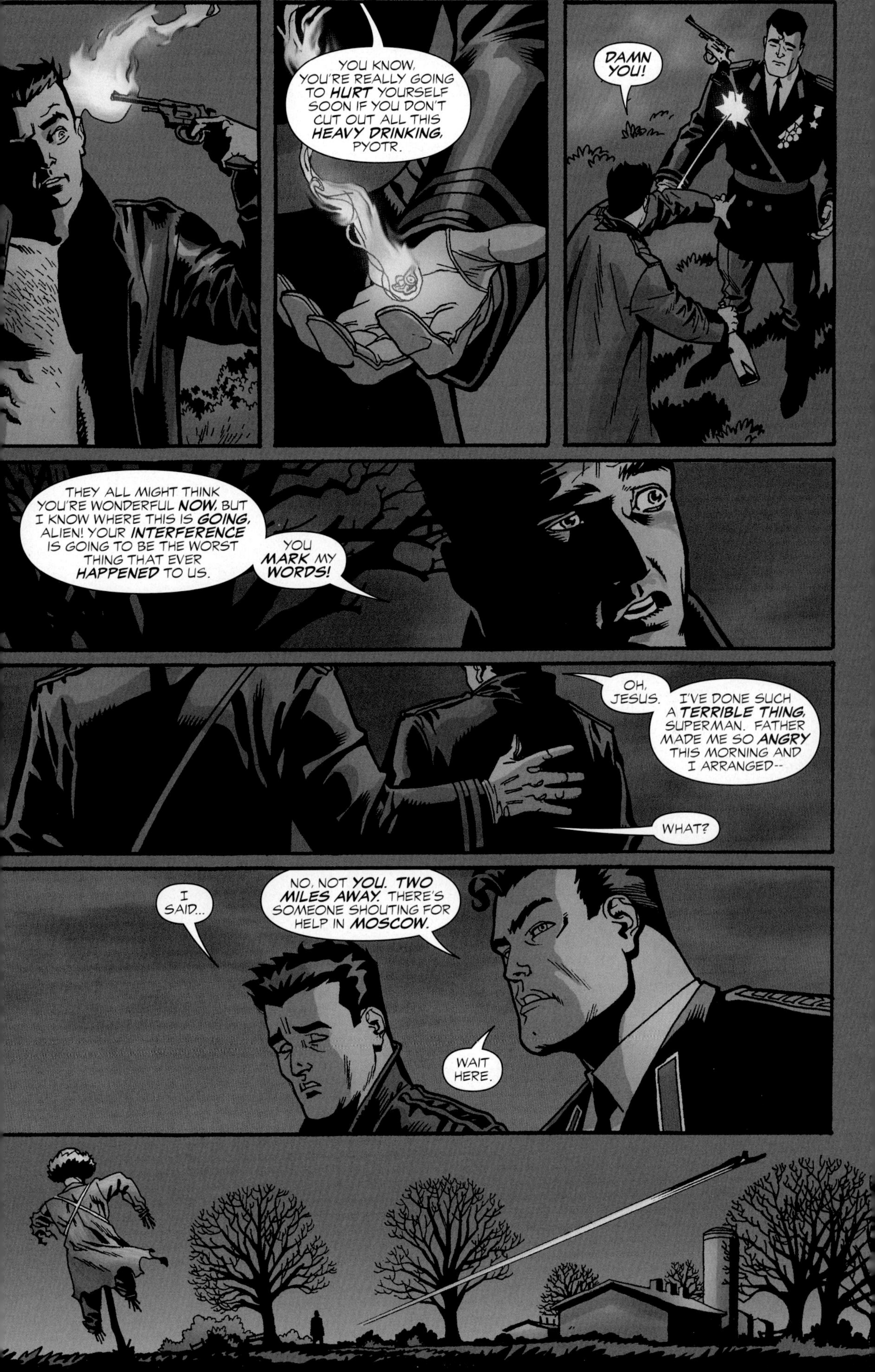
YOU KNOW, YOU'RE REALLY GOING TO HURT YOURSELF SOON IF YOU DON'T CUT OUT ALL THIS HEAVY DRINKING, PYOTR.
DAMN YOU!
THEY ALL MIGHT THINK YOU'RE WONDERFUL NOW, BUT I KNOW WHERE THIS IS GOING, ALIEN! YOUR INTERFERENCE IS GOING TO BE THE WORST THING THAT EVER HAPPENED TO US.
YOU MARK MY WORDS!
OH, JESUS.
I'VE DONE SUCH A TERRIBLE THING, SUPERMAN. FATHER MADE ME SO ANGRY THIS MORNING AND I ARRANGED--
WHAT?
I SAID...
NO, NOT YOU. TWO MILES AWAY. THERE'S SOMEONE SHOUTING FOR HELP IN MOSCOW.
WAIT HERE.

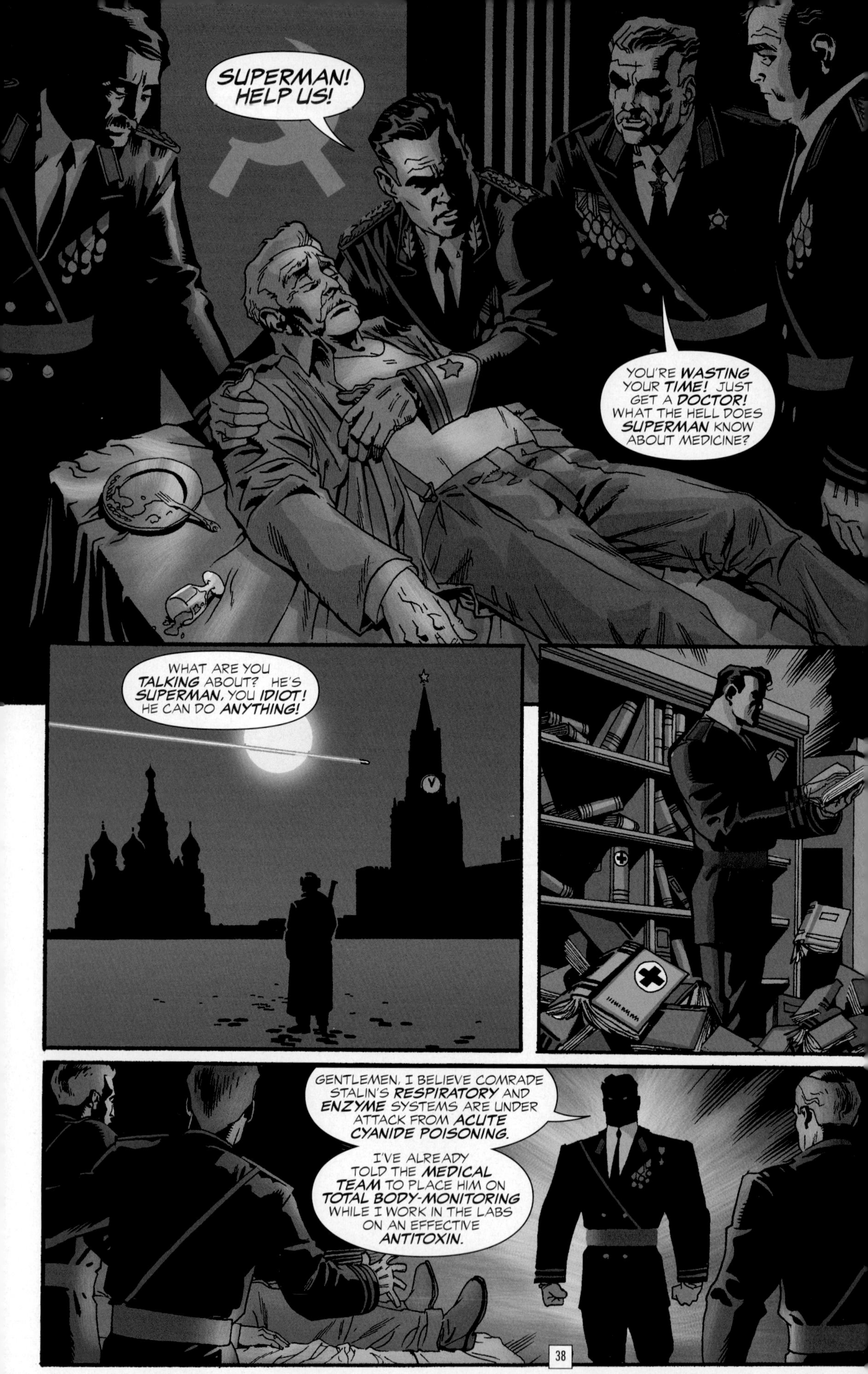
SUPERMAN! HELP US!
YOU'RE WASTING YOUR TIME! JUST GET A DOCTOR! WHAT THE HELL DOES SUPERMAN KNOW ABOUT MEDICINE?
WHAT ARE YOU TALKING ABOUT? HE'S SUPERMAN, YOU IDIOT! HE CAN DO ANYTHING!
GENTLEMEN, I BELIEVE COMRADE STALIN'S RESPIRATORY AND ENZYME SYSTEMS ARE UNDER ATTACK FROM ACUTE CYANIDE POISONING.
I'VE ALREADY TOLD THE MEDICAL TEAM TO PLACE HIM ON TOTAL BODY-MONITORING WHILE I WORK IN THE LABS ON AN EFFECTIVE ANTITOXIN.

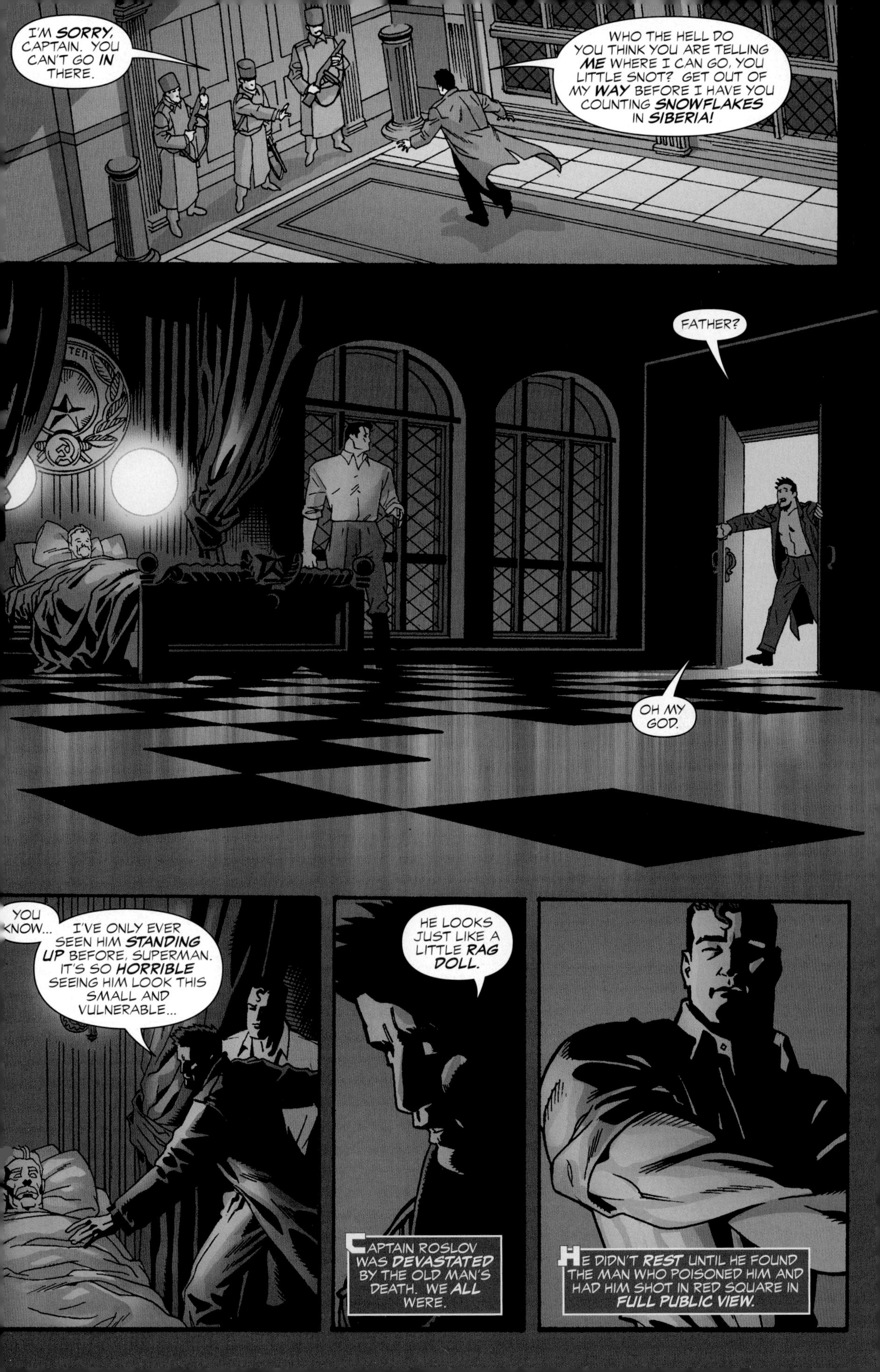
I'M SORRY, CAPTAIN. YOU CAN'T GO IN THERE.
WHO THE HELL DO YOU THINK YOU ARE TELLING ME WHERE I CAN GO, YOU LITTLE SNOT? GET OUT OF MY WAY BEFORE I HAVE YOU COUNTING SNOWFLAKES IN SIBERIA!
FATHER?
OH MY GOD.
YOU KNOW...
I'VE ONLY EVER SEEN HIM STANDING UP BEFORE, SUPERMAN. IT'S SO HORRIBLE SEEING HIM LOOK THIS SMALL AND VULNERABLE...
HE LOOKS JUST LIKE A LITTLE RAG DOLL.
CAPTAIN ROSLOV WAS DEVASTATED BY THE OLD MAN'S DEATH. WE ALL WERE.
HE DIDN'T REST UNTIL HE FOUND THE MAN WHO POISONED HIM AND HAD HIM SHOT IN RED SQUARE IN FULL PUBLIC VIEW.

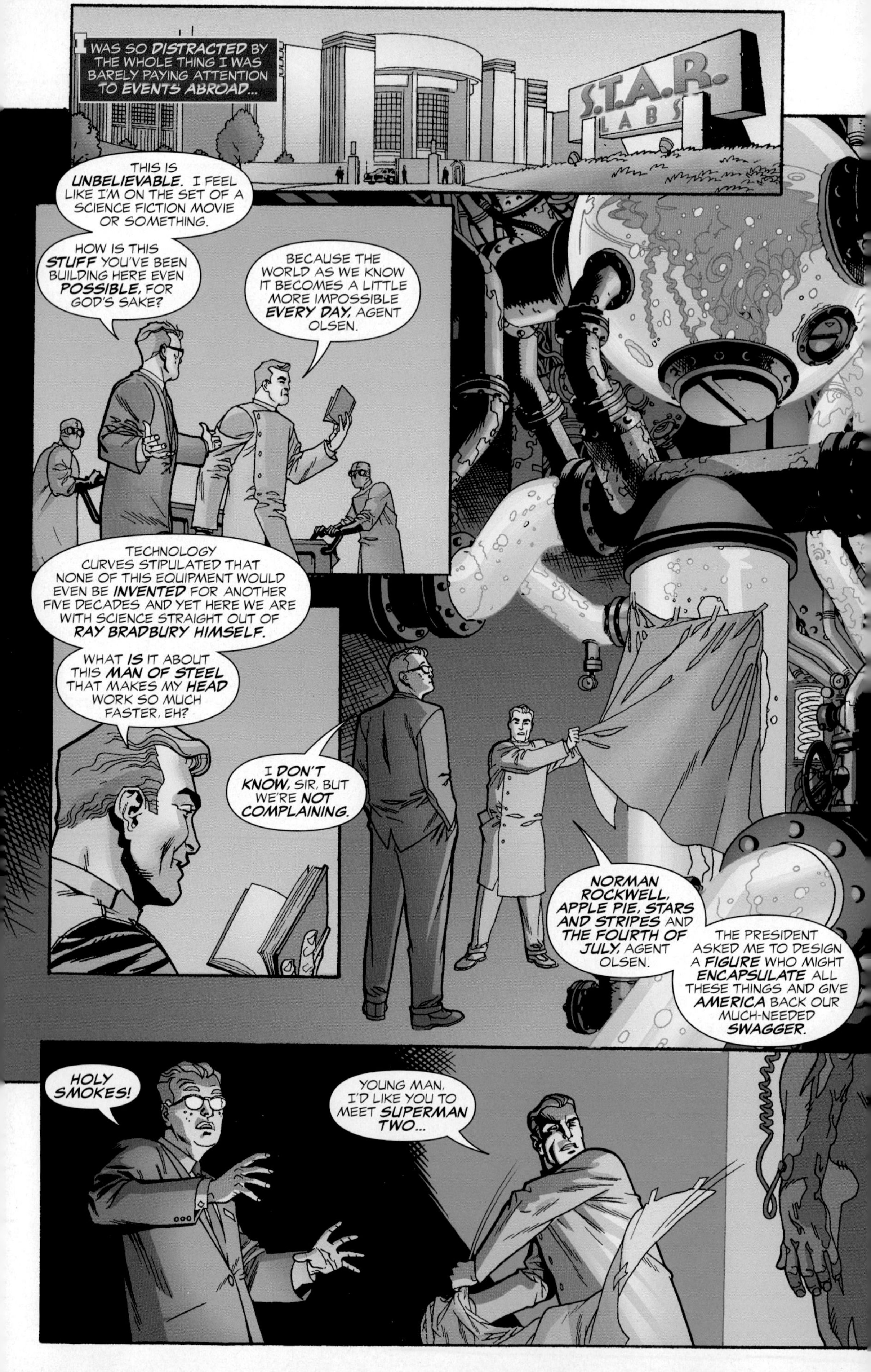
I WAS SO DISTRACTED BY THE WHOLE THING I WAS BARELY PAYING ATTENTION TO EVENTS ABROAD...
S.T.A.R. LABS
THIS IS UNBELIEVABLE. I FEEL LIKE I'M ON THE SET OF A SCIENCE FICTION MOVIE OR SOMETHING.
HOW IS THIS STUFF YOU'VE BEEN BUILDING HERE EVEN POSSIBLE, FOR GOD'S SAKE?
BECAUSE THE WORLD AS WE KNOW IT BECOMES A LITTLE MORE IMPOSSIBLE EVERY DAY, AGENT OLSEN.
TECHNOLOGY CURVES STIPULATED THAT NONE OF THIS EQUIPMENT WOULD EVEN BE INVENTED FOR ANOTHER FIVE DECADES AND YET HERE WE ARE WITH SCIENCE STRAIGHT OUT OF RAY BRADBURY HIMSELF.
WHAT IS IT ABOUT THIS MAN OF STEEL THAT MAKES MY HEAD WORK SO MUCH FASTER, EH?
I DON'T KNOW, SIR, BUT WE'RE NOT COMPLAINING.
NORMAN ROCKWELL, APPLE PIE, STARS AND STRIPES AND THE FOURTH OF JULY, AGENT OLSEN.
THE PRESIDENT ASKED ME TO DESIGN A FIGURE WHO MIGHT ENCAPSULATE ALL THESE THINGS AND GIVE AMERICA BACK OUR MUCH-NEEDED SWAGGER.
HOLY SMOKES!
YOUNG MAN, I'D LIKE YOU TO MEET SUPERMAN TWO...

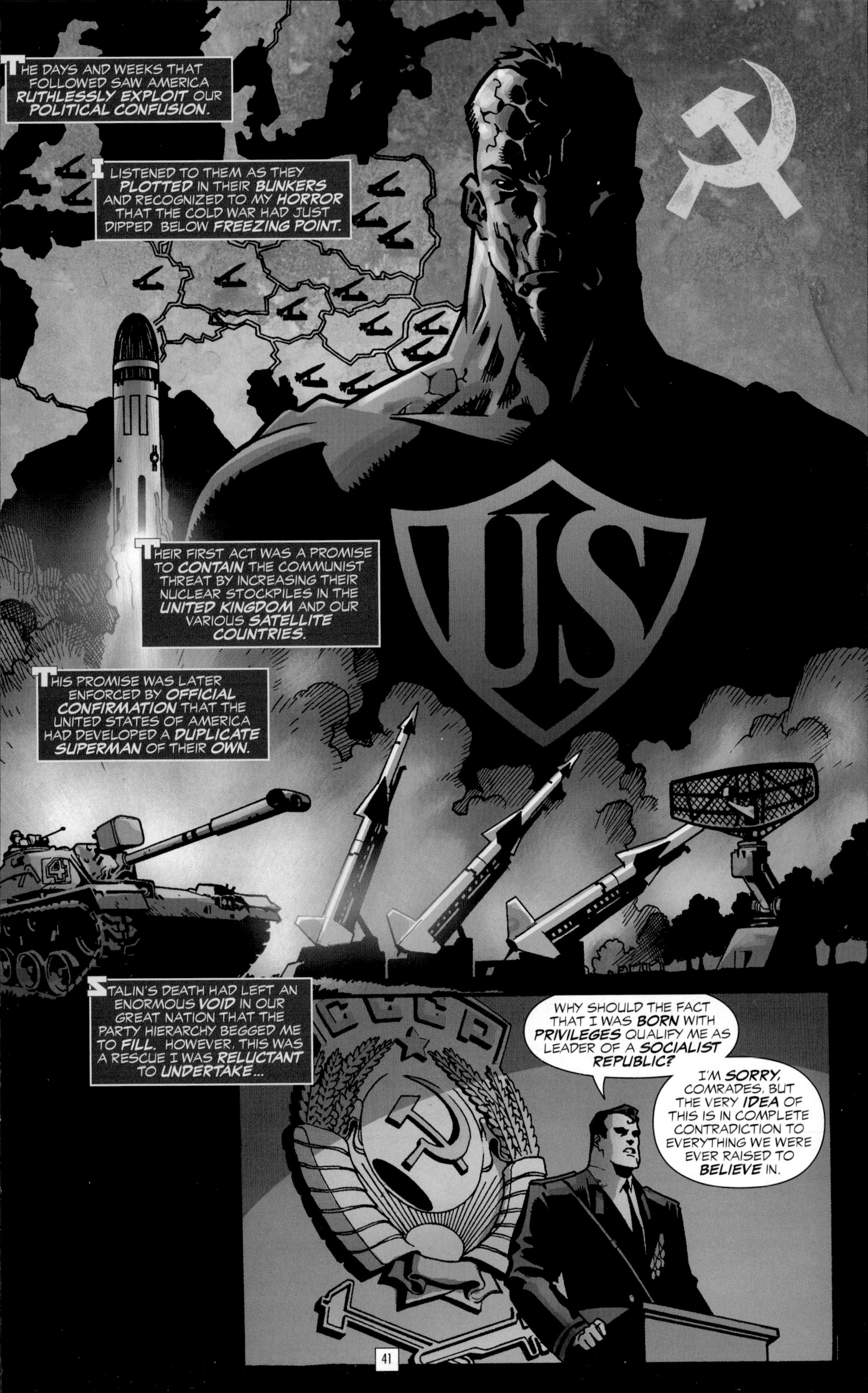
THE DAYS AND WEEKS THAT FOLLOWED SAW AMERICA RUTHLESSLY EXPLOIT OUR POLITICAL CONFUSION.
I LISTENED TO THEM AS THEY PLOTTED IN THEIR BUNKERS AND RECOGNIZED TO MY HORROR THAT THE COLD WAR HAD JUST DIPPED BELOW FREEZING POINT.
THEIR FIRST ACT WAS A PROMISE TO CONTAIN THE COMMUNIST THREAT BY INCREASING THEIR NUCLEAR STOCKPILES IN THE UNITED KINGDOM AND OUR VARIOUS SATELLITE COUNTRIES.
THIS PROMISE WAS LATER ENFORCED BY OFFICIAL CONFIRMATION THAT THE UNITED STATES OF AMERICA HAD DEVELOPED A DUPLICATE SUPERMAN OF THEIR OWN.
STALIN'S DEATH HAD LEFT AN ENORMOUS VOID IN OUR GREAT NATION THAT THE PARTY HIERARCHY BEGGED ME TO FILL. HOWEVER, THIS WAS A RESCUE I WAS RELUCTANT TO UNDERTAKE...
WHY SHOULD THE FACT THAT I WAS BORN WITH PRIVILEGES QUALIFY ME AS LEADER OF A SOCIALIST REPUBLIC?
I'M SORRY, COMRADES, BUT THE VERY IDEA OF THIS IS IN COMPLETE CONTRADICTION TO EVERYTHING WE WERE EVER RAISED TO BELIEVE IN.

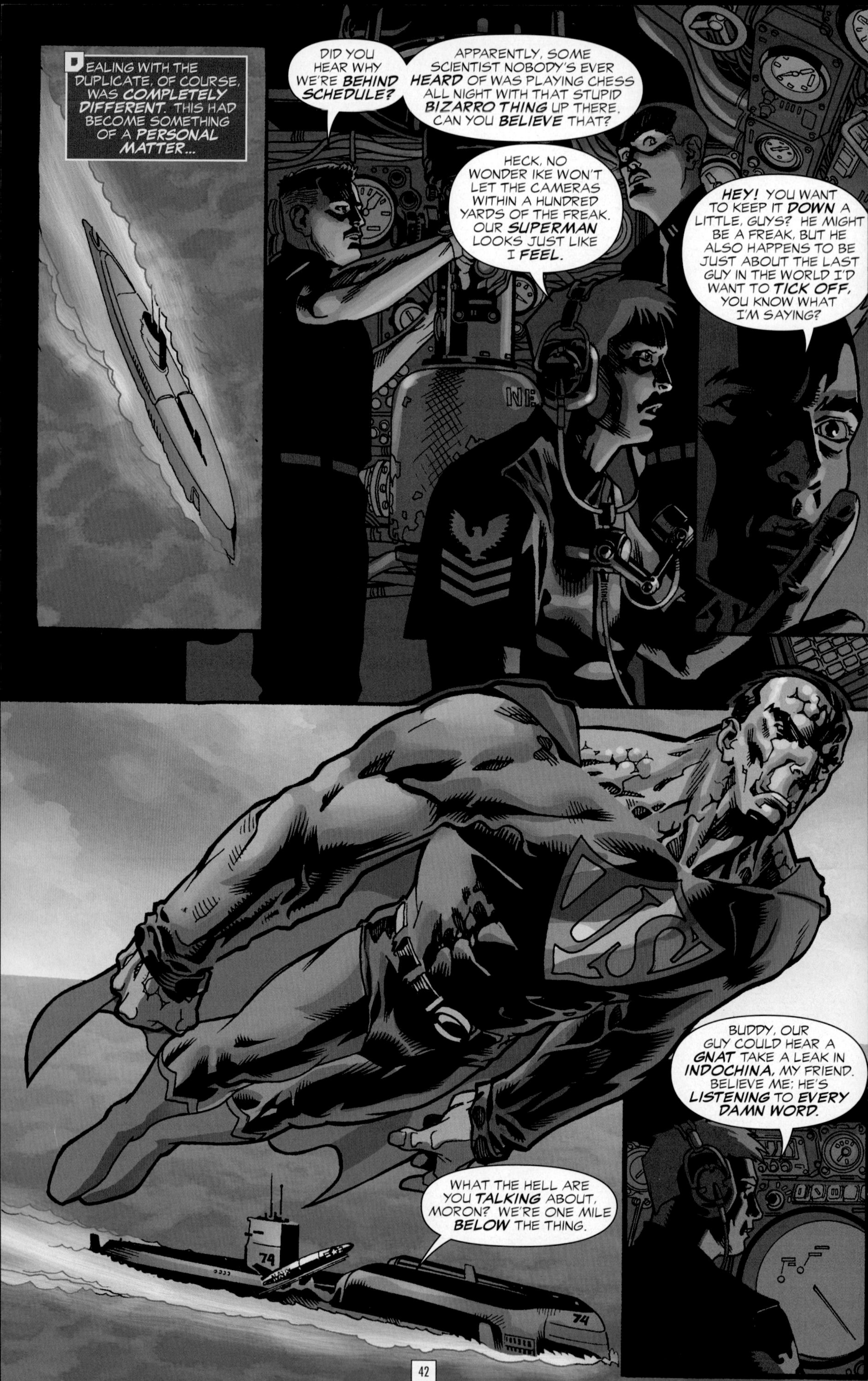
DEALING WITH THE DUPLICATE, OF COURSE, WAS COMPLETELY DIFFERENT. THIS HAD BECOME SOMETHING OF A PERSONAL MATTER...
DID YOU HEAR WHY WE'RE BEHIND SCHEDULE?
APPARENTLY, SOME SCIENTIST NOBODY'S EVER HEARD OF WAS PLAYING CHESS ALL NIGHT WITH THAT STUPID BIZARRO THING UP THERE. CAN YOU BELIEVE THAT?
HECK, NO WONDER IKE WON'T LET THE CAMERAS WITHIN A HUNDRED YARDS OF THE FREAK. OUR SUPERMAN LOOKS JUST LIKE I FEEL.
HEY! YOU WANT TO KEEP IT DOWN A LITTLE, GUYS? HE MIGHT BE A FREAK, BUT HE ALSO HAPPENS TO BE JUST ABOUT THE LAST GUY IN THE WORLD I'D WANT TO TICK OFF, YOU KNOW WHAT I'M SAYING?
WHAT THE HELL ARE YOU TALKING ABOUT, MORON? WE'RE ONE MILE BELOW THE THING.
BUDDY, OUR GUY COULD HEAR A GNAT TAKE A LEAK IN INDOCHINA, MY FRIEND. BELIEVE ME; HE'S LISTENING TO EVERY DAMN WORD.

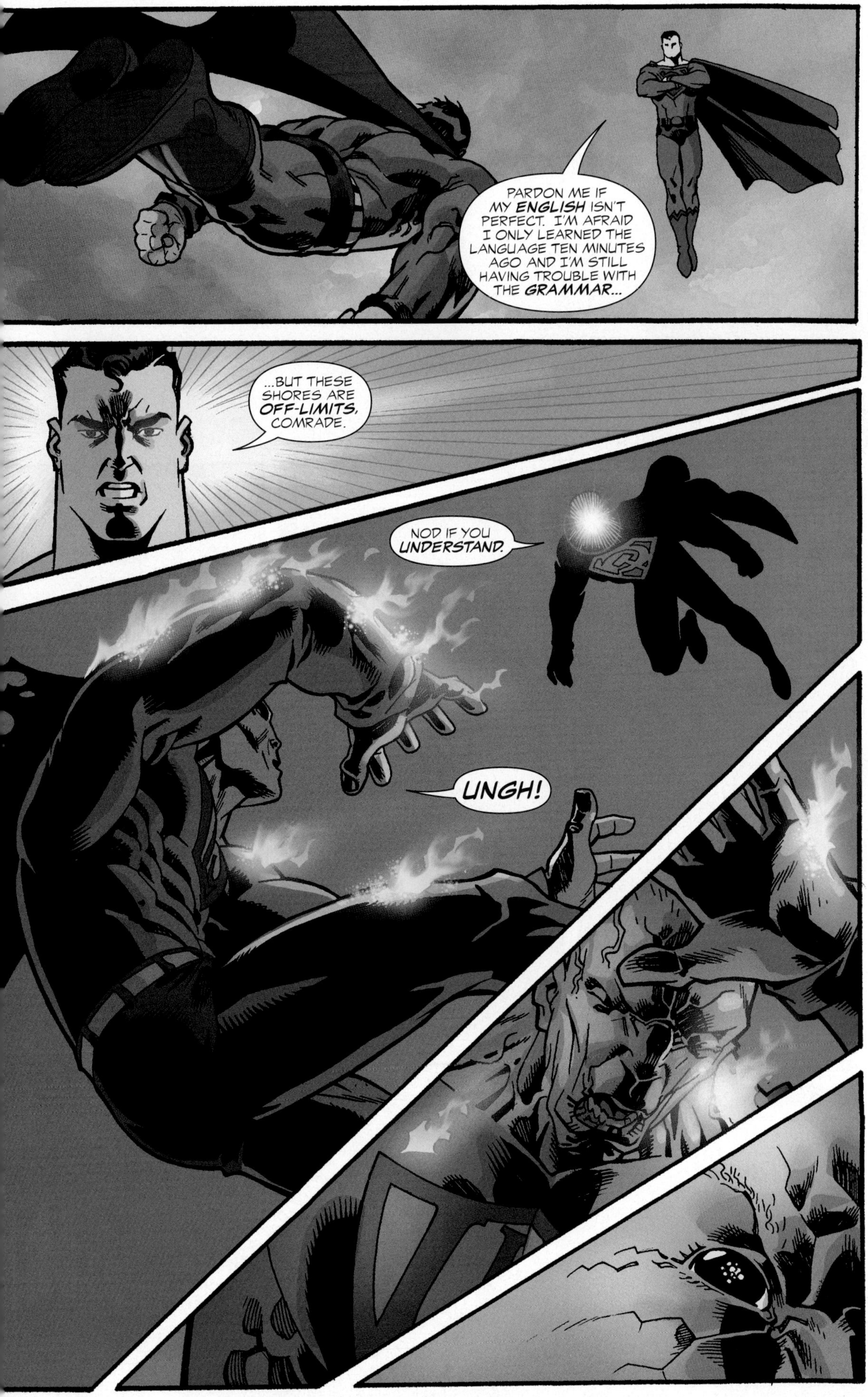
PARDON ME IF MY ENGLISH ISN'T PERFECT. I'M AFRAID I ONLY LEARNED THE LANGUAGE TEN MINUTES AGO AND I'M STILL HAVING TROUBLE WITH THE GRAMMAR...
...BUT THESE SHORES ARE OFF-LIMITS, COMRADE.
NOD IF YOU UNDERSTAND.
UNGH!

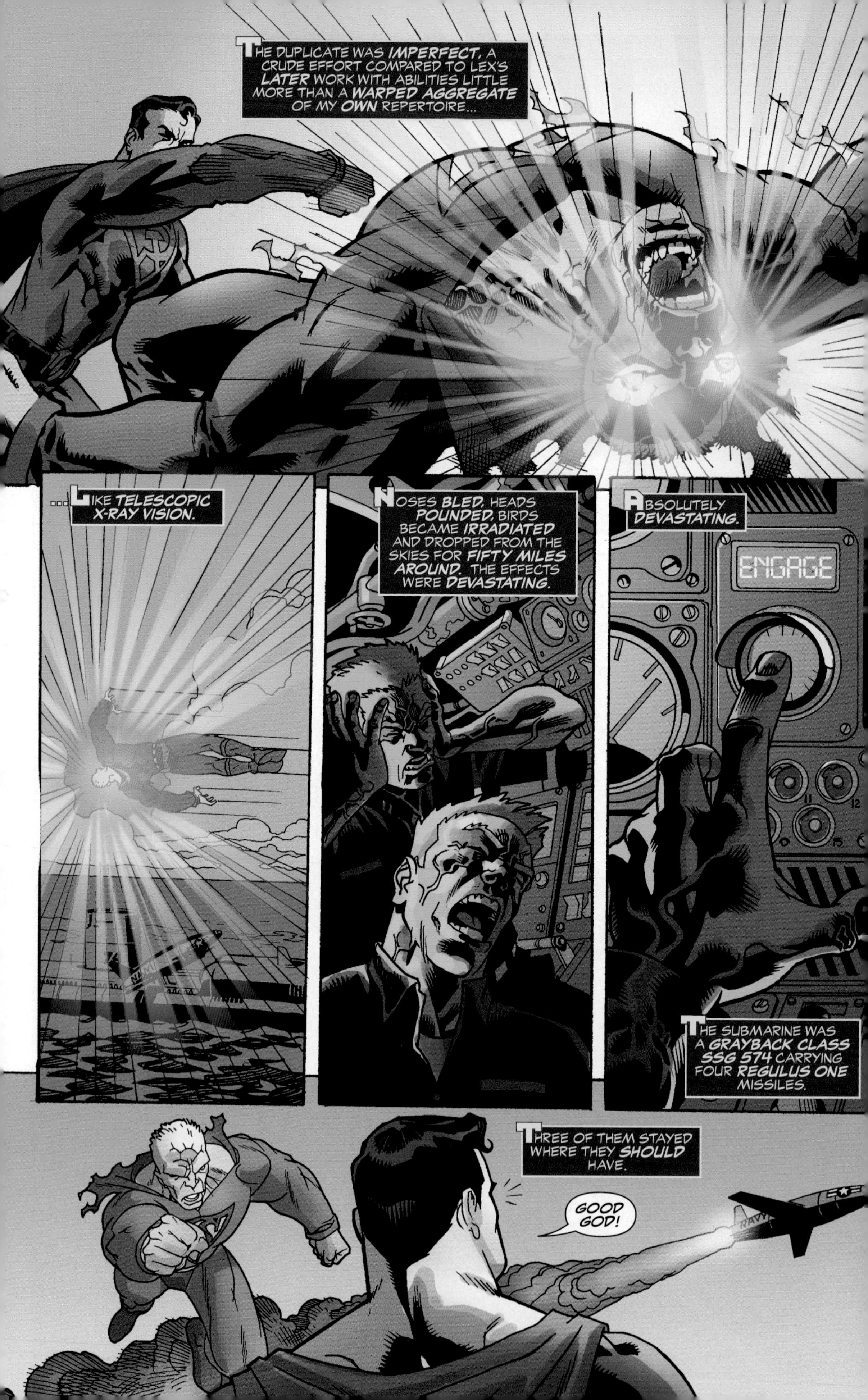
THE DUPLICATE WAS IMPERFECT, A CRUDE EFFORT COMPARED TO LEX'S LATER WORK WITH ABILITIES LITTLE MORE THAN A WARPED AGGREGATE OF MY OWN REPERTOIRE...
...LIKE TELESCOPIC X-RAY VISION.
NOSES BLED, HEADS POUNDED, BIRDS BECAME IRRADIATED AND DROPPED FROM THE SKIES FOR FIFTY MILES AROUND. THE EFFECTS WERE DEVASTATING.
ABSOLUTELY DEVASTATING.
ENGAGE
THE SUBMARINE WAS A GRAYBACK CLASS SSG 574 CARRYING FOUR REGULUS ONE MISSILES.
THREE OF THEM STAYED WHERE THEY SHOULD HAVE.
GOOD GOD!
NAVY

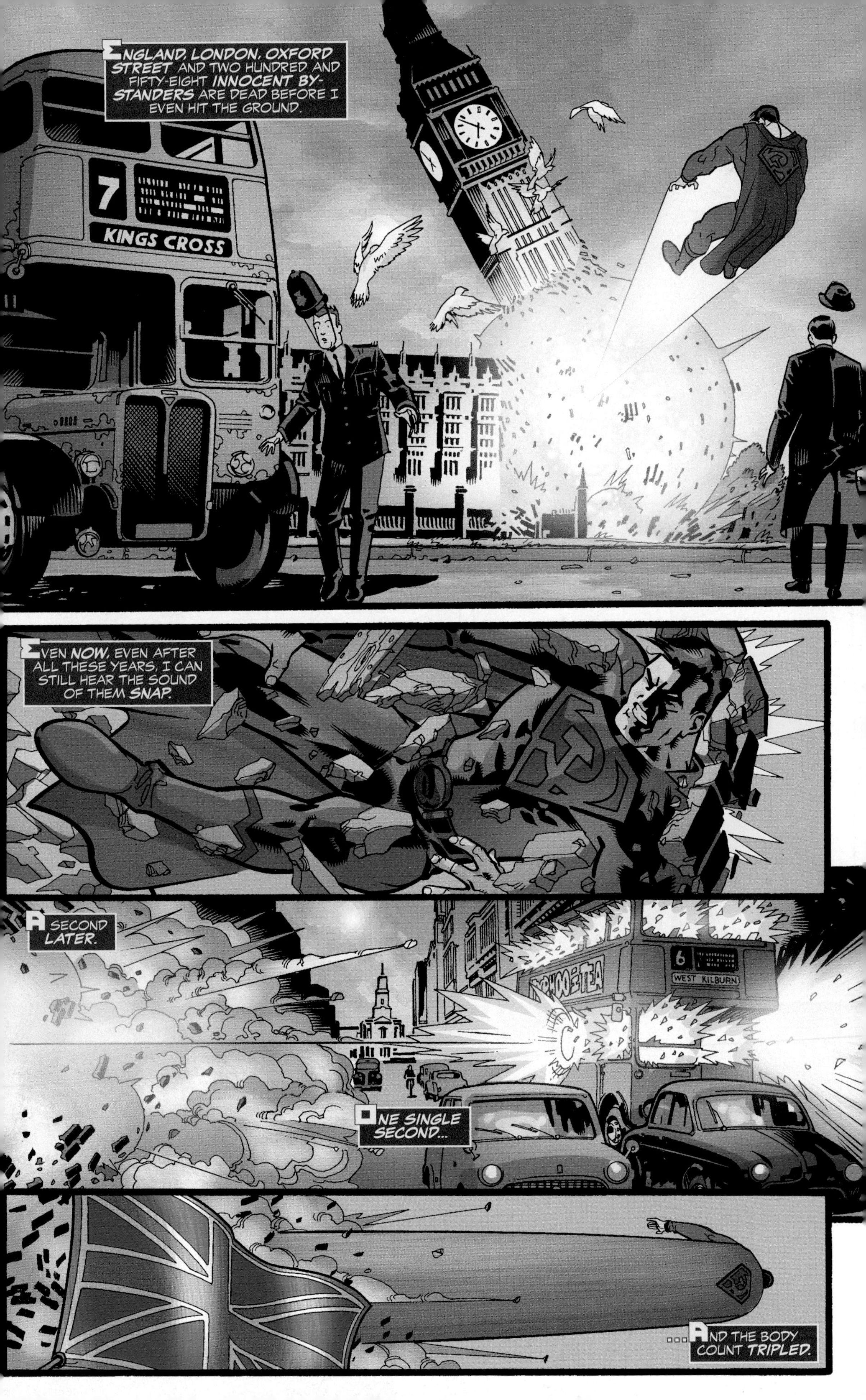
ENGLAND, LONDON, OXFORD STREET AND TWO HUNDRED AND FIFTY-EIGHT INNOCENT BY-STANDERS ARE DEAD BEFORE I EVEN HIT THE GROUND.
7
KINGS CROSS
EVEN NOW, EVEN AFTER ALL THESE YEARS, I CAN STILL HEAR THE SOUND OF THEM SNAP.
A SECOND LATER.
6
WEST KILBURN
ONE SINGLE SECOND...
...AND THE BODY COUNT TRIPLED.

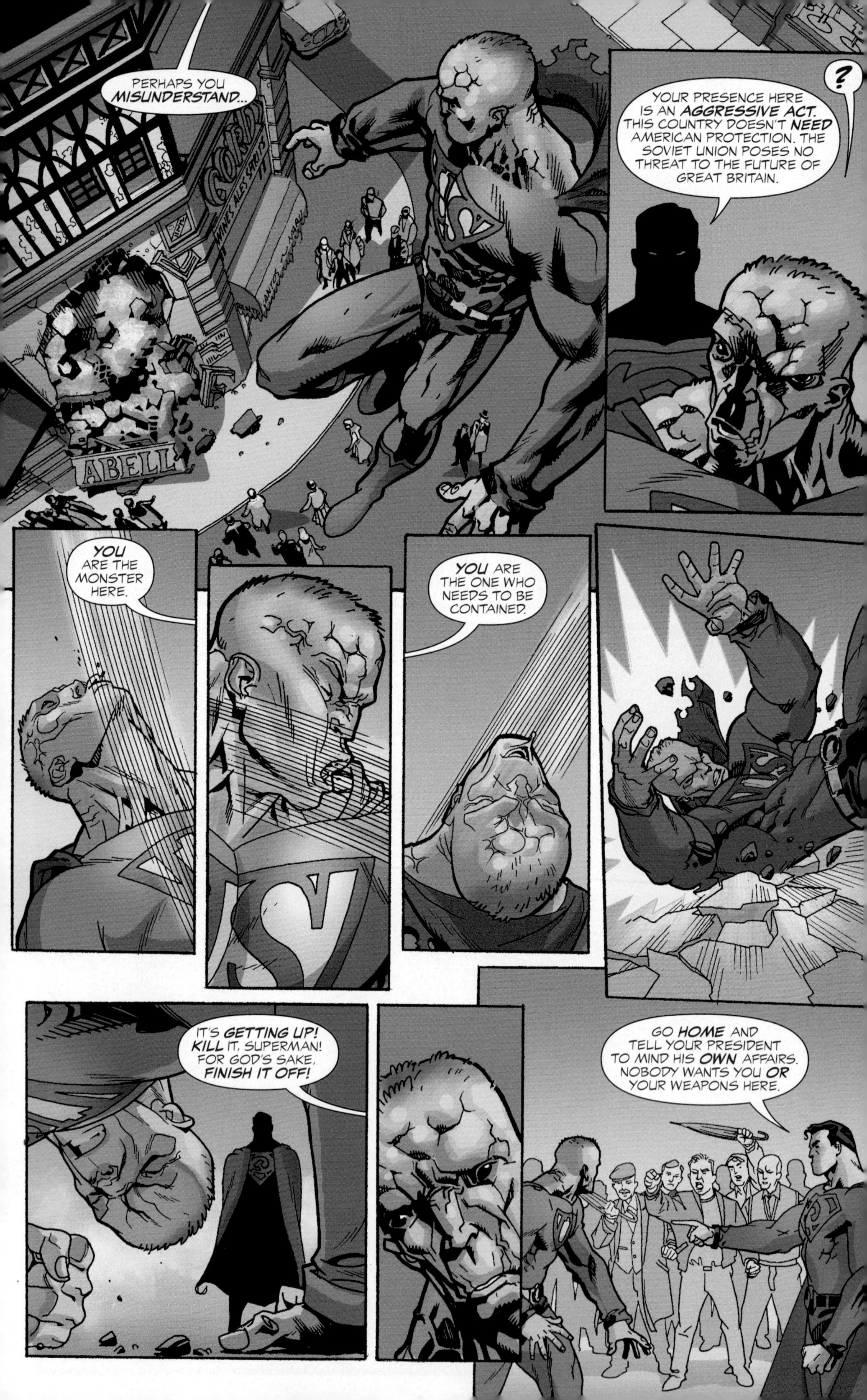
PERHAPS YOU MISUNDERSTAND...
GORDON
WINES ALES SPIRITS
ABELL
?
YOUR PRESENCE HERE IS AN AGGRESSIVE ACT. THIS COUNTRY DOESN'T NEED AMERICAN PROTECTION. THE SOVIET UNION POSES NO THREAT TO THE FUTURE OF GREAT BRITAIN.
YOU ARE THE MONSTER HERE.
YOU ARE THE ONE WHO NEEDS TO BE CONTAINED.
IT'S GETTING UP! KILL IT, SUPERMAN! FOR GOD'S SAKE, FINISH IT OFF!
GO HOME AND TELL YOUR PRESIDENT TO MIND HIS OWN AFFAIRS. NOBODY WANTS YOU OR YOUR WEAPONS HERE.

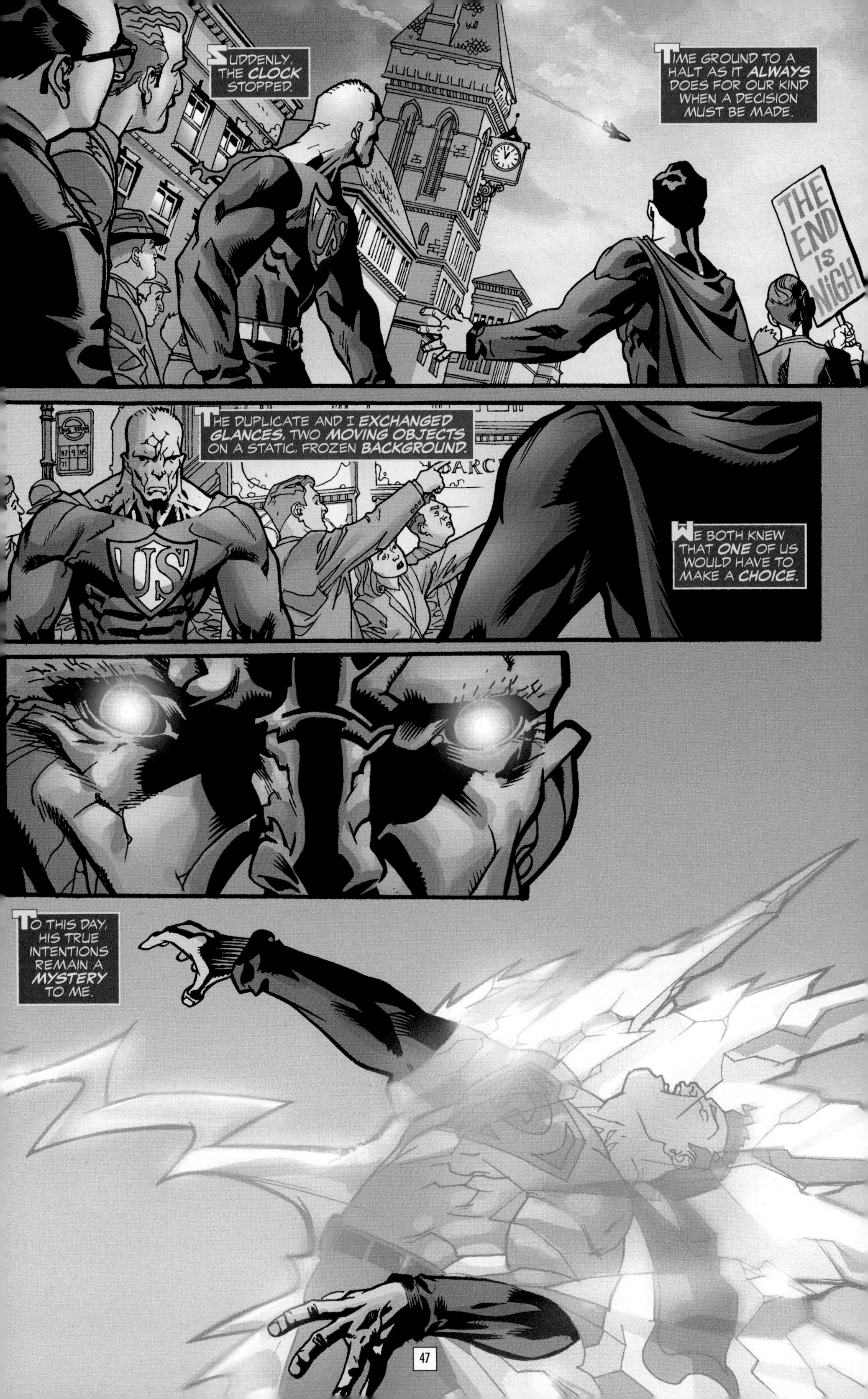
SUDDENLY, THE CLOCK STOPPED.
TIME GROUND TO A HALT AS IT ALWAYS DOES FOR OUR KIND WHEN A DECISION MUST BE MADE.
THE END IS NIGH
THE DUPLICATE AND I EXCHANGED GLANCES, TWO MOVING OBJECTS ON A STATIC, FROZEN BACKGROUND.
WE BOTH KNEW THAT ONE OF US WOULD HAVE TO MAKE A CHOICE.
TO THIS DAY, HIS TRUE INTENTIONS REMAIN A MYSTERY TO ME.

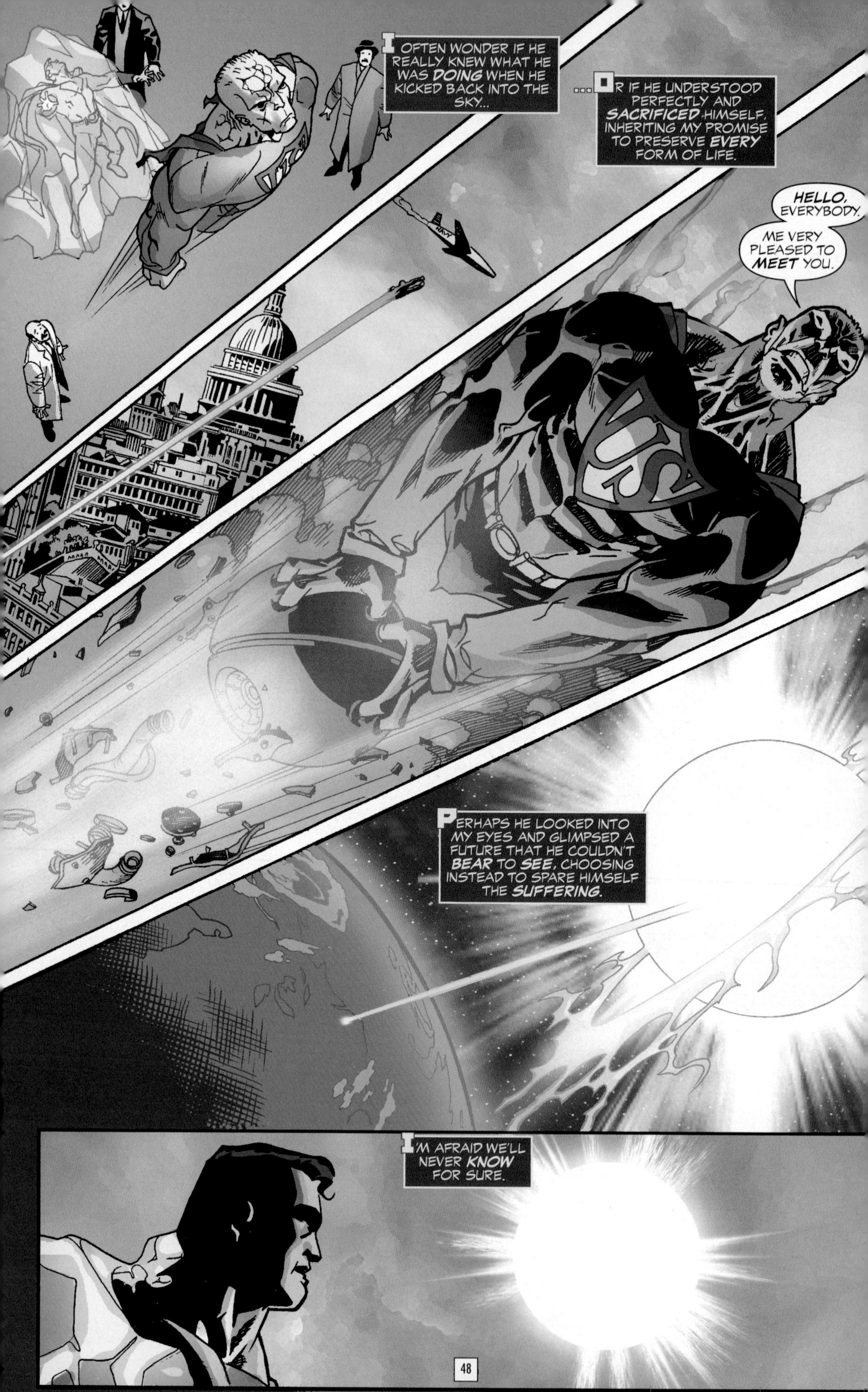
I OFTEN WONDER IF HE REALLY KNEW WHAT HE WAS DOING WHEN HE KICKED BACK INTO THE SKY...
...OR IF HE UNDERSTOOD PERFECTLY AND SACRIFICED HIMSELF, INHERITING MY PROMISE TO PRESERVE EVERY FORM OF LIFE.
NAVY
HELLO, EVERYBODY.
ME VERY PLEASED TO MEET YOU.
PERHAPS HE LOOKED INTO MY EYES AND GLIMPSED A FUTURE THAT HE COULDN'T BEAR TO SEE, CHOOSING INSTEAD TO SPARE HIMSELF THE SUFFERING.
I'M AFRAID WE'LL NEVER KNOW FOR SURE.

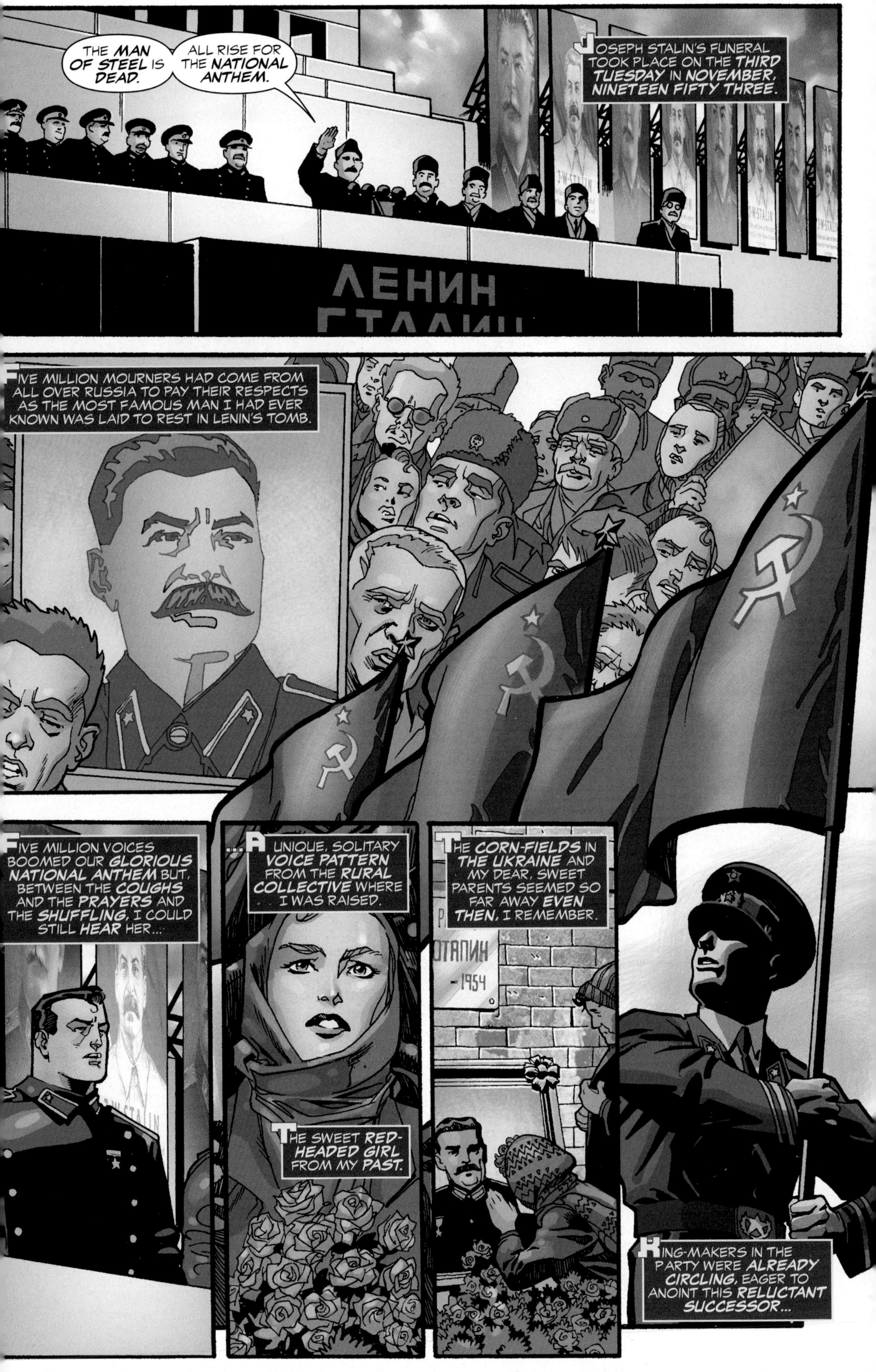
THE MAN OF STEEL IS DEAD.
ALL RISE FOR THE NATIONAL ANTHEM.
JOSEPH STALIN'S FUNERAL TOOK PLACE ON THE THIRD TUESDAY IN NOVEMBER, NINETEEN FIFTY THREE.
ЛЕНИН
FIVE MILLION MOURNERS HAD COME FROM ALL OVER RUSSIA TO PAY THEIR RESPECTS AS THE MOST FAMOUS MAN I HAD EVER KNOWN WAS LAID TO REST IN LENIN'S TOMB.
FIVE MILLION VOICES BOOMED OUR GLORIOUS NATIONAL ANTHEM BUT, BETWEEN THE COUGHS AND THE PRAYERS AND THE SHUFFLING, I COULD STILL HEAR HER...
...A UNIQUE, SOLITARY VOICE PATTERN FROM THE RURAL COLLECTIVE WHERE I WAS RAISED.
THE SWEET RED-HEADED GIRL FROM MY PAST.
THE CORN-FIELDS IN THE UKRAINE AND MY DEAR, SWEET PARENTS SEEMED SO FAR AWAY EVEN THEN, I REMEMBER.
KING-MAKERS IN THE PARTY WERE ALREADY CIRCLING, EAGER TO ANOINT THIS RELUCTANT SUCCESSOR...

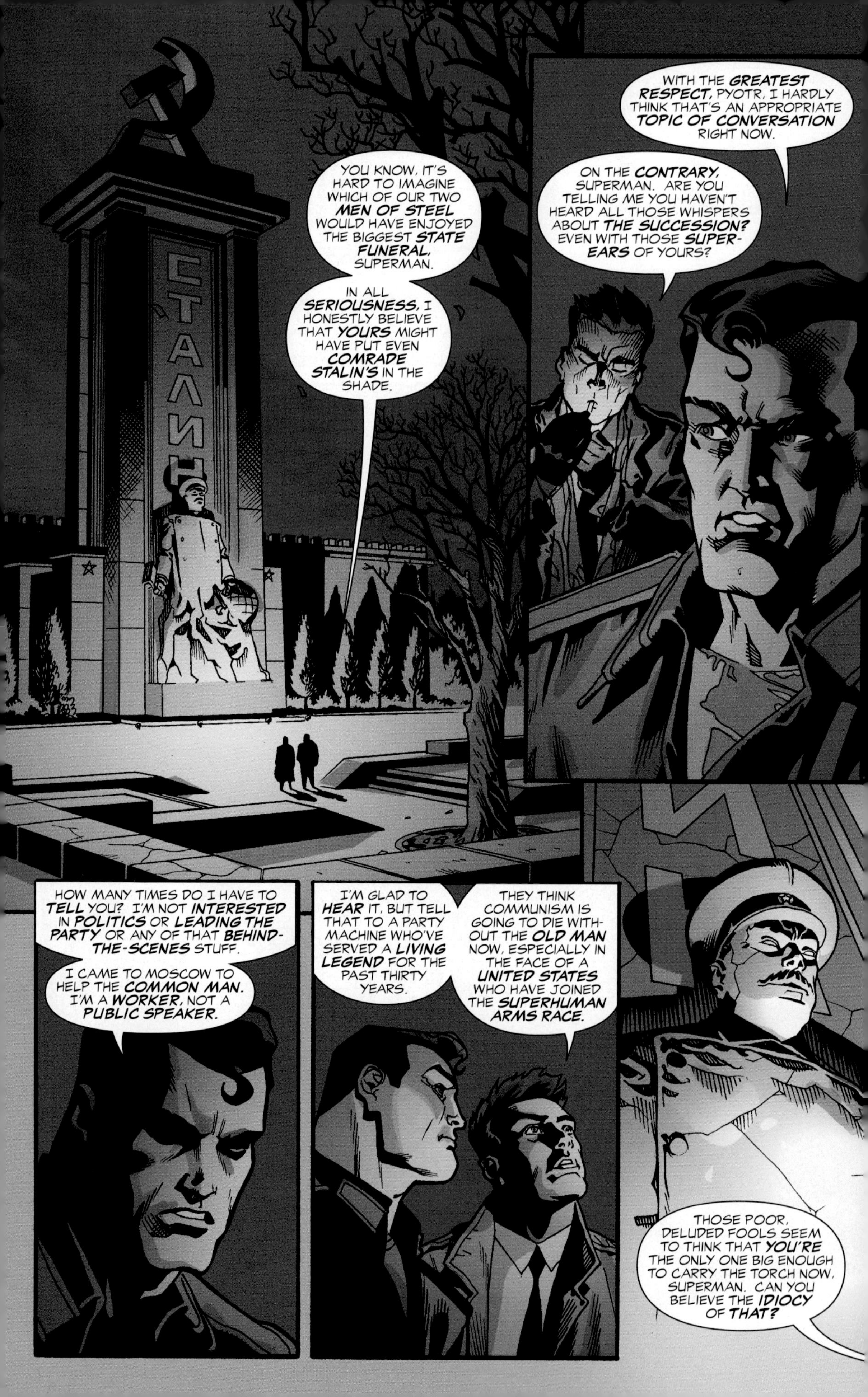

СТАЛИН
YOU KNOW, IT'S HARD TO IMAGINE WHICH OF OUR TWO MEN OF STEEL WOULD HAVE ENJOYED THE BIGGEST STATE FUNERAL, SUPERMAN.
IN ALL SERIOUSNESS, I HONESTLY BELIEVE THAT YOURS MIGHT HAVE PUT EVEN COMRADE STALIN'S IN THE SHADE.
WITH THE GREATEST RESPECT, PYOTR, I HARDLY THINK THAT'S AN APPROPRIATE TOPIC OF CONVERSATION RIGHT NOW.
ON THE CONTRARY, SUPERMAN. ARE YOU TELLING ME YOU HAVEN'T HEARD ALL THOSE WHISPERS ABOUT THE SUCCESSION? EVEN WITH THOSE SUPER-EARS OF YOURS?
HOW MANY TIMES DO I HAVE TO TELL YOU? I'M NOT INTERESTED IN POLITICS OR LEADING THE PARTY OR ANY OF THAT BEHIND-THE-SCENES STUFF.
I CAME TO MOSCOW TO HELP THE COMMON MAN. I'M A WORKER, NOT A PUBLIC SPEAKER.
I'M GLAD TO HEAR IT, BUT TELL THAT TO A PARTY MACHINE WHO'VE SERVED A LIVING LEGEND FOR THE PAST THIRTY YEARS.
THEY THINK COMMUNISM IS GOING TO DIE WITHOUT THE OLD MAN NOW, ESPECIALLY IN THE FACE OF A UNITED STATES WHO HAVE JOINED THE SUPERHUMAN ARMS RACE.
THOSE POOR, DELUDED FOOLS SEEM TO THINK THAT YOU'RE THE ONLY ONE BIG ENOUGH TO CARRY THE TORCH NOW, SUPERMAN. CAN YOU BELIEVE THE IDIOCY OF THAT?

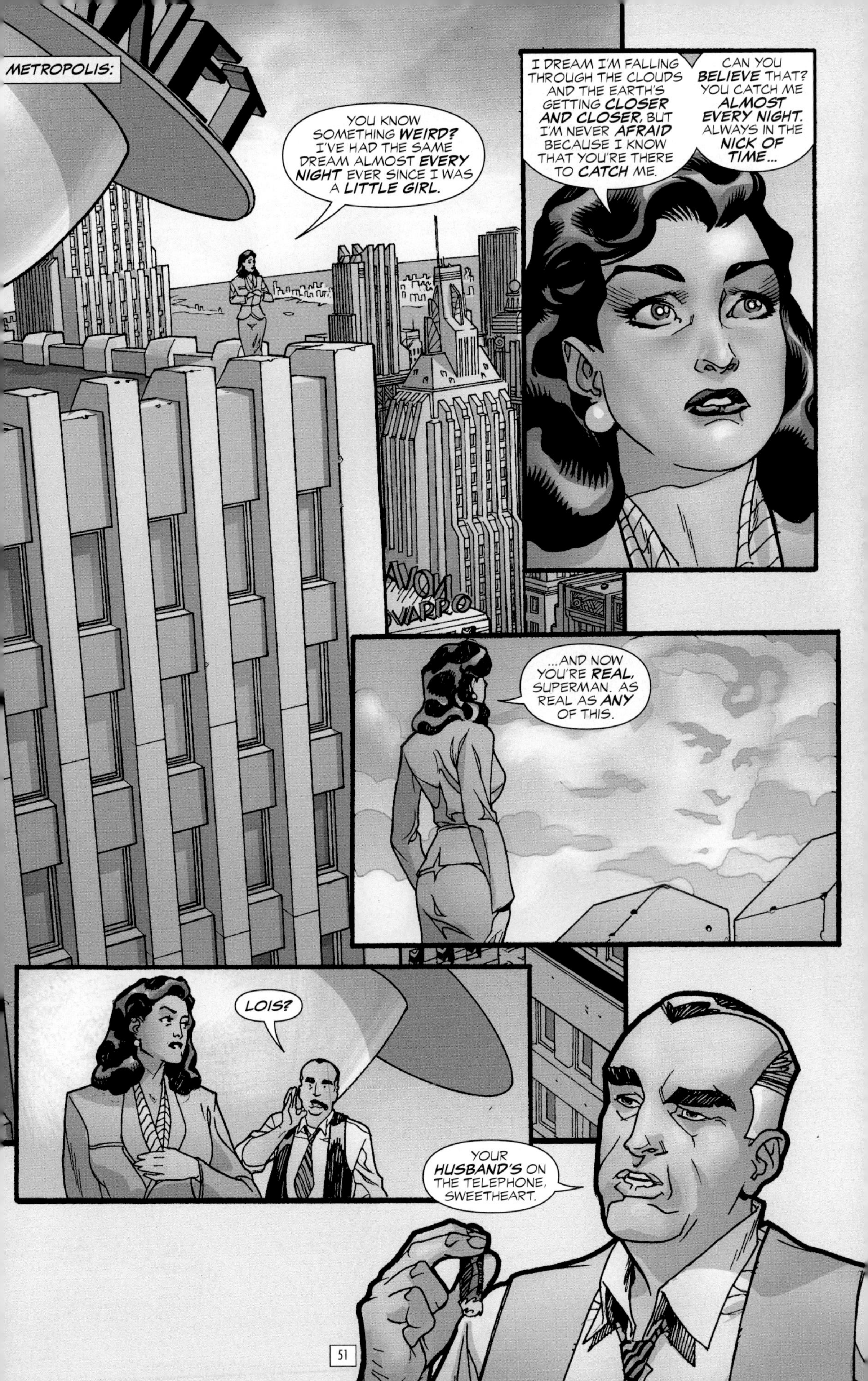
METROPOLIS:
YOU KNOW SOMETHING WEIRD? I'VE HAD THE SAME DREAM ALMOST EVERY NIGHT EVER SINCE I WAS A LITTLE GIRL.
I DREAM I'M FALLING THROUGH THE CLOUDS AND THE EARTH'S GETTING CLOSER AND CLOSER, BUT I'M NEVER AFRAID BECAUSE I KNOW THAT YOU'RE THERE TO CATCH ME.
CAN YOU BELIEVE THAT? YOU CATCH ME ALMOST EVERY NIGHT. ALWAYS IN THE NICK OF TIME...
...AND NOW YOU'RE REAL, SUPERMAN. AS REAL AS ANY OF THIS.
LOIS?
YOUR HUSBAND'S ON THE TELEPHONE, SWEETHEART.

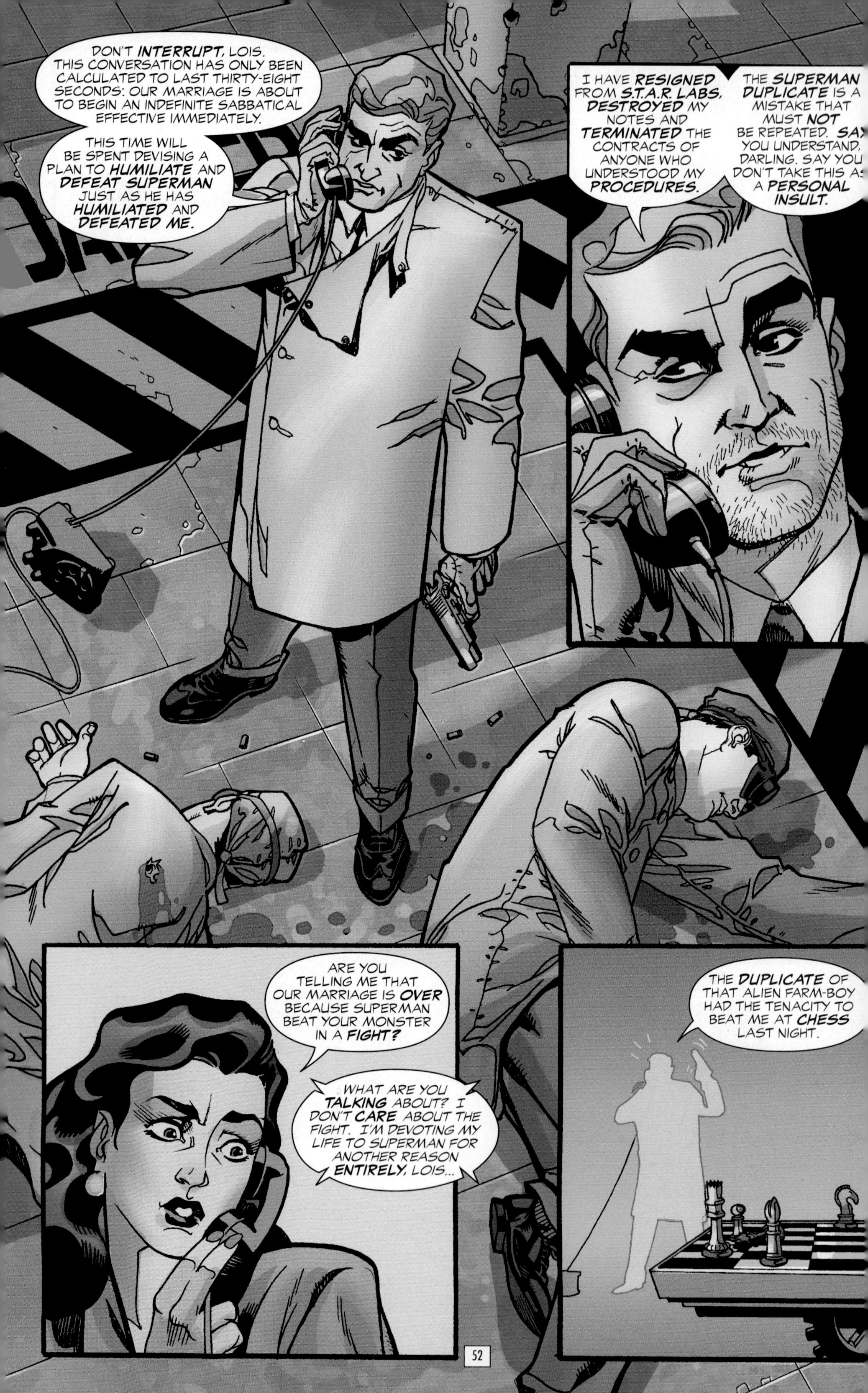

DON'T INTERRUPT, LOIS. THIS CONVERSATION HAS ONLY BEEN CALCULATED TO LAST THIRTY-EIGHT SECONDS: OUR MARRIAGE IS ABOUT TO BEGIN AN INDEFINITE SABBATICAL EFFECTIVE IMMEDIATELY.
THIS TIME WILL BE SPENT DEVISING A PLAN TO HUMILIATE AND DEFEAT SUPERMAN JUST AS HE HAS HUMILIATED AND DEFEATED ME.
I HAVE RESIGNED FROM S.T.A.R. LABS, DESTROYED MY NOTES AND TERMINATED THE CONTRACTS OF ANYONE WHO UNDERSTOOD MY PROCEDURES.
THE SUPERMAN DUPLICATE IS A MISTAKE THAT MUST NOT BE REPEATED. SAY YOU UNDERSTAND, DARLING. SAY YOU DON'T TAKE THIS AS A PERSONAL INSULT.
ARE YOU TELLING ME THAT OUR MARRIAGE IS OVER BECAUSE SUPERMAN BEAT YOUR MONSTER IN A FIGHT?
WHAT ARE YOU TALKING ABOUT? I DON'T CARE ABOUT THE FIGHT. I'M DEVOTING MY LIFE TO SUPERMAN FOR ANOTHER REASON ENTIRELY, LOIS...
THE DUPLICATE OF THAT ALIEN FARM-BOY HAD THE TENACITY TO BEAT ME AT CHESS LAST NIGHT.

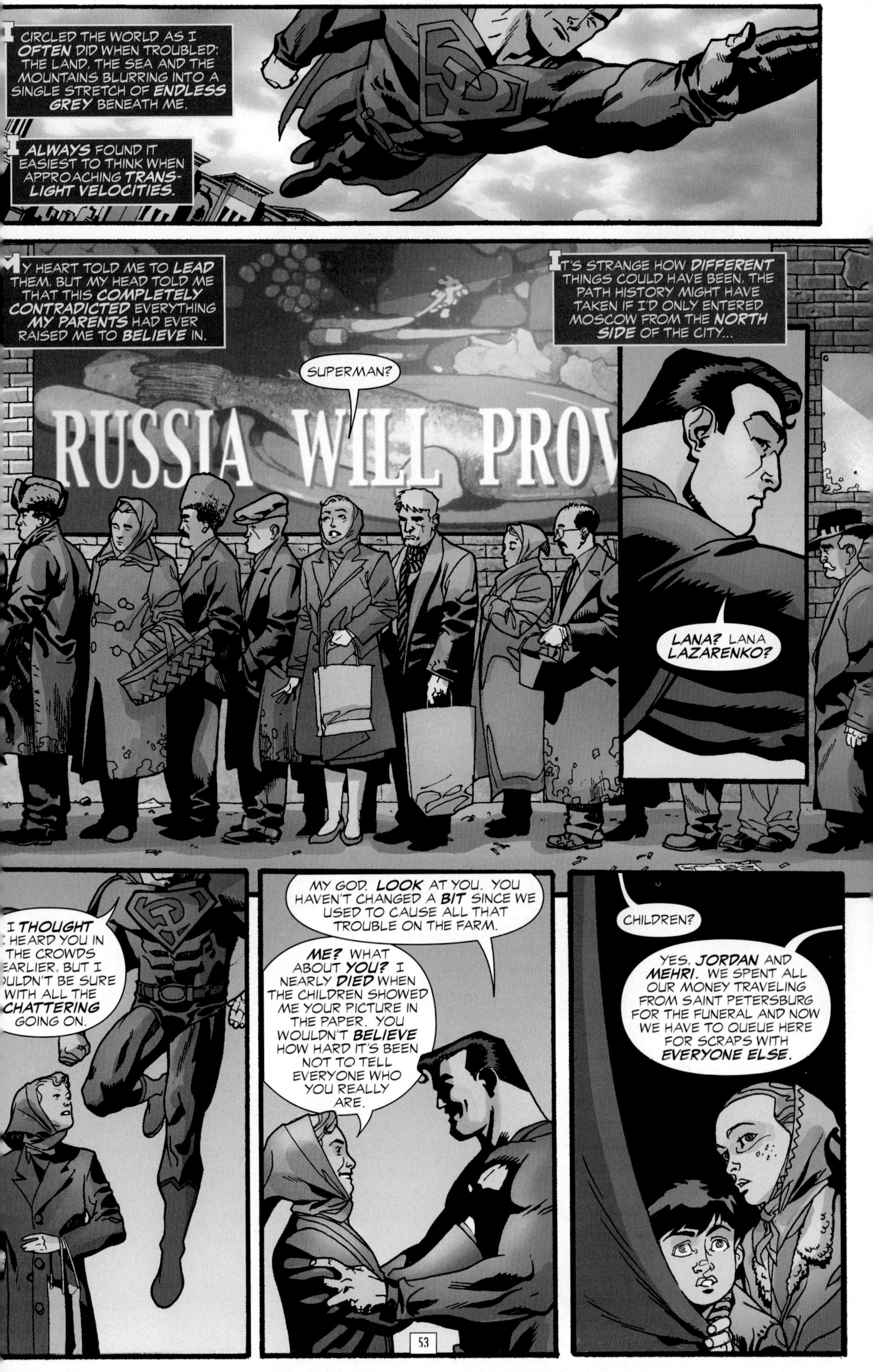
I CIRCLED THE WORLD AS I OFTEN DID WHEN TROUBLED: THE LAND, THE SEA AND THE MOUNTAINS BLURRING INTO A SINGLE STRETCH OF ENDLESS GREY BENEATH ME.
I ALWAYS FOUND IT EASIEST TO THINK WHEN APPROACHING TRANS-LIGHT VELOCITIES.
MY HEART TOLD ME TO LEAD THEM, BUT MY HEAD TOLD ME THAT THIS COMPLETELY CONTRADICTED EVERYTHING MY PARENTS HAD EVER RAISED ME TO BELIEVE IN.
RUSSIA WILL PROV
SUPERMAN?
IT'S STRANGE HOW DIFFERENT THINGS COULD HAVE BEEN, THE PATH HISTORY MIGHT HAVE TAKEN IF I'D ONLY ENTERED MOSCOW FROM THE NORTH SIDE OF THE CITY...
LANA? LANA LAZARENKO?
I THOUGHT HEARD YOU IN THE CROWDS EARLIER, BUT I ULDN'T BE SURE WITH ALL THE CHATTERING GOING ON.
MY GOD. LOOK AT YOU. YOU HAVEN'T CHANGED A BIT SINCE WE USED TO CAUSE ALL THAT TROUBLE ON THE FARM.
ME? WHAT ABOUT YOU? I NEARLY DIED WHEN THE CHILDREN SHOWED ME YOUR PICTURE IN THE PAPER. YOU WOULDN'T BELIEVE HOW HARD IT'S BEEN NOT TO TELL EVERYONE WHO YOU REALLY ARE.
CHILDREN?
YES, JORDAN AND MEHRI. WE SPENT ALL OUR MONEY TRAVELING FROM SAINT PETERSBURG FOR THE FUNERAL AND NOW WE HAVE TO QUEUE HERE FOR SCRAPS WITH EVERYONE ELSE.

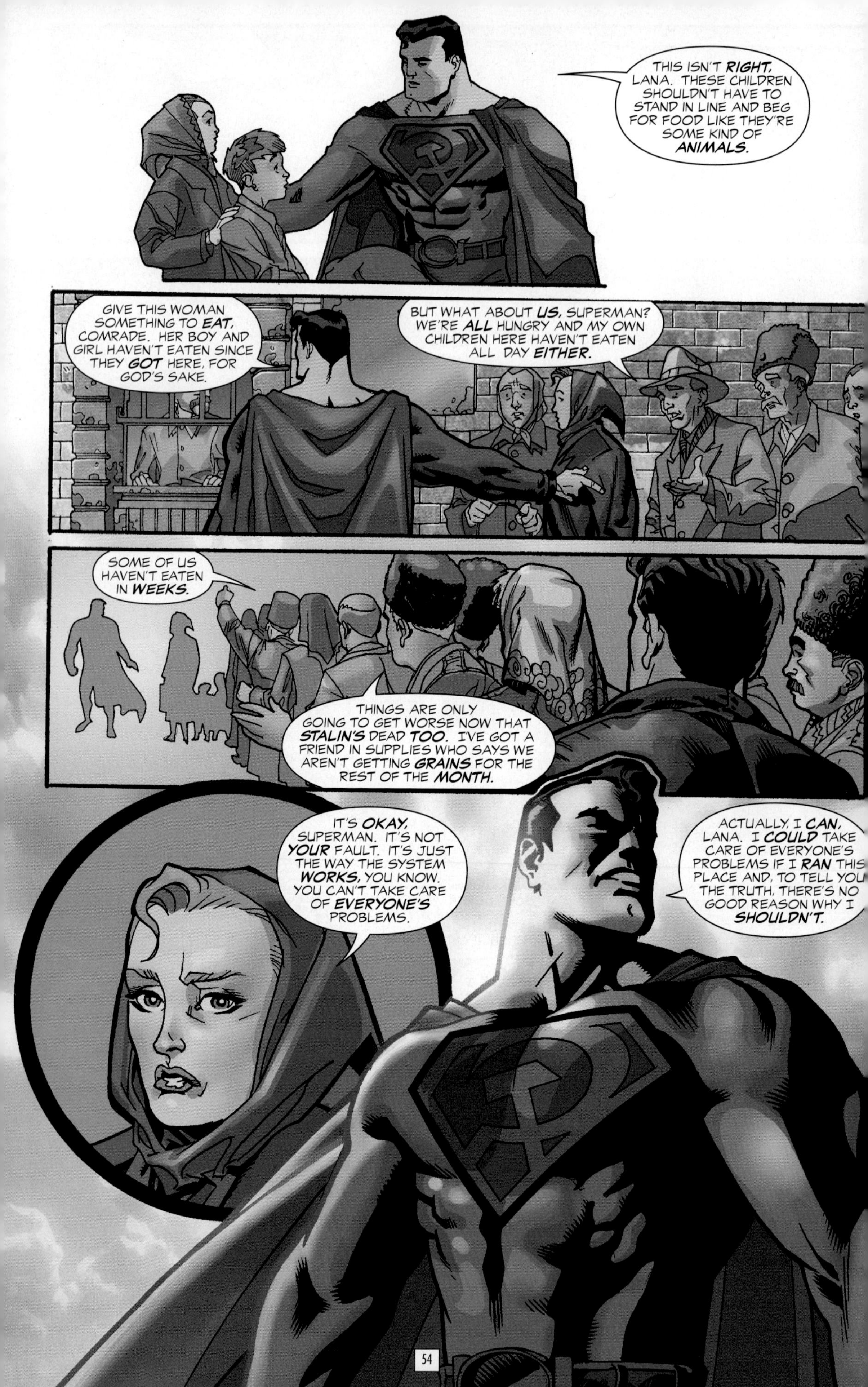
THIS ISN'T RIGHT, LANA. THESE CHILDREN SHOULDN'T HAVE TO STAND IN LINE AND BEG FOR FOOD LIKE THEY'RE SOME KIND OF ANIMALS.
GIVE THIS WOMAN SOMETHING TO EAT, COMRADE. HER BOY AND GIRL HAVEN'T EATEN SINCE THEY GOT HERE, FOR GOD'S SAKE.
BUT WHAT ABOUT US, SUPERMAN? WE'RE ALL HUNGRY AND MY OWN CHILDREN HERE HAVEN'T EATEN ALL DAY EITHER.
SOME OF US HAVEN'T EATEN IN WEEKS.
THINGS ARE ONLY GOING TO GET WORSE NOW THAT STALIN'S DEAD TOO. I'VE GOT A FRIEND IN SUPPLIES WHO SAYS WE AREN'T GETTING GRAINS FOR THE REST OF THE MONTH.
IT'S OKAY, SUPERMAN. IT'S NOT YOUR FAULT. IT'S JUST THE WAY THE SYSTEM WORKS, YOU KNOW. YOU CAN'T TAKE CARE OF EVERYONE'S PROBLEMS.
ACTUALLY, I CAN, LANA. I COULD TAKE CARE OF EVERYONE'S PROBLEMS IF I RAN THIS PLACE AND, TO TELL YOU THE TRUTH, THERE'S NO GOOD REASON WHY I SHOULDN'T.

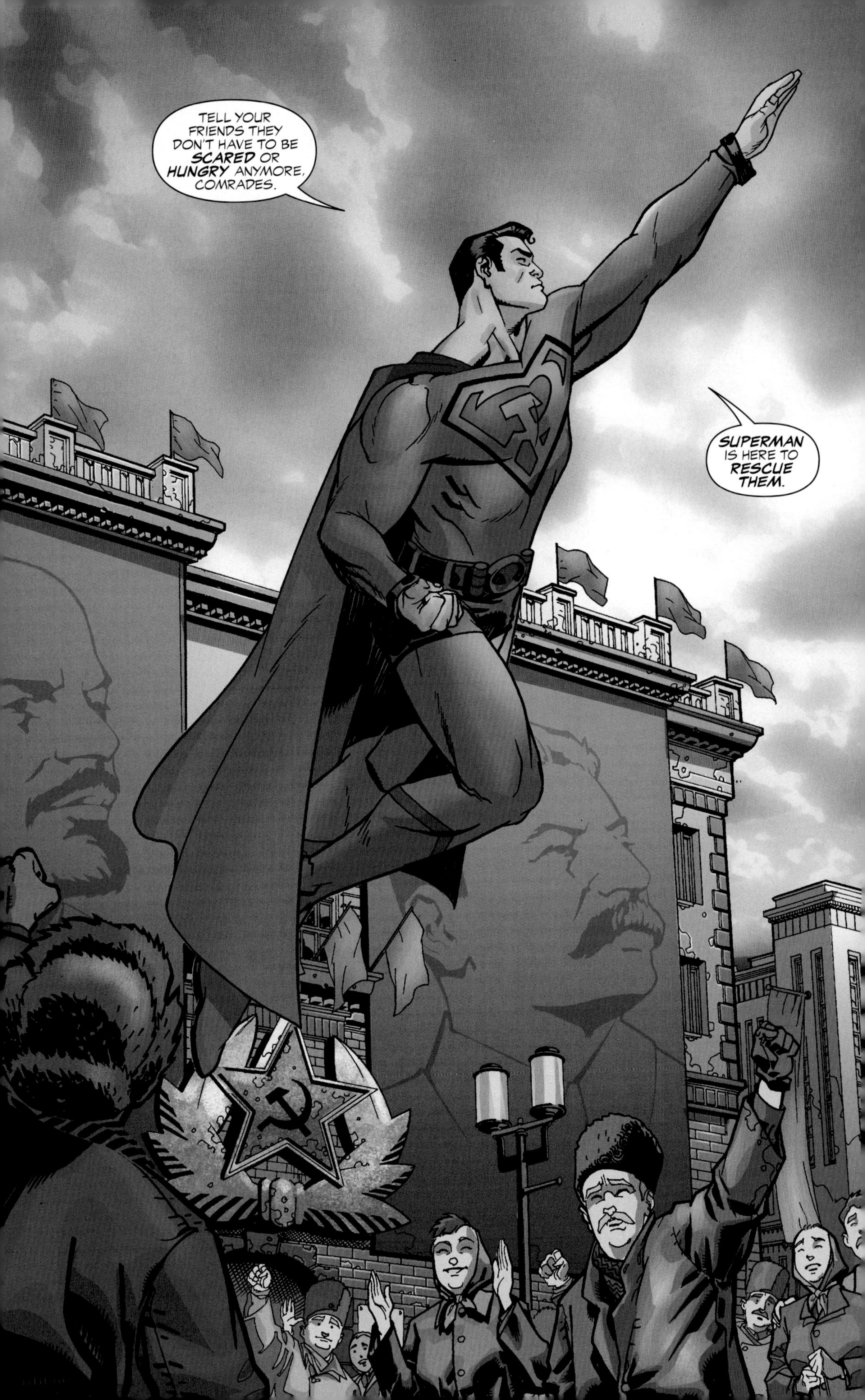
TELL YOUR FRIENDS THEY DON'T HAVE TO BE SCARED OR HUNGRY ANYMORE, COMRADES.
SUPERMAN IS HERE TO RESCUE THEM.

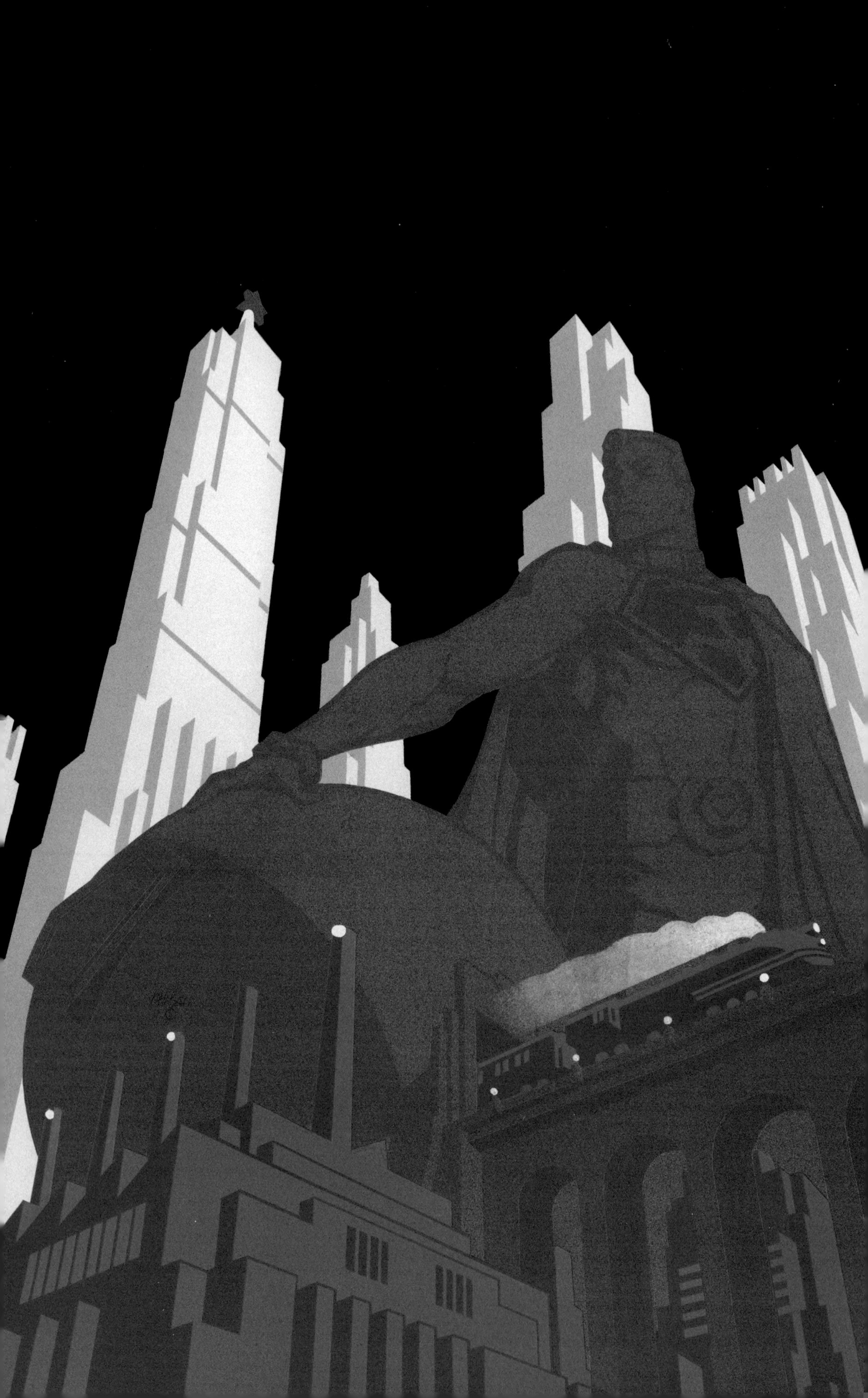

SUPERMAN RED SON

RED SON ASCENDANT

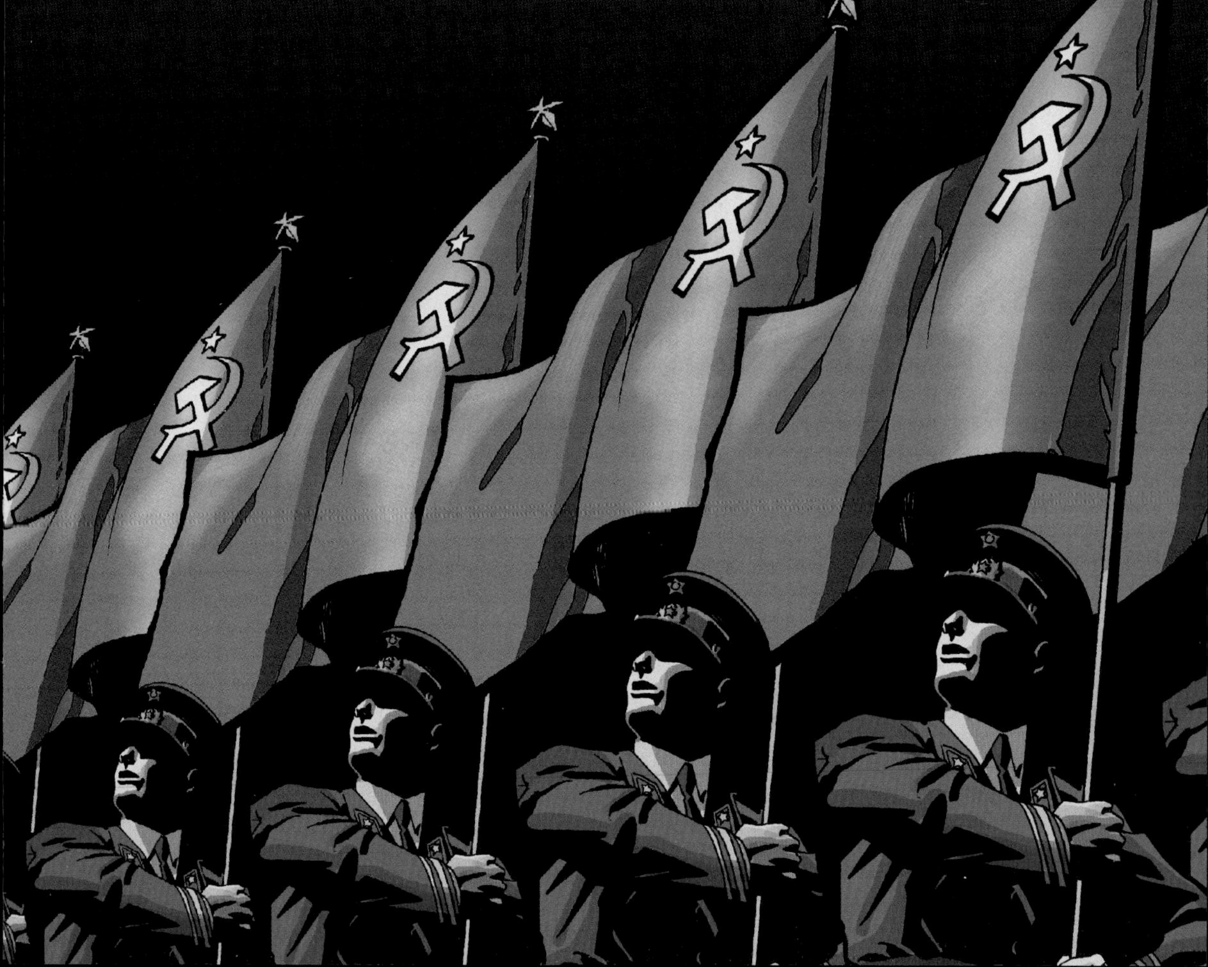

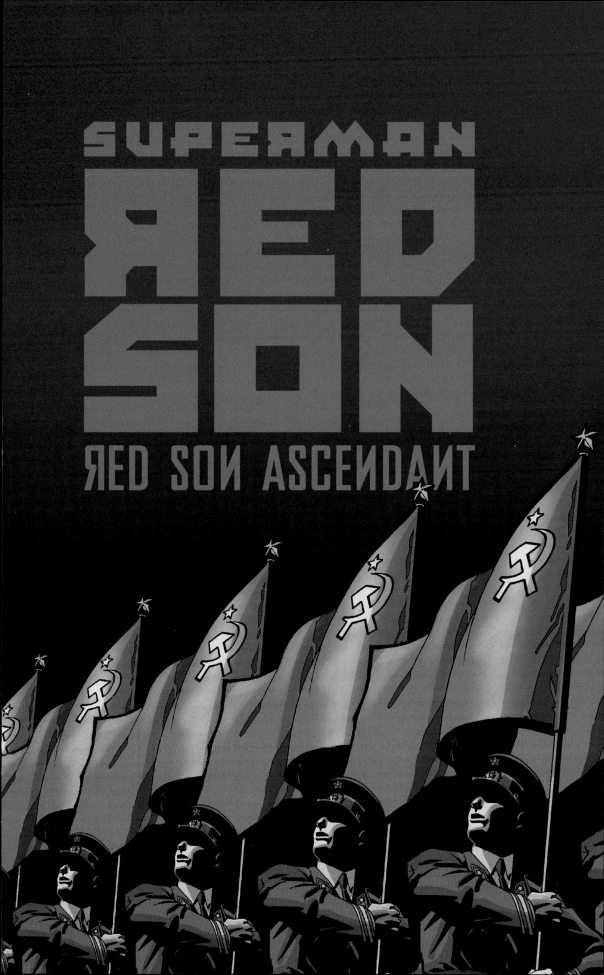

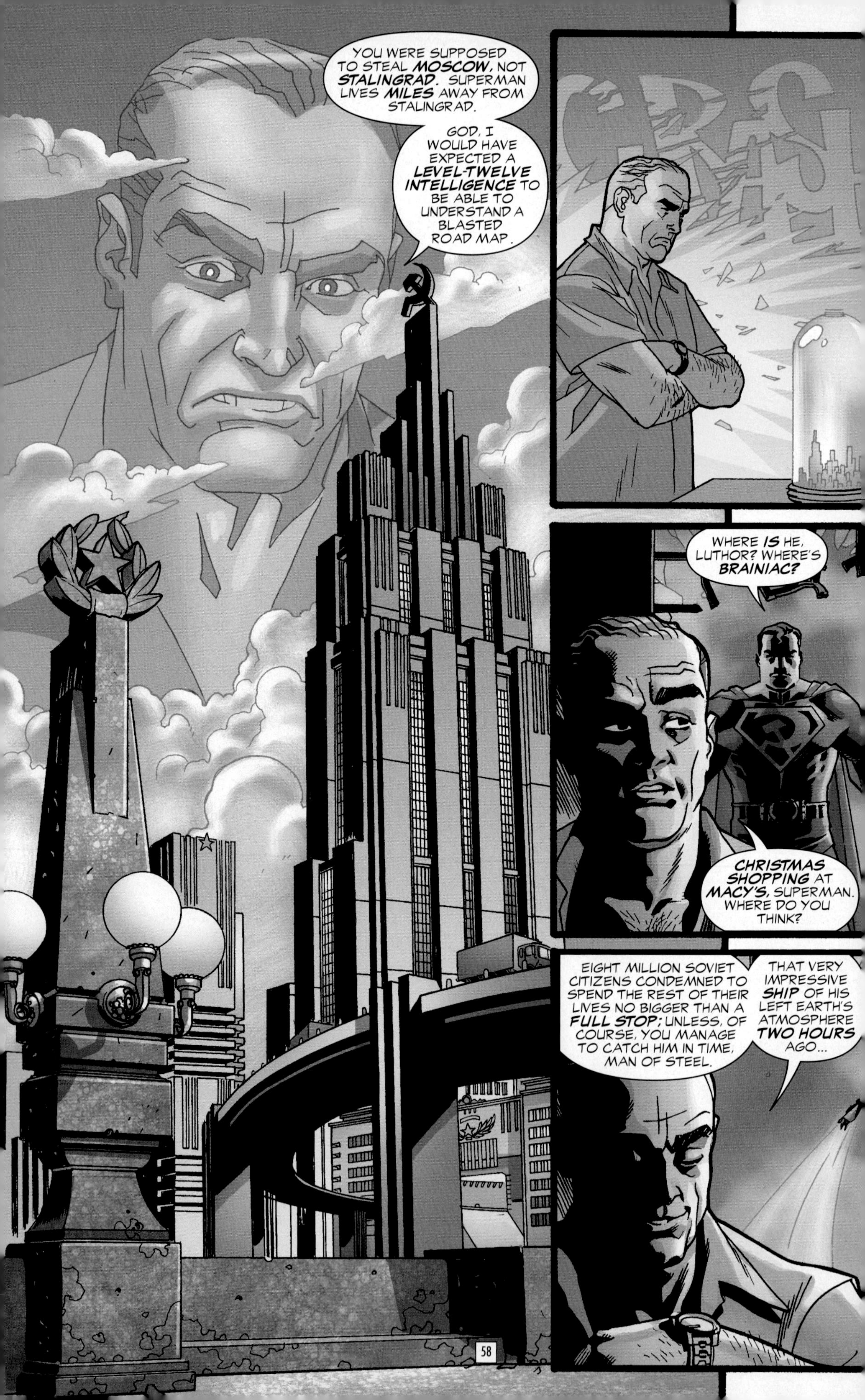
YOU WERE SUPPOSED TO STEAL MOSCOW, NOT STALINGRAD. SUPERMAN LIVES MILES AWAY FROM STALINGRAD.
GOD, I WOULD HAVE EXPECTED A LEVEL-TWELVE INTELLIGENCE TO BE ABLE TO UNDERSTAND A BLASTED ROAD MAP.
WHERE IS HE, LUTHOR? WHERE'S BRAINIAC?
CHRISTMAS SHOPPING AT MACY'S, SUPERMAN. WHERE DO YOU THINK?
THAT VERY IMPRESSIVE SHIP OF HIS LEFT EARTH'S ATMOSPHERE TWO HOURS AGO...
EIGHT MILLION SOVIET CITIZENS CONDEMNED TO SPEND THE REST OF THEIR LIVES NO BIGGER THAN A FULL STOP; UNLESS, OF COURSE, YOU MANAGE TO CATCH HIM IN TIME, MAN OF STEEL.

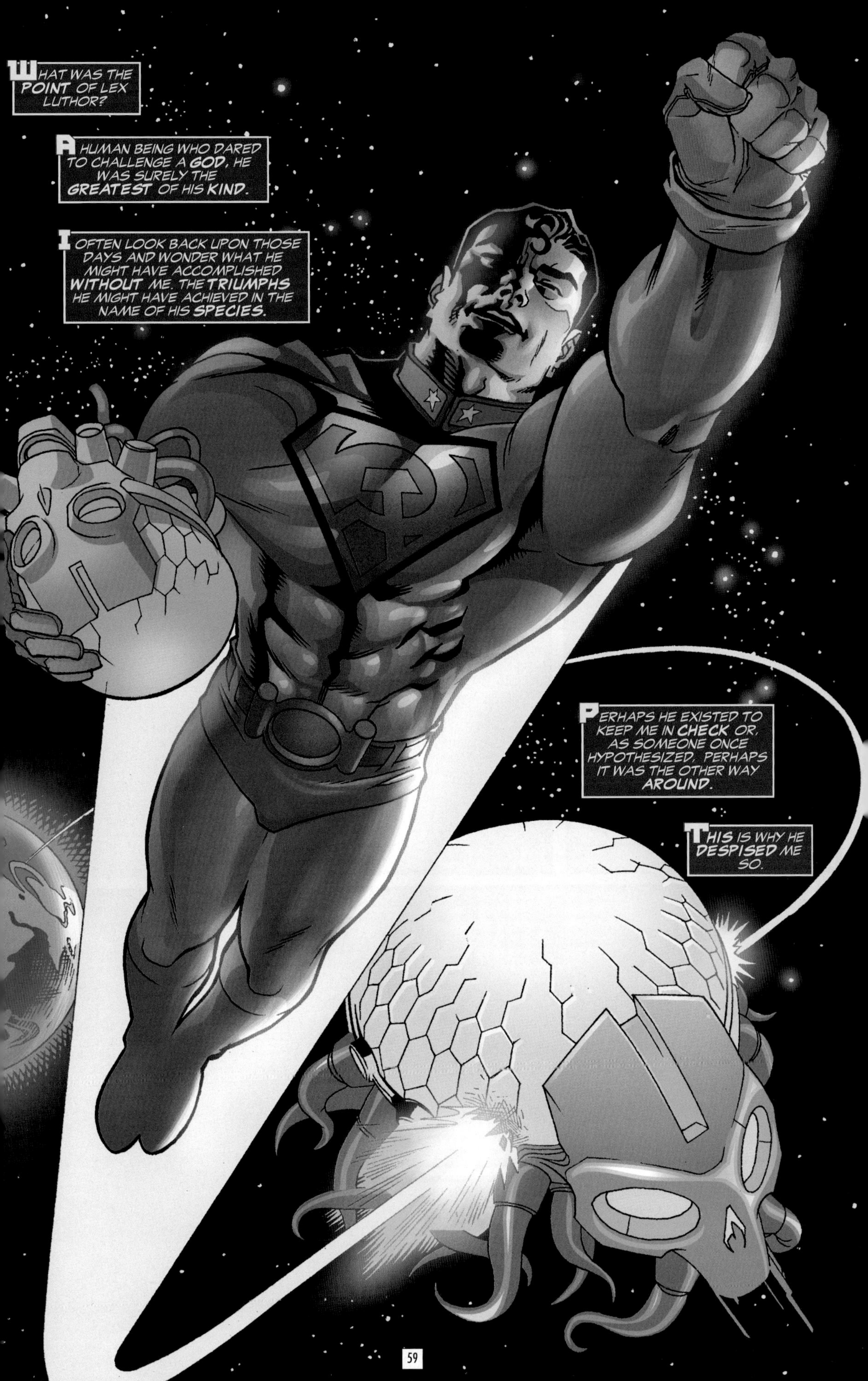
WHAT WAS THE POINT OF LEX LUTHOR?
A HUMAN BEING WHO DARED TO CHALLENGE A GOD, HE WAS SURELY THE GREATEST OF HIS KIND.
I OFTEN LOOK BACK UPON THOSE DAYS AND WONDER WHAT HE MIGHT HAVE ACCOMPLISHED WITHOUT ME. THE TRIUMPHS HE MIGHT HAVE ACHIEVED IN THE NAME OF HIS SPECIES.
PERHAPS HE EXISTED TO KEEP ME IN CHECK OR, AS SOMEONE ONCE HYPOTHESIZED, PERHAPS IT WAS THE OTHER WAY AROUND.
THIS IS WHY HE DESPISED ME SO.

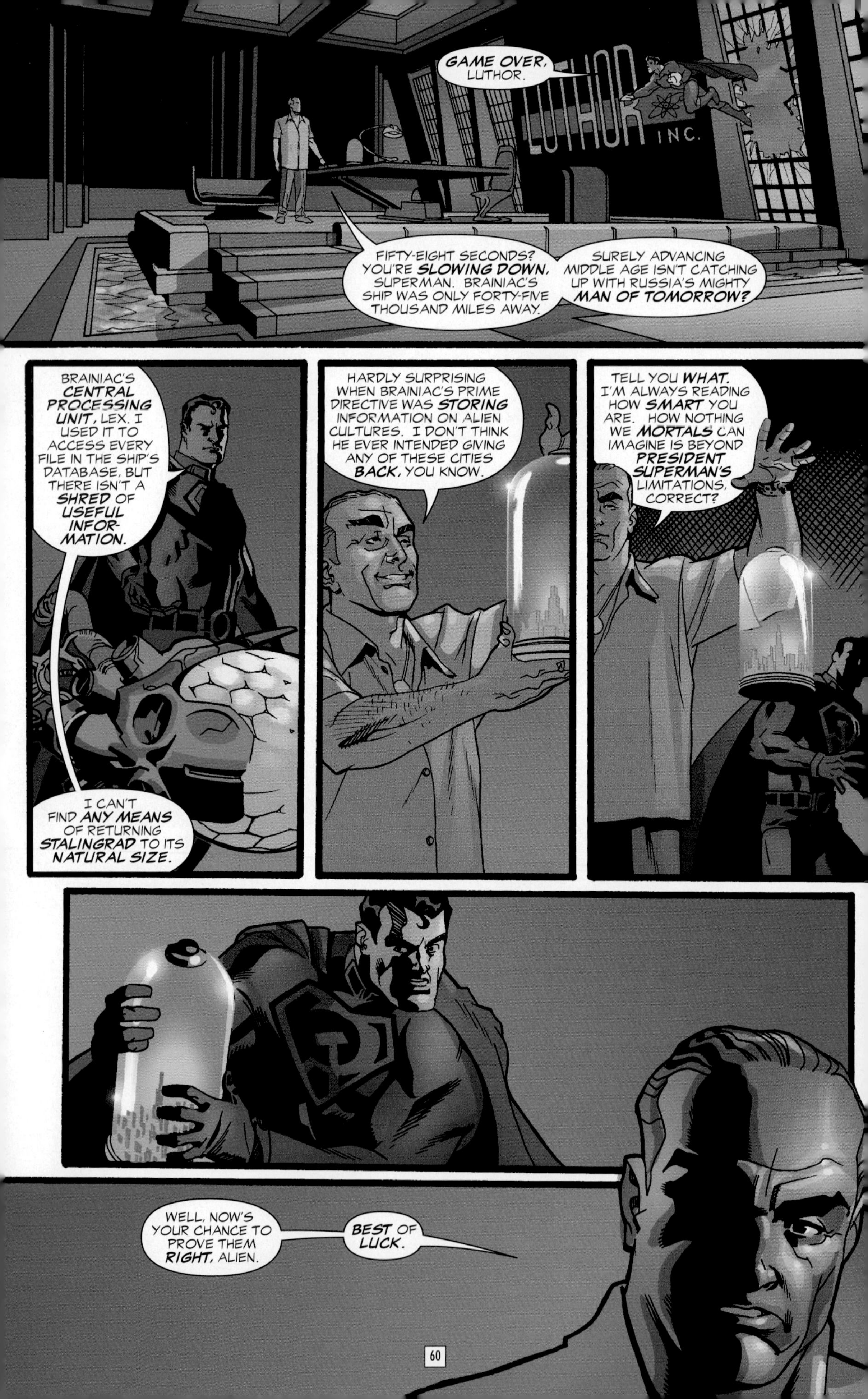
GAME OVER, LUTHOR.
LUTHOR INC.
FIFTY-EIGHT SECONDS? YOU'RE SLOWING DOWN, SUPERMAN. BRAINIAC'S SHIP WAS ONLY FORTY-FIVE THOUSAND MILES AWAY.
SURELY ADVANCING MIDDLE AGE ISN'T CATCHING UP WITH RUSSIA'S MIGHTY MAN OF TOMORROW?
BRAINIAC'S CENTRAL PROCESSING UNIT, LEX. I USED IT TO ACCESS EVERY FILE IN THE SHIP'S DATABASE, BUT THERE ISN'T A SHRED OF USEFUL INFORMATION.
I CAN'T FIND ANY MEANS OF RETURNING STALINGRAD TO ITS NATURAL SIZE.
HARDLY SURPRISING WHEN BRAINIAC'S PRIME DIRECTIVE WAS STORING INFORMATION ON ALIEN CULTURES. I DON'T THINK HE EVER INTENDED GIVING ANY OF THESE CITIES BACK, YOU KNOW.
TELL YOU WHAT. I'M ALWAYS READING HOW SMART YOU ARE. HOW NOTHING WE MORTALS CAN IMAGINE IS BEYOND PRESIDENT SUPERMAN'S LIMITATIONS, CORRECT?
WELL, NOW'S YOUR CHANCE TO PROVE THEM RIGHT, ALIEN.
BEST OF LUCK.

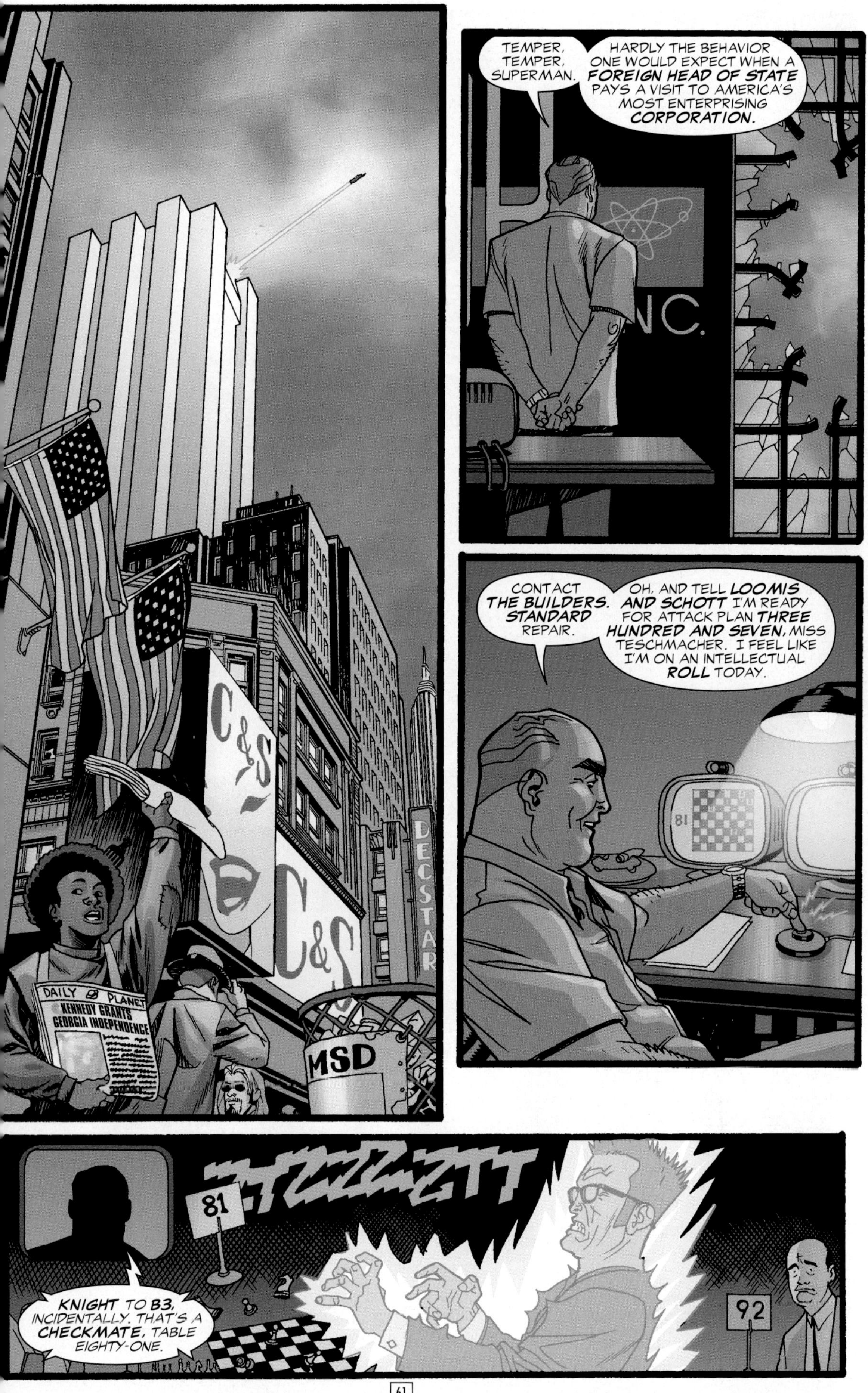
C&S
DECSTAR
DAILY PLANET
KENNEDY GRANTS GEORGIA INDEPENDENCE
MSD
TEMPER, TEMPER, SUPERMAN.
HARDLY THE BEHAVIOR ONE WOULD EXPECT WHEN A FOREIGN HEAD OF STATE PAYS A VISIT TO AMERICA'S MOST ENTERPRISING CORPORATION.
INC.
CONTACT THE BUILDERS. STANDARD REPAIR.
OH, AND TELL LOOMIS AND SCHOTT I'M READY FOR ATTACK PLAN THREE HUNDRED AND SEVEN, MISS TESCHMACHER. I FEEL LIKE I'M ON AN INTELLECTUAL ROLL TODAY.
81
ZTZZZZTT
81
KNIGHT TO B3. INCIDENTALLY, THAT'S A CHECKMATE, TABLE EIGHTY-ONE.
92

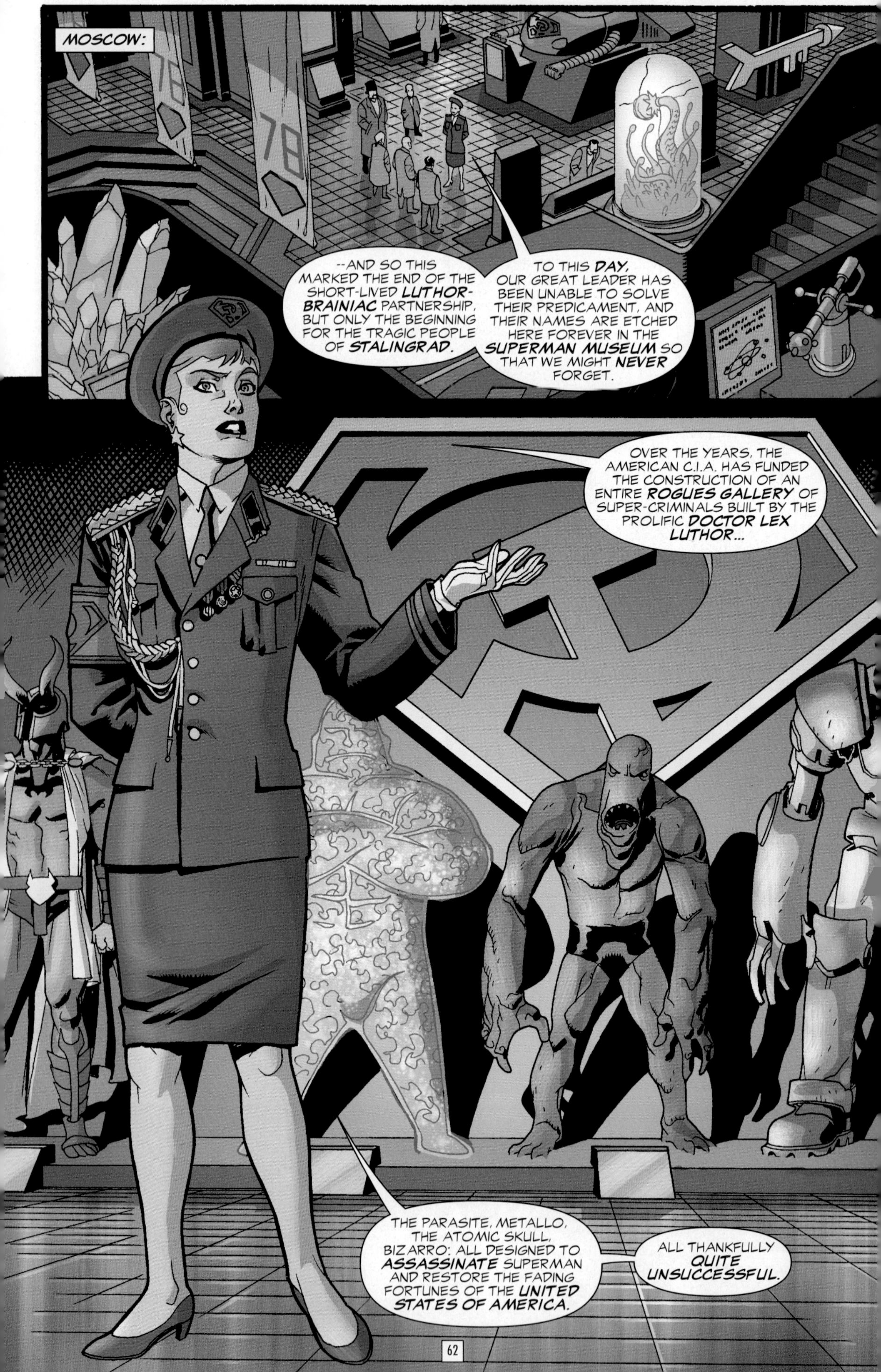
MOSCOW:
--AND SO THIS MARKED THE END OF THE SHORT-LIVED LUTHOR-BRAINIAC PARTNERSHIP, BUT ONLY THE BEGINNING FOR THE TRAGIC PEOPLE OF STALINGRAD.
TO THIS DAY, OUR GREAT LEADER HAS BEEN UNABLE TO SOLVE THEIR PREDICAMENT, AND THEIR NAMES ARE ETCHED HERE FOREVER IN THE SUPERMAN MUSEUM SO THAT WE MIGHT NEVER FORGET.
OVER THE YEARS, THE AMERICAN C.I.A. HAS FUNDED THE CONSTRUCTION OF AN ENTIRE ROGUES GALLERY OF SUPER-CRIMINALS BUILT BY THE PROLIFIC DOCTOR LEX LUTHOR...
THE PARASITE, METALLO, THE ATOMIC SKULL, BIZARRO: ALL DESIGNED TO ASSASSINATE SUPERMAN AND RESTORE THE FADING FORTUNES OF THE UNITED STATES OF AMERICA.
ALL THANKFULLY QUITE UNSUCCESSFUL.

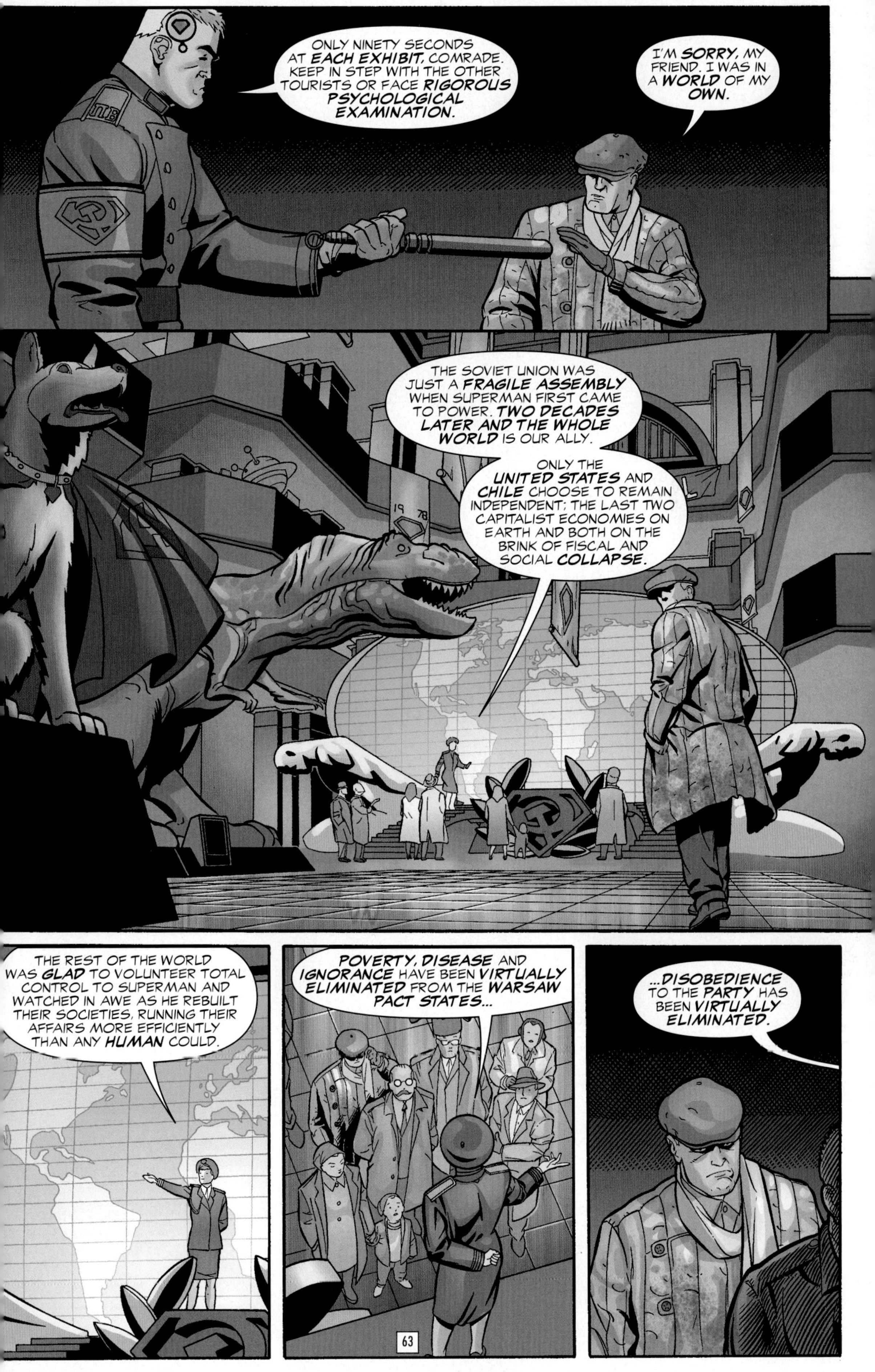
ONLY NINETY SECONDS AT EACH EXHIBIT, COMRADE. KEEP IN STEP WITH THE OTHER TOURISTS OR FACE RIGOROUS PSYCHOLOGICAL EXAMINATION.
I'M SORRY, MY FRIEND. I WAS IN A WORLD OF MY OWN.
THE SOVIET UNION WAS JUST A FRAGILE ASSEMBLY WHEN SUPERMAN FIRST CAME TO POWER. TWO DECADES LATER AND THE WHOLE WORLD IS OUR ALLY.
ONLY THE UNITED STATES AND CHILE CHOOSE TO REMAIN INDEPENDENT; THE LAST TWO CAPITALIST ECONOMIES ON EARTH AND BOTH ON THE BRINK OF FISCAL AND SOCIAL COLLAPSE.
THE REST OF THE WORLD WAS GLAD TO VOLUNTEER TOTAL CONTROL TO SUPERMAN AND WATCHED IN AWE AS HE REBUILT THEIR SOCIETIES, RUNNING THEIR AFFAIRS MORE EFFICIENTLY THAN ANY HUMAN COULD.
POVERTY, DISEASE AND IGNORANCE HAVE BEEN VIRTUALLY ELIMINATED FROM THE WARSAW PACT STATES...
...DISOBEDIENCE TO THE PARTY HAS BEEN VIRTUALLY ELIMINATED.

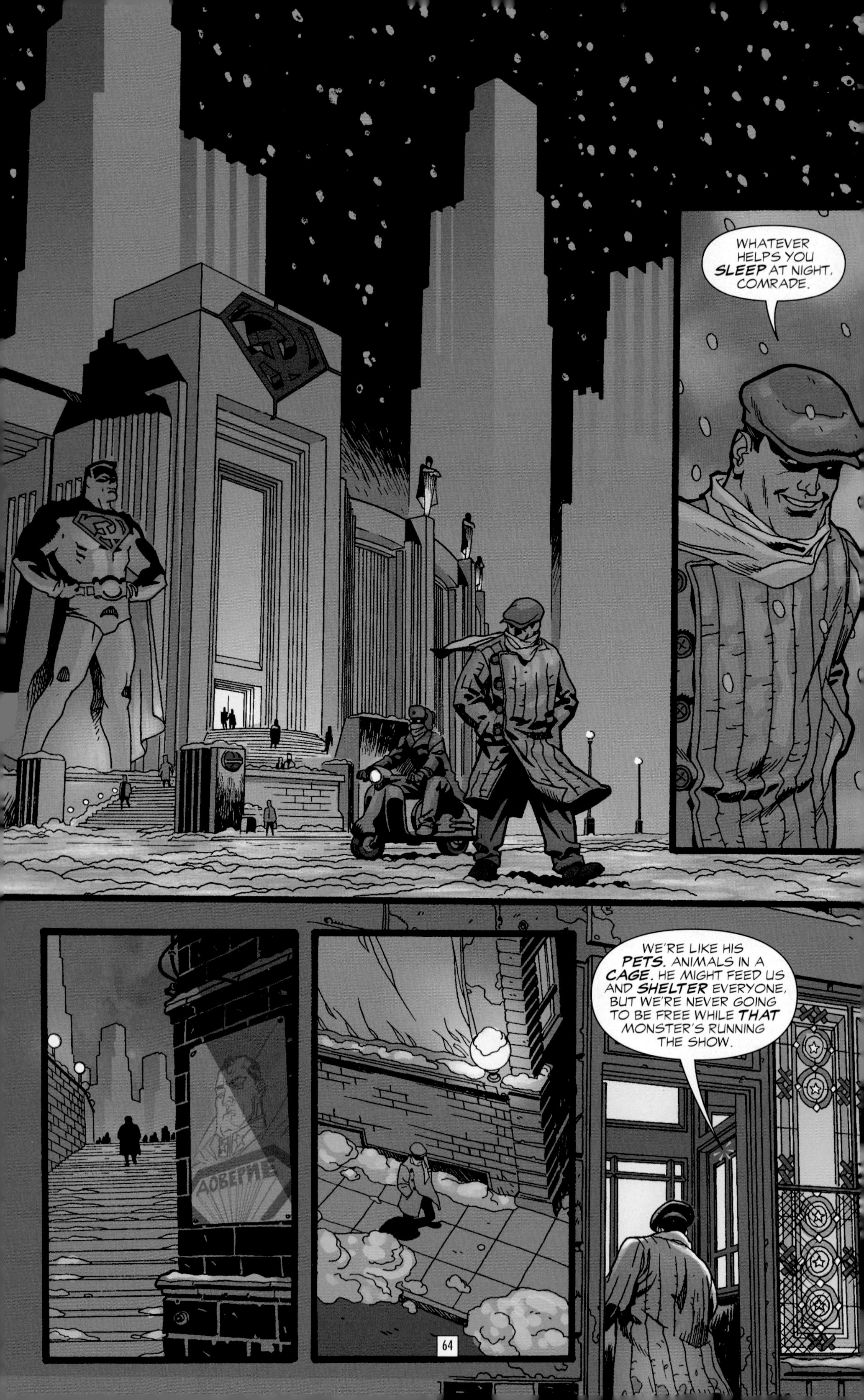
WHATEVER HELPS YOU SLEEP AT NIGHT, COMRADE.
ДОВЕРИЕ
WE'RE LIKE HIS PETS. ANIMALS IN A CAGE. HE MIGHT FEED US AND SHELTER EVERYONE, BUT WE'RE NEVER GOING TO BE FREE WHILE THAT MONSTER'S RUNNING THE SHOW.

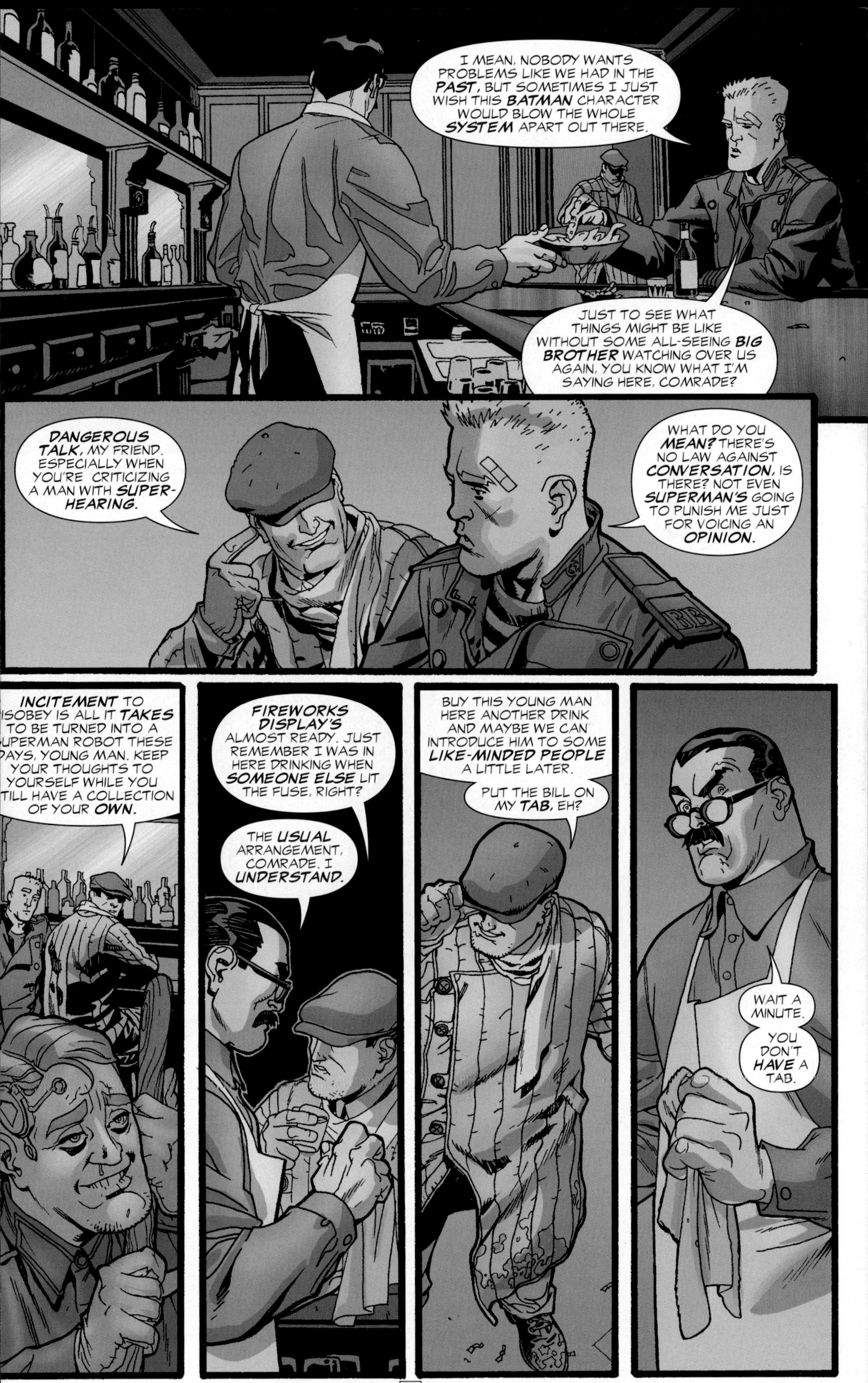
I MEAN, NOBODY WANTS PROBLEMS LIKE WE HAD IN THE PAST, BUT SOMETIMES I JUST WISH THIS BATMAN CHARACTER WOULD BLOW THE WHOLE SYSTEM APART OUT THERE.
JUST TO SEE WHAT THINGS MIGHT BE LIKE WITHOUT SOME ALL-SEEING BIG BROTHER WATCHING OVER US AGAIN, YOU KNOW WHAT I'M SAYING HERE, COMRADE?
DANGEROUS TALK, MY FRIEND. ESPECIALLY WHEN YOU'RE CRITICIZING A MAN WITH SUPER-HEARING.
WHAT DO YOU MEAN? THERE'S NO LAW AGAINST CONVERSATION, IS THERE? NOT EVEN SUPERMAN'S GOING TO PUNISH ME JUST FOR VOICING AN OPINION.
INCITEMENT TO ISOBEY IS ALL IT TAKES TO BE TURNED INTO A UPERMAN ROBOT THESE AYS, YOUNG MAN. KEEP YOUR THOUGHTS TO YOURSELF WHILE YOU TILL HAVE A COLLECTION OF YOUR OWN.
FIREWORKS DISPLAY'S ALMOST READY. JUST REMEMBER I WAS IN HERE DRINKING WHEN SOMEONE ELSE LIT THE FUSE, RIGHT?
THE USUAL ARRANGEMENT, COMRADE. I UNDERSTAND.
BUY THIS YOUNG MAN HERE ANOTHER DRINK AND MAYBE WE CAN INTRODUCE HIM TO SOME LIKE-MINDED PEOPLE A LITTLE LATER.
PUT THE BILL ON MY TAB, EH?
WAIT A MINUTE.
YOU DON'T HAVE A TAB.

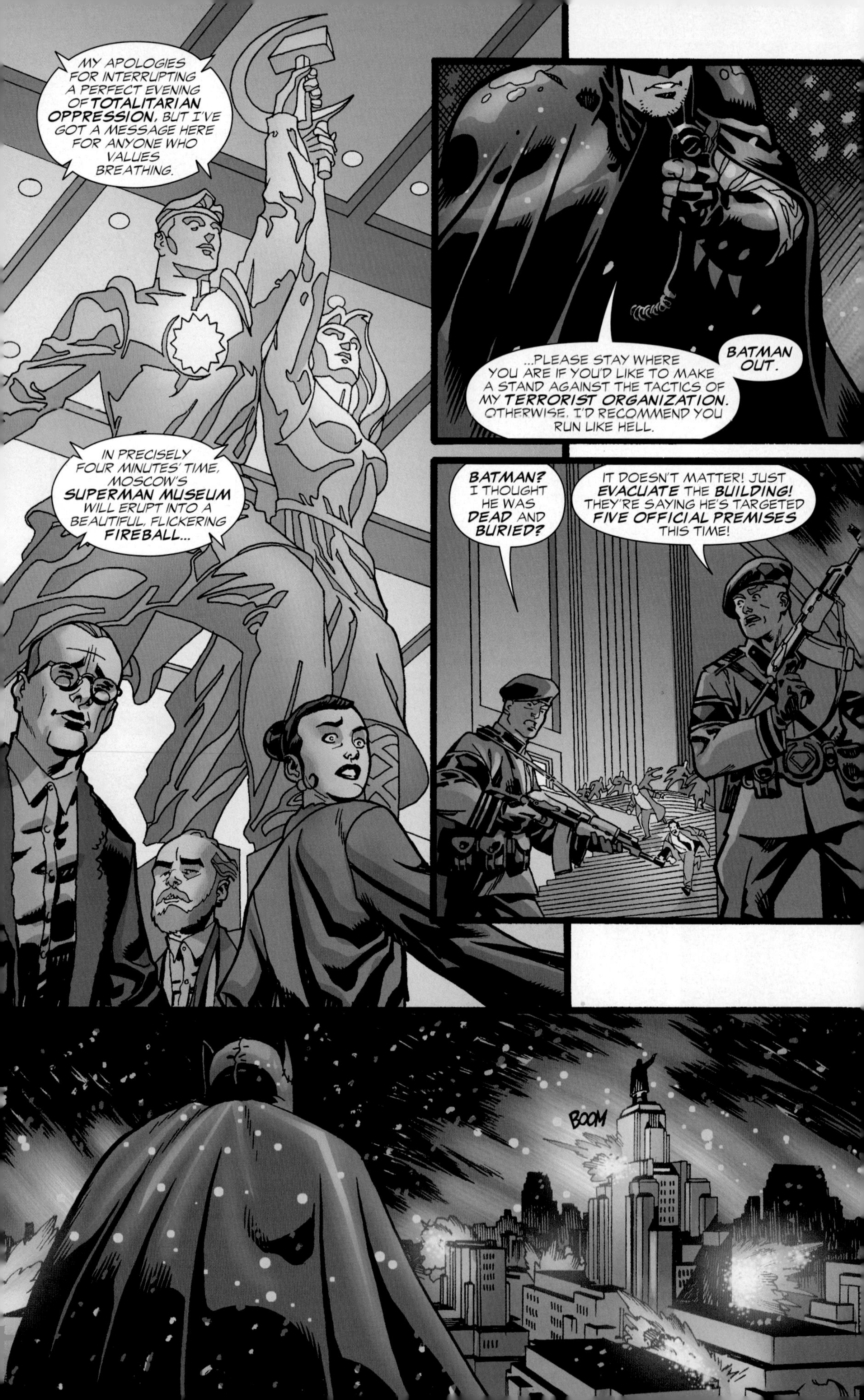
MY APOLOGIES FOR INTERRUPTING A PERFECT EVENING OF TOTALITARIAN OPPRESSION, BUT I'VE GOT A MESSAGE HERE FOR ANYONE WHO VALUES BREATHING.
IN PRECISELY FOUR MINUTES' TIME, MOSCOW'S SUPERMAN MUSEUM WILL ERUPT INTO A BEAUTIFUL, FLICKERING FIREBALL...
...PLEASE STAY WHERE YOU ARE IF YOU'D LIKE TO MAKE A STAND AGAINST THE TACTICS OF MY TERRORIST ORGANIZATION. OTHERWISE, I'D RECOMMEND YOU RUN LIKE HELL.
BATMAN OUT.
BATMAN? I THOUGHT HE WAS DEAD AND BURIED?
IT DOESN'T MATTER! JUST EVACUATE THE BUILDING! THEY'RE SAYING HE'S TARGETED FIVE OFFICIAL PREMISES THIS TIME!
BOOM

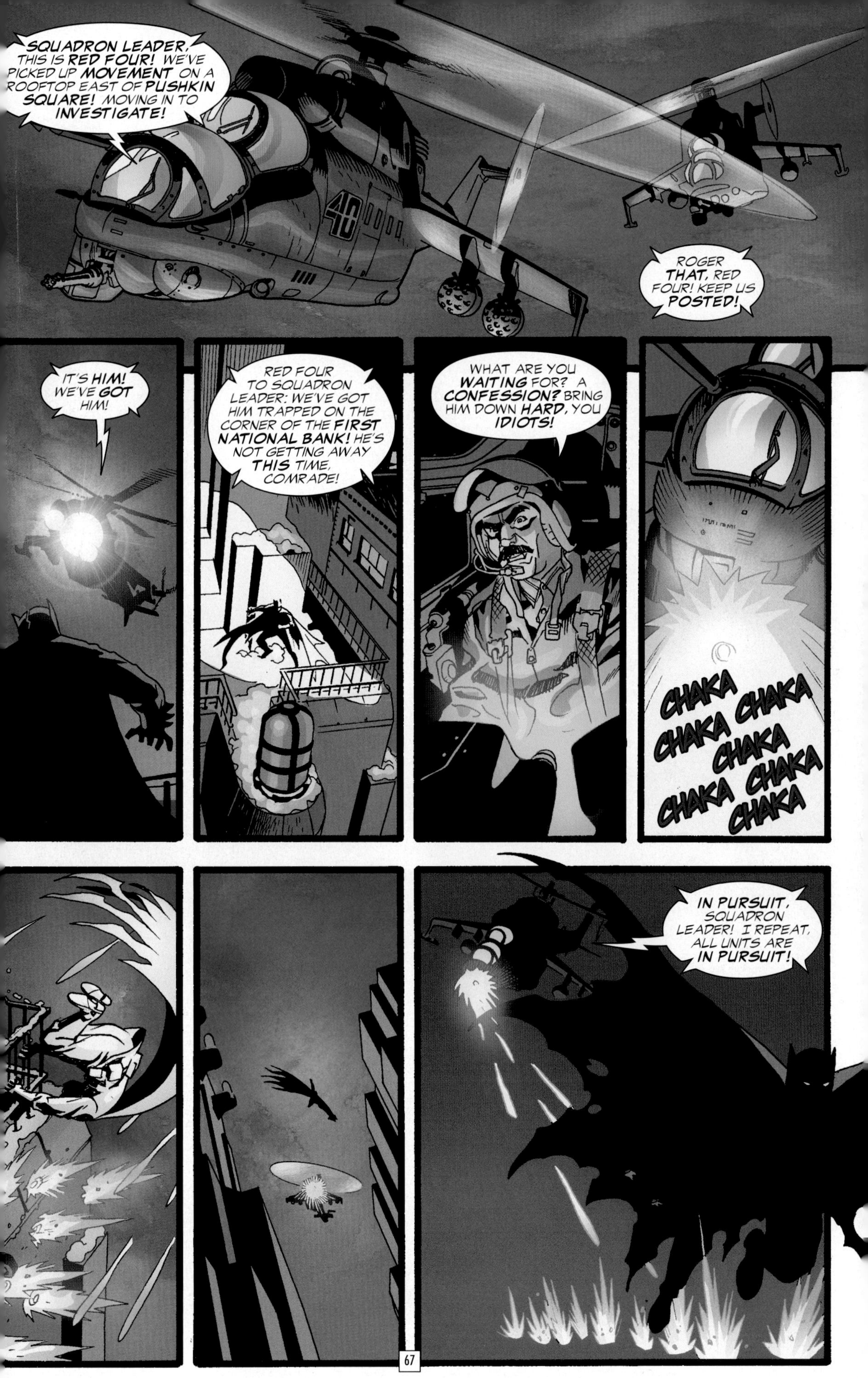
SQUADRON LEADER, THIS IS RED FOUR! WE'VE PICKED UP MOVEMENT ON A ROOFTOP EAST OF PUSHKIN SQUARE! MOVING IN TO INVESTIGATE!
ROGER THAT, RED FOUR! KEEP US POSTED!
IT'S HIM! WE'VE GOT HIM!
RED FOUR TO SQUADRON LEADER: WE'VE GOT HIM TRAPPED ON THE CORNER OF THE FIRST NATIONAL BANK! HE'S NOT GETTING AWAY THIS TIME, COMRADE!
WHAT ARE YOU WAITING FOR? A CONFESSION? BRING HIM DOWN HARD, YOU IDIOTS!
CHAKA CHAKA CHAKA CHAKA CHAKA CHAKA CHAKA
IN PURSUIT, SQUADRON LEADER! I REPEAT, ALL UNITS ARE IN PURSUIT!

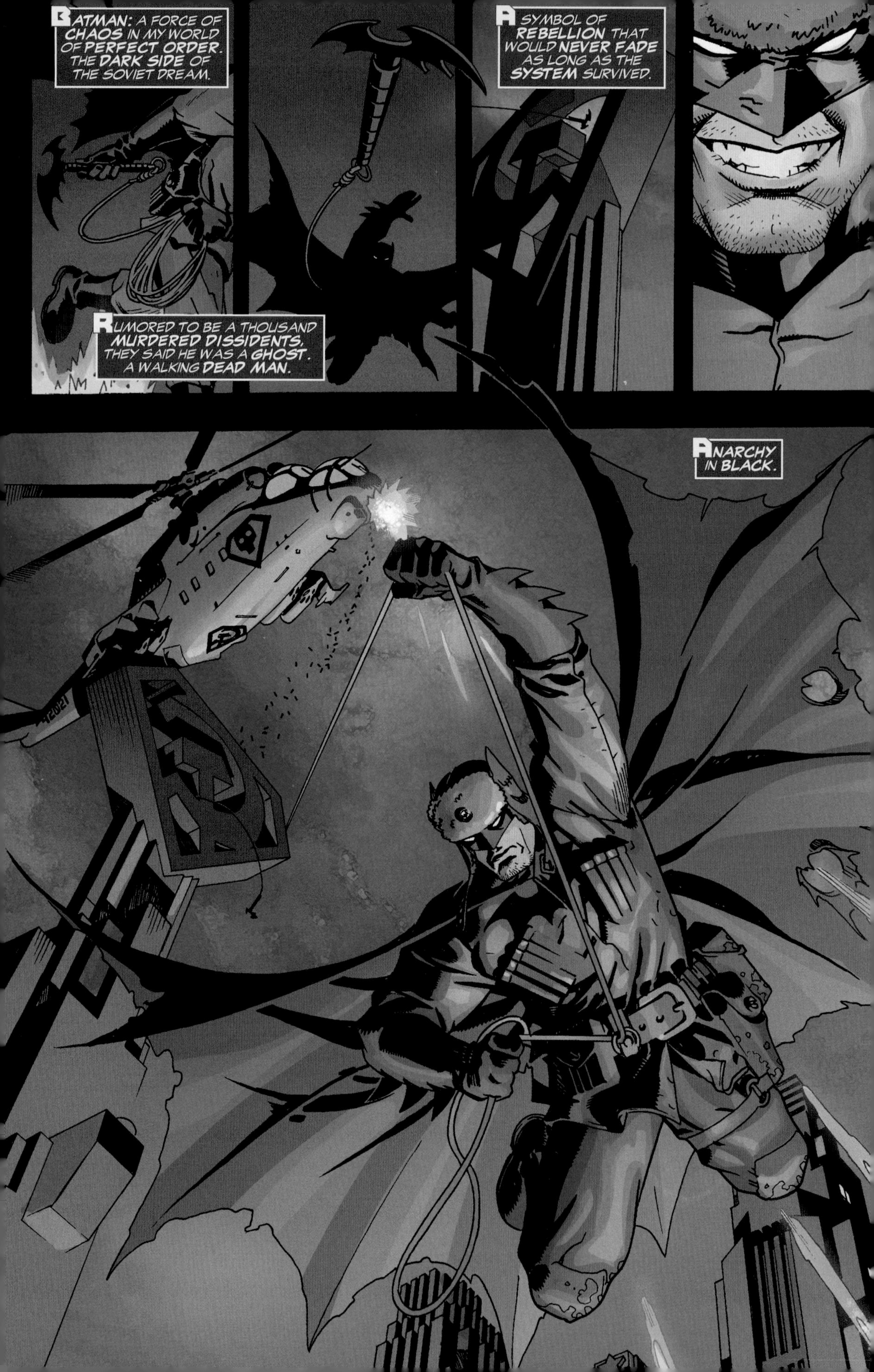
BATMAN: A FORCE OF CHAOS IN MY WORLD OF PERFECT ORDER. THE DARK SIDE OF THE SOVIET DREAM.
RUMORED TO BE A THOUSAND MURDERED DISSIDENTS. THEY SAID HE WAS A GHOST. A WALKING DEAD MAN.
A SYMBOL OF REBELLION THAT WOULD NEVER FADE AS LONG AS THE SYSTEM SURVIVED.
ANARCHY IN BLACK.

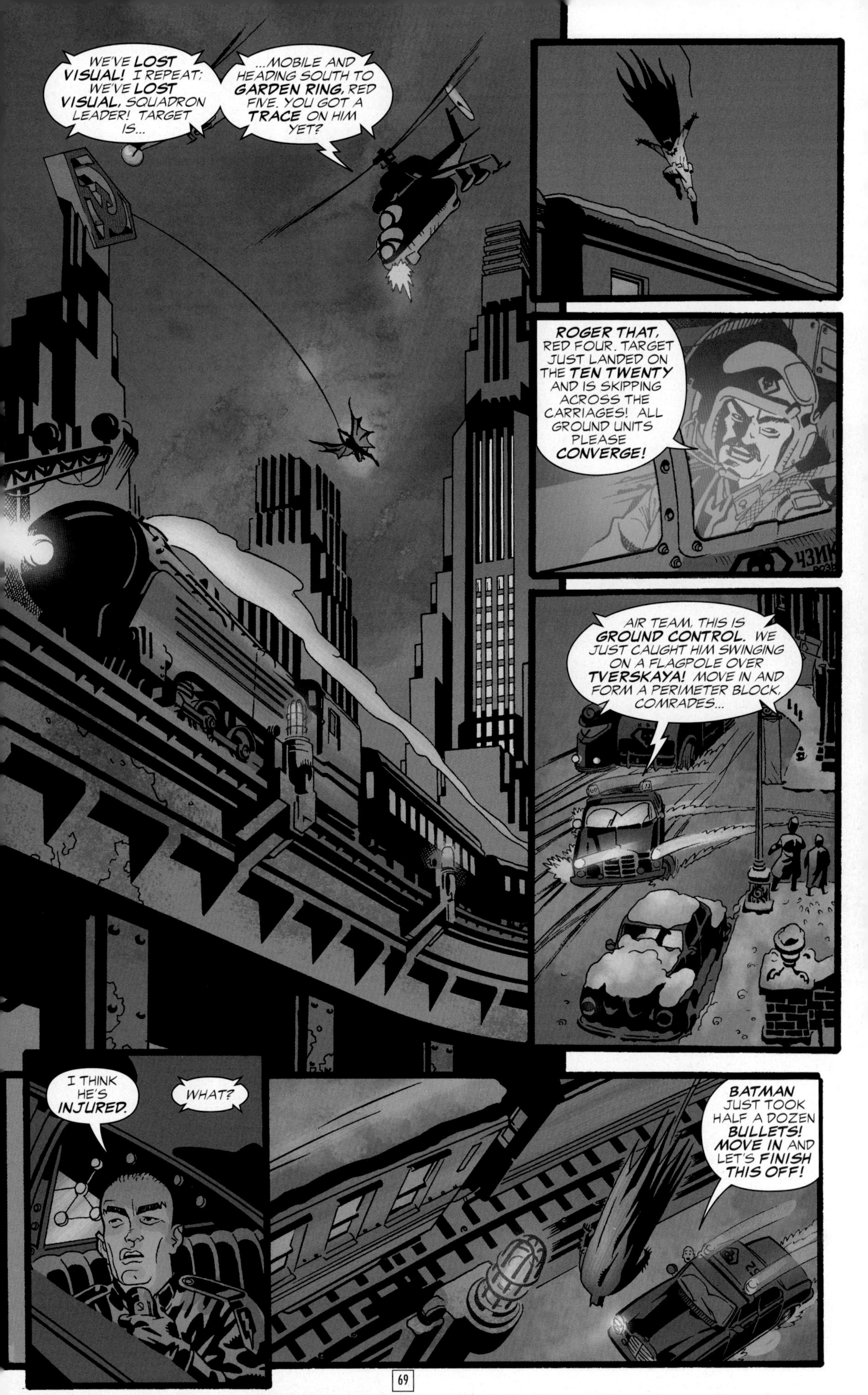

WE'VE LOST VISUAL! I REPEAT; WE'VE LOST VISUAL, SQUADRON LEADER! TARGET IS...
...MOBILE AND HEADING SOUTH TO GARDEN RING, RED FIVE. YOU GOT A TRACE ON HIM YET?
ROGER THAT, RED FOUR. TARGET JUST LANDED ON THE TEN TWENTY AND IS SKIPPING ACROSS THE CARRIAGES! ALL GROUND UNITS PLEASE CONVERGE!
AIR TEAM, THIS IS GROUND CONTROL. WE JUST CAUGHT HIM SWINGING ON A FLAGPOLE OVER TVERSKAYA! MOVE IN AND FORM A PERIMETER BLOCK, COMRADES...
I THINK HE'S INJURED.
WHAT?
BATMAN JUST TOOK HALF A DOZEN BULLETS! MOVE IN AND LET'S FINISH THIS OFF!

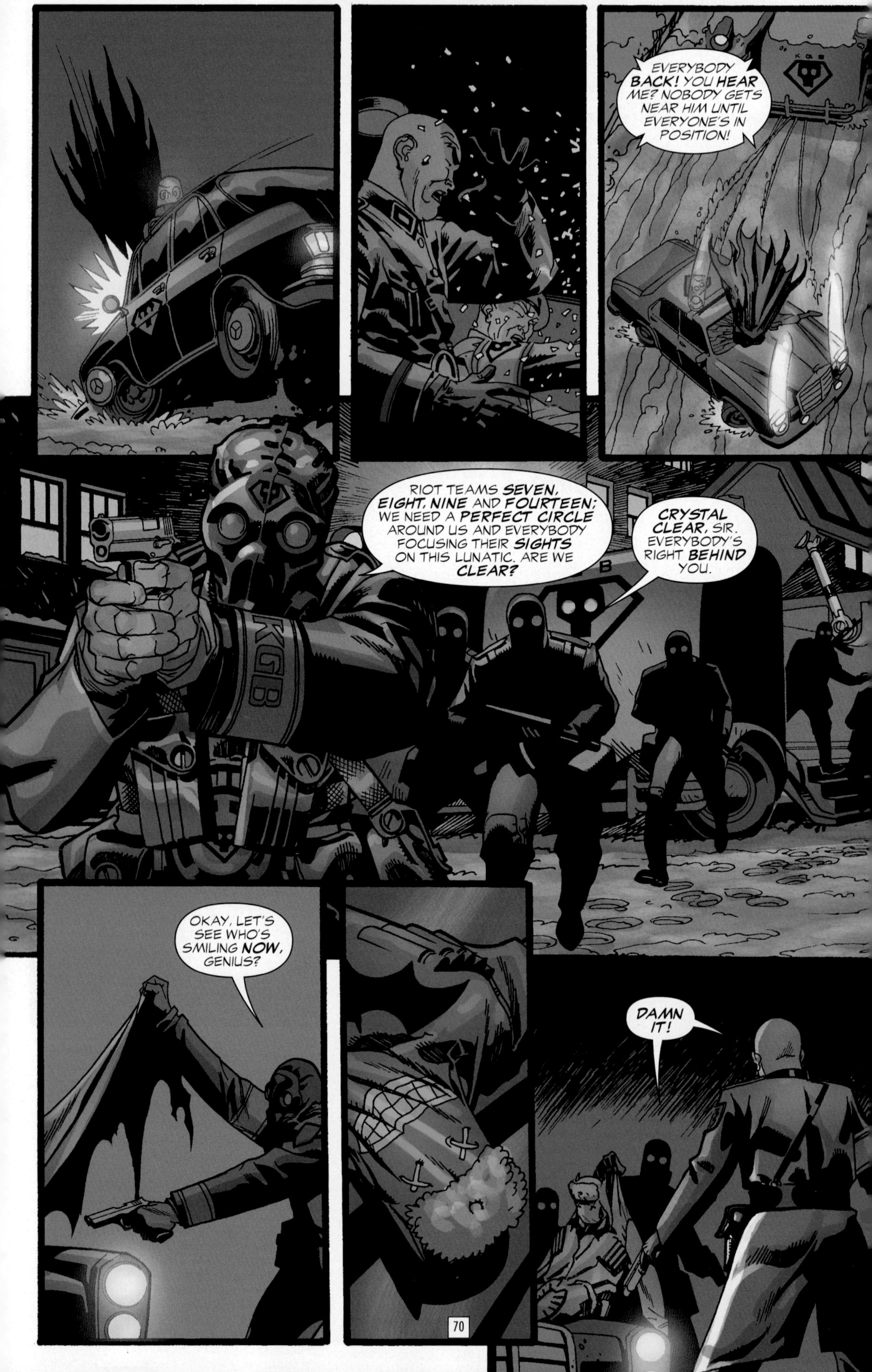
EVERYBODY **BACK!** YOU **HEAR** ME? NOBODY GETS NEAR HIM UNTIL EVERYONE'S IN POSITION!
RIOT TEAMS **SEVEN, EIGHT, NINE** AND **FOURTEEN;** WE NEED A **PERFECT CIRCLE** AROUND US AND EVERYBODY FOCUSING THEIR **SIGHTS** ON THIS LUNATIC. ARE WE **CLEAR?**
CRYSTAL CLEAR, SIR. EVERYBODY'S RIGHT **BEHIND** YOU.
KGB
OKAY, LET'S SEE WHO'S SMILING **NOW,** GENIUS?
DAMN IT!

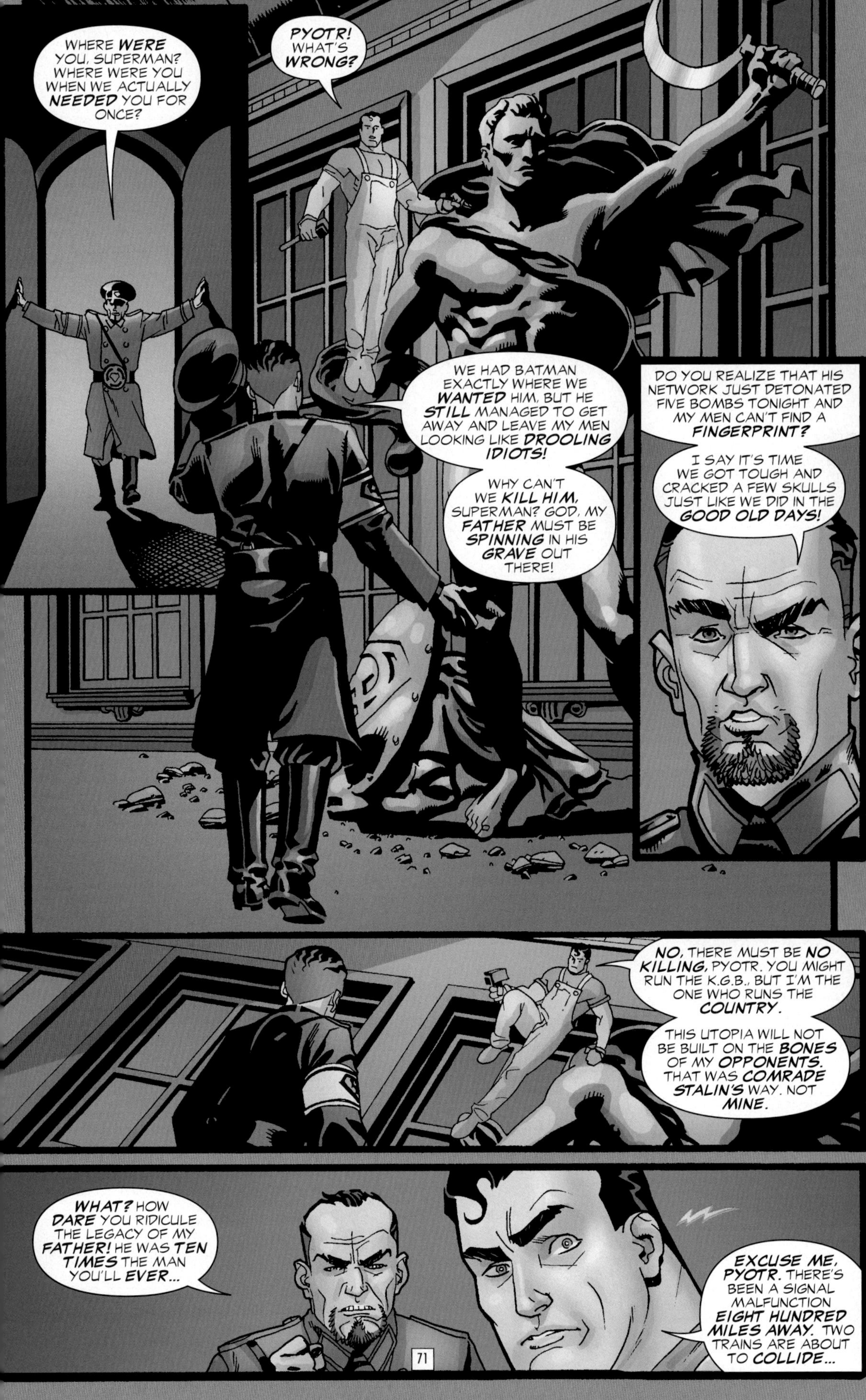
WHERE WERE YOU, SUPERMAN? WHERE WERE YOU WHEN WE ACTUALLY NEEDED YOU FOR ONCE?
PYOTR! WHAT'S WRONG?
WE HAD BATMAN EXACTLY WHERE WE WANTED HIM, BUT HE STILL MANAGED TO GET AWAY AND LEAVE MY MEN LOOKING LIKE DROOLING IDIOTS!
WHY CAN'T WE KILL HIM, SUPERMAN? GOD, MY FATHER MUST BE SPINNING IN HIS GRAVE OUT THERE!
DO YOU REALIZE THAT HIS NETWORK JUST DETONATED FIVE BOMBS TONIGHT AND MY MEN CAN'T FIND A FINGERPRINT?
I SAY IT'S TIME WE GOT TOUGH AND CRACKED A FEW SKULLS JUST LIKE WE DID IN THE GOOD OLD DAYS!
NO, THERE MUST BE NO KILLING, PYOTR. YOU MIGHT RUN THE K.G.B., BUT I'M THE ONE WHO RUNS THE COUNTRY.
THIS UTOPIA WILL NOT BE BUILT ON THE BONES OF MY OPPONENTS. THAT WAS COMRADE STALIN'S WAY. NOT MINE.
WHAT? HOW DARE YOU RIDICULE THE LEGACY OF MY FATHER! HE WAS TEN TIMES THE MAN YOU'LL EVER...
EXCUSE ME, PYOTR. THERE'S BEEN A SIGNAL MALFUNCTION EIGHT HUNDRED MILES AWAY. TWO TRAINS ARE ABOUT TO COLLIDE...

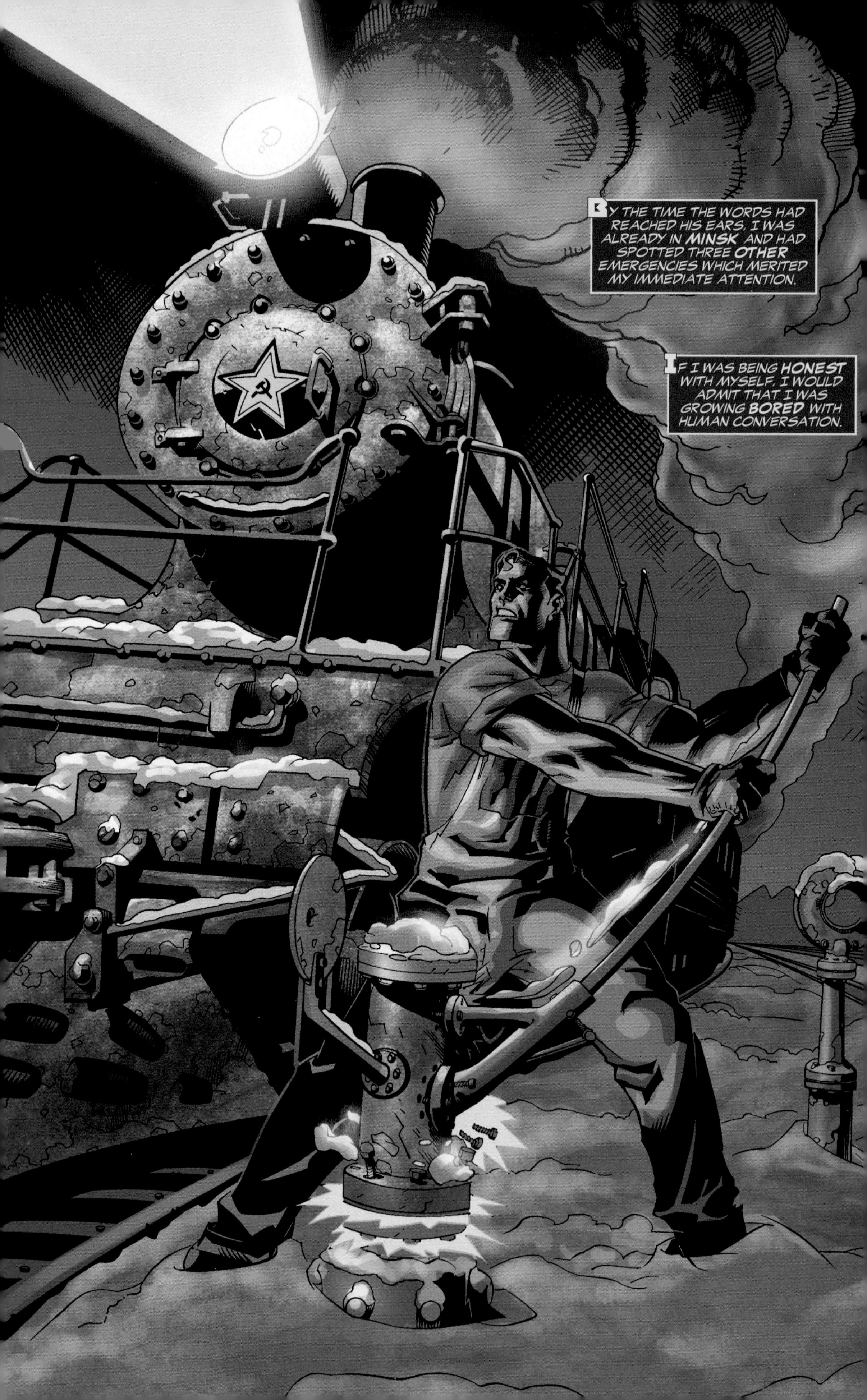
BY THE TIME THE WORDS HAD REACHED HIS EARS, I WAS ALREADY IN MINSK AND HAD SPOTTED THREE OTHER EMERGENCIES WHICH MERITED MY IMMEDIATE ATTENTION.
IF I WAS BEING HONEST WITH MYSELF, I WOULD ADMIT THAT I WAS GROWING BORED WITH HUMAN CONVERSATION.

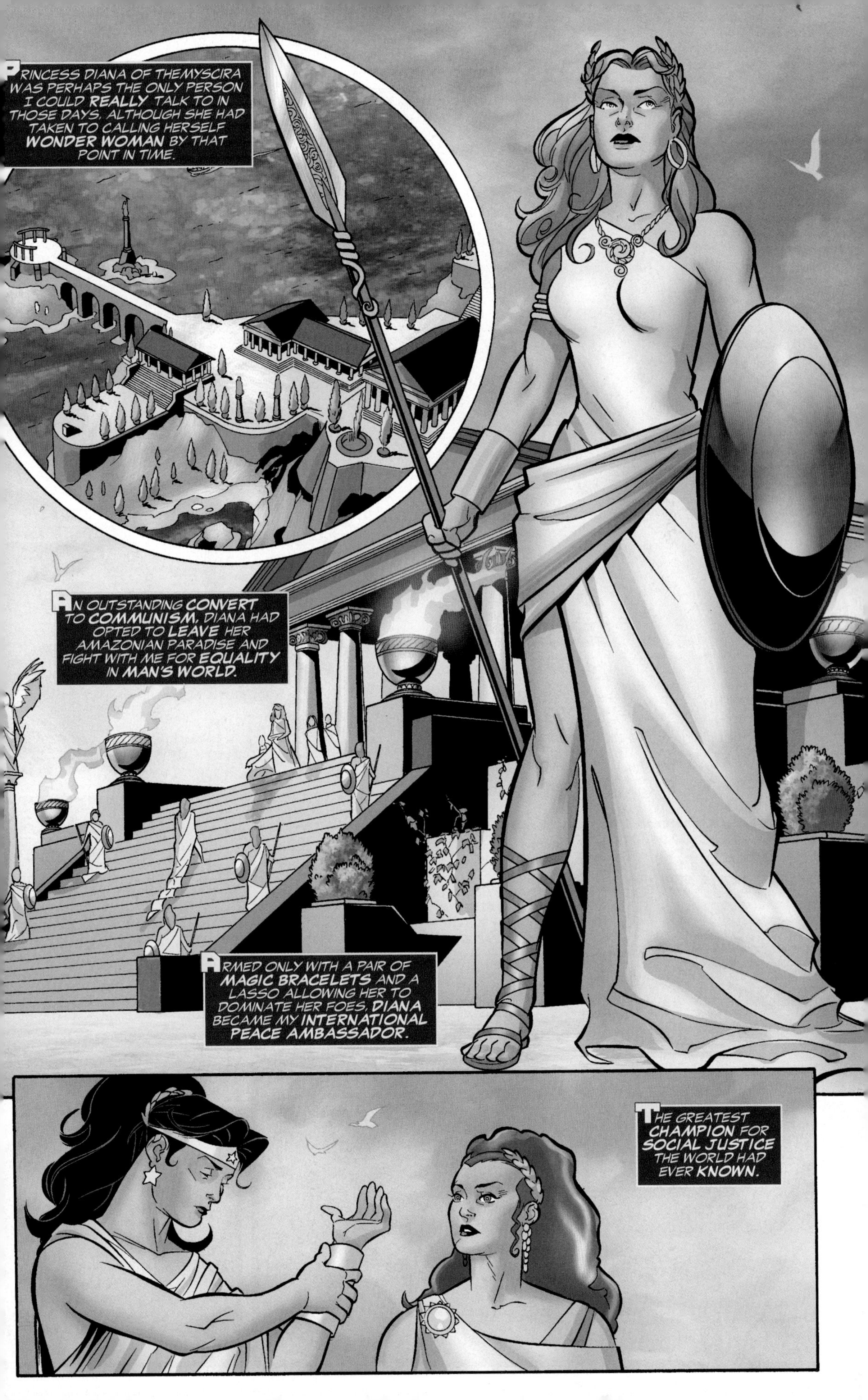

PRINCESS DIANA OF THEMYSCIRA WAS PERHAPS THE ONLY PERSON I COULD REALLY TALK TO IN THOSE DAYS, ALTHOUGH SHE HAD TAKEN TO CALLING HERSELF WONDER WOMAN BY THAT POINT IN TIME.
AN OUTSTANDING CONVERT TO COMMUNISM, DIANA HAD OPTED TO LEAVE HER AMAZONIAN PARADISE AND FIGHT WITH ME FOR EQUALITY IN MAN'S WORLD.
ARMED ONLY WITH A PAIR OF MAGIC BRACELETS AND A LASSO ALLOWING HER TO DOMINATE HER FOES, DIANA BECAME MY INTERNATIONAL PEACE AMBASSADOR.
THE GREATEST CHAMPION FOR SOCIAL JUSTICE THE WORLD HAD EVER KNOWN.

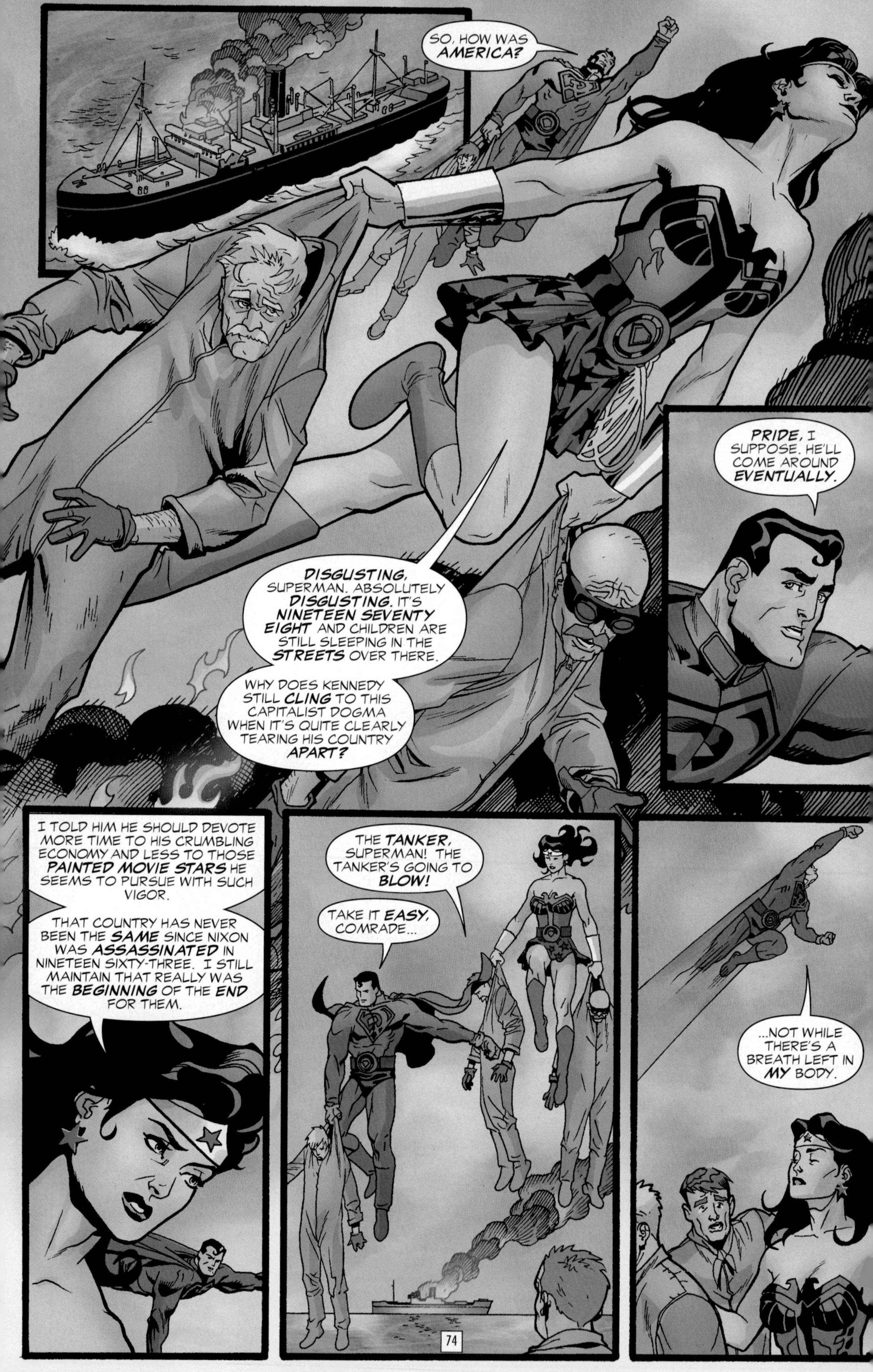
SO, HOW WAS AMERICA?
DISGUSTING, SUPERMAN. ABSOLUTELY DISGUSTING. IT'S NINETEEN SEVENTY EIGHT AND CHILDREN ARE STILL SLEEPING IN THE STREETS OVER THERE.
WHY DOES KENNEDY STILL CLING TO THIS CAPITALIST DOGMA WHEN IT'S QUITE CLEARLY TEARING HIS COUNTRY APART?
PRIDE, I SUPPOSE. HE'LL COME AROUND EVENTUALLY.
I TOLD HIM HE SHOULD DEVOTE MORE TIME TO HIS CRUMBLING ECONOMY AND LESS TO THOSE PAINTED MOVIE STARS HE SEEMS TO PURSUE WITH SUCH VIGOR.
THAT COUNTRY HAS NEVER BEEN THE SAME SINCE NIXON WAS ASSASSINATED IN NINETEEN SIXTY-THREE. I STILL MAINTAIN THAT REALLY WAS THE BEGINNING OF THE END FOR THEM.
THE TANKER, SUPERMAN! THE TANKER'S GOING TO BLOW!
TAKE IT EASY, COMRADE...
...NOT WHILE THERE'S A BREATH LEFT IN MY BODY.

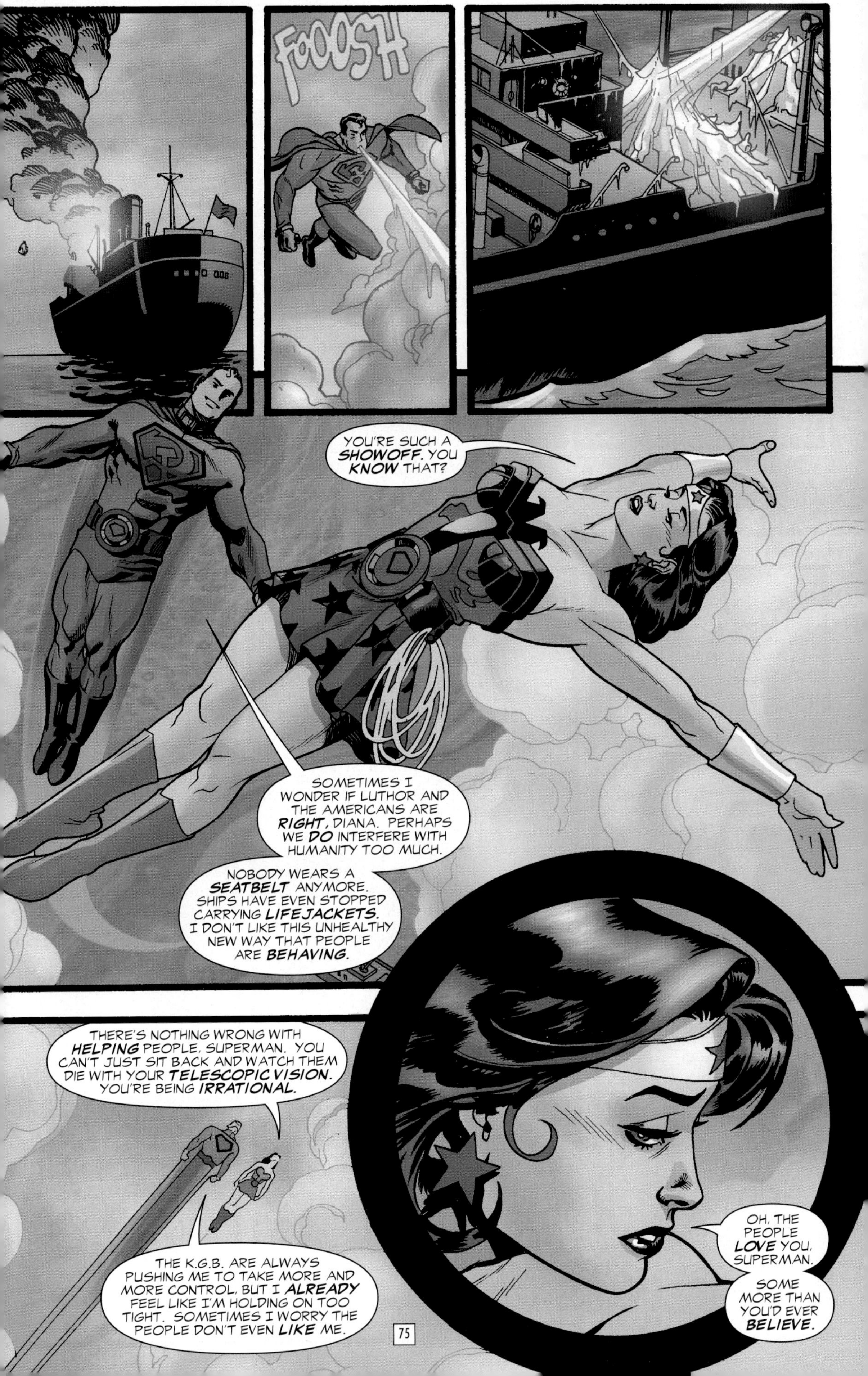
FOOOSH
YOU'RE SUCH A SHOWOFF. YOU KNOW THAT?
SOMETIMES I WONDER IF LUTHOR AND THE AMERICANS ARE RIGHT, DIANA. PERHAPS WE DO INTERFERE WITH HUMANITY TOO MUCH.
NOBODY WEARS A SEATBELT ANYMORE. SHIPS HAVE EVEN STOPPED CARRYING LIFEJACKETS. I DON'T LIKE THIS UNHEALTHY NEW WAY THAT PEOPLE ARE BEHAVING.
THERE'S NOTHING WRONG WITH HELPING PEOPLE, SUPERMAN. YOU CAN'T JUST SIT BACK AND WATCH THEM DIE WITH YOUR TELESCOPIC VISION. YOU'RE BEING IRRATIONAL.
THE K.G.B. ARE ALWAYS PUSHING ME TO TAKE MORE AND MORE CONTROL, BUT I ALREADY FEEL LIKE I'M HOLDING ON TOO TIGHT. SOMETIMES I WORRY THE PEOPLE DON'T EVEN LIKE ME.
OH, THE PEOPLE LOVE YOU, SUPERMAN.
SOME MORE THAN YOU'D EVER BELIEVE.

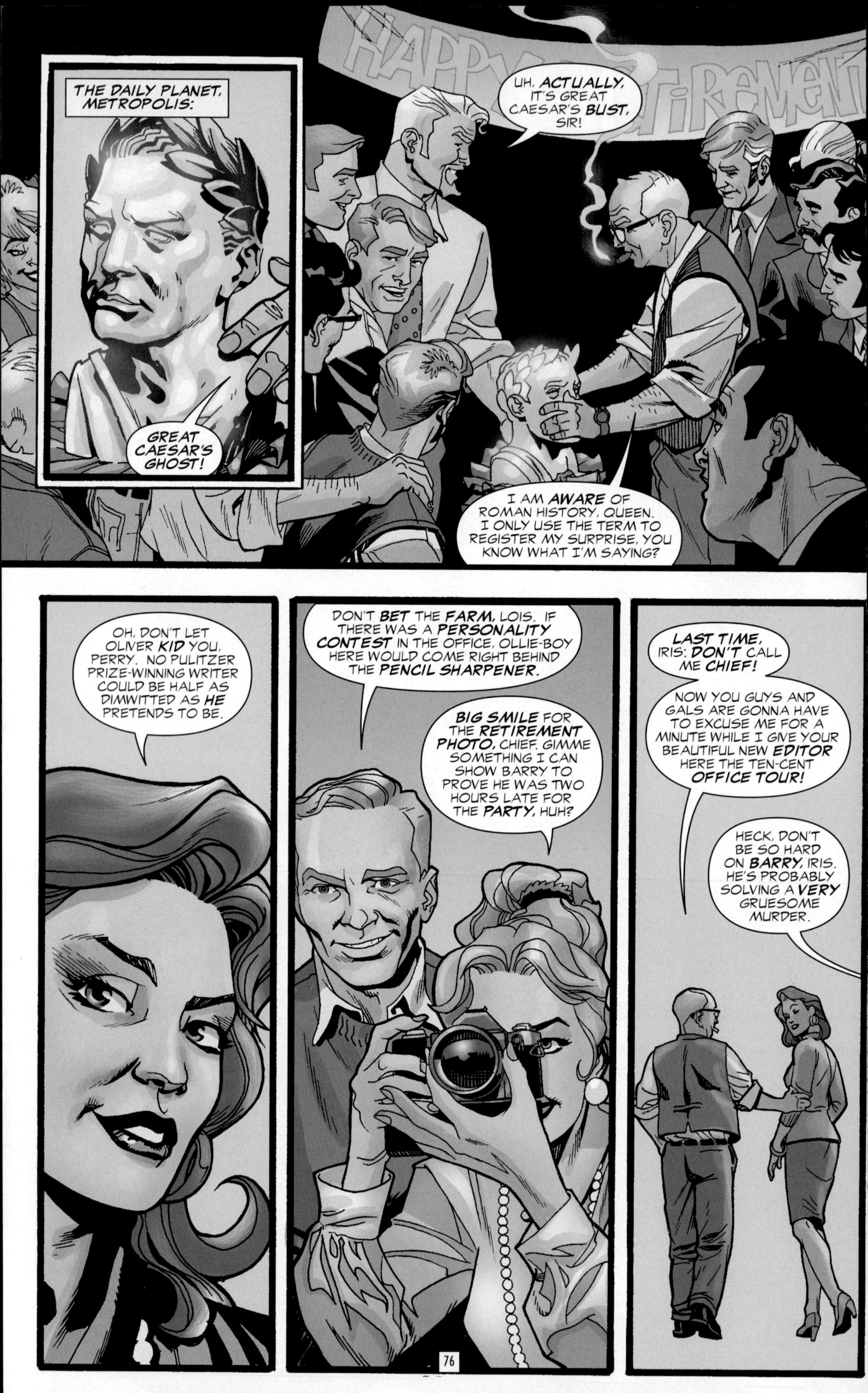
THE DAILY PLANET, METROPOLIS:
GREAT CAESAR'S GHOST!
UH, ACTUALLY, IT'S GREAT CAESAR'S BUST, SIR!
I AM AWARE OF ROMAN HISTORY, QUEEN. I ONLY USE THE TERM TO REGISTER MY SURPRISE, YOU KNOW WHAT I'M SAYING?
OH, DON'T LET OLIVER KID YOU, PERRY. NO PULITZER PRIZE-WINNING WRITER COULD BE HALF AS DIMWITTED AS HE PRETENDS TO BE.
DON'T BET THE FARM, LOIS. IF THERE WAS A PERSONALITY CONTEST IN THE OFFICE, OLLIE-BOY HERE WOULD COME RIGHT BEHIND THE PENCIL SHARPENER.
BIG SMILE FOR THE RETIREMENT PHOTO, CHIEF. GIMME SOMETHING I CAN SHOW BARRY TO PROVE HE WAS TWO HOURS LATE FOR THE PARTY, HUH?
LAST TIME, IRIS: DON'T CALL ME CHIEF!
NOW YOU GUYS AND GALS ARE GONNA HAVE TO EXCUSE ME FOR A MINUTE WHILE I GIVE YOUR BEAUTIFUL NEW EDITOR HERE THE TEN-CENT OFFICE TOUR!
HECK, DON'T BE SO HARD ON BARRY, IRIS. HE'S PROBABLY SOLVING A VERY GRUESOME MURDER.

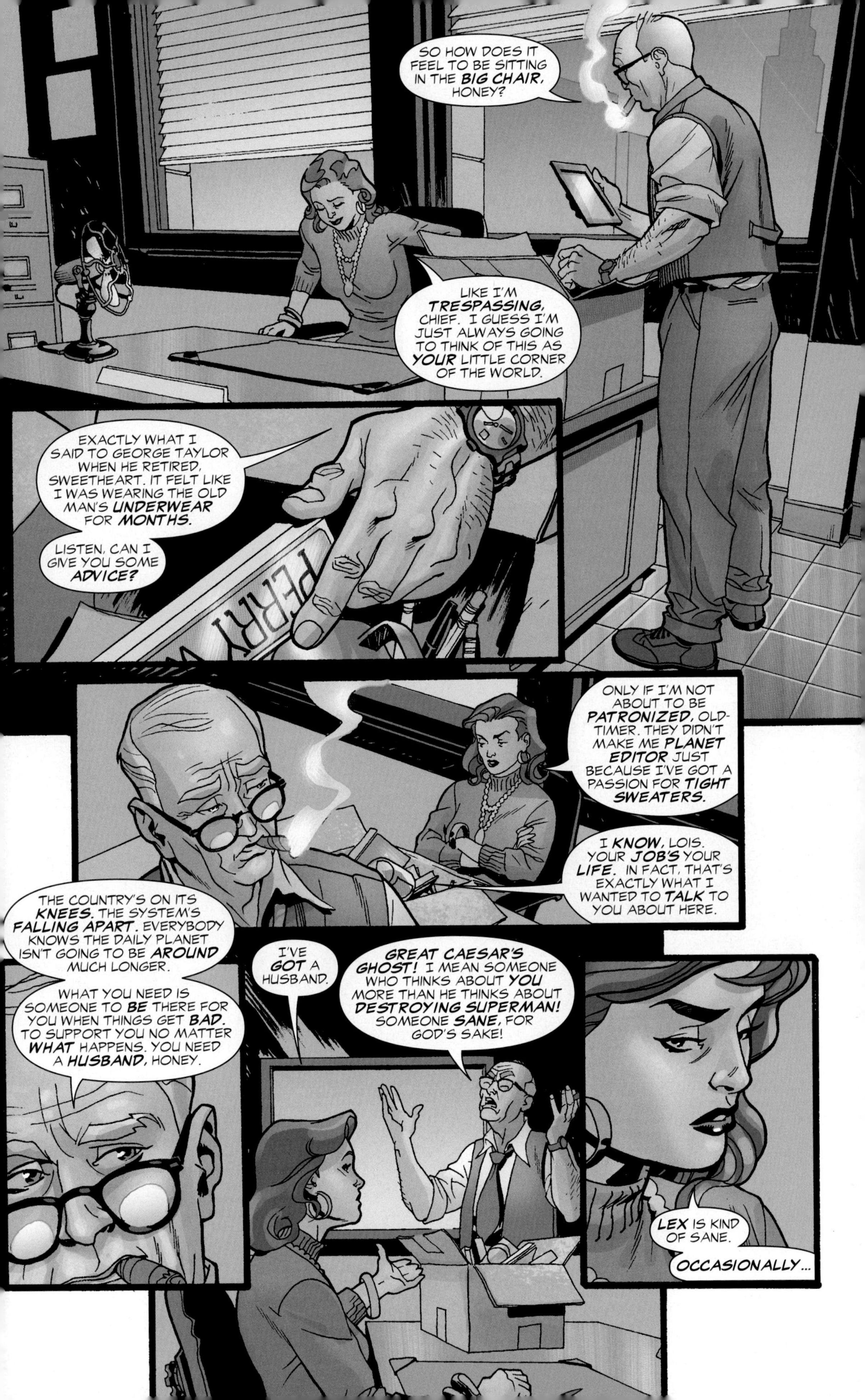
SO HOW DOES IT FEEL TO BE SITTING IN THE BIG CHAIR, HONEY?
LIKE I'M TRESPASSING, CHIEF. I GUESS I'M JUST ALWAYS GOING TO THINK OF THIS AS YOUR LITTLE CORNER OF THE WORLD.
EXACTLY WHAT I SAID TO GEORGE TAYLOR WHEN HE RETIRED, SWEETHEART. IT FELT LIKE I WAS WEARING THE OLD MAN'S UNDERWEAR FOR MONTHS.
LISTEN, CAN I GIVE YOU SOME ADVICE?
PERRY
ONLY IF I'M NOT ABOUT TO BE PATRONIZED, OLD-TIMER. THEY DIDN'T MAKE ME PLANET EDITOR JUST BECAUSE I'VE GOT A PASSION FOR TIGHT SWEATERS.
I KNOW, LOIS. YOUR JOB'S YOUR LIFE. IN FACT, THAT'S EXACTLY WHAT I WANTED TO TALK TO YOU ABOUT HERE.
THE COUNTRY'S ON ITS KNEES. THE SYSTEM'S FALLING APART. EVERYBODY KNOWS THE DAILY PLANET ISN'T GOING TO BE AROUND MUCH LONGER.
WHAT YOU NEED IS SOMEONE TO BE THERE FOR YOU WHEN THINGS GET BAD. TO SUPPORT YOU NO MATTER WHAT HAPPENS. YOU NEED A HUSBAND, HONEY.
I'VE GOT A HUSBAND.
GREAT CAESAR'S GHOST! I MEAN SOMEONE WHO THINKS ABOUT YOU MORE THAN HE THINKS ABOUT DESTROYING SUPERMAN! SOMEONE SANE, FOR GOD'S SAKE!
LEX IS KIND OF SANE.
OCCASIONALLY...

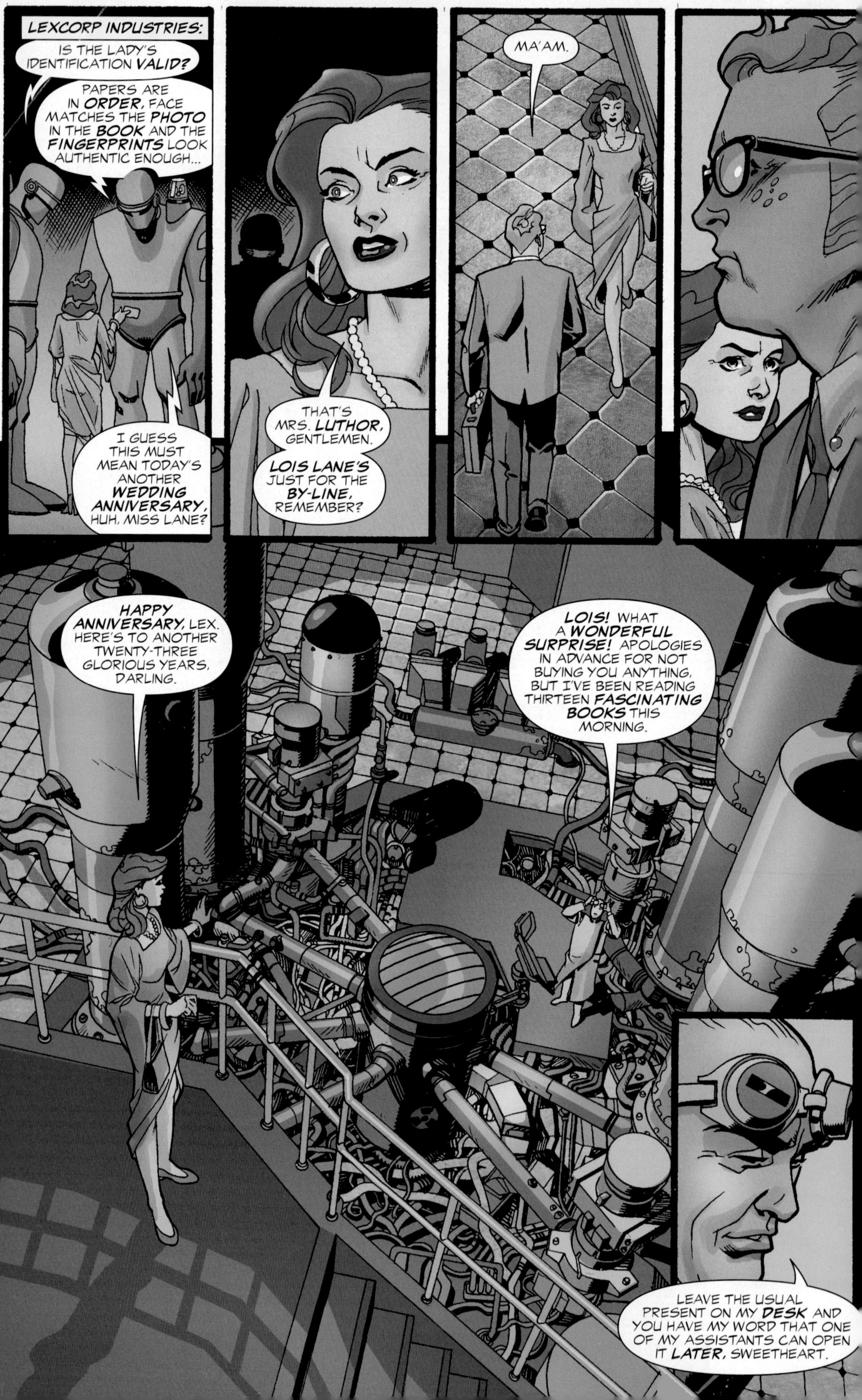
LEXCORP INDUSTRIES:
IS THE LADY'S IDENTIFICATION VALID?
PAPERS ARE IN ORDER, FACE MATCHES THE PHOTO IN THE BOOK AND THE FINGERPRINTS LOOK AUTHENTIC ENOUGH...
I GUESS THIS MUST MEAN TODAY'S ANOTHER WEDDING ANNIVERSARY, HUH, MISS LANE?
THAT'S MRS. LUTHOR, GENTLEMEN.
LOIS LANE'S JUST FOR THE BY-LINE, REMEMBER?
MA'AM.
HAPPY ANNIVERSARY, LEX. HERE'S TO ANOTHER TWENTY-THREE GLORIOUS YEARS, DARLING.
LOIS! WHAT A WONDERFUL SURPRISE! APOLOGIES IN ADVANCE FOR NOT BUYING YOU ANYTHING, BUT I'VE BEEN READING THIRTEEN FASCINATING BOOKS THIS MORNING.
LEAVE THE USUAL PRESENT ON MY DESK AND YOU HAVE MY WORD THAT ONE OF MY ASSISTANTS CAN OPEN IT LATER, SWEETHEART.

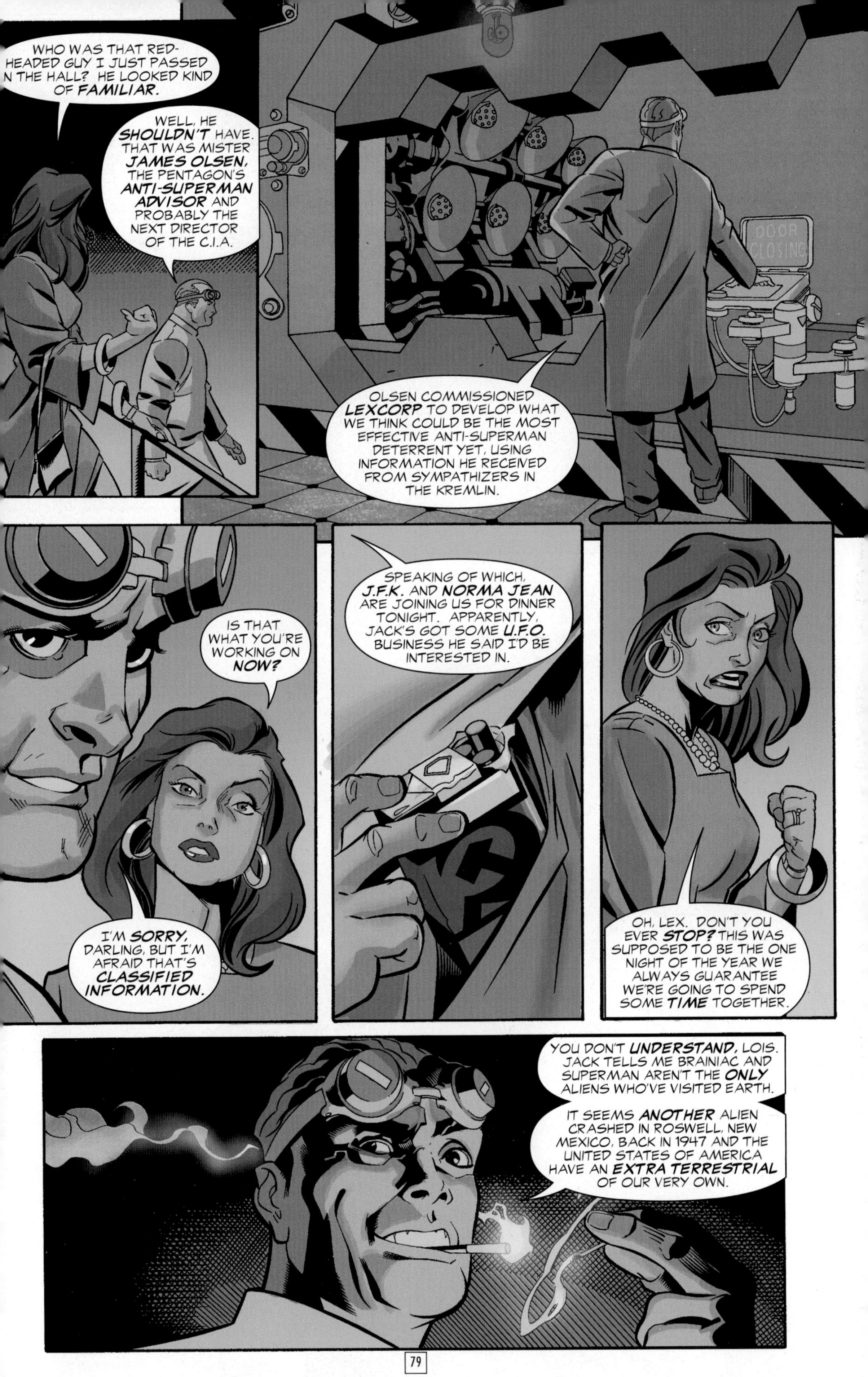
WHO WAS THAT RED-HEADED GUY I JUST PASSED IN THE HALL? HE LOOKED KIND OF FAMILIAR.
WELL, HE SHOULDN'T HAVE. THAT WAS MISTER JAMES OLSEN, THE PENTAGON'S ANTI-SUPERMAN ADVISOR AND PROBABLY THE NEXT DIRECTOR OF THE C.I.A.
DOOR CLOSING
OLSEN COMMISSIONED LEXCORP TO DEVELOP WHAT WE THINK COULD BE THE MOST EFFECTIVE ANTI-SUPERMAN DETERRENT YET, USING INFORMATION HE RECEIVED FROM SYMPATHIZERS IN THE KREMLIN.
IS THAT WHAT YOU'RE WORKING ON NOW?
I'M SORRY, DARLING, BUT I'M AFRAID THAT'S CLASSIFIED INFORMATION.
SPEAKING OF WHICH, J.F.K. AND NORMA JEAN ARE JOINING US FOR DINNER TONIGHT. APPARENTLY, JACK'S GOT SOME U.F.O. BUSINESS HE SAID I'D BE INTERESTED IN.
OH, LEX. DON'T YOU EVER STOP? THIS WAS SUPPOSED TO BE THE ONE NIGHT OF THE YEAR WE ALWAYS GUARANTEE WE'RE GOING TO SPEND SOME TIME TOGETHER.
YOU DON'T UNDERSTAND, LOIS. JACK TELLS ME BRAINIAC AND SUPERMAN AREN'T THE ONLY ALIENS WHO'VE VISITED EARTH.
IT SEEMS ANOTHER ALIEN CRASHED IN ROSWELL, NEW MEXICO, BACK IN 1947 AND THE UNITED STATES OF AMERICA HAVE AN EXTRA TERRESTRIAL OF OUR VERY OWN.

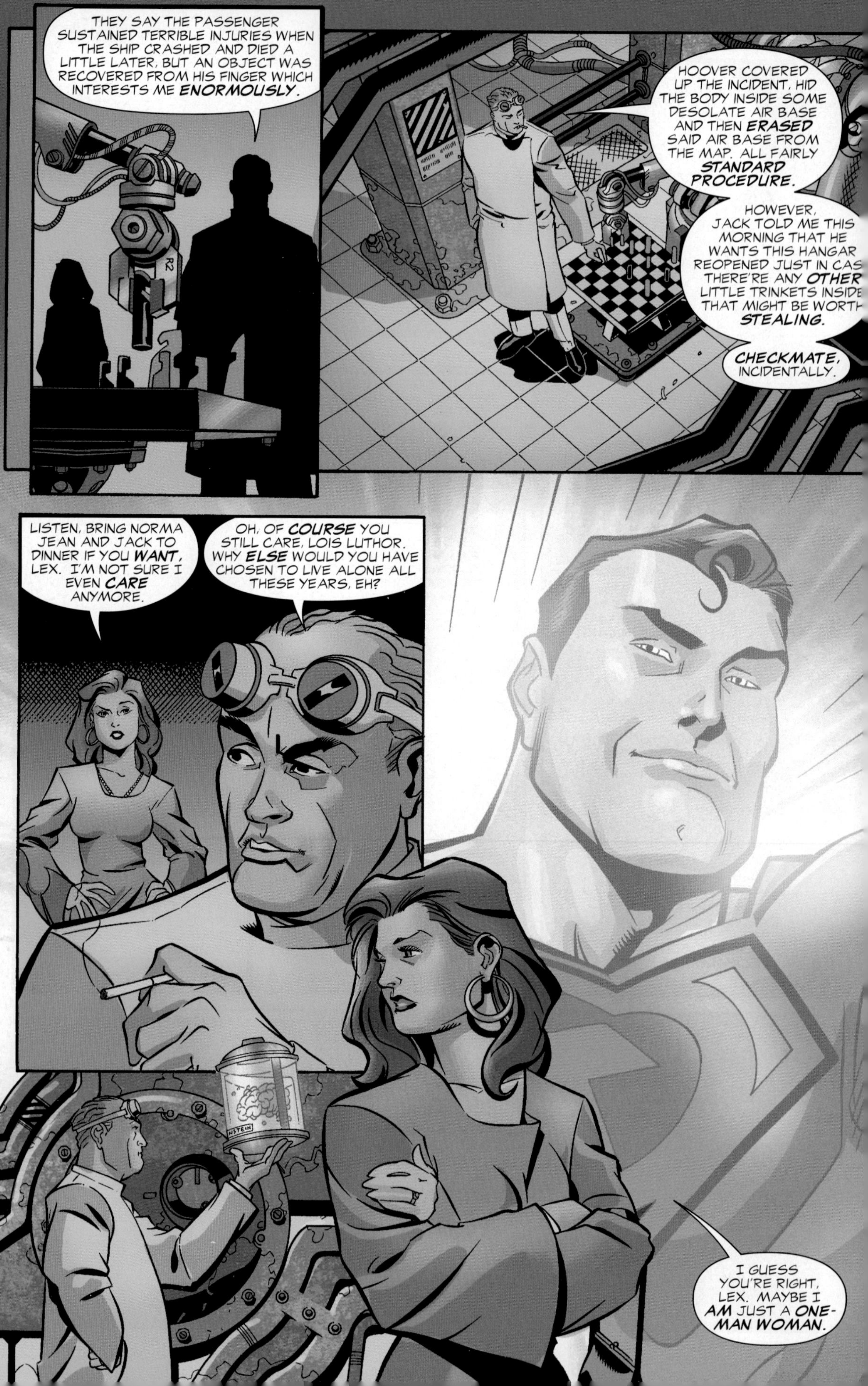
THEY SAY THE PASSENGER SUSTAINED TERRIBLE INJURIES WHEN THE SHIP CRASHED AND DIED A LITTLE LATER, BUT AN OBJECT WAS RECOVERED FROM HIS FINGER WHICH INTERESTS ME ENORMOUSLY.
HOOVER COVERED UP THE INCIDENT, HID THE BODY INSIDE SOME DESOLATE AIR BASE AND THEN ERASED SAID AIR BASE FROM THE MAP. ALL FAIRLY STANDARD PROCEDURE.
HOWEVER, JACK TOLD ME THIS MORNING THAT HE WANTS THIS HANGAR REOPENED JUST IN CASE THERE'RE ANY OTHER LITTLE TRINKETS INSIDE THAT MIGHT BE WORTH STEALING.
CHECKMATE, INCIDENTALLY.
LISTEN, BRING NORMA JEAN AND JACK TO DINNER IF YOU WANT, LEX. I'M NOT SURE I EVEN CARE ANYMORE.
OH, OF COURSE YOU STILL CARE, LOIS LUTHOR. WHY ELSE WOULD YOU HAVE CHOSEN TO LIVE ALONE ALL THESE YEARS, EH?
I GUESS YOU'RE RIGHT, LEX. MAYBE I AM JUST A ONE-MAN WOMAN.

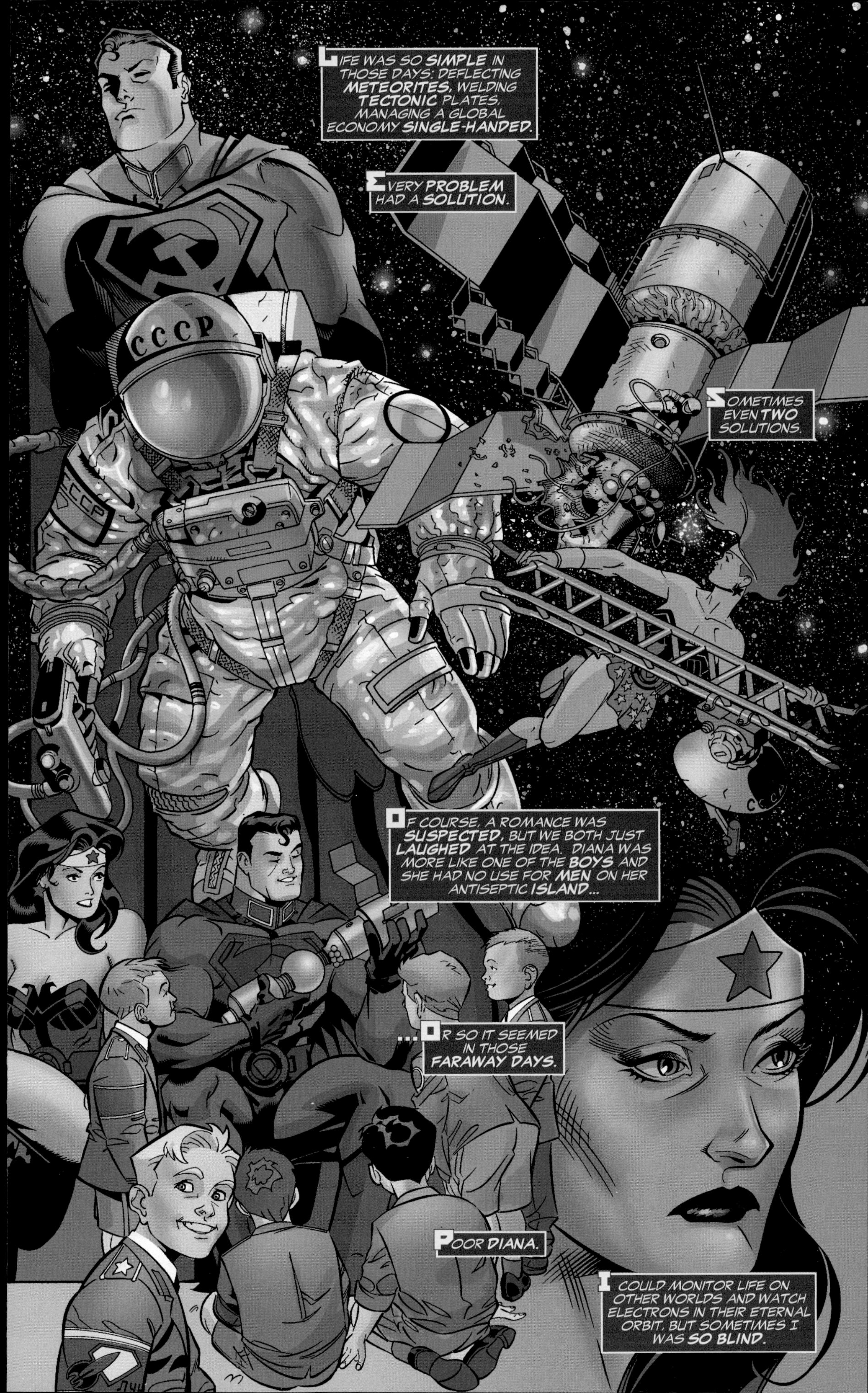
LIFE WAS SO SIMPLE IN THOSE DAYS: DEFLECTING METEORITES, WELDING TECTONIC PLATES, MANAGING A GLOBAL ECONOMY SINGLE-HANDED.
EVERY PROBLEM HAD A SOLUTION.
SOMETIMES EVEN TWO SOLUTIONS.
CCCP
OF COURSE, A ROMANCE WAS SUSPECTED, BUT WE BOTH JUST LAUGHED AT THE IDEA. DIANA WAS MORE LIKE ONE OF THE BOYS AND SHE HAD NO USE FOR MEN ON HER ANTISEPTIC ISLAND...
...OR SO IT SEEMED IN THOSE FARAWAY DAYS.
POOR DIANA.
I COULD MONITOR LIFE ON OTHER WORLDS AND WATCH ELECTRONS IN THEIR ETERNAL ORBIT, BUT SOMETIMES I WAS SO BLIND.

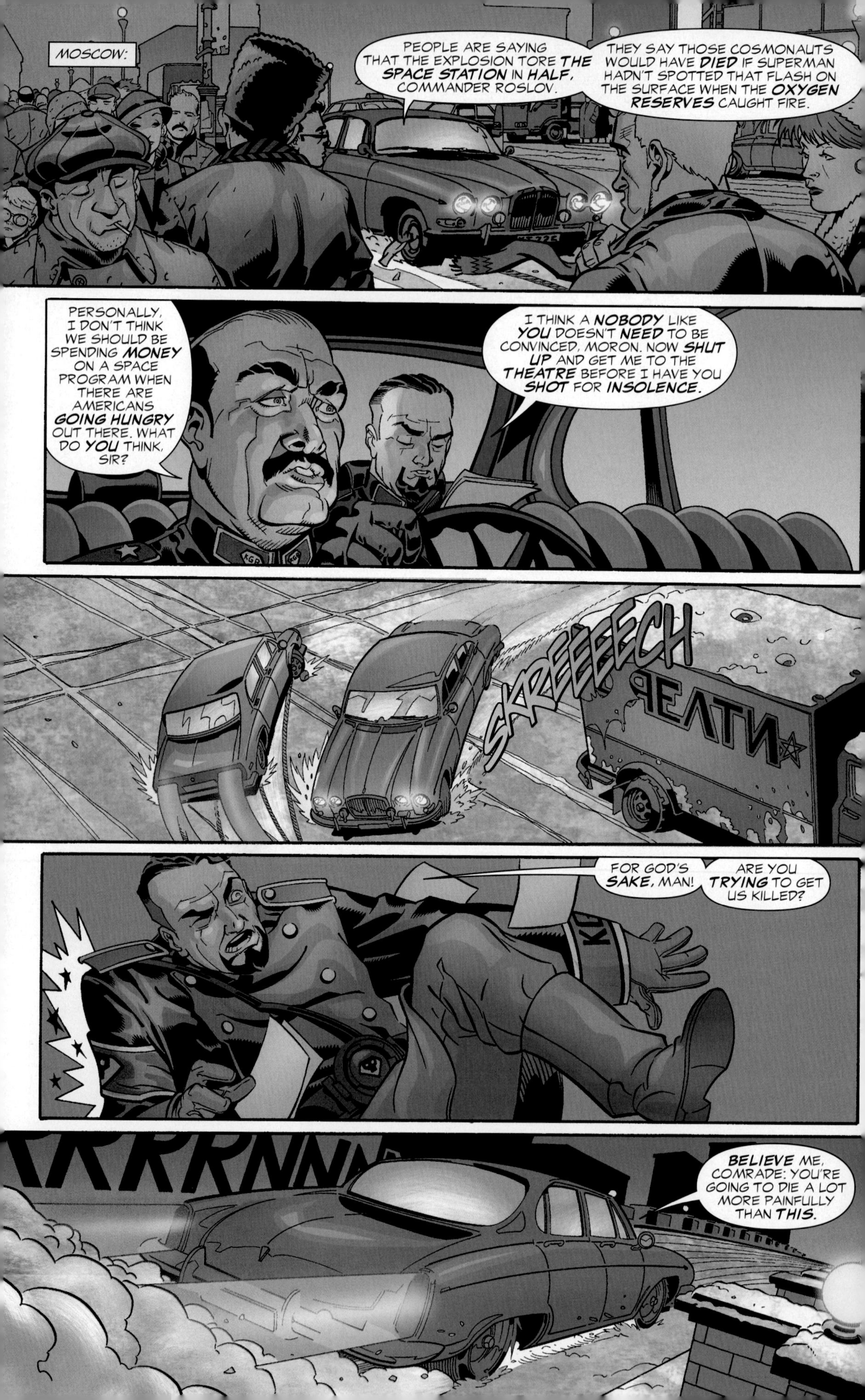
MOSCOW:
PEOPLE ARE SAYING THAT THE EXPLOSION TORE THE SPACE STATION IN HALF, COMMANDER ROSLOV.
THEY SAY THOSE COSMONAUTS WOULD HAVE DIED IF SUPERMAN HADN'T SPOTTED THAT FLASH ON THE SURFACE WHEN THE OXYGEN RESERVES CAUGHT FIRE.
PERSONALLY, I DON'T THINK WE SHOULD BE SPENDING MONEY ON A SPACE PROGRAM WHEN THERE ARE AMERICANS GOING HUNGRY OUT THERE. WHAT DO YOU THINK, SIR?
I THINK A NOBODY LIKE YOU DOESN'T NEED TO BE CONVINCED, MORON. NOW SHUT UP AND GET ME TO THE THEATRE BEFORE I HAVE YOU SHOT FOR INSOLENCE.
SKREEEECH
FOR GOD'S SAKE, MAN!
ARE YOU TRYING TO GET US KILLED?
RRRRNNN
BELIEVE ME, COMRADE: YOU'RE GOING TO DIE A LOT MORE PAINFULLY THAN THIS.

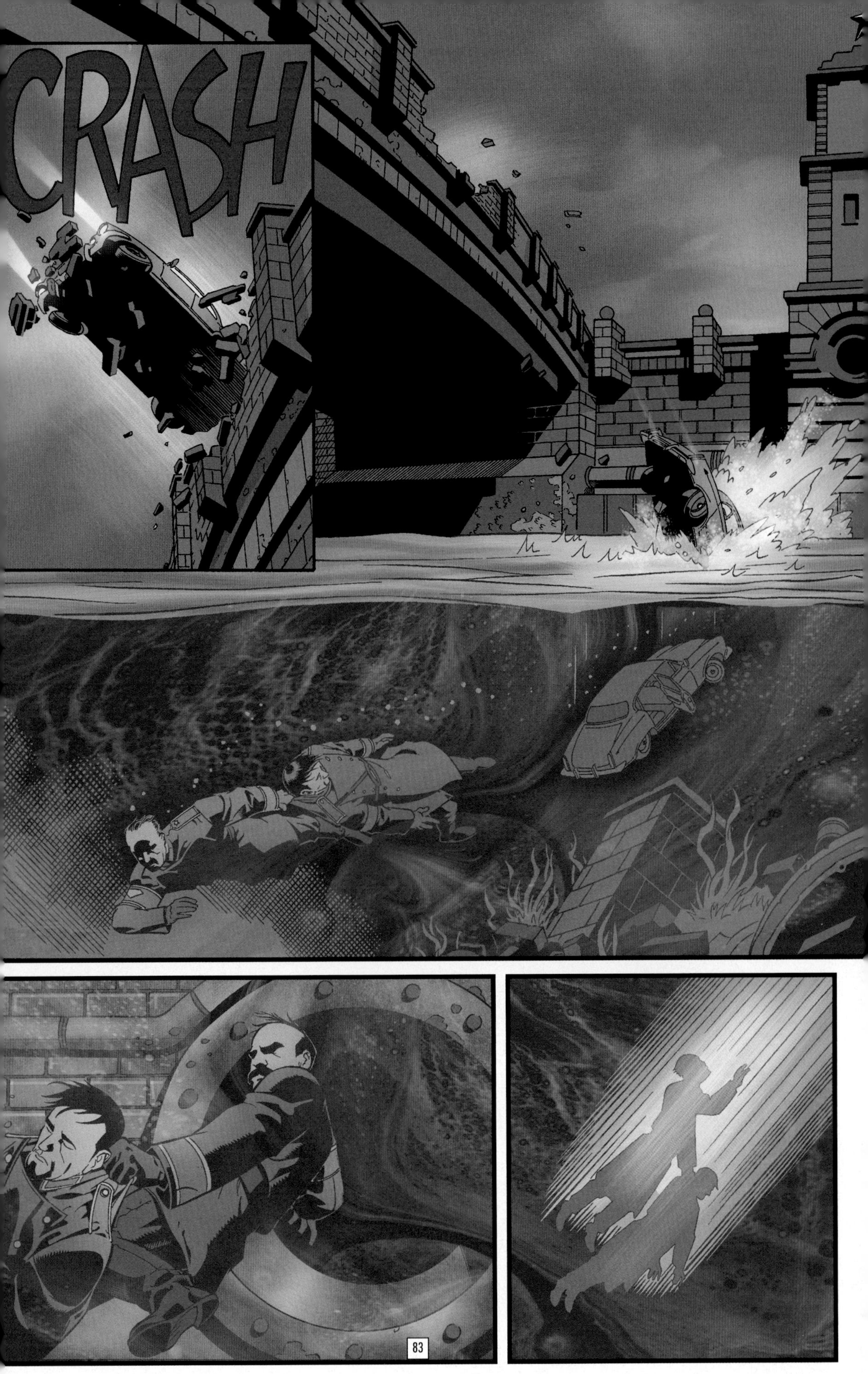
CRASH

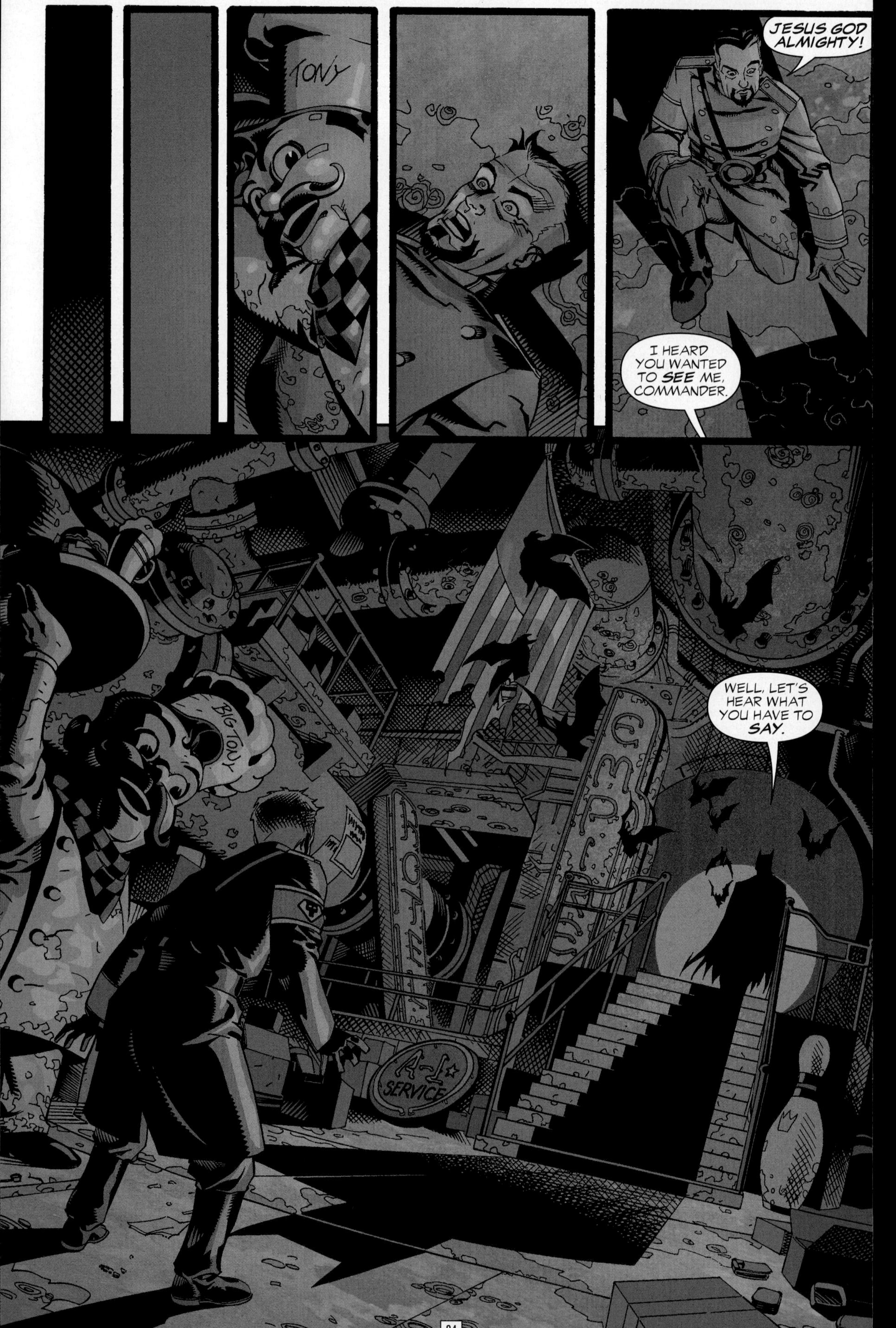
TONY
JESUS GOD ALMIGHTY!
I HEARD YOU WANTED TO SEE ME, COMMANDER.
BIG TONY
WELL, LET'S HEAR WHAT YOU HAVE TO SAY.
A-1 SERVICE

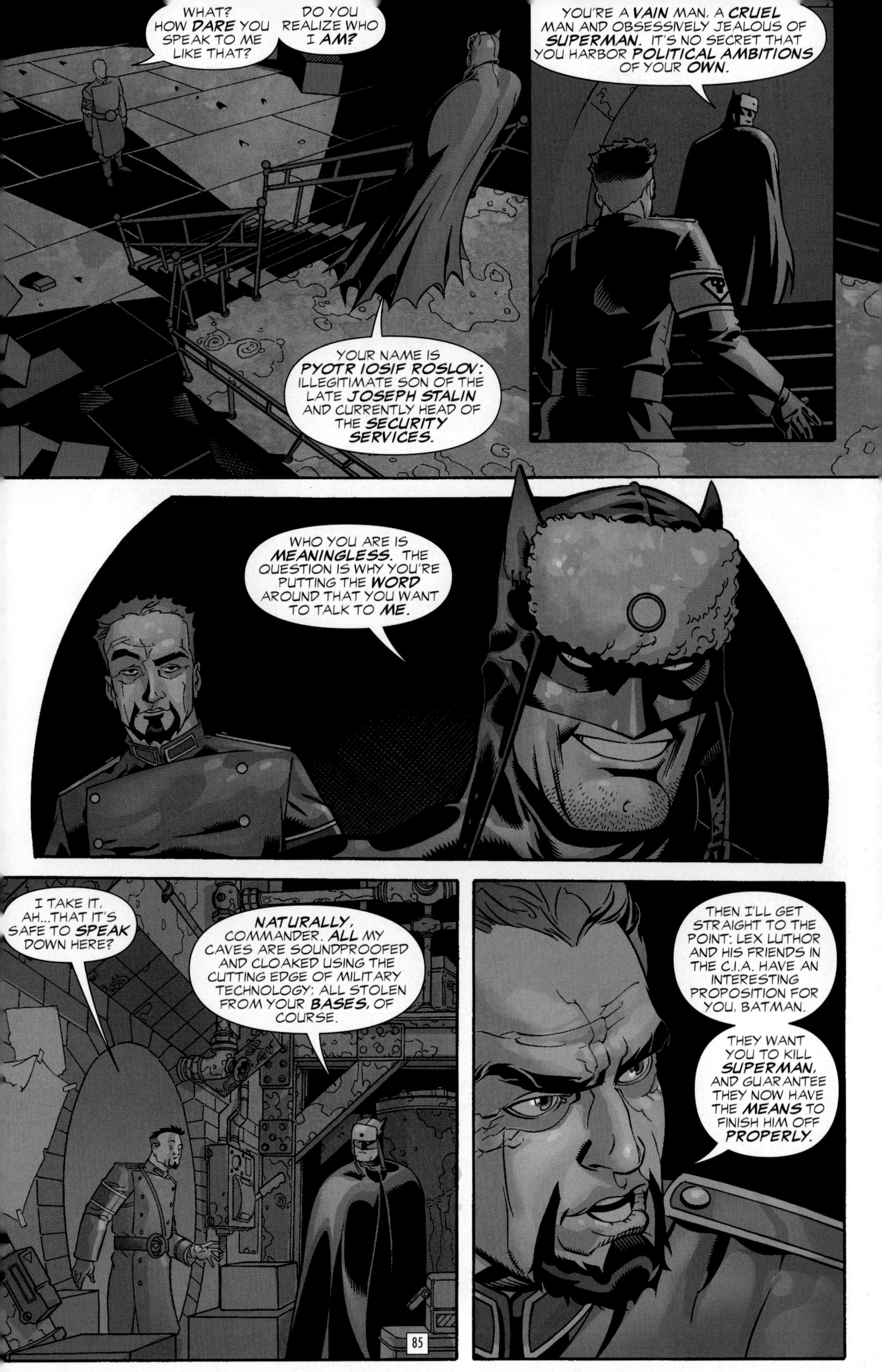

WHAT? HOW DARE YOU SPEAK TO ME LIKE THAT?
DO YOU REALIZE WHO I AM?
YOUR NAME IS PYOTR IOSIF ROSLOV: ILLEGITIMATE SON OF THE LATE JOSEPH STALIN AND CURRENTLY HEAD OF THE SECURITY SERVICES.
YOU'RE A VAIN MAN, A CRUEL MAN AND OBSESSIVELY JEALOUS OF SUPERMAN. IT'S NO SECRET THAT YOU HARBOR POLITICAL AMBITIONS OF YOUR OWN.
WHO YOU ARE IS MEANINGLESS. THE QUESTION IS WHY YOU'RE PUTTING THE WORD AROUND THAT YOU WANT TO TALK TO ME.
I TAKE IT, AH...THAT IT'S SAFE TO SPEAK DOWN HERE?
NATURALLY, COMMANDER. ALL MY CAVES ARE SOUNDPROOFED AND CLOAKED USING THE CUTTING EDGE OF MILITARY TECHNOLOGY; ALL STOLEN FROM YOUR BASES, OF COURSE.
THEN I'LL GET STRAIGHT TO THE POINT: LEX LUTHOR AND HIS FRIENDS IN THE C.I.A. HAVE AN INTERESTING PROPOSITION FOR YOU, BATMAN.
THEY WANT YOU TO KILL SUPERMAN, AND GUARANTEE THEY NOW HAVE THE MEANS TO FINISH HIM OFF PROPERLY.

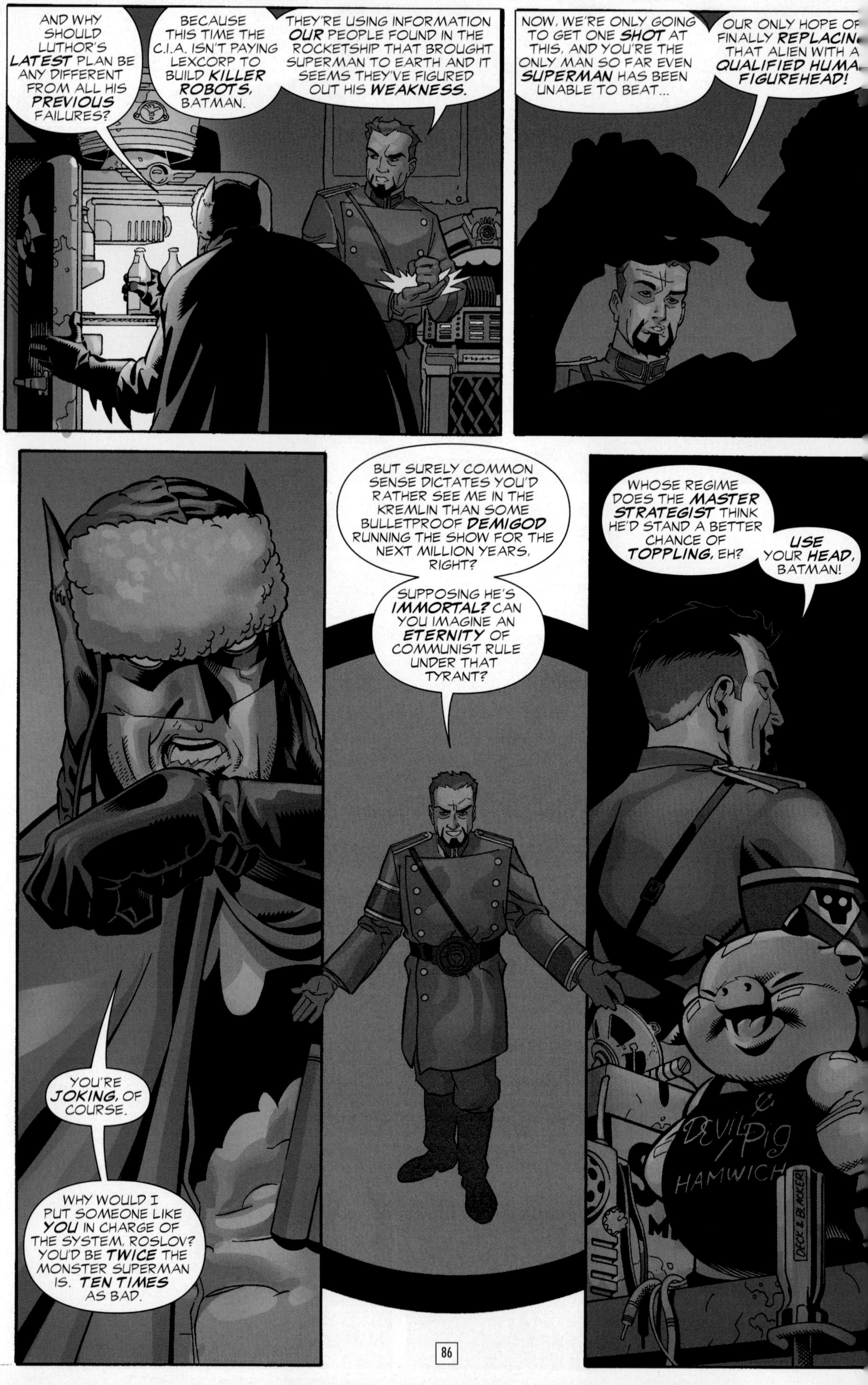
AND WHY SHOULD LUTHOR'S LATEST PLAN BE ANY DIFFERENT FROM ALL HIS PREVIOUS FAILURES?
BECAUSE THIS TIME THE C.I.A. ISN'T PAYING LEXCORP TO BUILD KILLER ROBOTS, BATMAN.
THEY'RE USING INFORMATION OUR PEOPLE FOUND IN THE ROCKETSHIP THAT BROUGHT SUPERMAN TO EARTH AND IT SEEMS THEY'VE FIGURED OUT HIS WEAKNESS.
NOW, WE'RE ONLY GOING TO GET ONE SHOT AT THIS, AND YOU'RE THE ONLY MAN SO FAR EVEN SUPERMAN HAS BEEN UNABLE TO BEAT...
OUR ONLY HOPE OF FINALLY REPLACIN THAT ALIEN WITH A QUALIFIED HUMA FIGUREHEAD!
YOU'RE JOKING, OF COURSE.
WHY WOULD I PUT SOMEONE LIKE YOU IN CHARGE OF THE SYSTEM, ROSLOV? YOU'D BE TWICE THE MONSTER SUPERMAN IS. TEN TIMES AS BAD.
BUT SURELY COMMON SENSE DICTATES YOU'D RATHER SEE ME IN THE KREMLIN THAN SOME BULLETPROOF DEMIGOD RUNNING THE SHOW FOR THE NEXT MILLION YEARS, RIGHT?
SUPPOSING HE'S IMMORTAL? CAN YOU IMAGINE AN ETERNITY OF COMMUNIST RULE UNDER THAT TYRANT?
WHOSE REGIME DOES THE MASTER STRATEGIST THINK HE'D STAND A BETTER CHANCE OF TOPPLING, EH?
USE YOUR HEAD, BATMAN!
DEVIL PIG
HAMWICH
DECK & BLACKER

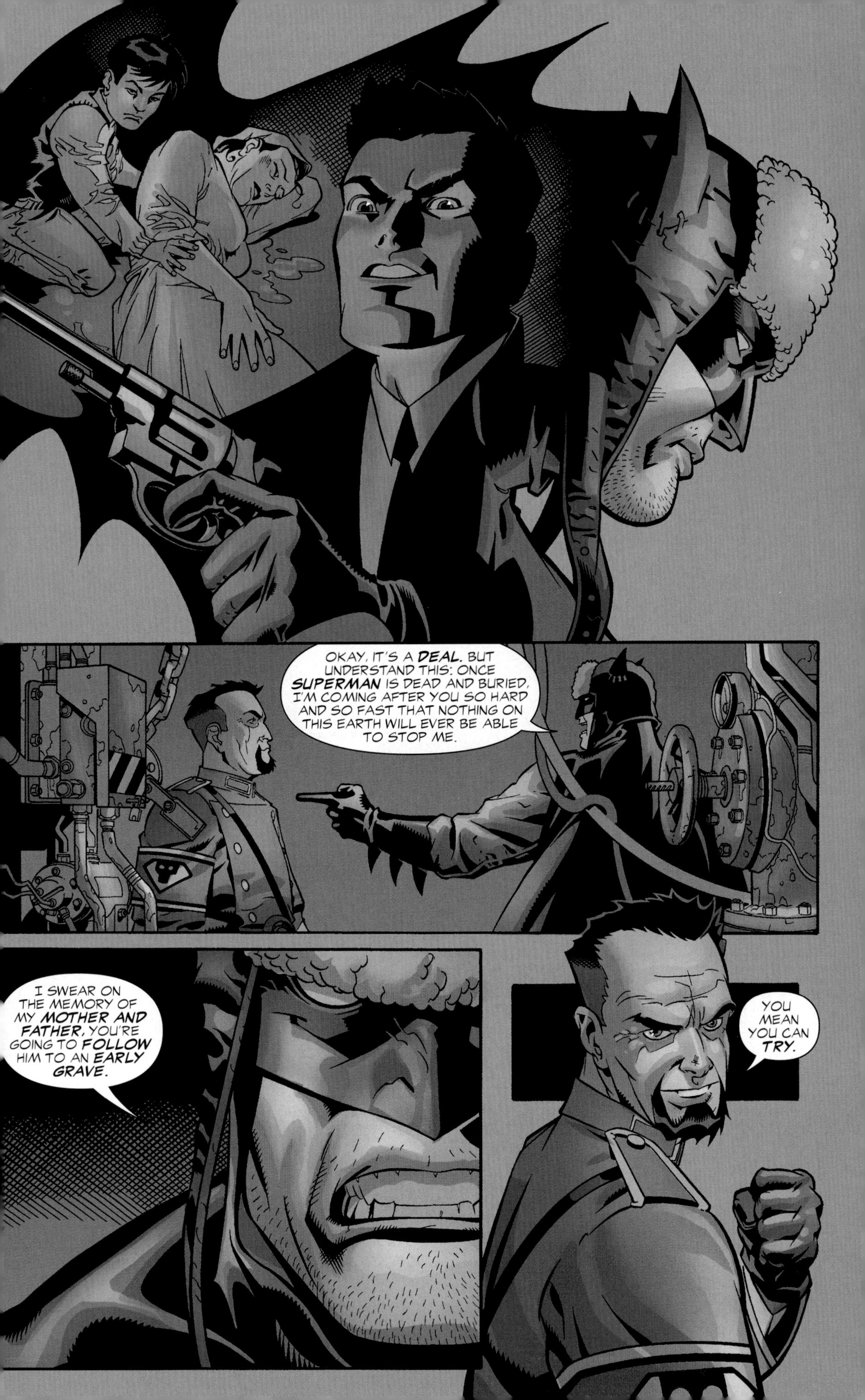
OKAY, IT'S A DEAL. BUT UNDERSTAND THIS: ONCE SUPERMAN IS DEAD AND BURIED, I'M COMING AFTER YOU SO HARD AND SO FAST THAT NOTHING ON THIS EARTH WILL EVER BE ABLE TO STOP ME.
I SWEAR ON THE MEMORY OF MY MOTHER AND FATHER, YOU'RE GOING TO FOLLOW HIM TO AN EARLY GRAVE.
YOU MEAN YOU CAN TRY.

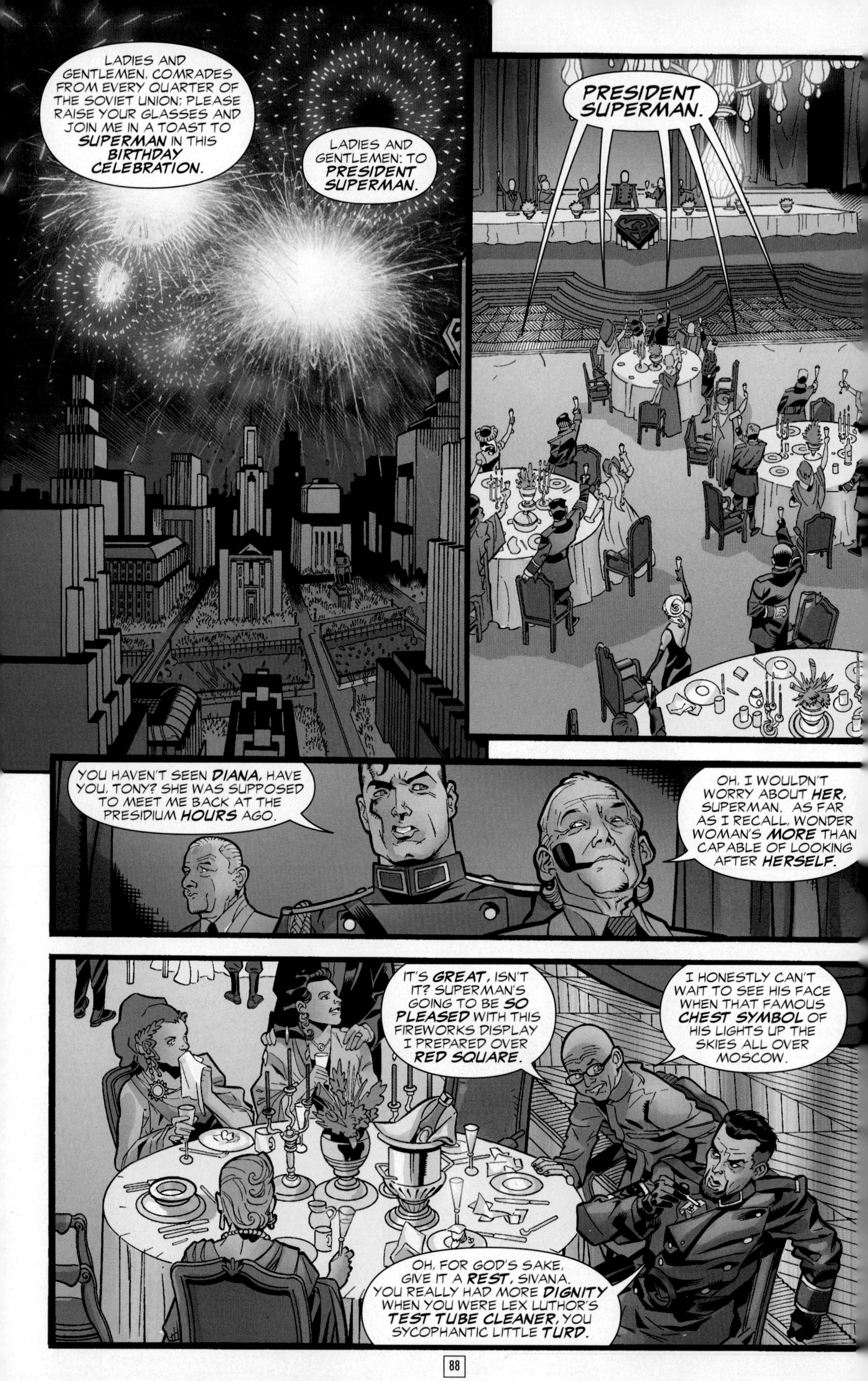

LADIES AND GENTLEMEN, COMRADES FROM EVERY QUARTER OF THE SOVIET UNION: PLEASE RAISE YOUR GLASSES AND JOIN ME IN A TOAST TO SUPERMAN IN THIS BIRTHDAY CELEBRATION.
LADIES AND GENTLEMEN: TO PRESIDENT SUPERMAN.
PRESIDENT SUPERMAN.
YOU HAVEN'T SEEN DIANA, HAVE YOU, TONY? SHE WAS SUPPOSED TO MEET ME BACK AT THE PRESIDIUM HOURS AGO.
OH, I WOULDN'T WORRY ABOUT HER, SUPERMAN. AS FAR AS I RECALL, WONDER WOMAN'S MORE THAN CAPABLE OF LOOKING AFTER HERSELF.
IT'S GREAT, ISN'T IT? SUPERMAN'S GOING TO BE SO PLEASED WITH THIS FIREWORKS DISPLAY I PREPARED OVER RED SQUARE.
I HONESTLY CAN'T WAIT TO SEE HIS FACE WHEN THAT FAMOUS CHEST SYMBOL OF HIS LIGHTS UP THE SKIES ALL OVER MOSCOW.
OH, FOR GOD'S SAKE, GIVE IT A REST, SIVANA. YOU REALLY HAD MORE DIGNITY WHEN YOU WERE LEX LUTHOR'S TEST TUBE CLEANER, YOU SYCOPHANTIC LITTLE TURD.

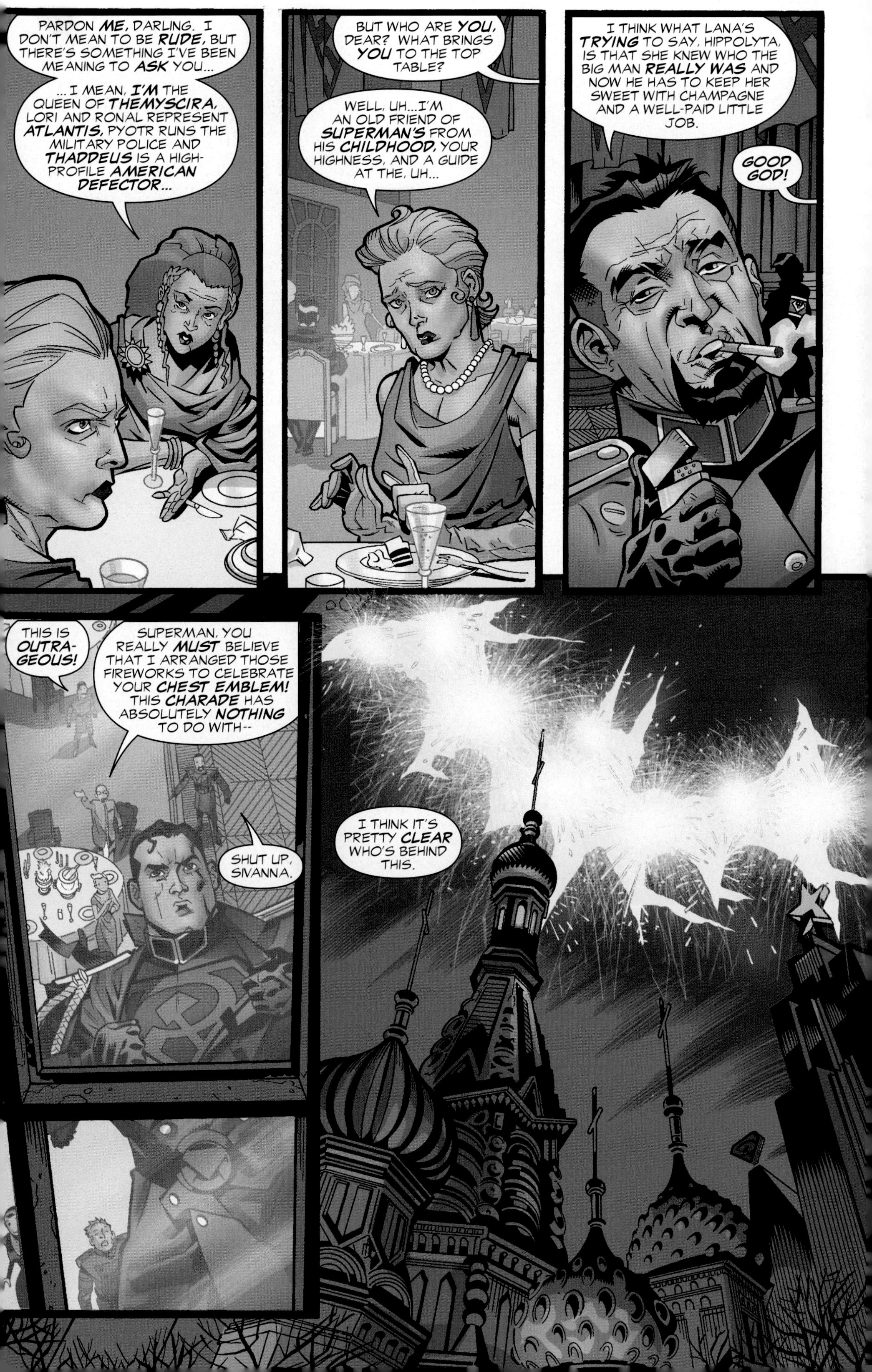
PARDON ME, DARLING. I DON'T MEAN TO BE RUDE, BUT THERE'S SOMETHING I'VE BEEN MEANING TO ASK YOU...
... I MEAN, I'M THE QUEEN OF THEMYSCIRA, LORI AND RONAL REPRESENT ATLANTIS, PYOTR RUNS THE MILITARY POLICE AND THADDEUS IS A HIGH-PROFILE AMERICAN DEFECTOR...
BUT WHO ARE YOU, DEAR? WHAT BRINGS YOU TO THE TOP TABLE?
WELL, UH...I'M AN OLD FRIEND OF SUPERMAN'S FROM HIS CHILDHOOD, YOUR HIGHNESS, AND A GUIDE AT THE, UH...
I THINK WHAT LANA'S TRYING TO SAY, HIPPOLYTA, IS THAT SHE KNEW WHO THE BIG MAN REALLY WAS AND NOW HE HAS TO KEEP HER SWEET WITH CHAMPAGNE AND A WELL-PAID LITTLE JOB.
GOOD GOD!
THIS IS OUTRAGEOUS!
SUPERMAN, YOU REALLY MUST BELIEVE THAT I ARRANGED THOSE FIREWORKS TO CELEBRATE YOUR CHEST EMBLEM! THIS CHARADE HAS ABSOLUTELY NOTHING TO DO WITH--
SHUT UP, SIVANNA.
I THINK IT'S PRETTY CLEAR WHO'S BEHIND THIS.

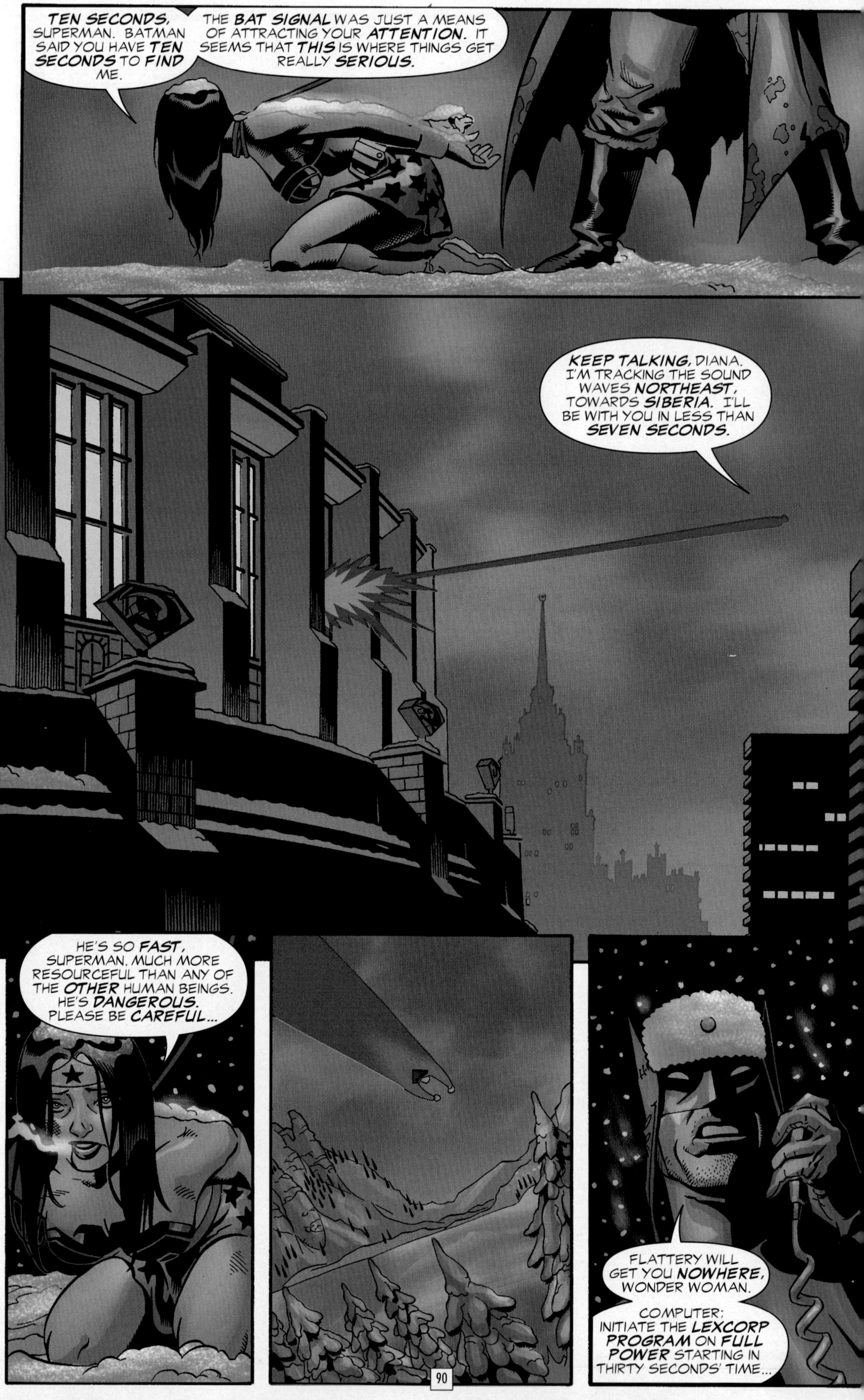

TEN SECONDS, SUPERMAN. BATMAN SAID YOU HAVE TEN SECONDS TO FIND ME.
THE BAT SIGNAL WAS JUST A MEANS OF ATTRACTING YOUR ATTENTION. IT SEEMS THAT THIS IS WHERE THINGS GET REALLY SERIOUS.
KEEP TALKING, DIANA. I'M TRACKING THE SOUND WAVES NORTHEAST, TOWARDS SIBERIA. I'LL BE WITH YOU IN LESS THAN SEVEN SECONDS.
HE'S SO FAST, SUPERMAN. MUCH MORE RESOURCEFUL THAN ANY OF THE OTHER HUMAN BEINGS. HE'S DANGEROUS. PLEASE BE CAREFUL...
FLATTERY WILL GET YOU NOWHERE, WONDER WOMAN.
COMPUTER; INITIATE THE LEXCORP PROGRAM ON FULL POWER STARTING IN THIRTY SECONDS' TIME...

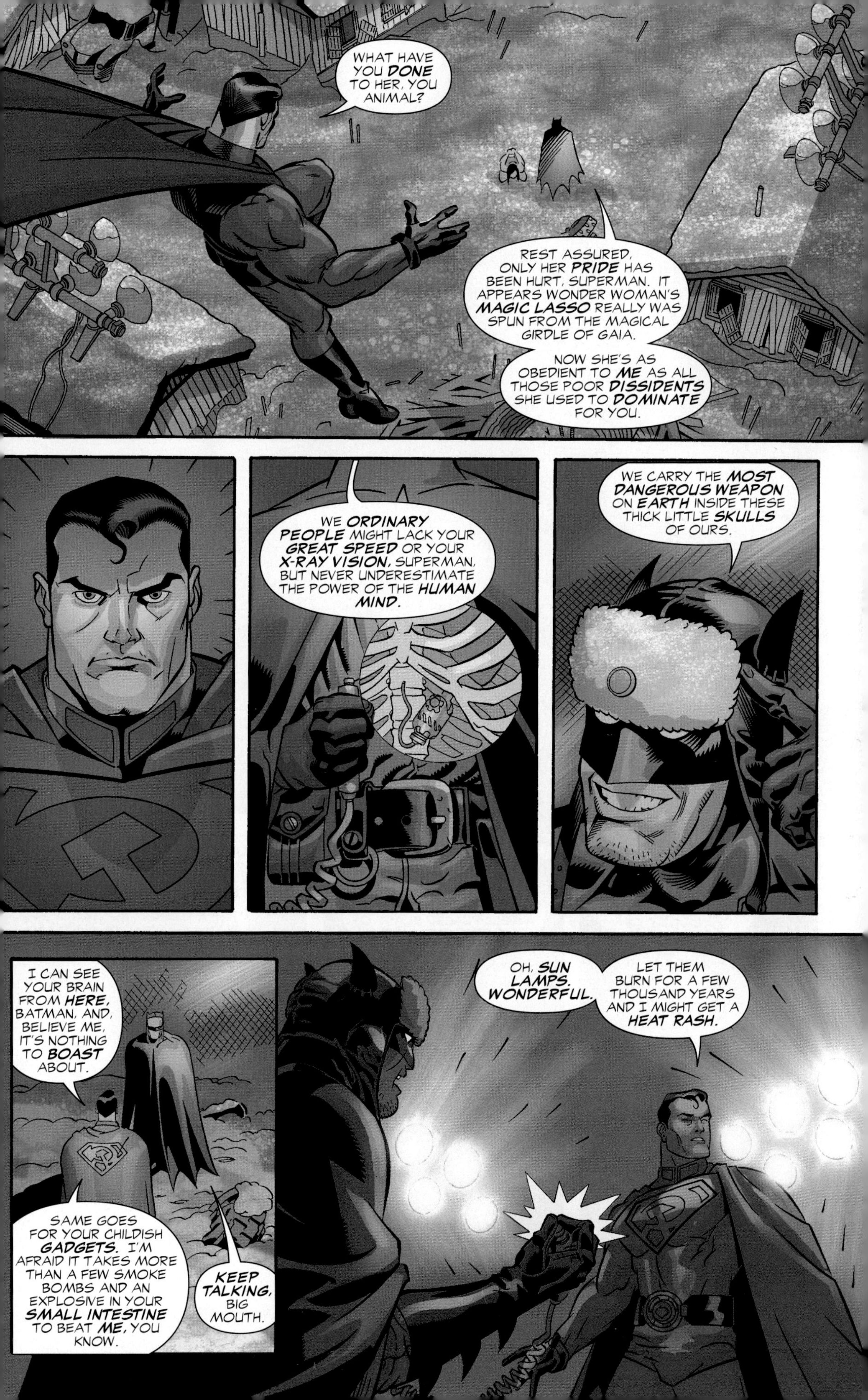
WHAT HAVE YOU DONE TO HER, YOU ANIMAL?
REST ASSURED, ONLY HER PRIDE HAS BEEN HURT, SUPERMAN. IT APPEARS WONDER WOMAN'S MAGIC LASSO REALLY WAS SPUN FROM THE MAGICAL GIRDLE OF GAIA.
NOW SHE'S AS OBEDIENT TO ME AS ALL THOSE POOR DISSIDENTS SHE USED TO DOMINATE FOR YOU.
WE ORDINARY PEOPLE MIGHT LACK YOUR GREAT SPEED OR YOUR X-RAY VISION, SUPERMAN, BUT NEVER UNDERESTIMATE THE POWER OF THE HUMAN MIND.
WE CARRY THE MOST DANGEROUS WEAPON ON EARTH INSIDE THESE THICK LITTLE SKULLS OF OURS.
I CAN SEE YOUR BRAIN FROM HERE, BATMAN, AND, BELIEVE ME, IT'S NOTHING TO BOAST ABOUT.
SAME GOES FOR YOUR CHILDISH GADGETS. I'M AFRAID IT TAKES MORE THAN A FEW SMOKE BOMBS AND AN EXPLOSIVE IN YOUR SMALL INTESTINE TO BEAT ME, YOU KNOW.
KEEP TALKING, BIG MOUTH.
OH, SUN LAMPS. WONDERFUL.
LET THEM BURN FOR A FEW THOUSAND YEARS AND I MIGHT GET A HEAT RASH.

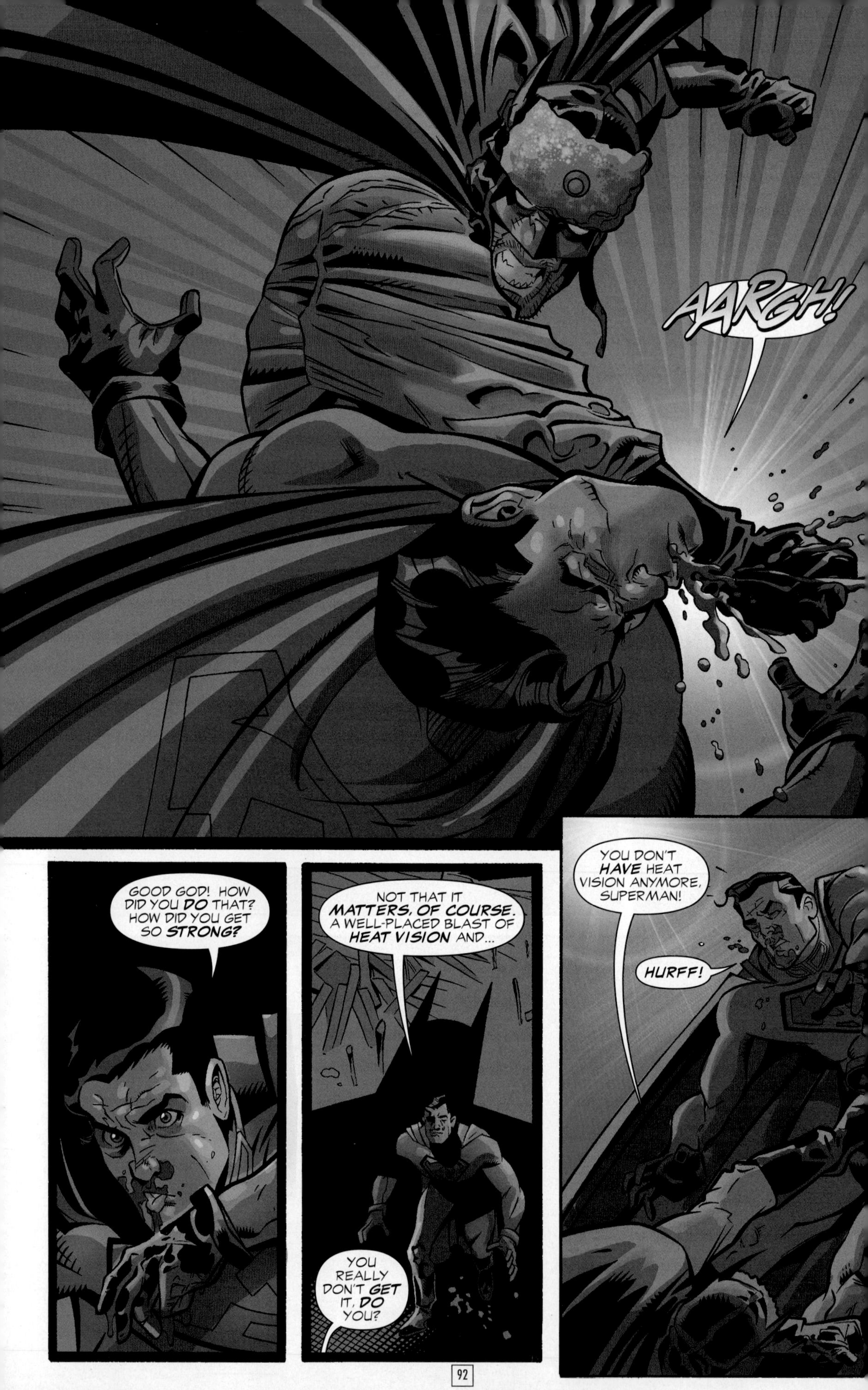
AARGH!
GOOD GOD! HOW DID YOU DO THAT? HOW DID YOU GET SO STRONG?
NOT THAT IT MATTERS, OF COURSE. A WELL-PLACED BLAST OF HEAT VISION AND...
YOU REALLY DON'T GET IT, DO YOU?
YOU DON'T HAVE HEAT VISION ANYMORE, SUPERMAN!
HURFF!

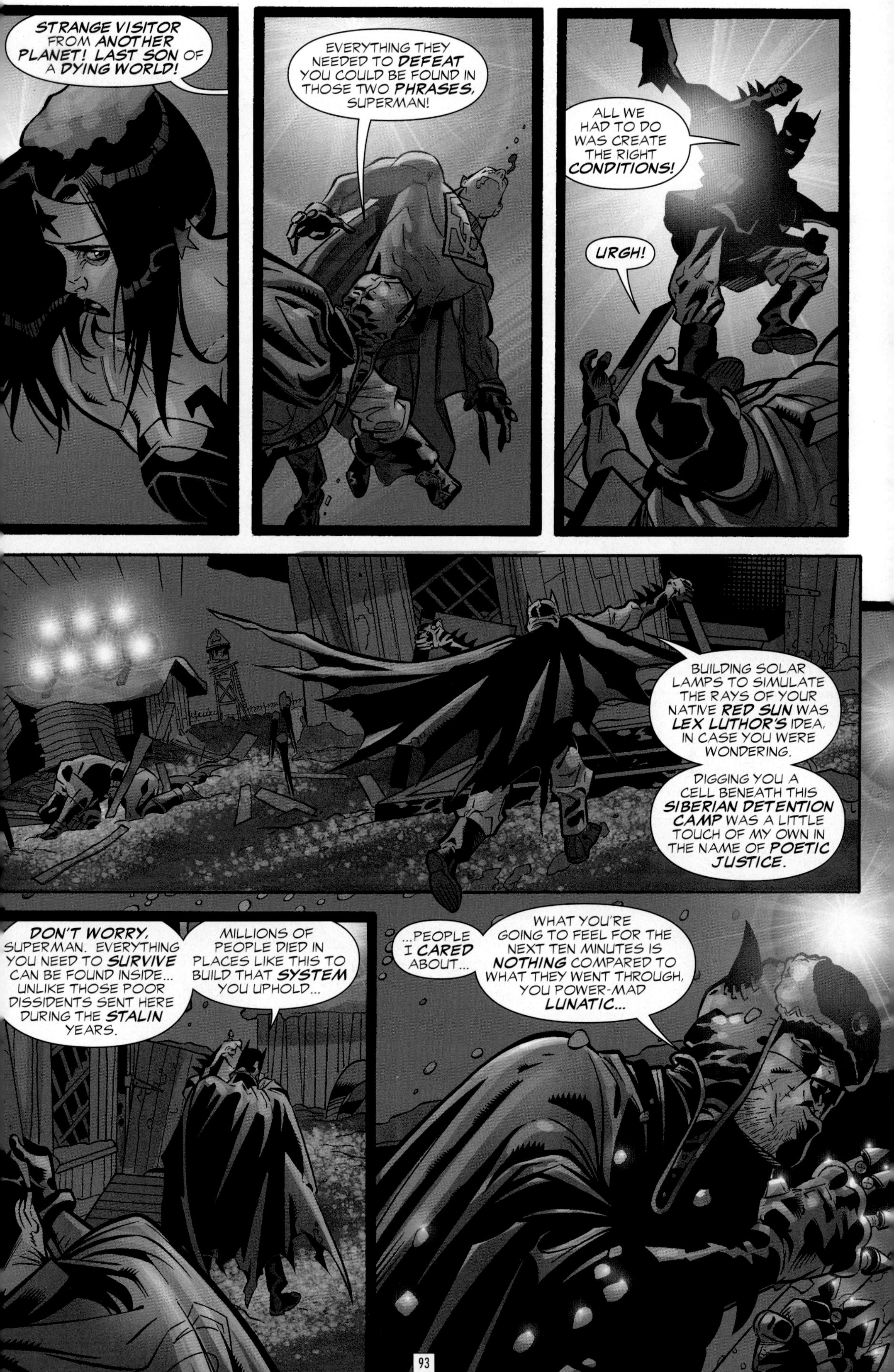
STRANGE VISITOR FROM ANOTHER PLANET! LAST SON OF A DYING WORLD!
EVERYTHING THEY NEEDED TO DEFEAT YOU COULD BE FOUND IN THOSE TWO PHRASES, SUPERMAN!
ALL WE HAD TO DO WAS CREATE THE RIGHT CONDITIONS!
URGH!
BUILDING SOLAR LAMPS TO SIMULATE THE RAYS OF YOUR NATIVE RED SUN WAS LEX LUTHOR'S IDEA, IN CASE YOU WERE WONDERING.
DIGGING YOU A CELL BENEATH THIS SIBERIAN DETENTION CAMP WAS A LITTLE TOUCH OF MY OWN IN THE NAME OF POETIC JUSTICE.
DON'T WORRY, SUPERMAN. EVERYTHING YOU NEED TO SURVIVE CAN BE FOUND INSIDE... UNLIKE THOSE POOR DISSIDENTS SENT HERE DURING THE STALIN YEARS.
MILLIONS OF PEOPLE DIED IN PLACES LIKE THIS TO BUILD THAT SYSTEM YOU UPHOLD...
...PEOPLE I CARED ABOUT...
WHAT YOU'RE GOING TO FEEL FOR THE NEXT TEN MINUTES IS NOTHING COMPARED TO WHAT THEY WENT THROUGH, YOU POWER-MAD LUNATIC...

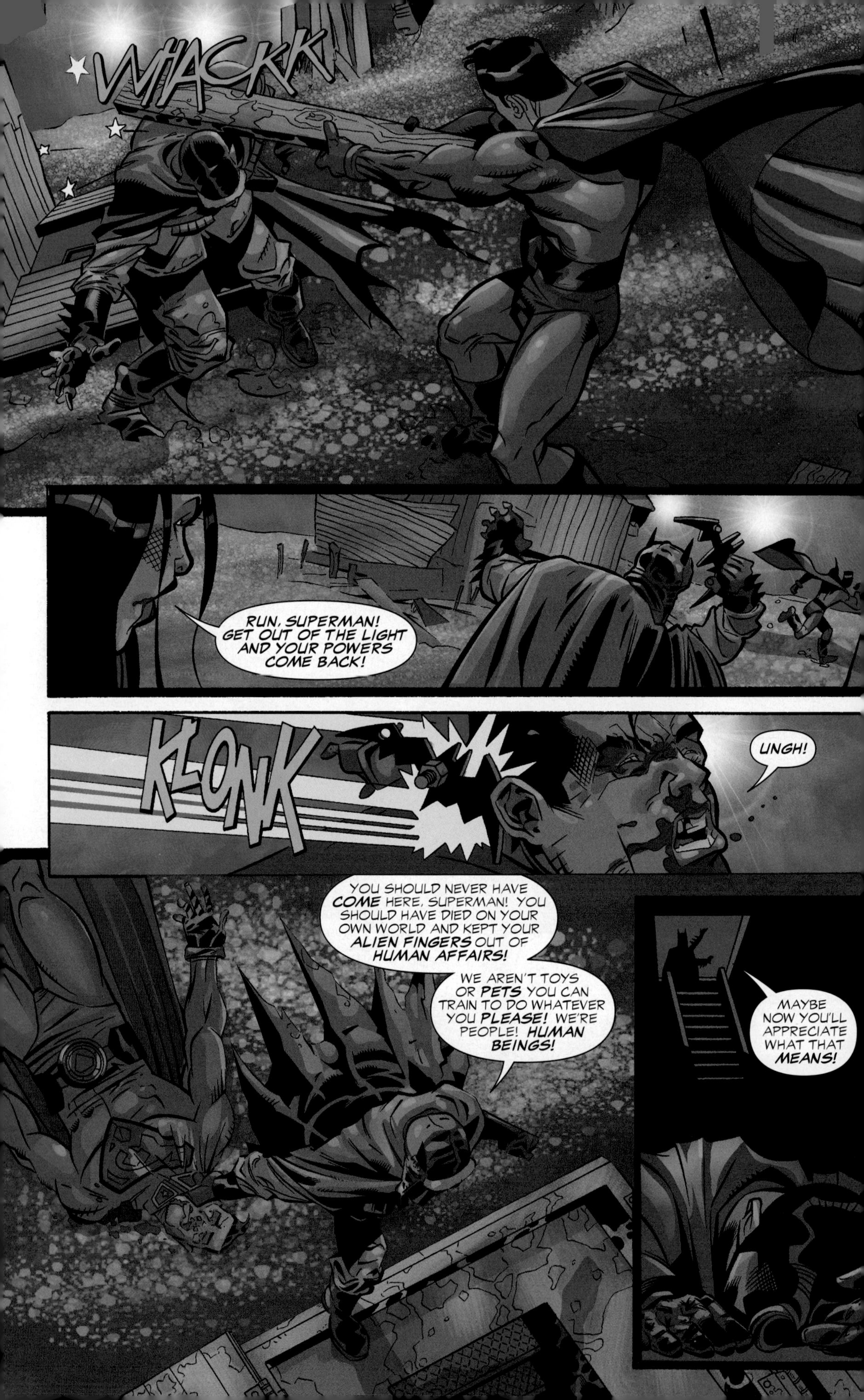
WHACKK
RUN, SUPERMAN! GET OUT OF THE LIGHT AND YOUR POWERS COME BACK!
KLONK
UNGH!
YOU SHOULD NEVER HAVE COME HERE, SUPERMAN! YOU SHOULD HAVE DIED ON YOUR OWN WORLD AND KEPT YOUR ALIEN FINGERS OUT OF HUMAN AFFAIRS!
WE AREN'T TOYS OR PETS YOU CAN TRAIN TO DO WHATEVER YOU PLEASE! WE'RE PEOPLE! HUMAN BEINGS!
MAYBE NOW YOU'LL APPRECIATE WHAT THAT MEANS!

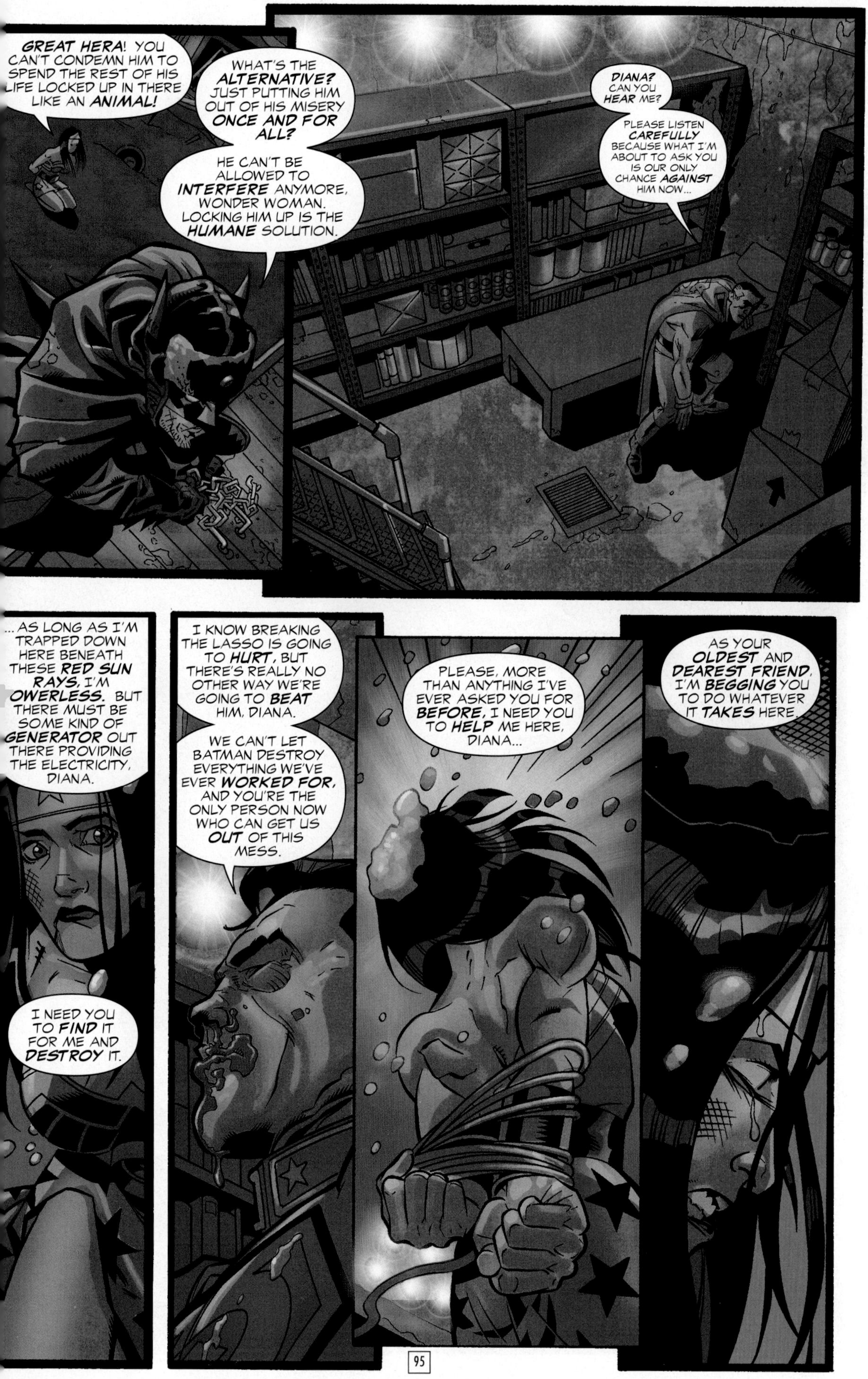
GREAT HERA! YOU CAN'T CONDEMN HIM TO SPEND THE REST OF HIS LIFE LOCKED UP IN THERE LIKE AN ANIMAL!
WHAT'S THE ALTERNATIVE? JUST PUTTING HIM OUT OF HIS MISERY ONCE AND FOR ALL?
HE CAN'T BE ALLOWED TO INTERFERE ANYMORE, WONDER WOMAN. LOCKING HIM UP IS THE HUMANE SOLUTION.
DIANA? CAN YOU HEAR ME?
PLEASE LISTEN CAREFULLY BECAUSE WHAT I'M ABOUT TO ASK YOU IS OUR ONLY CHANCE AGAINST HIM NOW...
...AS LONG AS I'M TRAPPED DOWN HERE BENEATH THESE RED SUN RAYS, I'M OWERLESS. BUT THERE MUST BE SOME KIND OF GENERATOR OUT THERE PROVIDING THE ELECTRICITY, DIANA.
I NEED YOU TO FIND IT FOR ME AND DESTROY IT.
I KNOW BREAKING THE LASSO IS GOING TO HURT, BUT THERE'S REALLY NO OTHER WAY WE'RE GOING TO BEAT HIM, DIANA.
WE CAN'T LET BATMAN DESTROY EVERYTHING WE'VE EVER WORKED FOR, AND YOU'RE THE ONLY PERSON NOW WHO CAN GET US OUT OF THIS MESS.
PLEASE, MORE THAN ANYTHING I'VE EVER ASKED YOU FOR BEFORE, I NEED YOU TO HELP ME HERE, DIANA...
AS YOUR OLDEST AND DEAREST FRIEND, I'M BEGGING YOU TO DO WHATEVER IT TAKES HERE.

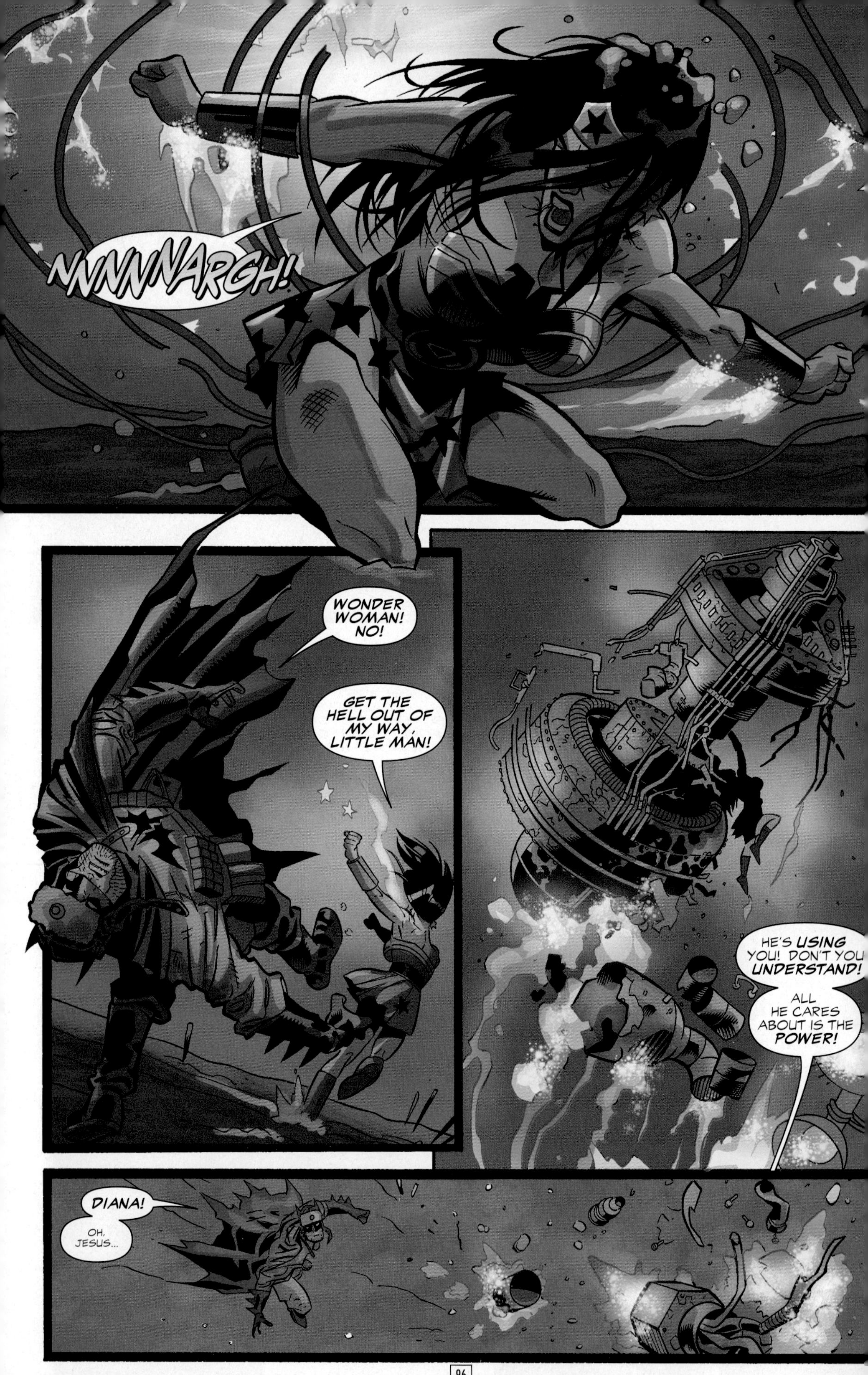
NNNNNARGH!
WONDER WOMAN! NO!
GET THE HELL OUT OF MY WAY, LITTLE MAN!
HE'S USING YOU! DON'T YOU UNDERSTAND!
ALL HE CARES ABOUT IS THE POWER!
DIANA!
OH, JESUS...

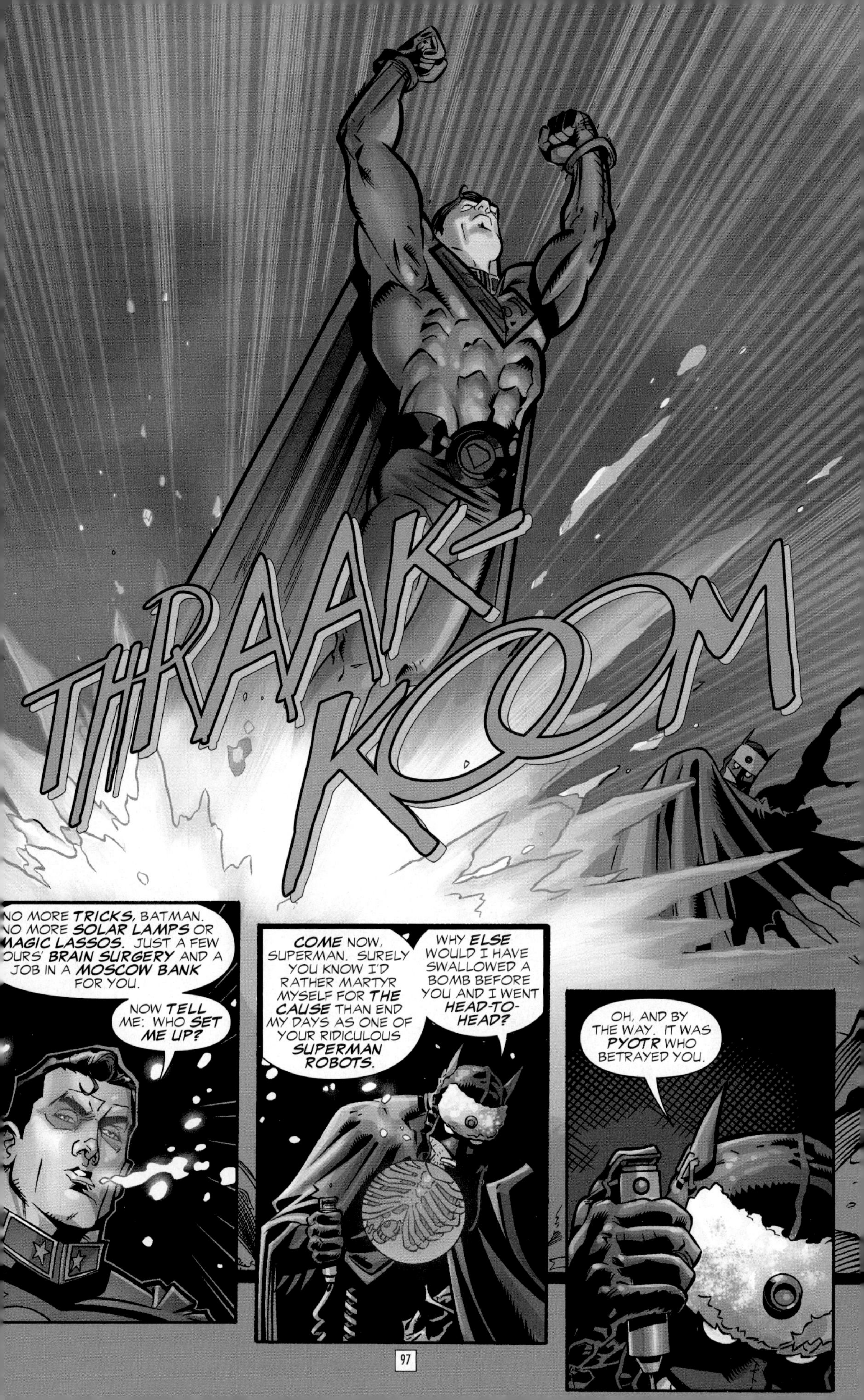
THRAAK-KOOM
NO MORE TRICKS, BATMAN. NO MORE SOLAR LAMPS OR MAGIC LASSOS. JUST A FEW OURS' BRAIN SURGERY AND A JOB IN A MOSCOW BANK FOR YOU.
NOW TELL ME: WHO SET ME UP?
COME NOW, SUPERMAN. SURELY YOU KNOW I'D RATHER MARTYR MYSELF FOR THE CAUSE THAN END MY DAYS AS ONE OF YOUR RIDICULOUS SUPERMAN ROBOTS.
WHY ELSE WOULD I HAVE SWALLOWED A BOMB BEFORE YOU AND I WENT HEAD-TO-HEAD?
OH, AND BY THE WAY, IT WAS PYOTR WHO BETRAYED YOU.

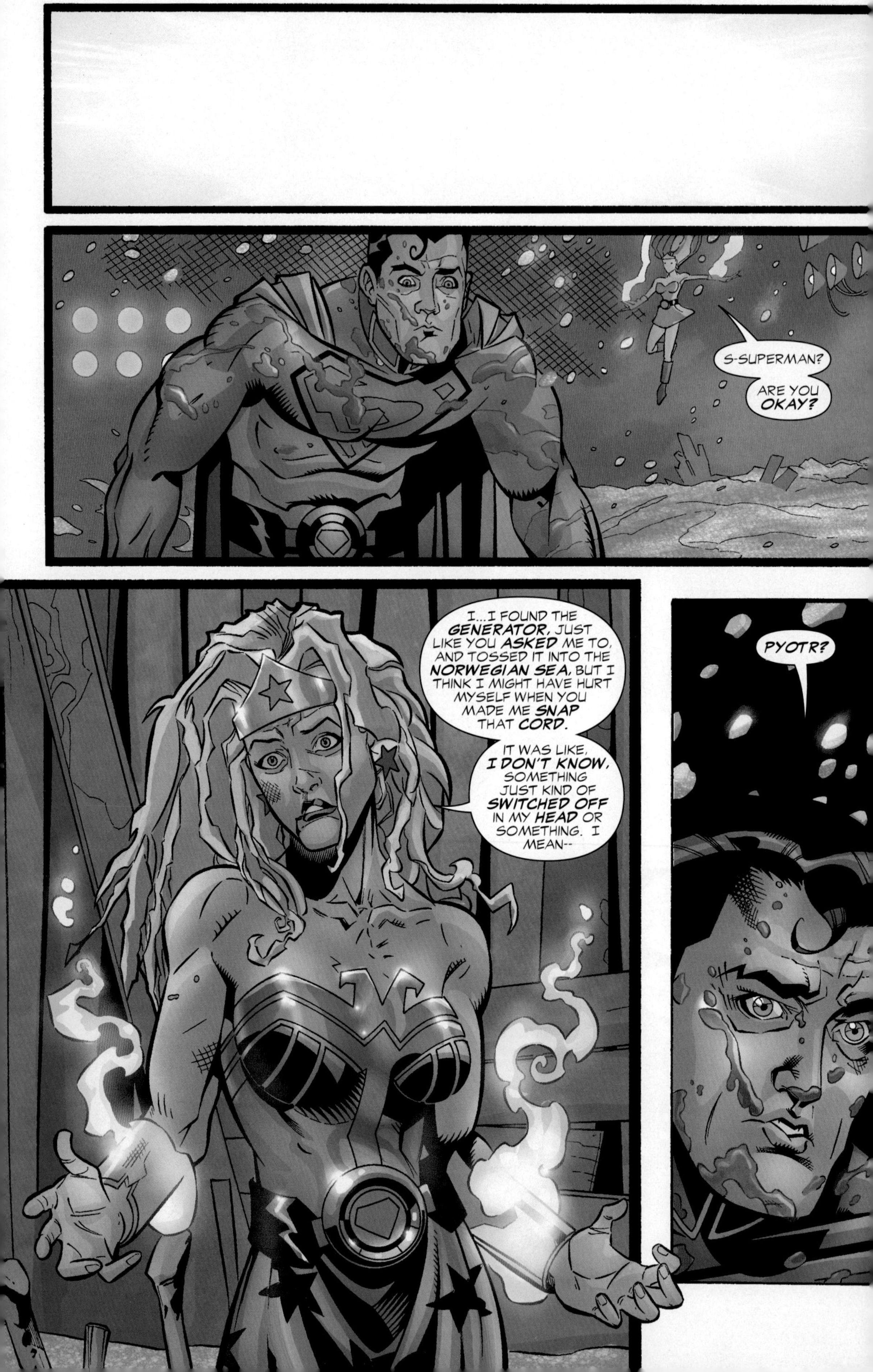
S-SUPERMAN?
ARE YOU OKAY?
I...I FOUND THE GENERATOR, JUST LIKE YOU ASKED ME TO, AND TOSSED IT INTO THE NORWEGIAN SEA, BUT I THINK I MIGHT HAVE HURT MYSELF WHEN YOU MADE ME SNAP THAT CORD.
IT WAS LIKE, I DON'T KNOW, SOMETHING JUST KIND OF SWITCHED OFF IN MY HEAD OR SOMETHING. I MEAN--
PYOTR?

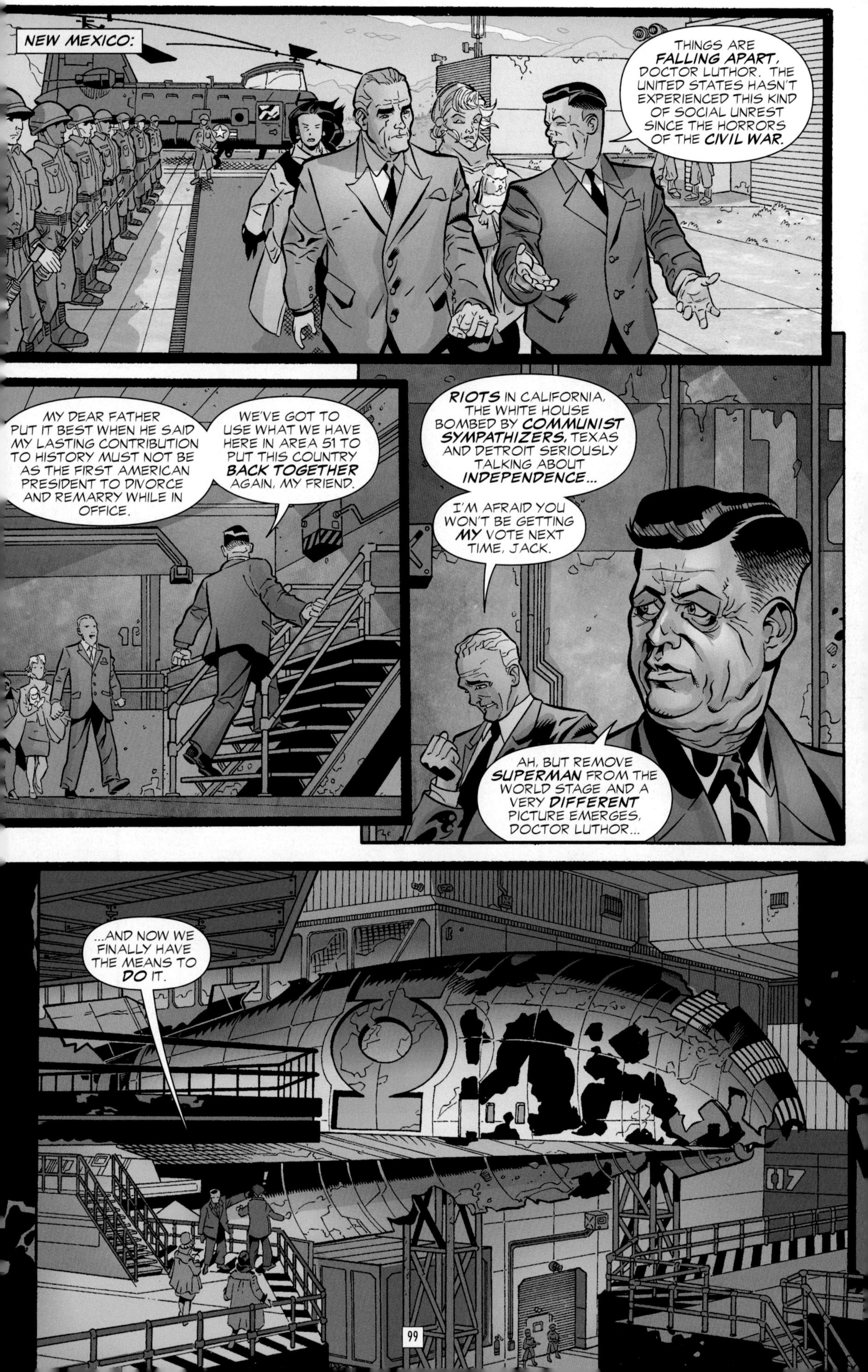
NEW MEXICO:
THINGS ARE FALLING APART, DOCTOR LUTHOR. THE UNITED STATES HASN'T EXPERIENCED THIS KIND OF SOCIAL UNREST SINCE THE HORRORS OF THE CIVIL WAR.
MY DEAR FATHER PUT IT BEST WHEN HE SAID MY LASTING CONTRIBUTION TO HISTORY MUST NOT BE AS THE FIRST AMERICAN PRESIDENT TO DIVORCE AND REMARRY WHILE IN OFFICE.
WE'VE GOT TO USE WHAT WE HAVE HERE IN AREA 51 TO PUT THIS COUNTRY BACK TOGETHER AGAIN, MY FRIEND.
RIOTS IN CALIFORNIA, THE WHITE HOUSE BOMBED BY COMMUNIST SYMPATHIZERS, TEXAS AND DETROIT SERIOUSLY TALKING ABOUT INDEPENDENCE...
I'M AFRAID YOU WON'T BE GETTING MY VOTE NEXT TIME, JACK.
AH, BUT REMOVE SUPERMAN FROM THE WORLD STAGE AND A VERY DIFFERENT PICTURE EMERGES, DOCTOR LUTHOR...
...AND NOW WE FINALLY HAVE THE MEANS TO DO IT.

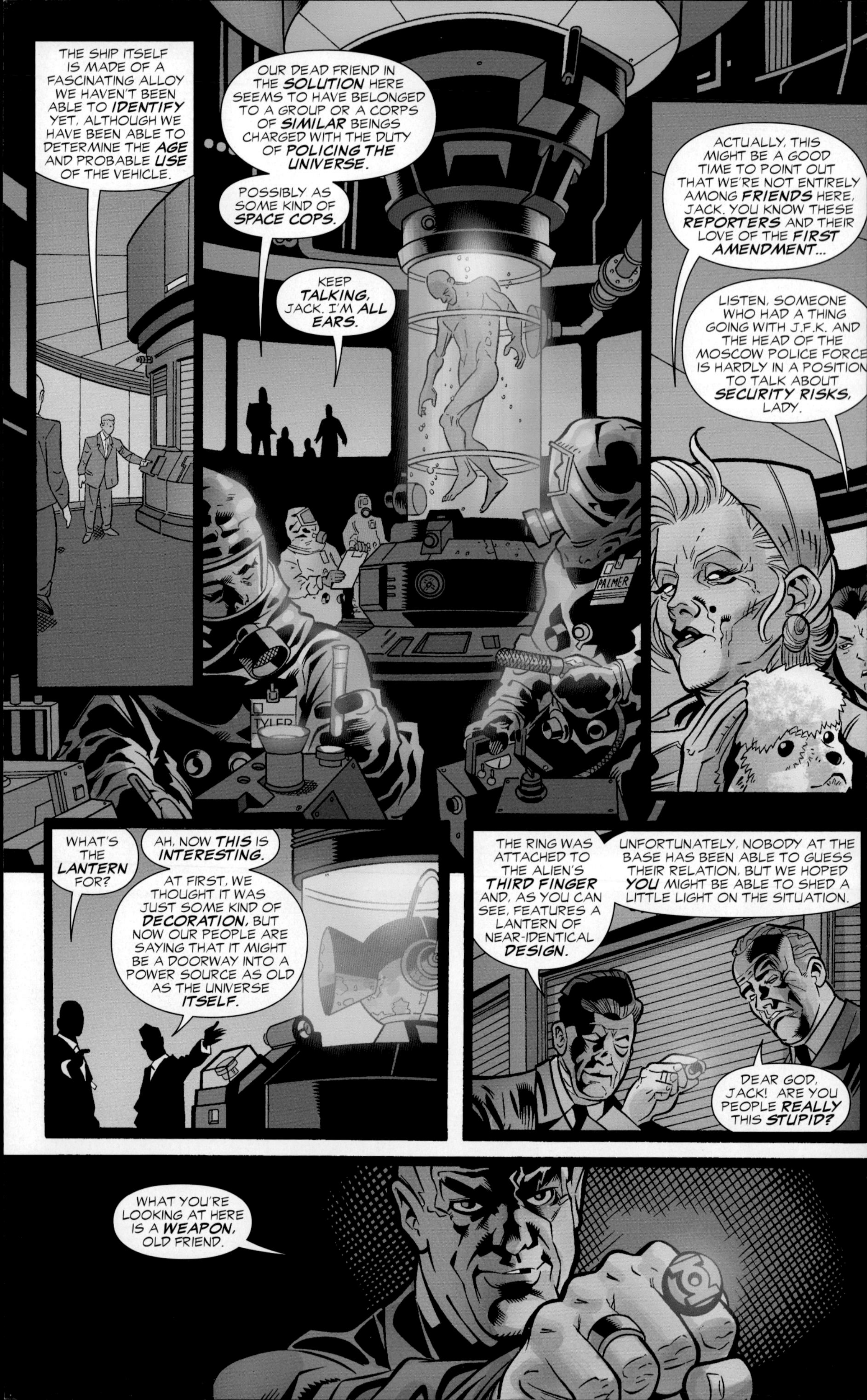
THE SHIP ITSELF IS MADE OF A FASCINATING ALLOY WE HAVEN'T BEEN ABLE TO IDENTIFY YET, ALTHOUGH WE HAVE BEEN ABLE TO DETERMINE THE AGE AND PROBABLE USE OF THE VEHICLE.
OUR DEAD FRIEND IN THE SOLUTION HERE SEEMS TO HAVE BELONGED TO A GROUP OR A CORPS OF SIMILAR BEINGS CHARGED WITH THE DUTY OF POLICING THE UNIVERSE.
POSSIBLY AS SOME KIND OF SPACE COPS.
KEEP TALKING, JACK. I'M ALL EARS.
ACTUALLY, THIS MIGHT BE A GOOD TIME TO POINT OUT THAT WE'RE NOT ENTIRELY AMONG FRIENDS HERE, JACK. YOU KNOW THESE REPORTERS AND THEIR LOVE OF THE FIRST AMENDMENT...
LISTEN, SOMEONE WHO HAD A THING GOING WITH J.F.K. AND THE HEAD OF THE MOSCOW POLICE FORCE IS HARDLY IN A POSITION TO TALK ABOUT SECURITY RISKS, LADY.
PALMER
TYLER
WHAT'S THE LANTERN FOR?
AH, NOW THIS IS INTERESTING.
AT FIRST, WE THOUGHT IT WAS JUST SOME KIND OF DECORATION, BUT NOW OUR PEOPLE ARE SAYING THAT IT MIGHT BE A DOORWAY INTO A POWER SOURCE AS OLD AS THE UNIVERSE ITSELF.
THE RING WAS ATTACHED TO THE ALIEN'S THIRD FINGER AND, AS YOU CAN SEE, FEATURES A LANTERN OF NEAR-IDENTICAL DESIGN.
UNFORTUNATELY, NOBODY AT THE BASE HAS BEEN ABLE TO GUESS THEIR RELATION, BUT WE HOPED YOU MIGHT BE ABLE TO SHED A LITTLE LIGHT ON THE SITUATION.
DEAR GOD, JACK! ARE YOU PEOPLE REALLY THIS STUPID?
WHAT YOU'RE LOOKING AT HERE IS A WEAPON, OLD FRIEND.

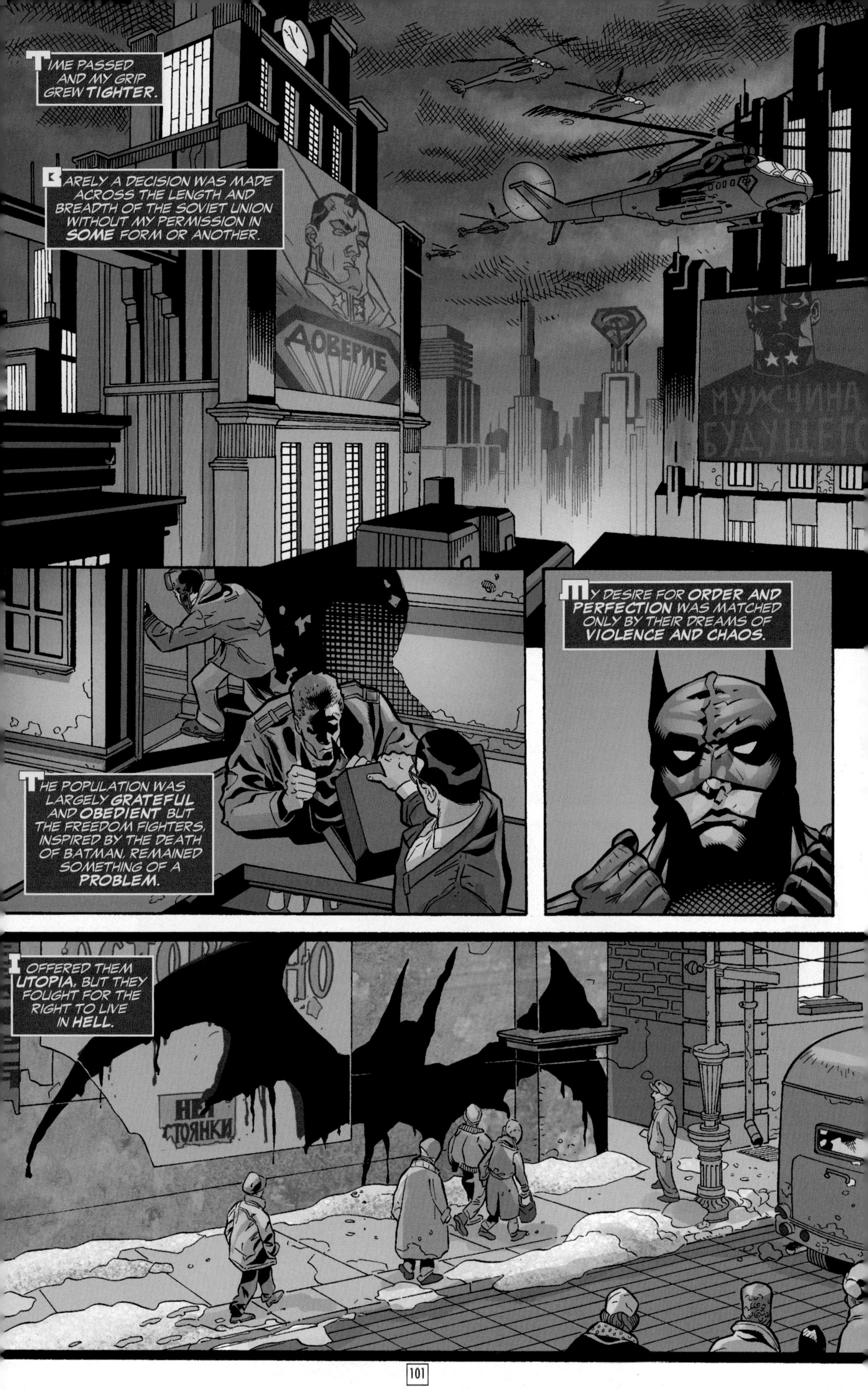
TIME PASSED AND MY GRIP GREW TIGHTER.
BARELY A DECISION WAS MADE ACROSS THE LENGTH AND BREADTH OF THE SOVIET UNION WITHOUT MY PERMISSION IN SOME FORM OR ANOTHER.
ДОВЕРИЕ
МУЖЧИНА
THE POPULATION WAS LARGELY GRATEFUL AND OBEDIENT BUT THE FREEDOM FIGHTERS, INSPIRED BY THE DEATH OF BATMAN, REMAINED SOMETHING OF A PROBLEM.
MY DESIRE FOR ORDER AND PERFECTION WAS MATCHED ONLY BY THEIR DREAMS OF VIOLENCE AND CHAOS.
I OFFERED THEM UTOPIA, BUT THEY FOUGHT FOR THE RIGHT TO LIVE IN HELL.
НЕТ
СТОЯНКИ

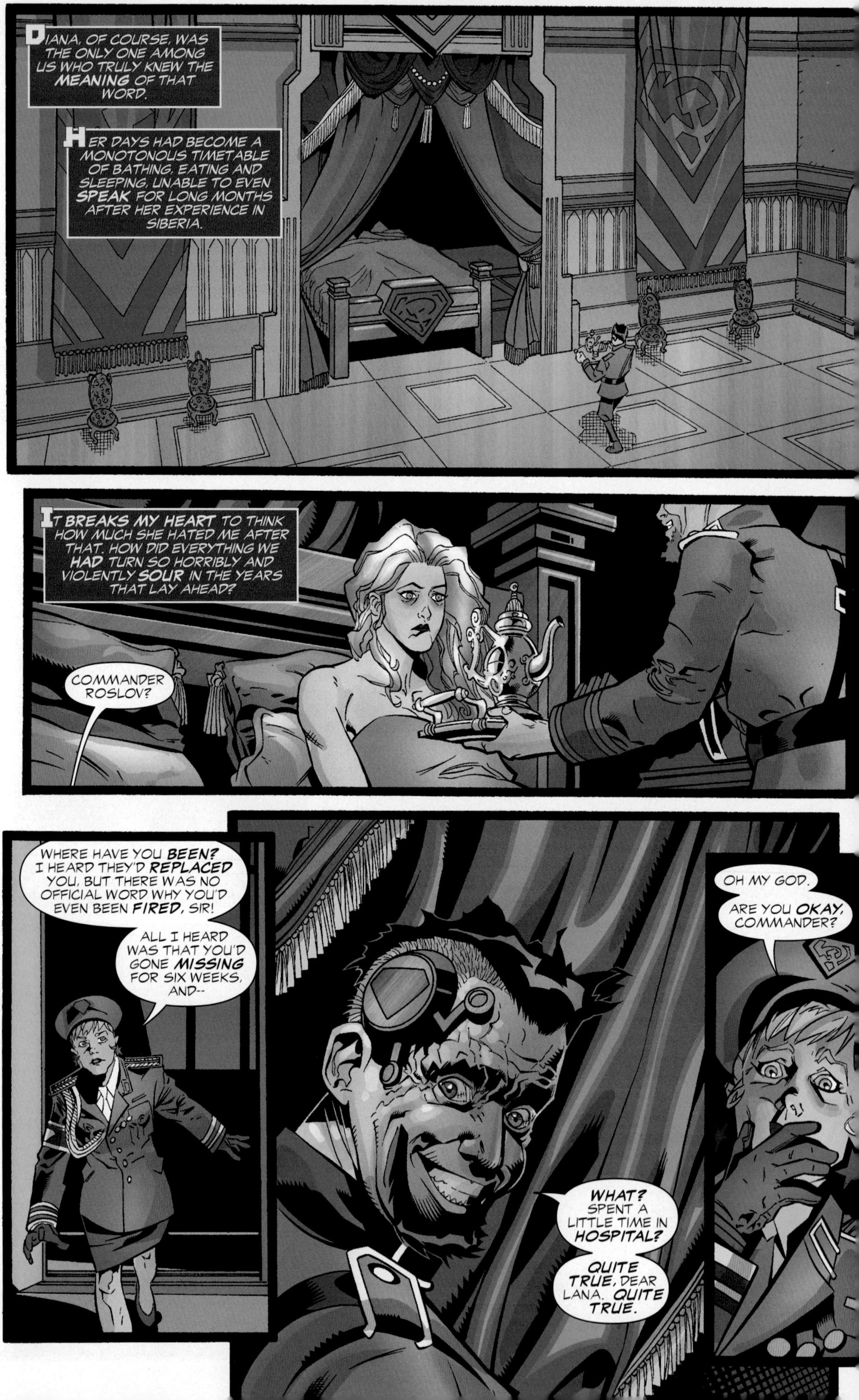
DIANA, OF COURSE, WAS THE ONLY ONE AMONG US WHO TRULY KNEW THE MEANING OF THAT WORD.
HER DAYS HAD BECOME A MONOTONOUS TIMETABLE OF BATHING, EATING AND SLEEPING, UNABLE TO EVEN SPEAK FOR LONG MONTHS AFTER HER EXPERIENCE IN SIBERIA.
IT BREAKS MY HEART TO THINK HOW MUCH SHE HATED ME AFTER THAT. HOW DID EVERYTHING WE HAD TURN SO HORRIBLY AND VIOLENTLY SOUR IN THE YEARS THAT LAY AHEAD?
COMMANDER ROSLOV?
WHERE HAVE YOU BEEN? I HEARD THEY'D REPLACED YOU, BUT THERE WAS NO OFFICIAL WORD WHY YOU'D EVEN BEEN FIRED, SIR!
ALL I HEARD WAS THAT YOU'D GONE MISSING FOR SIX WEEKS, AND--
WHAT? SPENT A LITTLE TIME IN HOSPITAL?
QUITE TRUE, DEAR LANA. QUITE TRUE.
OH MY GOD.
ARE YOU OKAY, COMMANDER?

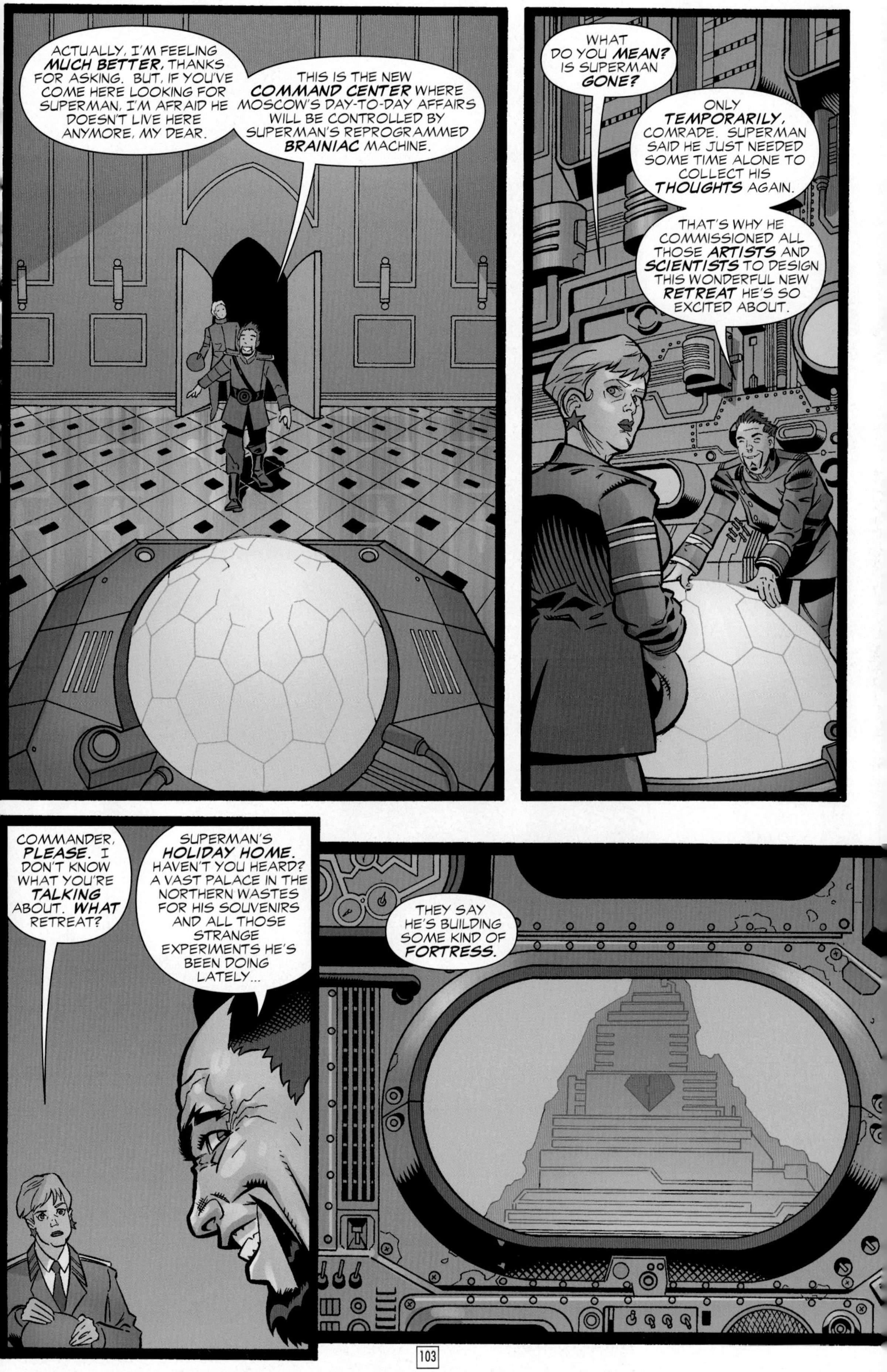
ACTUALLY, I'M FEELING MUCH BETTER, THANKS FOR ASKING. BUT, IF YOU'VE COME HERE LOOKING FOR SUPERMAN, I'M AFRAID HE DOESN'T LIVE HERE ANYMORE, MY DEAR.
THIS IS THE NEW COMMAND CENTER WHERE MOSCOW'S DAY-TO-DAY AFFAIRS WILL BE CONTROLLED BY SUPERMAN'S REPROGRAMMED BRAINIAC MACHINE.
WHAT DO YOU MEAN? IS SUPERMAN GONE?
ONLY TEMPORARILY, COMRADE. SUPERMAN SAID HE JUST NEEDED SOME TIME ALONE TO COLLECT HIS THOUGHTS AGAIN.
THAT'S WHY HE COMMISSIONED ALL THOSE ARTISTS AND SCIENTISTS TO DESIGN THIS WONDERFUL NEW RETREAT HE'S SO EXCITED ABOUT.
COMMANDER, PLEASE. I DON'T KNOW WHAT YOU'RE TALKING ABOUT. WHAT RETREAT?
SUPERMAN'S HOLIDAY HOME. HAVEN'T YOU HEARD? A VAST PALACE IN THE NORTHERN WASTES FOR HIS SOUVENIRS AND ALL THOSE STRANGE EXPERIMENTS HE'S BEEN DOING LATELY...
THEY SAY HE'S BUILDING SOME KIND OF FORTRESS.

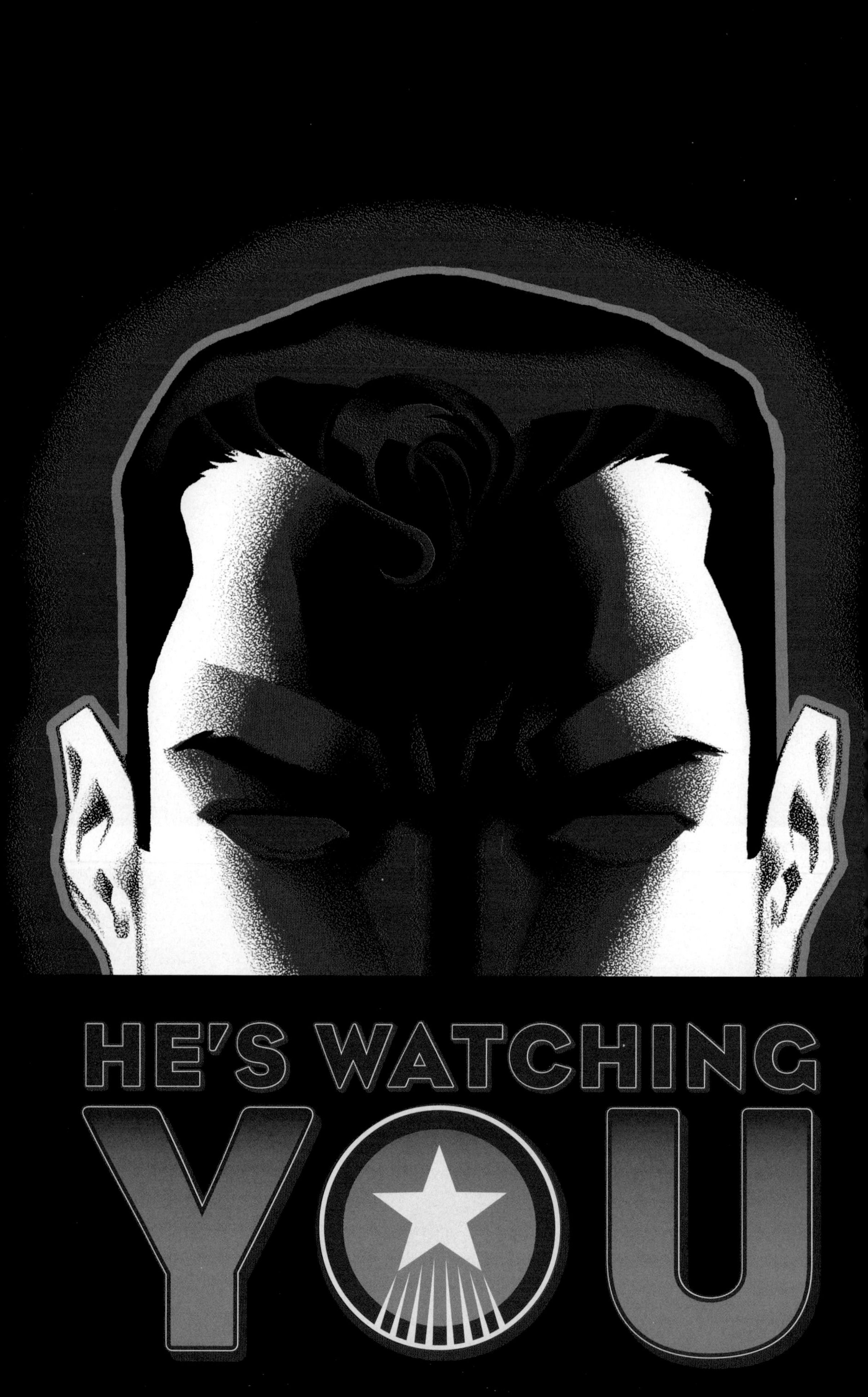
HE'S WATCHING
YOU

SUPERMAN RED SON

RED SON SETTING

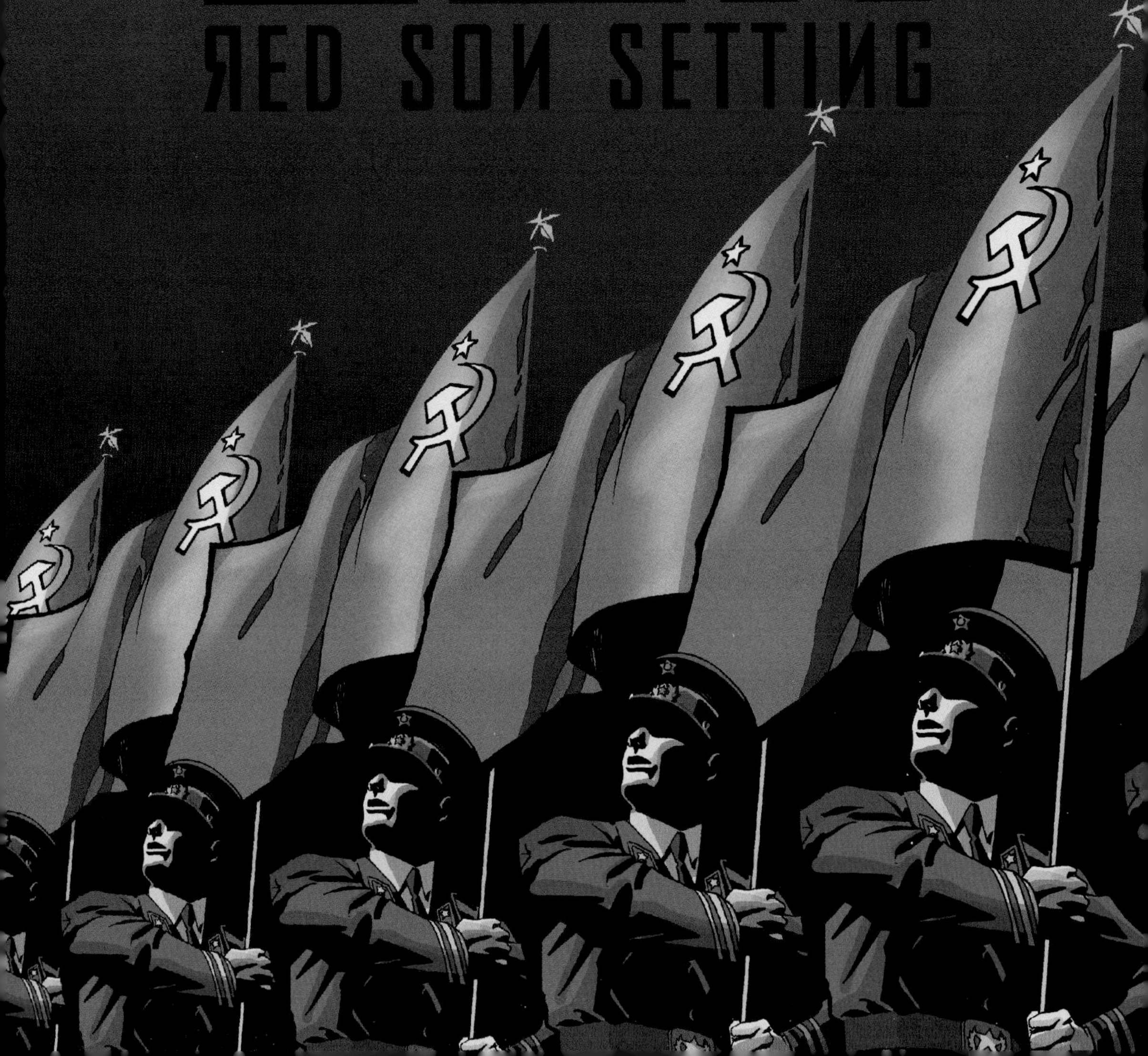

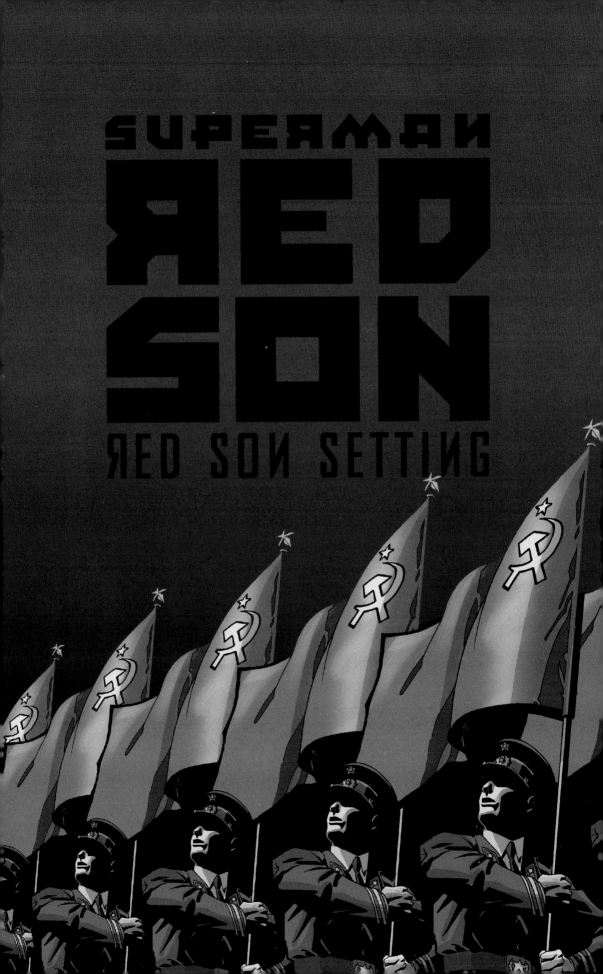

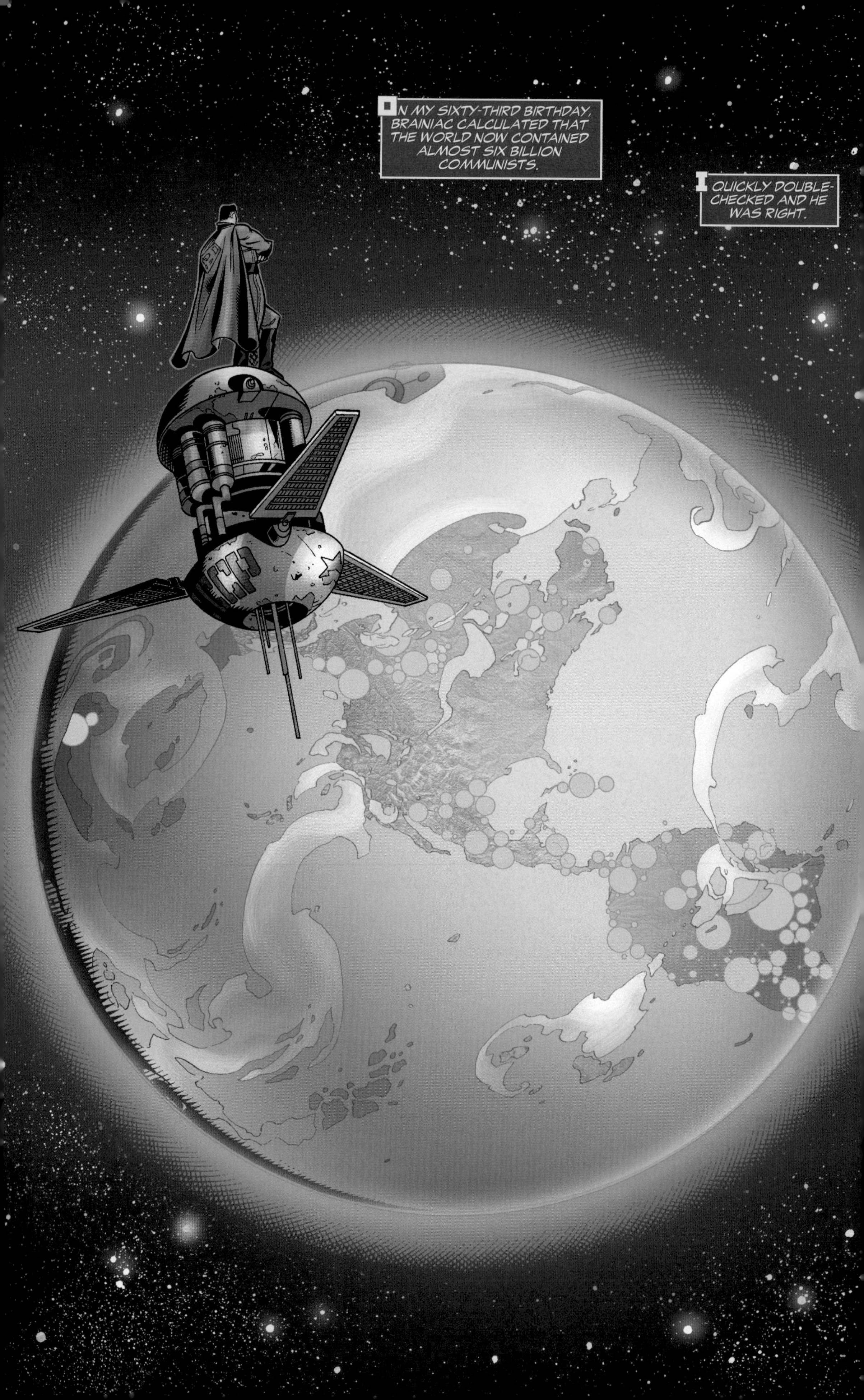
ON MY SIXTY-THIRD BIRTHDAY, BRAINIAC CALCULATED THAT THE WORLD NOW CONTAINED ALMOST SIX BILLION COMMUNISTS.
I QUICKLY DOUBLE-CHECKED AND HE WAS RIGHT.

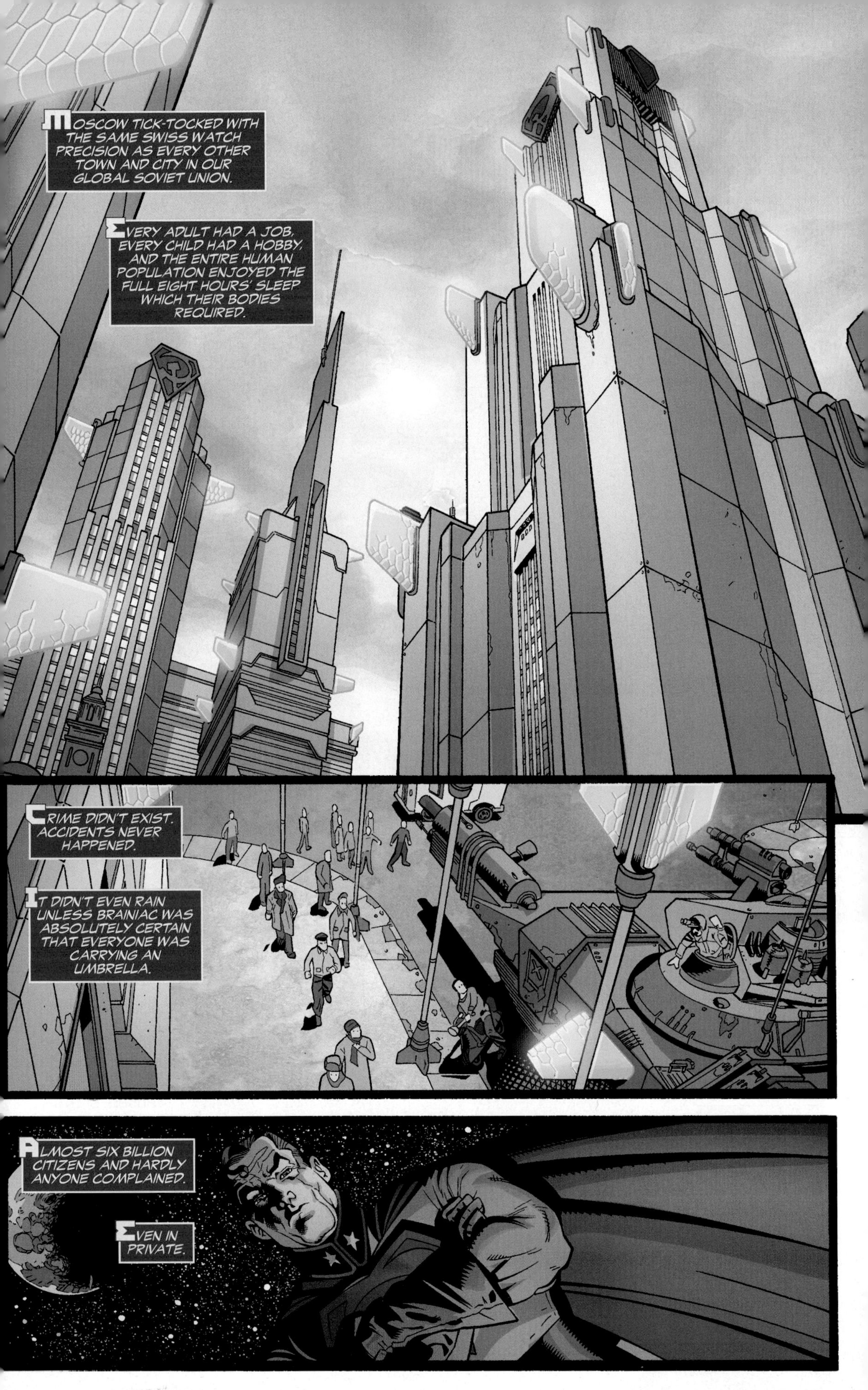

MOSCOW TICK-TOCKED WITH THE SAME SWISS WATCH PRECISION AS EVERY OTHER TOWN AND CITY IN OUR GLOBAL SOVIET UNION.
EVERY ADULT HAD A JOB, EVERY CHILD HAD A HOBBY, AND THE ENTIRE HUMAN POPULATION ENJOYED THE FULL EIGHT HOURS' SLEEP WHICH THEIR BODIES REQUIRED.
CRIME DIDN'T EXIST. ACCIDENTS NEVER HAPPENED.
IT DIDN'T EVEN RAIN UNLESS BRAINIAC WAS ABSOLUTELY CERTAIN THAT EVERYONE WAS CARRYING AN UMBRELLA.
ALMOST SIX BILLION CITIZENS AND HARDLY ANYONE COMPLAINED.
EVEN IN PRIVATE.

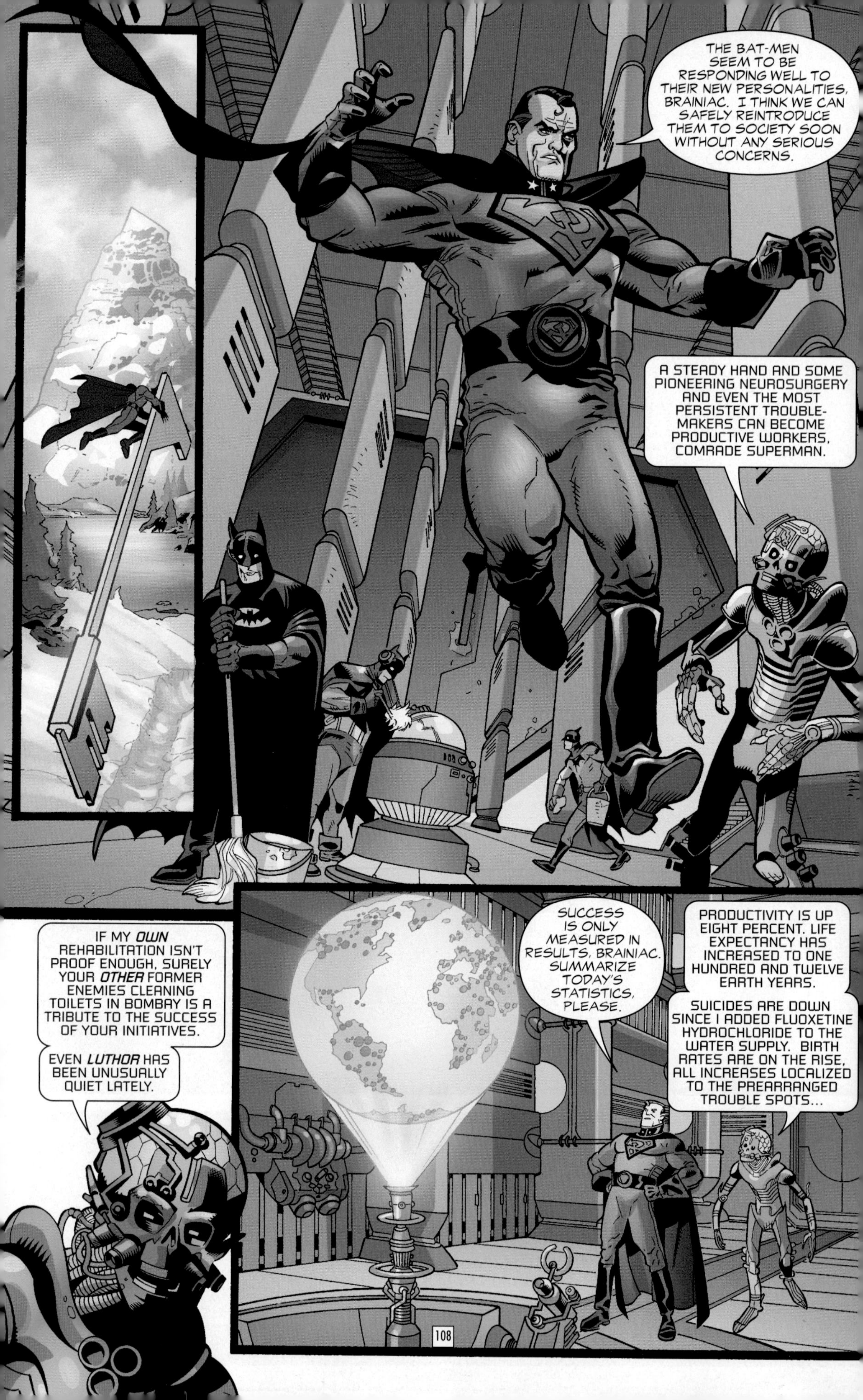
THE BAT-MEN SEEM TO BE RESPONDING WELL TO THEIR NEW PERSONALITIES, BRAINIAC. I THINK WE CAN SAFELY REINTRODUCE THEM TO SOCIETY SOON WITHOUT ANY SERIOUS CONCERNS.
A STEADY HAND AND SOME PIONEERING NEUROSURGERY AND EVEN THE MOST PERSISTENT TROUBLE-MAKERS CAN BECOME PRODUCTIVE WORKERS, COMRADE SUPERMAN.
IF MY *OWN* REHABILITATION ISN'T PROOF ENOUGH, SURELY YOUR *OTHER* FORMER ENEMIES CLEANING TOILETS IN BOMBAY IS A TRIBUTE TO THE SUCCESS OF YOUR INITIATIVES.
EVEN *LUTHOR* HAS BEEN UNUSUALLY QUIET LATELY.
SUCCESS IS ONLY MEASURED IN RESULTS, BRAINIAC. SUMMARIZE TODAY'S STATISTICS, PLEASE.
PRODUCTIVITY IS UP EIGHT PERCENT. LIFE EXPECTANCY HAS INCREASED TO ONE HUNDRED AND TWELVE EARTH YEARS.
SUICIDES ARE DOWN SINCE I ADDED FLUOXETINE HYDROCHLORIDE TO THE WATER SUPPLY. BIRTH RATES ARE ON THE RISE, ALL INCREASES LOCALIZED TO THE PREARRANGED TROUBLE SPOTS...

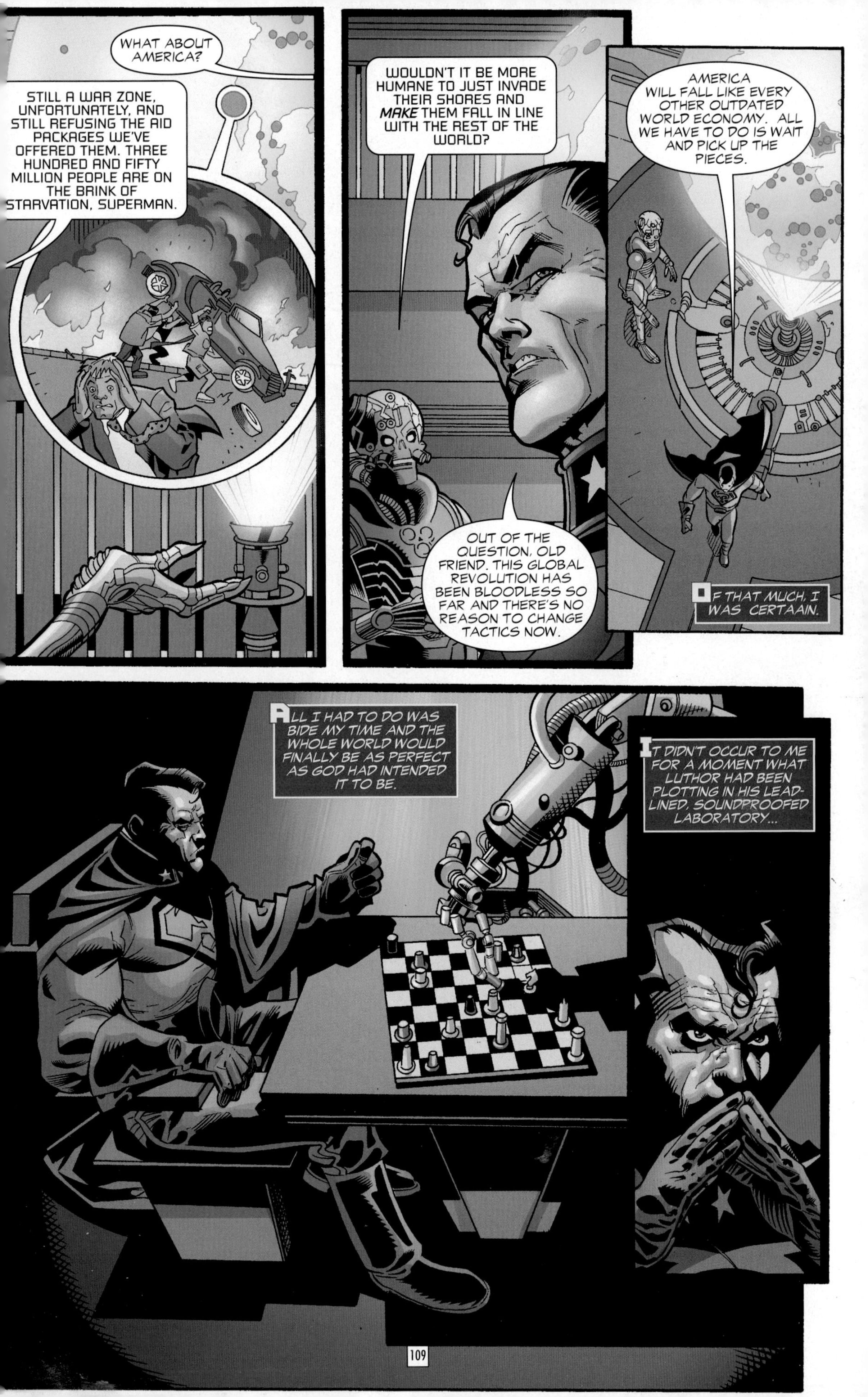

WHAT ABOUT AMERICA?
STILL A WAR ZONE, UNFORTUNATELY, AND STILL REFUSING THE AID PACKAGES WE'VE OFFERED THEM. THREE HUNDRED AND FIFTY MILLION PEOPLE ARE ON THE BRINK OF STARVATION, SUPERMAN.
WOULDN'T IT BE MORE HUMANE TO JUST INVADE THEIR SHORES AND MAKE THEM FALL IN LINE WITH THE REST OF THE WORLD?
OUT OF THE QUESTION, OLD FRIEND. THIS GLOBAL REVOLUTION HAS BEEN BLOODLESS SO FAR AND THERE'S NO REASON TO CHANGE TACTICS NOW.
AMERICA WILL FALL LIKE EVERY OTHER OUTDATED WORLD ECONOMY. ALL WE HAVE TO DO IS WAIT AND PICK UP THE PIECES.
OF THAT MUCH, I WAS CERTAAIN.
ALL I HAD TO DO WAS BIDE MY TIME AND THE WHOLE WORLD WOULD FINALLY BE AS PERFECT AS GOD HAD INTENDED IT TO BE.
IT DIDN'T OCCUR TO ME FOR A MOMENT WHAT LUTHOR HAD BEEN PLOTTING IN HIS LEAD-LINED, SOUNDPROOFED LABORATORY...

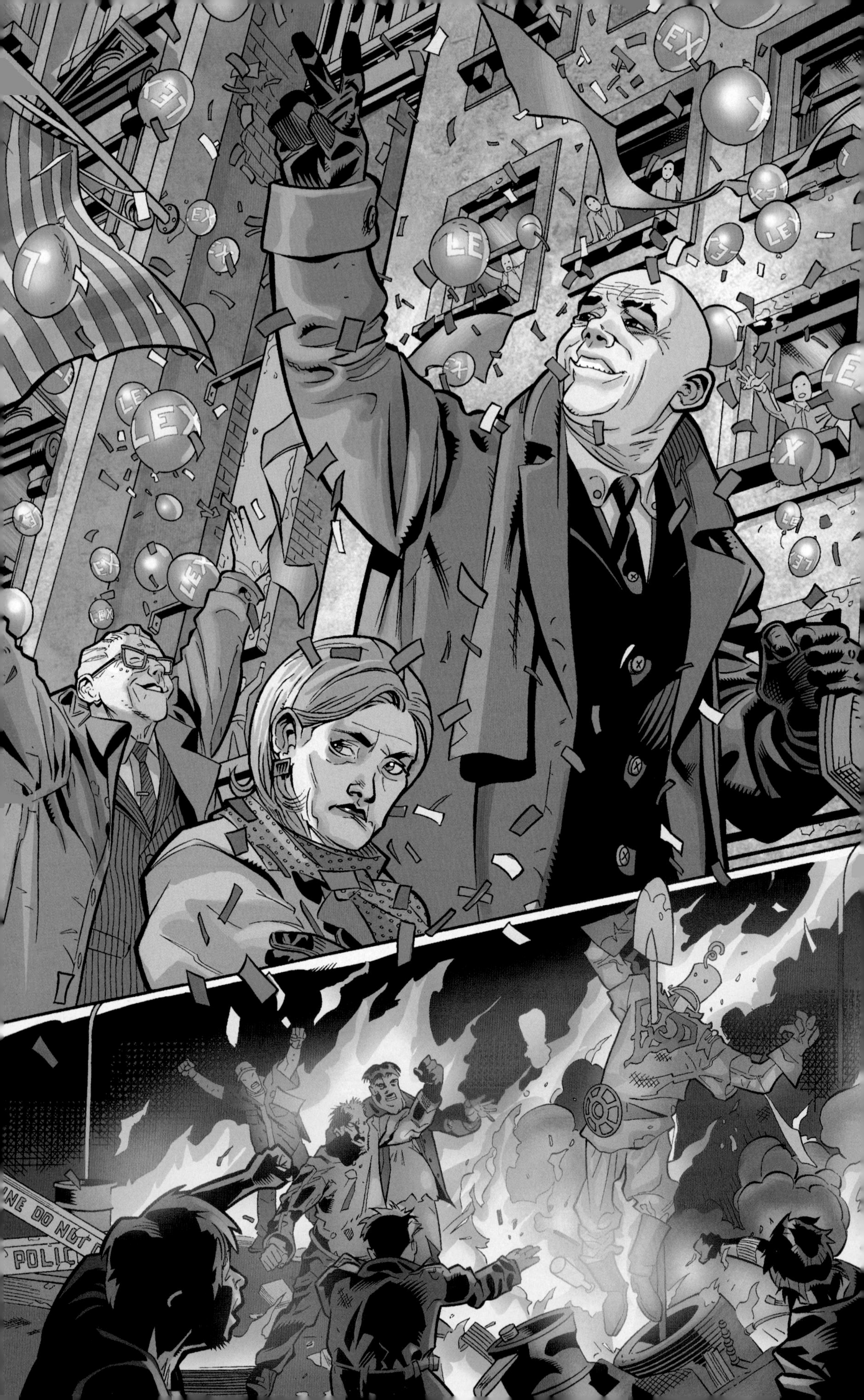
LEX

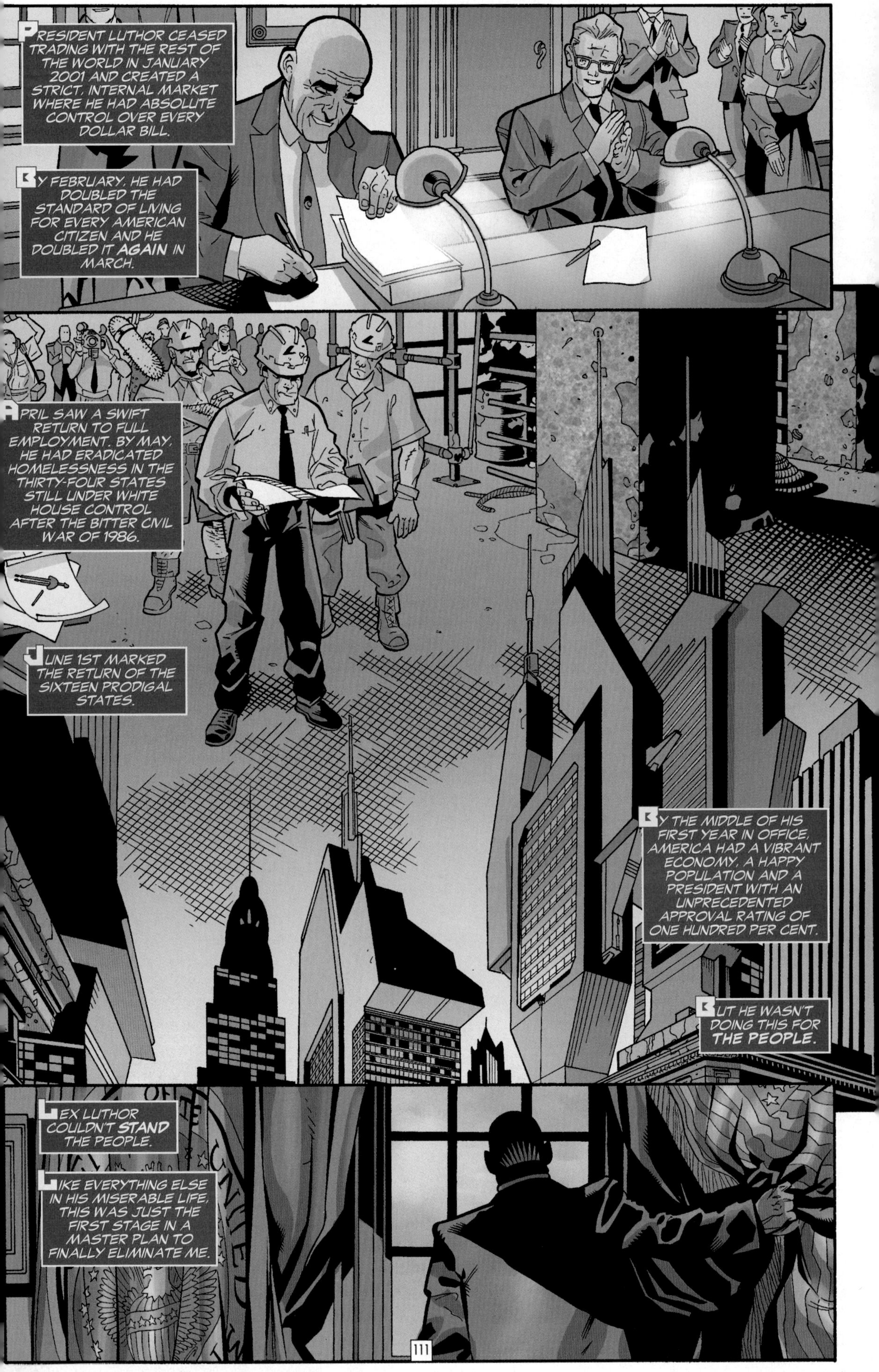
PRESIDENT LUTHOR CEASED TRADING WITH THE REST OF THE WORLD IN JANUARY 2001 AND CREATED A STRICT, INTERNAL MARKET WHERE HE HAD ABSOLUTE CONTROL OVER EVERY DOLLAR BILL.
BY FEBRUARY, HE HAD DOUBLED THE STANDARD OF LIVING FOR EVERY AMERICAN CITIZEN AND HE DOUBLED IT AGAIN IN MARCH.
APRIL SAW A SWIFT RETURN TO FULL EMPLOYMENT. BY MAY, HE HAD ERADICATED HOMELESSNESS IN THE THIRTY-FOUR STATES STILL UNDER WHITE HOUSE CONTROL AFTER THE BITTER CIVIL WAR OF 1986.
JUNE 1ST MARKED THE RETURN OF THE SIXTEEN PRODIGAL STATES.
BY THE MIDDLE OF HIS FIRST YEAR IN OFFICE, AMERICA HAD A VIBRANT ECONOMY, A HAPPY POPULATION AND A PRESIDENT WITH AN UNPRECEDENTED APPROVAL RATING OF ONE HUNDRED PER CENT.
BUT HE WASN'T DOING THIS FOR THE PEOPLE.
LEX LUTHOR COULDN'T STAND THE PEOPLE.
LIKE EVERYTHING ELSE IN HIS MISERABLE LIFE, THIS WAS JUST THE FIRST STAGE IN A MASTER PLAN TO FINALLY ELIMINATE ME.

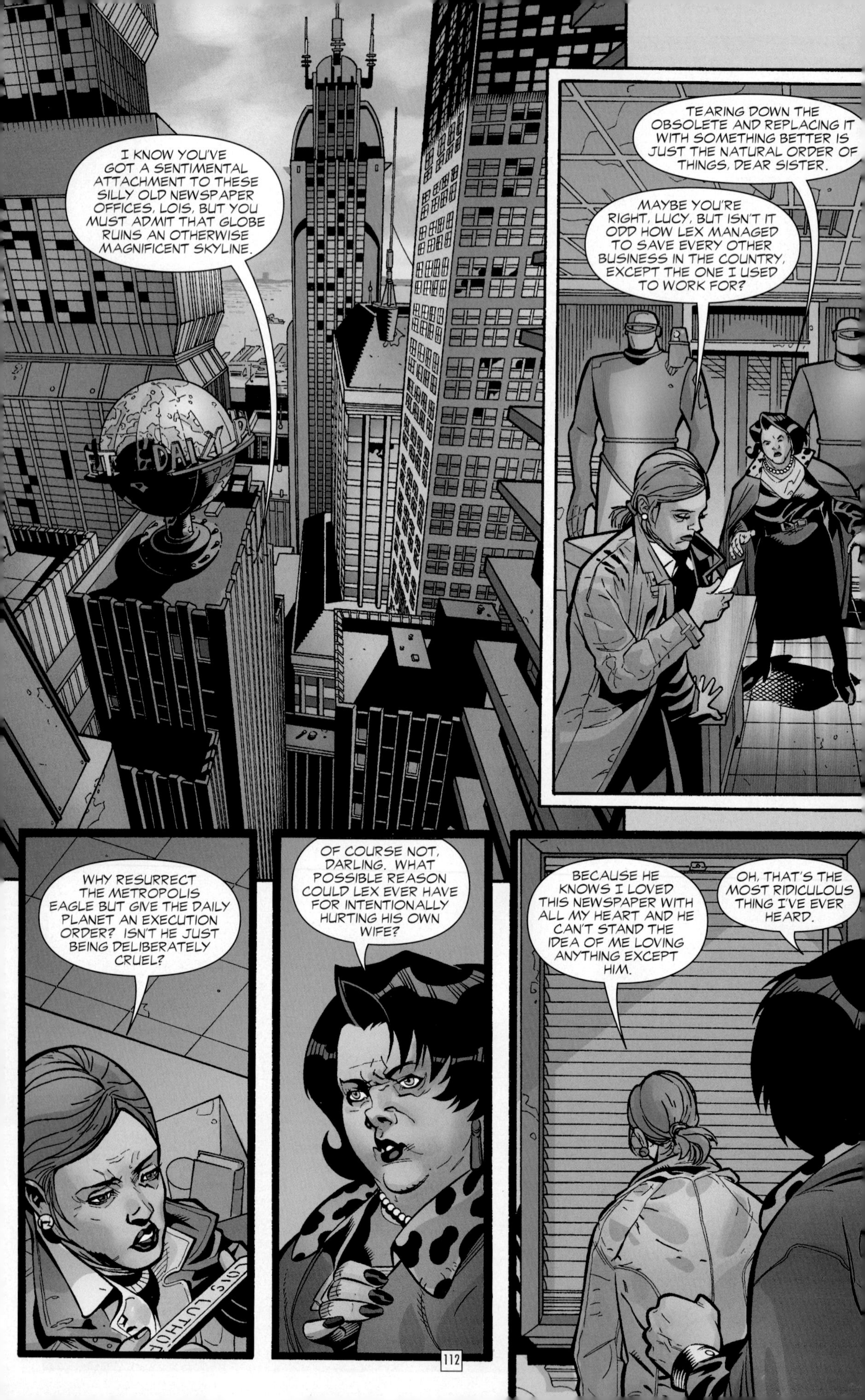
I KNOW YOU'VE GOT A SENTIMENTAL ATTACHMENT TO THESE SILLY OLD NEWSPAPER OFFICES, LOIS, BUT YOU MUST ADMIT THAT GLOBE RUINS AN OTHERWISE MAGNIFICENT SKYLINE.
TEARING DOWN THE OBSOLETE AND REPLACING IT WITH SOMETHING BETTER IS JUST THE NATURAL ORDER OF THINGS, DEAR SISTER.
MAYBE YOU'RE RIGHT, LUCY, BUT ISN'T IT ODD HOW LEX MANAGED TO SAVE EVERY OTHER BUSINESS IN THE COUNTRY, EXCEPT THE ONE I USED TO WORK FOR?
WHY RESURRECT THE METROPOLIS EAGLE BUT GIVE THE DAILY PLANET AN EXECUTION ORDER? ISN'T HE JUST BEING DELIBERATELY CRUEL?
OF COURSE NOT, DARLING. WHAT POSSIBLE REASON COULD LEX EVER HAVE FOR INTENTIONALLY HURTING HIS OWN WIFE?
BECAUSE HE KNOWS I LOVED THIS NEWSPAPER WITH ALL MY HEART AND HE CAN'T STAND THE IDEA OF ME LOVING ANYTHING EXCEPT HIM.
OH, THAT'S THE MOST RIDICULOUS THING I'VE EVER HEARD.

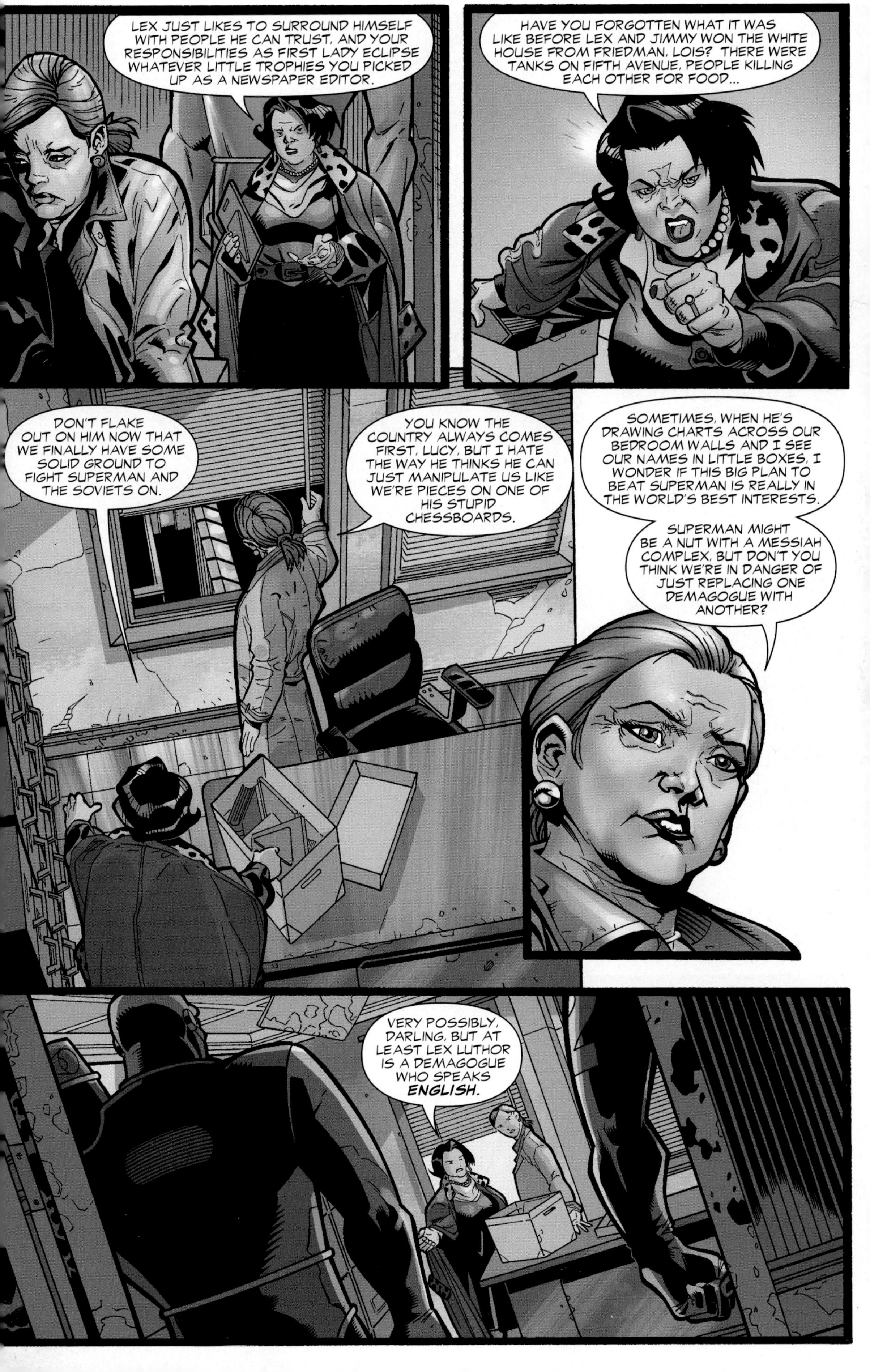
LEX JUST LIKES TO SURROUND HIMSELF WITH PEOPLE HE CAN TRUST, AND YOUR RESPONSIBILITIES AS FIRST LADY ECLIPSE WHATEVER LITTLE TROPHIES YOU PICKED UP AS A NEWSPAPER EDITOR.
HAVE YOU FORGOTTEN WHAT IT WAS LIKE BEFORE LEX AND JIMMY WON THE WHITE HOUSE FROM FRIEDMAN, LOIS? THERE WERE TANKS ON FIFTH AVENUE, PEOPLE KILLING EACH OTHER FOR FOOD...
DON'T FLAKE OUT ON HIM NOW THAT WE FINALLY HAVE SOME SOLID GROUND TO FIGHT SUPERMAN AND THE SOVIETS ON.
YOU KNOW THE COUNTRY ALWAYS COMES FIRST, LUCY, BUT I HATE THE WAY HE THINKS HE CAN JUST MANIPULATE US LIKE WE'RE PIECES ON ONE OF HIS STUPID CHESSBOARDS.
SOMETIMES, WHEN HE'S DRAWING CHARTS ACROSS OUR BEDROOM WALLS AND I SEE OUR NAMES IN LITTLE BOXES, I WONDER IF THIS BIG PLAN TO BEAT SUPERMAN IS REALLY IN THE WORLD'S BEST INTERESTS.
SUPERMAN MIGHT BE A NUT WITH A MESSIAH COMPLEX, BUT DON'T YOU THINK WE'RE IN DANGER OF JUST REPLACING ONE DEMAGOGUE WITH ANOTHER?
VERY POSSIBLY, DARLING, BUT AT LEAST LEX LUTHOR IS A DEMAGOGUE WHO SPEAKS ENGLISH.

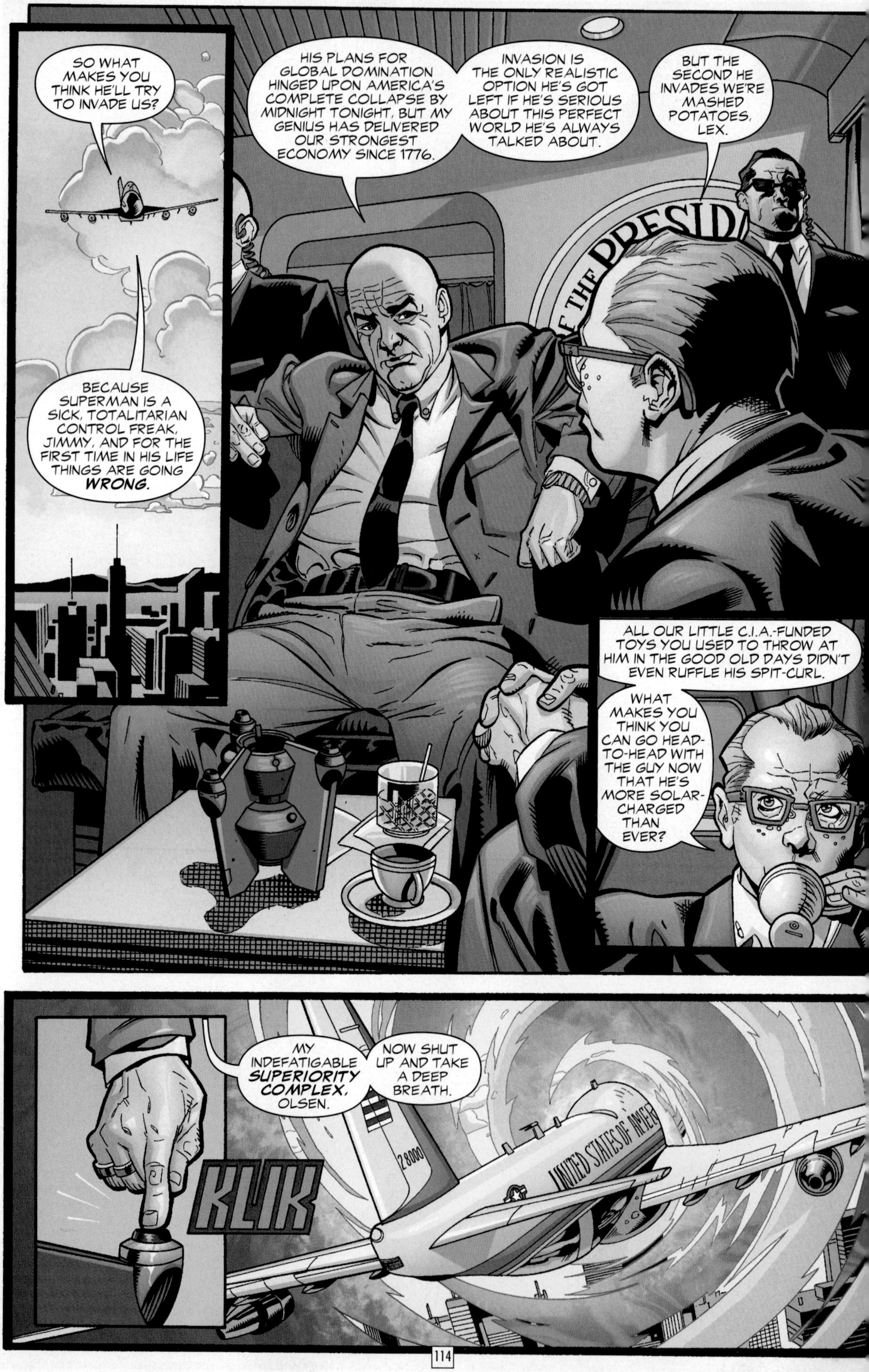

SO WHAT MAKES YOU THINK HE'LL TRY TO INVADE US?
BECAUSE SUPERMAN IS A SICK, TOTALITARIAN CONTROL FREAK, JIMMY, AND FOR THE FIRST TIME IN HIS LIFE THINGS ARE GOING **WRONG.**
HIS PLANS FOR GLOBAL DOMINATION HINGED UPON AMERICA'S COMPLETE COLLAPSE BY MIDNIGHT TONIGHT, BUT MY GENIUS HAS DELIVERED OUR STRONGEST ECONOMY SINCE 1776.
INVASION IS THE ONLY REALISTIC OPTION HE'S GOT LEFT IF HE'S SERIOUS ABOUT THIS PERFECT WORLD HE'S ALWAYS TALKED ABOUT.
BUT THE SECOND HE INVADES WE'RE MASHED POTATOES, LEX.
ALL OUR LITTLE C.I.A.-FUNDED TOYS YOU USED TO THROW AT HIM IN THE GOOD OLD DAYS DIDN'T EVEN RUFFLE HIS SPIT-CURL.
WHAT MAKES YOU THINK YOU CAN GO HEAD-TO-HEAD WITH THE GUY NOW THAT HE'S MORE SOLAR-CHARGED THAN EVER?
MY INDEFATIGABLE ***SUPERIORITY COMPLEX,*** OLSEN.
NOW SHUT UP AND TAKE A DEEP BREATH.
KLIK
UNITED STATES OF AMER
28000

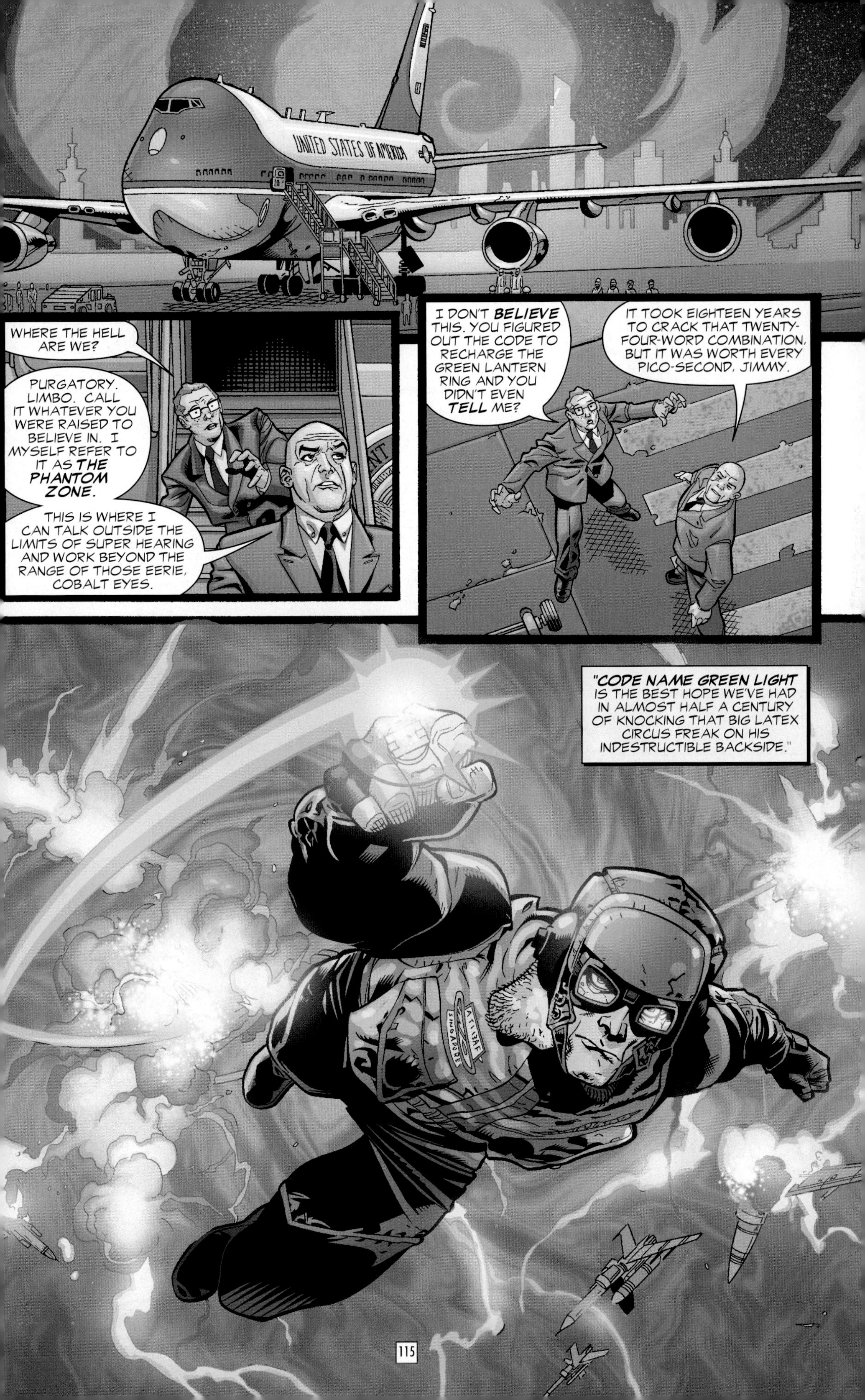
UNITED STATES OF AMERICA
WHERE THE HELL ARE WE?
PURGATORY. LIMBO. CALL IT WHATEVER YOU WERE RAISED TO BELIEVE IN. I MYSELF REFER TO IT AS THE PHANTOM ZONE.
THIS IS WHERE I CAN TALK OUTSIDE THE LIMITS OF SUPER HEARING AND WORK BEYOND THE RANGE OF THOSE EERIE, COBALT EYES.
I DON'T BELIEVE THIS. YOU FIGURED OUT THE CODE TO RECHARGE THE GREEN LANTERN RING AND YOU DIDN'T EVEN TELL ME?
IT TOOK EIGHTEEN YEARS TO CRACK THAT TWENTY-FOUR-WORD COMBINATION, BUT IT WAS WORTH EVERY PICO-SECOND, JIMMY.
"CODE NAME GREEN LIGHT IS THE BEST HOPE WE'VE HAD IN ALMOST HALF A CENTURY OF KNOCKING THAT BIG LATEX CIRCUS FREAK ON HIS INDESTRUCTIBLE BACKSIDE."

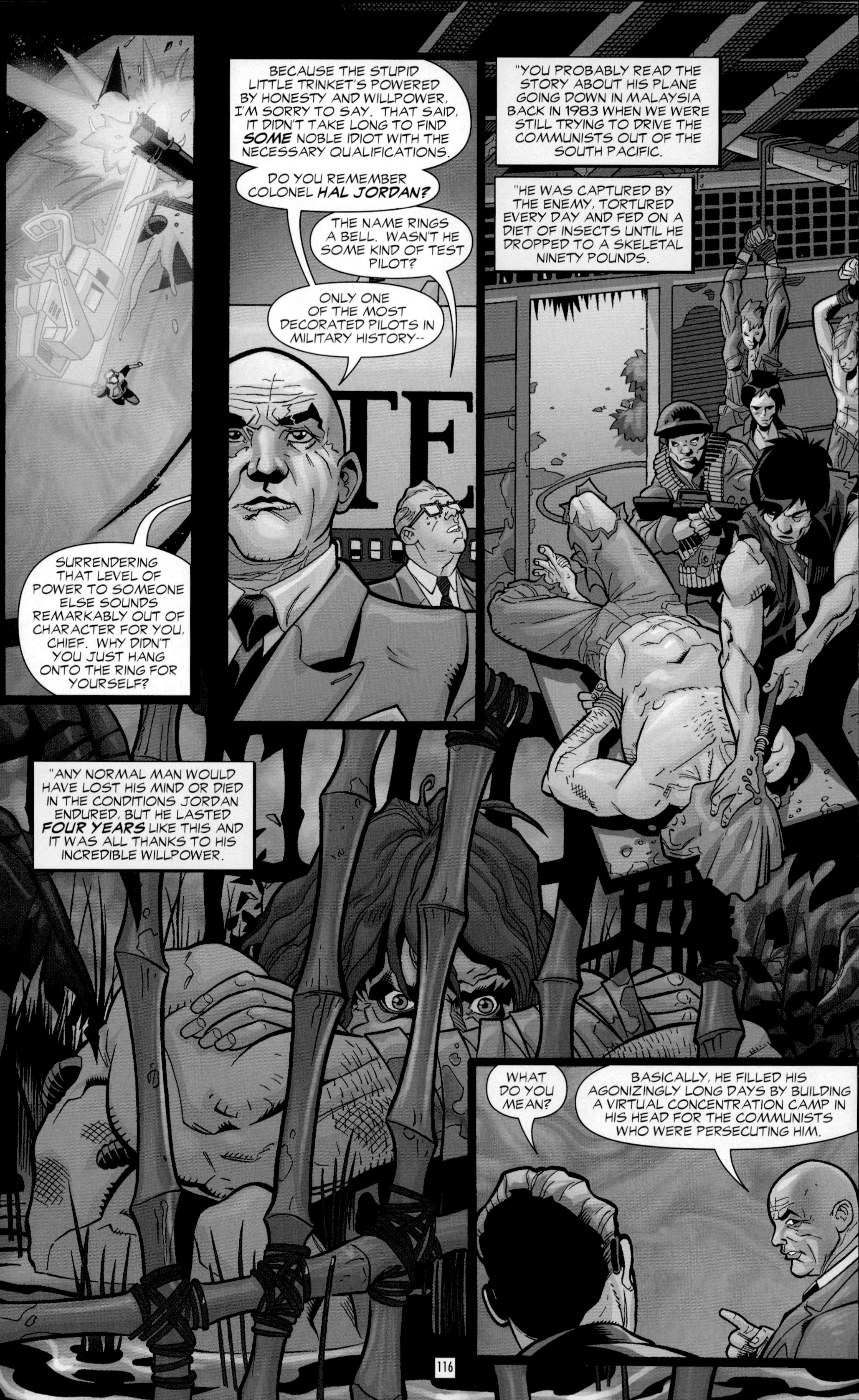
BECAUSE THE STUPID LITTLE TRINKET'S POWERED BY HONESTY AND WILLPOWER, I'M SORRY TO SAY. THAT SAID, IT DIDN'T TAKE LONG TO FIND SOME NOBLE IDIOT WITH THE NECESSARY QUALIFICATIONS.
DO YOU REMEMBER COLONEL HAL JORDAN?
THE NAME RINGS A BELL. WASN'T HE SOME KIND OF TEST PILOT?
ONLY ONE OF THE MOST DECORATED PILOTS IN MILITARY HISTORY--
SURRENDERING THAT LEVEL OF POWER TO SOMEONE ELSE SOUNDS REMARKABLY OUT OF CHARACTER FOR YOU, CHIEF. WHY DIDN'T YOU JUST HANG ONTO THE RING FOR YOURSELF?
"YOU PROBABLY READ THE STORY ABOUT HIS PLANE GOING DOWN IN MALAYSIA BACK IN 1983 WHEN WE WERE STILL TRYING TO DRIVE THE COMMUNISTS OUT OF THE SOUTH PACIFIC.
"HE WAS CAPTURED BY THE ENEMY, TORTURED EVERY DAY AND FED ON A DIET OF INSECTS UNTIL HE DROPPED TO A SKELETAL NINETY POUNDS.
"ANY NORMAL MAN WOULD HAVE LOST HIS MIND OR DIED IN THE CONDITIONS JORDAN ENDURED, BUT HE LASTED FOUR YEARS LIKE THIS AND IT WAS ALL THANKS TO HIS INCREDIBLE WILLPOWER.
WHAT DO YOU MEAN?
BASICALLY, HE FILLED HIS AGONIZINGLY LONG DAYS BY BUILDING A VIRTUAL CONCENTRATION CAMP IN HIS HEAD FOR THE COMMUNISTS WHO WERE PERSECUTING HIM.

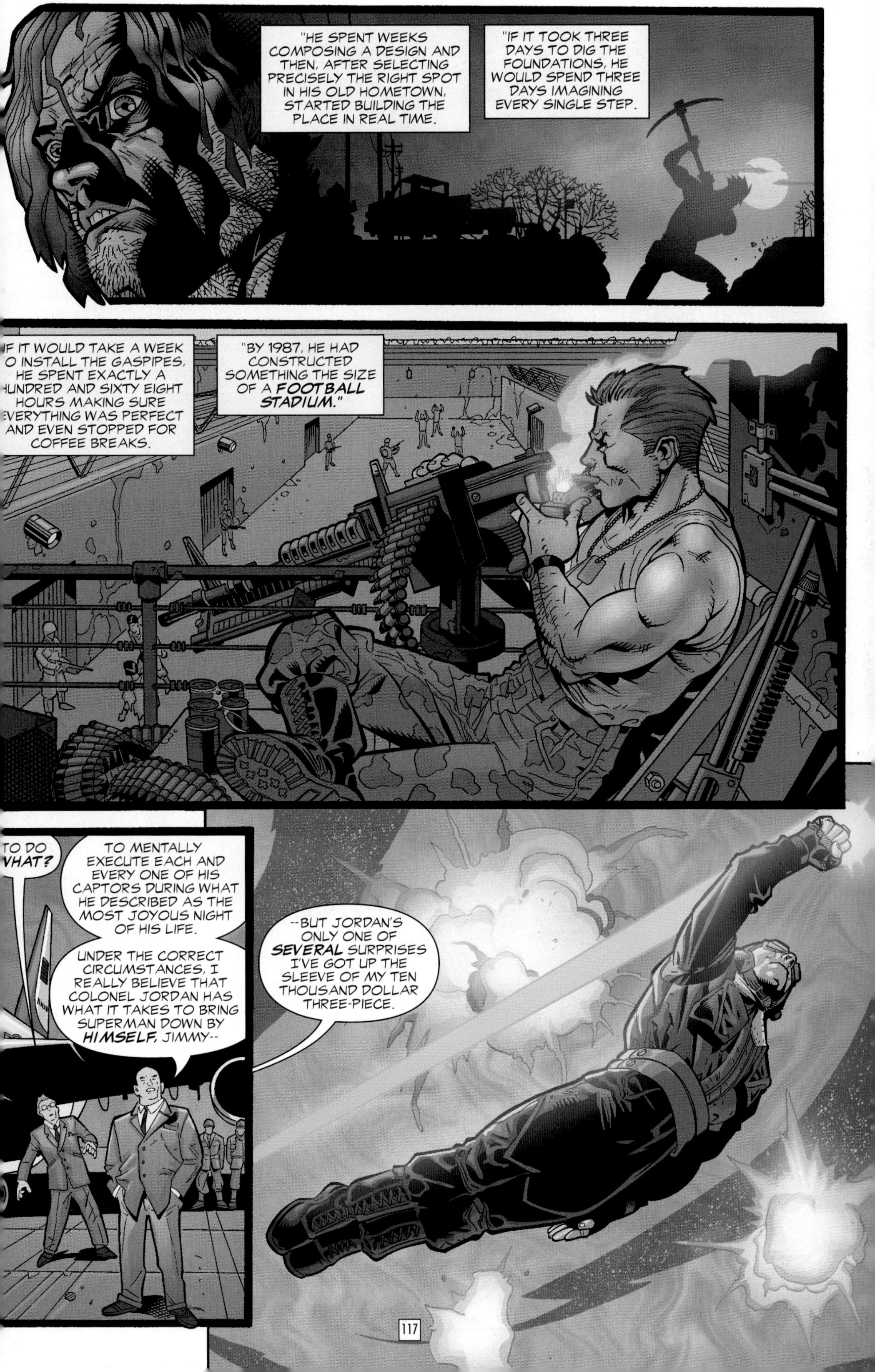
"HE SPENT WEEKS COMPOSING A DESIGN AND THEN, AFTER SELECTING PRECISELY THE RIGHT SPOT IN HIS OLD HOMETOWN, STARTED BUILDING THE PLACE IN REAL TIME.
"IF IT TOOK THREE DAYS TO DIG THE FOUNDATIONS, HE WOULD SPEND THREE DAYS IMAGINING EVERY SINGLE STEP.
IF IT WOULD TAKE A WEEK TO INSTALL THE GASPIPES, HE SPENT EXACTLY A HUNDRED AND SIXTY EIGHT HOURS MAKING SURE EVERYTHING WAS PERFECT AND EVEN STOPPED FOR COFFEE BREAKS.
"BY 1987, HE HAD CONSTRUCTED SOMETHING THE SIZE OF A FOOTBALL STADIUM."
TO DO WHAT?
TO MENTALLY EXECUTE EACH AND EVERY ONE OF HIS CAPTORS DURING WHAT HE DESCRIBED AS THE MOST JOYOUS NIGHT OF HIS LIFE.
UNDER THE CORRECT CIRCUMSTANCES, I REALLY BELIEVE THAT COLONEL JORDAN HAS WHAT IT TAKES TO BRING SUPERMAN DOWN BY HIMSELF, JIMMY--
--BUT JORDAN'S ONLY ONE OF SEVERAL SURPRISES I'VE GOT UP THE SLEEVE OF MY TEN THOUSAND DOLLAR THREE-PIECE.

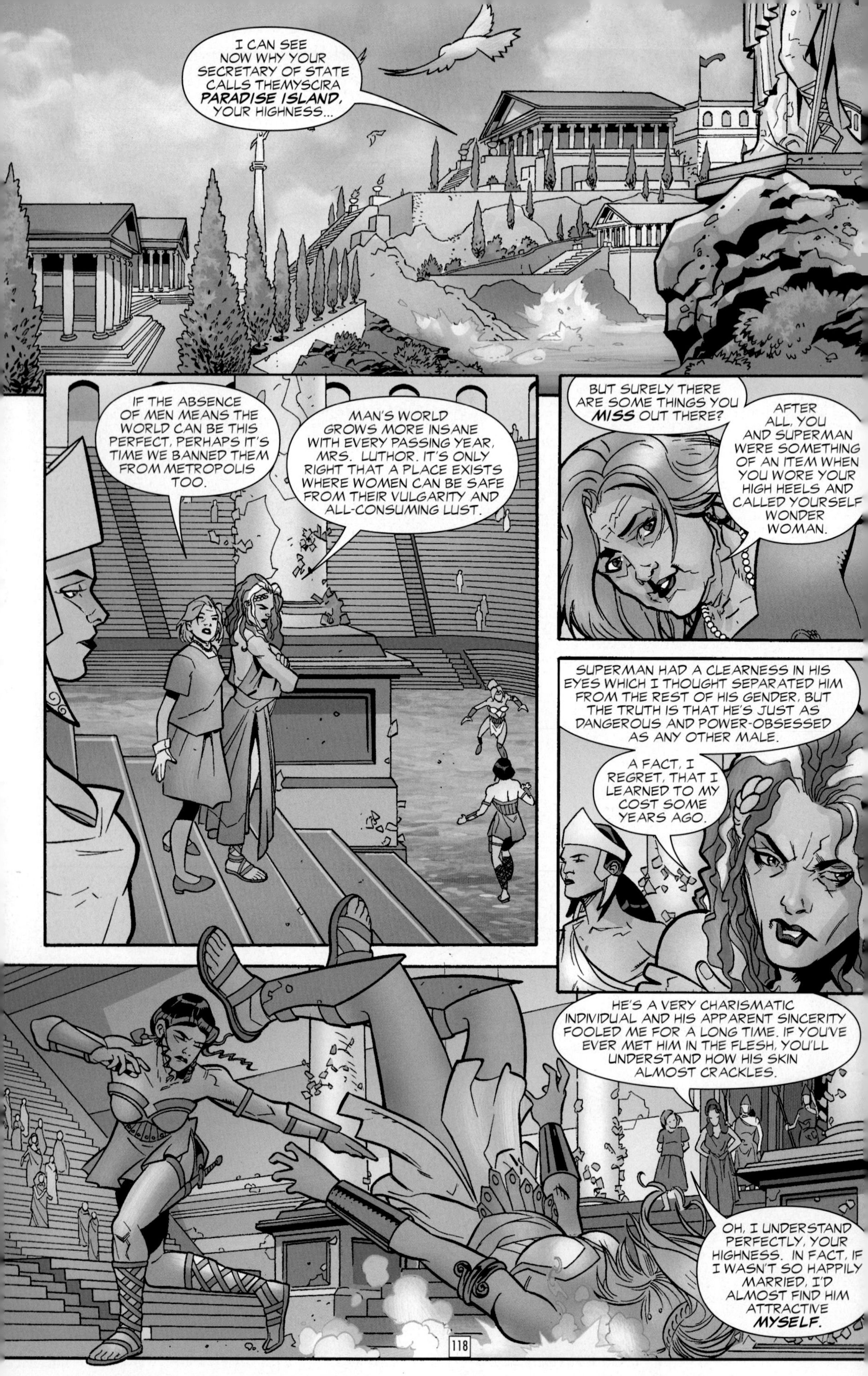
I CAN SEE NOW WHY YOUR SECRETARY OF STATE CALLS THEMYSCIRA PARADISE ISLAND, YOUR HIGHNESS...
IF THE ABSENCE OF MEN MEANS THE WORLD CAN BE THIS PERFECT, PERHAPS IT'S TIME WE BANNED THEM FROM METROPOLIS TOO.
MAN'S WORLD GROWS MORE INSANE WITH EVERY PASSING YEAR, MRS. LUTHOR. IT'S ONLY RIGHT THAT A PLACE EXISTS WHERE WOMEN CAN BE SAFE FROM THEIR VULGARITY AND ALL-CONSUMING LUST.
BUT SURELY THERE ARE SOME THINGS YOU MISS OUT THERE?
AFTER ALL, YOU AND SUPERMAN WERE SOMETHING OF AN ITEM WHEN YOU WORE YOUR HIGH HEELS AND CALLED YOURSELF WONDER WOMAN.
SUPERMAN HAD A CLEARNESS IN HIS EYES WHICH I THOUGHT SEPARATED HIM FROM THE REST OF HIS GENDER, BUT THE TRUTH IS THAT HE'S JUST AS DANGEROUS AND POWER-OBSESSED AS ANY OTHER MALE.
A FACT, I REGRET, THAT I LEARNED TO MY COST SOME YEARS AGO.
HE'S A VERY CHARISMATIC INDIVIDUAL AND HIS APPARENT SINCERITY FOOLED ME FOR A LONG TIME. IF YOU'VE EVER MET HIM IN THE FLESH, YOU'LL UNDERSTAND HOW HIS SKIN ALMOST CRACKLES.
OH, I UNDERSTAND PERFECTLY, YOUR HIGHNESS. IN FACT, IF I WASN'T SO HAPPILY MARRIED, I'D ALMOST FIND HIM ATTRACTIVE MYSELF.

I'VE OFTEN WONDERED WHY A WOMAN OF YOUR CHARACTER REMAINS BY THE SIDE OF THAT HAIRLESS MACHIAVELLI, MRS. LUTHOR.

HE MIGHT HAVE RESTORED THE DIGNITY OF YOUR COUNTRY, BUT I'VE FOUGHT ENOUGH OF HIS KILLER ROBOTS OVER THE YEARS TO REALIZE LEX LUTHOR HAS LITTLE OR NO REGARD FOR HUMAN LIFE.

IT'S QUITE CLEAR THAT THE ONLY REASON HE EVEN RAN FOR PRESIDENT WAS TO CREATE A MORE EFFECTIVE PLATFORM FROM WHICH HE MIGHT ULTIMATELY DESTROY SUPERMAN.

THEN THE END JUSTIFIES THE MEANS.

FOR ALL WE KNOW, ROOSEVELT ONLY RAN FOR OFFICE BECAUSE HE LIKED SKIDDING AROUND THE WHITE HOUSE IN A WHEELCHAIR, BUT HE STILL BEAT HITLER, RIGHT?

WHY DID YOU COME HERE, MRS. LUTHOR? AND I DON'T WANT TO HEAR YOUR EXCUSE ABOUT A DIPLOMATIC VISIT FROM THE FIRST LADY ON BEHALF OF THE WONDER WOMEN OF AMERICA.

WHY ARE YOU *REALLY* HERE?

TO MAKE SURE LEX HAS YOUR SUPPORT WHEN HE LAUNCHES HIS BIG ATTACK ON SUPERMAN INSIDE THE NEXT TWENTY-FOUR HOURS.

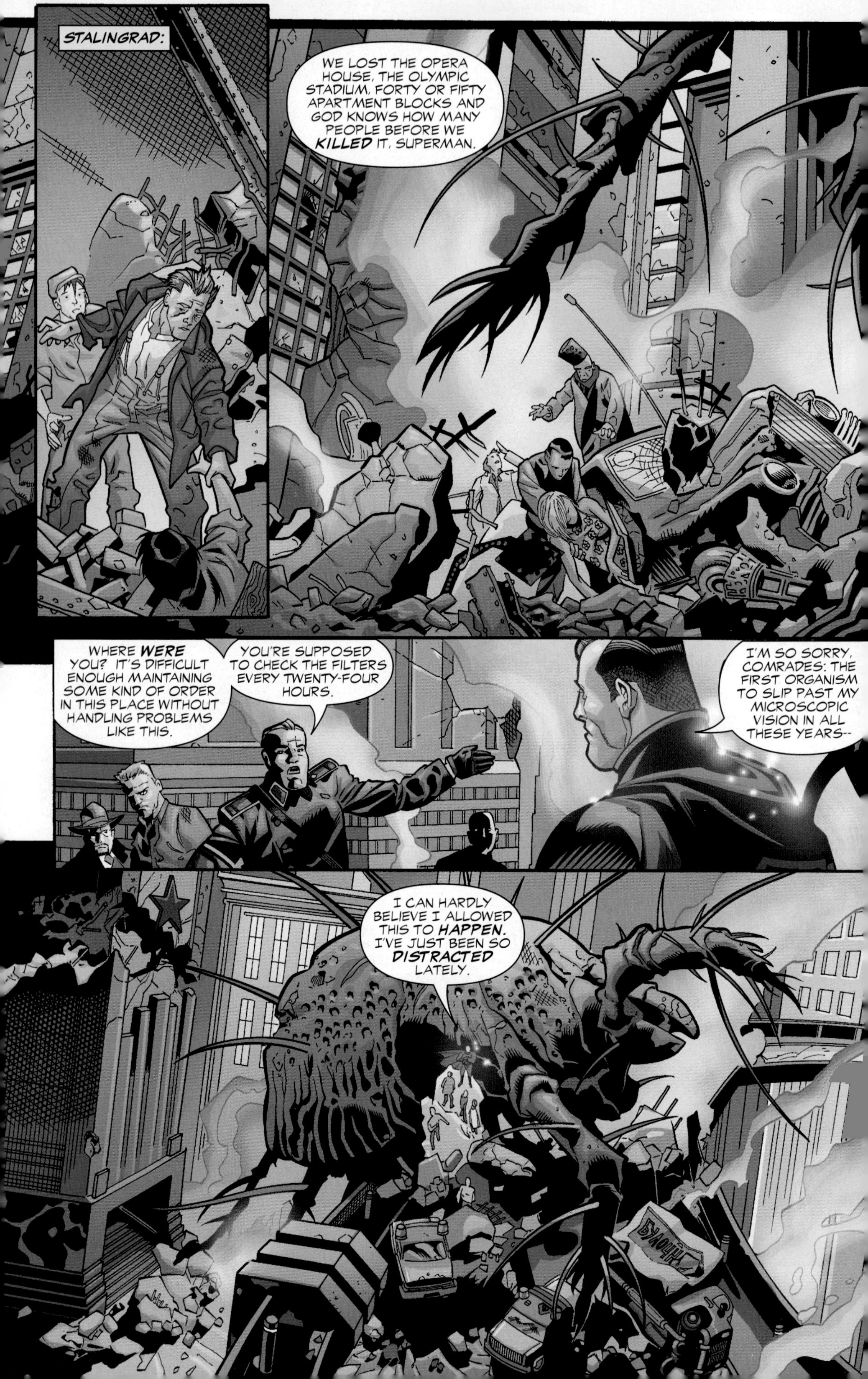
STALINGRAD:
WE LOST THE OPERA HOUSE, THE OLYMPIC STADIUM, FORTY OR FIFTY APARTMENT BLOCKS AND GOD KNOWS HOW MANY PEOPLE BEFORE WE KILLED IT, SUPERMAN.
WHERE WERE YOU? IT'S DIFFICULT ENOUGH MAINTAINING SOME KIND OF ORDER IN THIS PLACE WITHOUT HANDLING PROBLEMS LIKE THIS.
YOU'RE SUPPOSED TO CHECK THE FILTERS EVERY TWENTY-FOUR HOURS.
I'M SO SORRY, COMRADES: THE FIRST ORGANISM TO SLIP PAST MY MICROSCOPIC VISION IN ALL THESE YEARS--
I CAN HARDLY BELIEVE I ALLOWED THIS TO HAPPEN. I'VE JUST BEEN SO DISTRACTED LATELY.

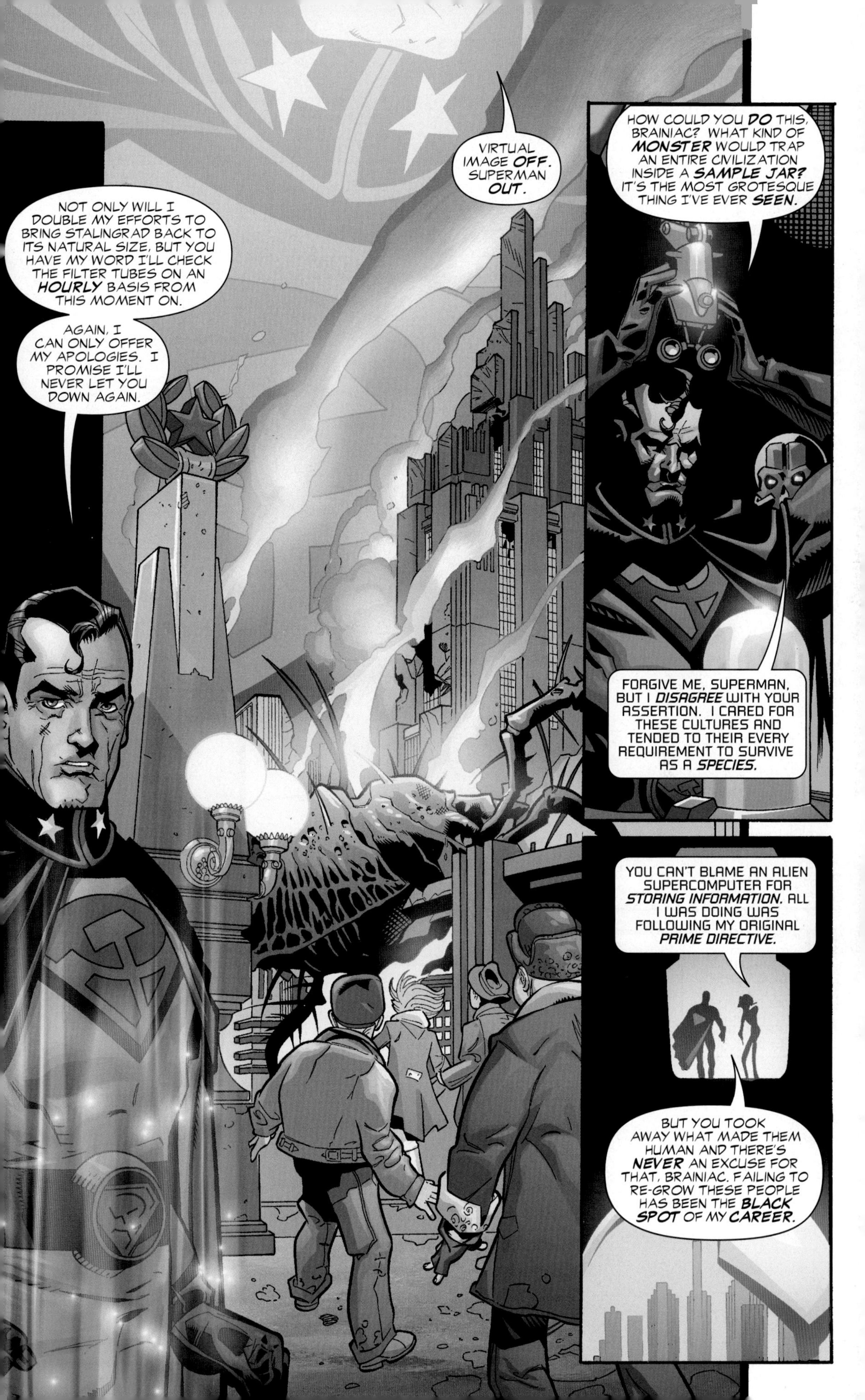

NOT ONLY WILL I DOUBLE MY EFFORTS TO BRING STALINGRAD BACK TO ITS NATURAL SIZE, BUT YOU HAVE MY WORD I'LL CHECK THE FILTER TUBES ON AN HOURLY BASIS FROM THIS MOMENT ON.
AGAIN, I CAN ONLY OFFER MY APOLOGIES. I PROMISE I'LL NEVER LET YOU DOWN AGAIN.
VIRTUAL IMAGE OFF. SUPERMAN OUT.
HOW COULD YOU DO THIS, BRAINIAC? WHAT KIND OF MONSTER WOULD TRAP AN ENTIRE CIVILIZATION INSIDE A SAMPLE JAR? IT'S THE MOST GROTESQUE THING I'VE EVER SEEN.
FORGIVE ME, SUPERMAN, BUT I DISAGREE WITH YOUR ASSERTION. I CARED FOR THESE CULTURES AND TENDED TO THEIR EVERY REQUIREMENT TO SURVIVE AS A SPECIES.
YOU CAN'T BLAME AN ALIEN SUPERCOMPUTER FOR STORING INFORMATION. ALL I WAS DOING WAS FOLLOWING MY ORIGINAL PRIME DIRECTIVE.
BUT YOU TOOK AWAY WHAT MADE THEM HUMAN AND THERE'S NEVER AN EXCUSE FOR THAT, BRAINIAC. FAILING TO RE-GROW THESE PEOPLE HAS BEEN THE BLACK SPOT OF MY CAREER.

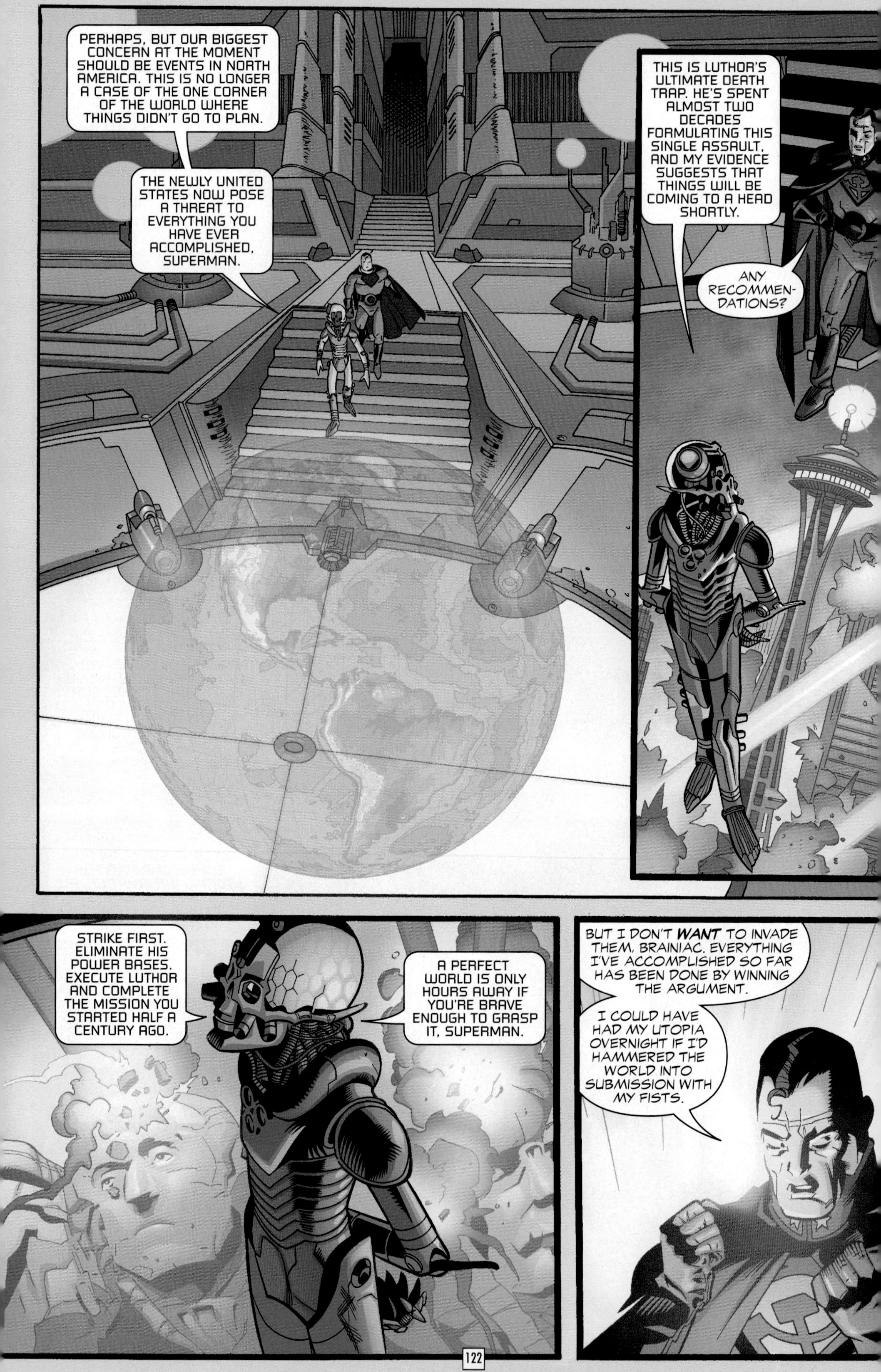
PERHAPS, BUT OUR BIGGEST CONCERN AT THE MOMENT SHOULD BE EVENTS IN NORTH AMERICA. THIS IS NO LONGER A CASE OF THE ONE CORNER OF THE WORLD WHERE THINGS DIDN'T GO TO PLAN.
THE NEWLY UNITED STATES NOW POSE A THREAT TO EVERYTHING YOU HAVE EVER ACCOMPLISHED, SUPERMAN.
THIS IS LUTHOR'S ULTIMATE DEATH TRAP. HE'S SPENT ALMOST TWO DECADES FORMULATING THIS SINGLE ASSAULT, AND MY EVIDENCE SUGGESTS THAT THINGS WILL BE COMING TO A HEAD SHORTLY.
ANY RECOMMEN-DATIONS?
STRIKE FIRST. ELIMINATE HIS POWER BASES. EXECUTE LUTHOR AND COMPLETE THE MISSION YOU STARTED HALF A CENTURY AGO.
A PERFECT WORLD IS ONLY HOURS AWAY IF YOU'RE BRAVE ENOUGH TO GRASP IT, SUPERMAN.
BUT I DON'T WANT TO INVADE THEM, BRAINIAC. EVERYTHING I'VE ACCOMPLISHED SO FAR HAS BEEN DONE BY WINNING THE ARGUMENT.
I COULD HAVE HAD MY UTOPIA OVERNIGHT IF I'D HAMMERED THE WORLD INTO SUBMISSION WITH MY FISTS.

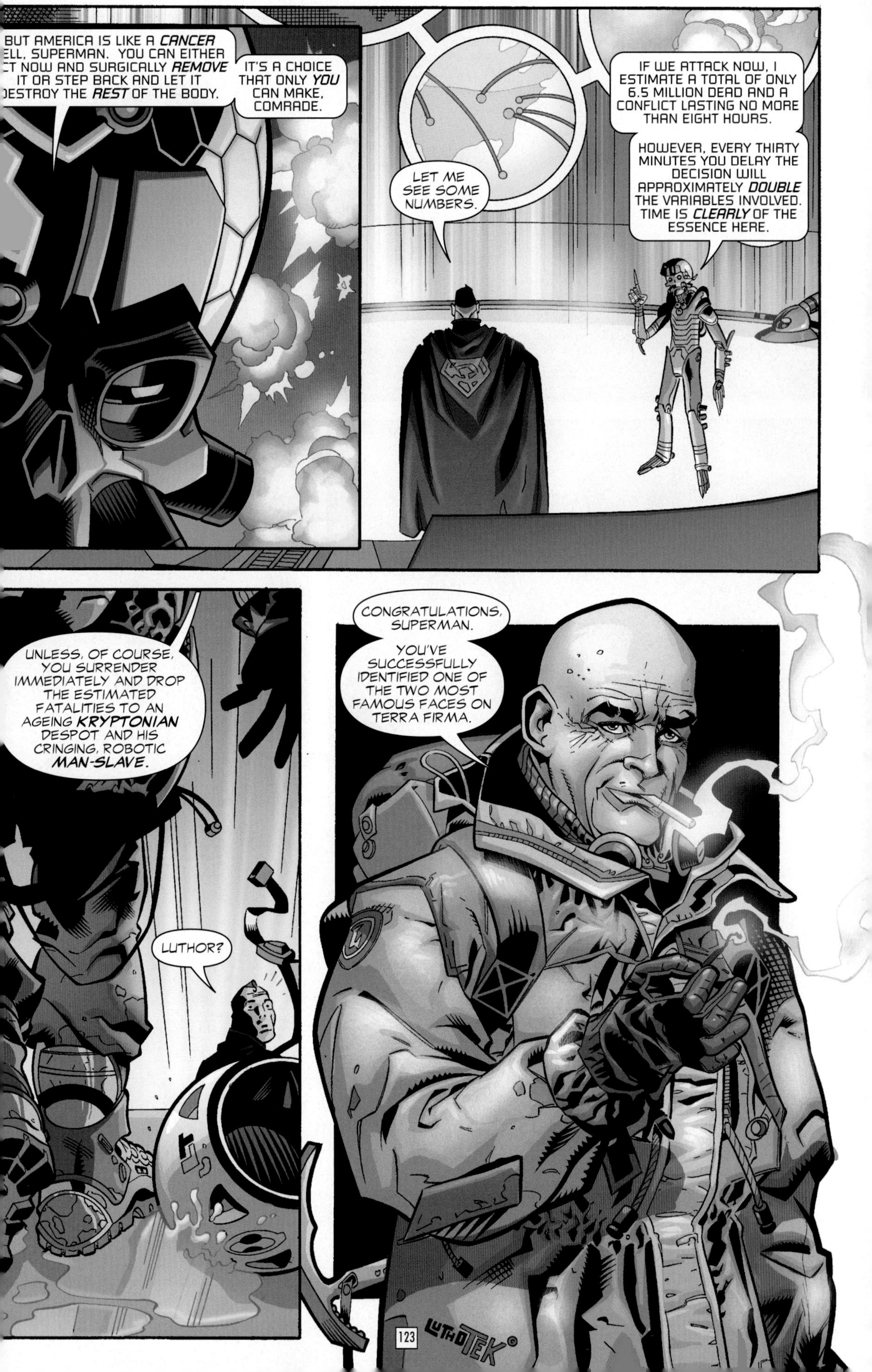
BUT AMERICA IS LIKE A CANCER
ELL, SUPERMAN. YOU CAN EITHER
CT NOW AND SURGICALLY REMOVE IT OR STEP BACK AND LET IT DESTROY THE REST OF THE BODY.
IT'S A CHOICE THAT ONLY YOU CAN MAKE, COMRADE.
LET ME SEE SOME NUMBERS.
IF WE ATTACK NOW, I ESTIMATE A TOTAL OF ONLY 6.5 MILLION DEAD AND A CONFLICT LASTING NO MORE THAN EIGHT HOURS.
HOWEVER, EVERY THIRTY MINUTES YOU DELAY THE DECISION WILL APPROXIMATELY DOUBLE THE VARIABLES INVOLVED. TIME IS CLEARLY OF THE ESSENCE HERE.
UNLESS, OF COURSE, YOU SURRENDER IMMEDIATELY AND DROP THE ESTIMATED FATALITIES TO AN AGEING KRYPTONIAN DESPOT AND HIS CRINGING, ROBOTIC MAN-SLAVE.
LUTHOR?
CONGRATULATIONS, SUPERMAN.
YOU'VE SUCCESSFULLY IDENTIFIED ONE OF THE TWO MOST FAMOUS FACES ON TERRA FIRMA.
LUTHOTEK®

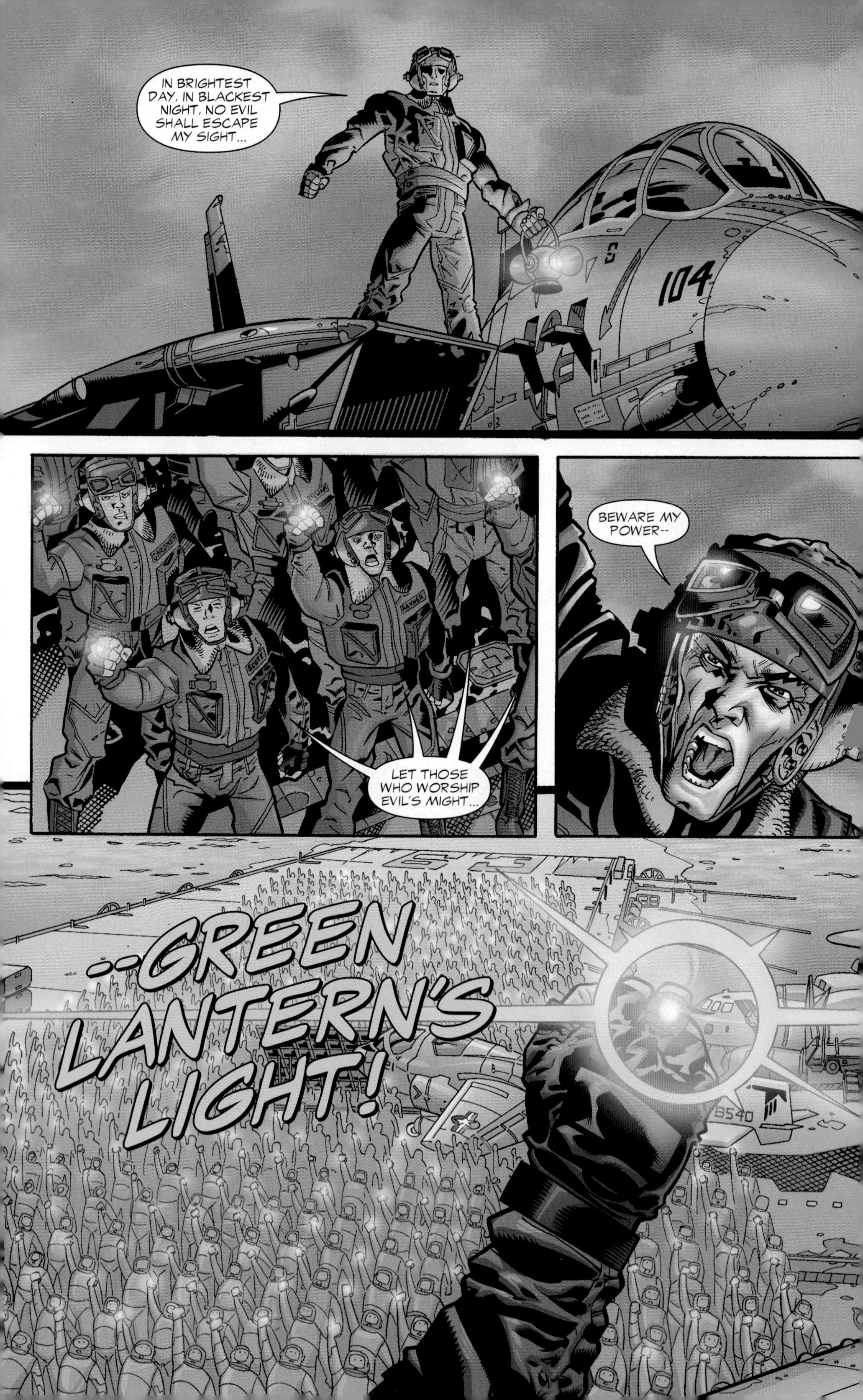
IN BRIGHTEST DAY, IN BLACKEST NIGHT, NO EVIL SHALL ESCAPE MY SIGHT...
104
LET THOSE WHO WORSHIP EVIL'S MIGHT...
BEWARE MY POWER--
--GREEN LANTERN'S LIGHT!

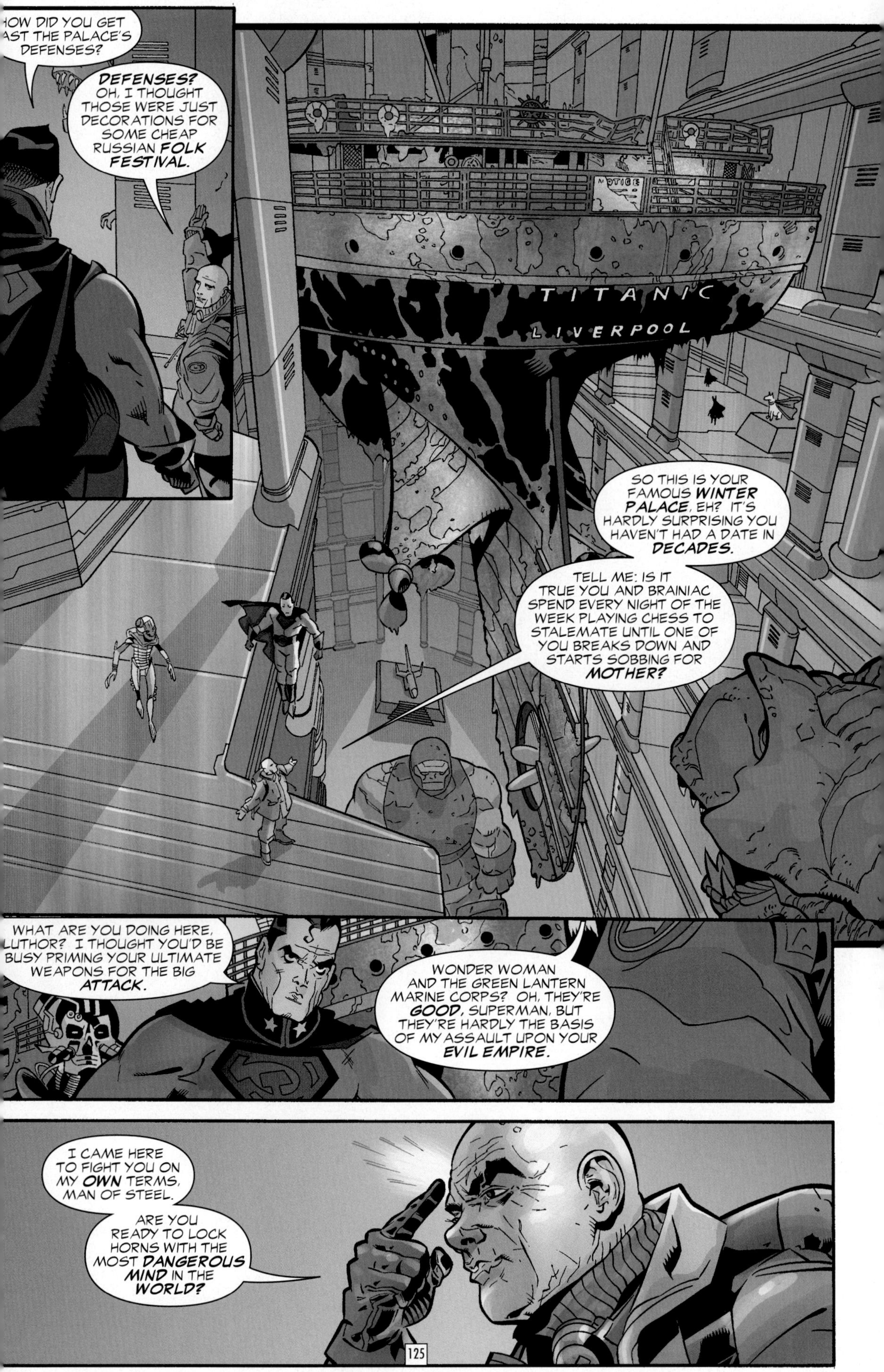
HOW DID YOU GET PAST THE PALACE'S DEFENSES?
DEFENSES? OH, I THOUGHT THOSE WERE JUST DECORATIONS FOR SOME CHEAP RUSSIAN FOLK FESTIVAL.
NOTICE
TITANIC
LIVERPOOL
SO THIS IS YOUR FAMOUS WINTER PALACE, EH? IT'S HARDLY SURPRISING YOU HAVEN'T HAD A DATE IN DECADES.
TELL ME: IS IT TRUE YOU AND BRAINIAC SPEND EVERY NIGHT OF THE WEEK PLAYING CHESS TO STALEMATE UNTIL ONE OF YOU BREAKS DOWN AND STARTS SOBBING FOR MOTHER?
WHAT ARE YOU DOING HERE, LUTHOR? I THOUGHT YOU'D BE BUSY PRIMING YOUR ULTIMATE WEAPONS FOR THE BIG ATTACK.
WONDER WOMAN AND THE GREEN LANTERN MARINE CORPS? OH, THEY'RE GOOD, SUPERMAN, BUT THEY'RE HARDLY THE BASIS OF MY ASSAULT UPON YOUR EVIL EMPIRE.
I CAME HERE TO FIGHT YOU ON MY OWN TERMS, MAN OF STEEL.
ARE YOU READY TO LOCK HORNS WITH THE MOST DANGEROUS MIND IN THE WORLD?

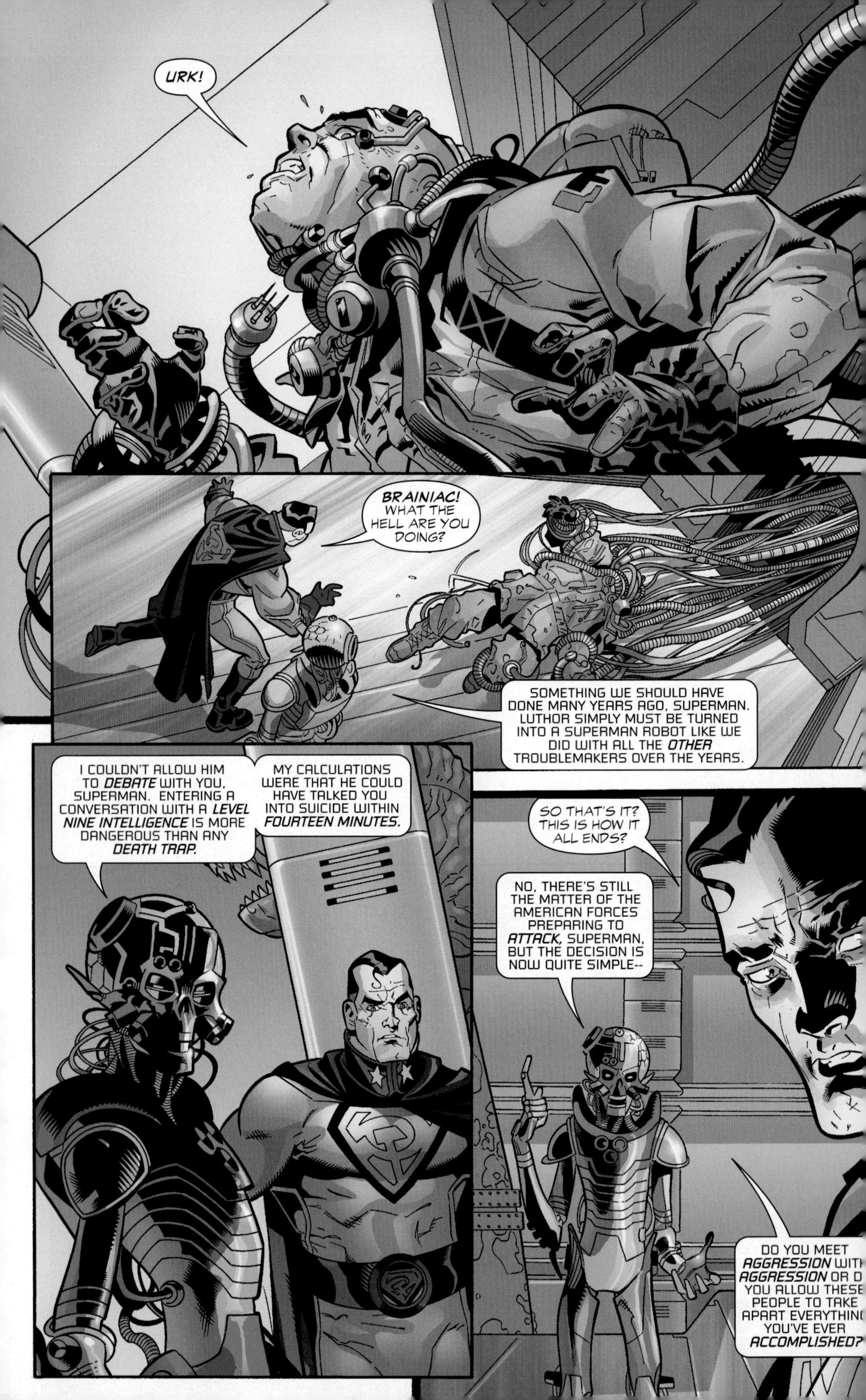
URK!
BRAINIAC! WHAT THE HELL ARE YOU DOING?
SOMETHING WE SHOULD HAVE DONE MANY YEARS AGO, SUPERMAN. LUTHOR SIMPLY MUST BE TURNED INTO A SUPERMAN ROBOT LIKE WE DID WITH ALL THE OTHER TROUBLEMAKERS OVER THE YEARS.
I COULDN'T ALLOW HIM TO DEBATE WITH YOU, SUPERMAN. ENTERING A CONVERSATION WITH A LEVEL NINE INTELLIGENCE IS MORE DANGEROUS THAN ANY DEATH TRAP.
MY CALCULATIONS WERE THAT HE COULD HAVE TALKED YOU INTO SUICIDE WITHIN FOURTEEN MINUTES.
SO THAT'S IT? THIS IS HOW IT ALL ENDS?
NO, THERE'S STILL THE MATTER OF THE AMERICAN FORCES PREPARING TO ATTACK, SUPERMAN, BUT THE DECISION IS NOW QUITE SIMPLE--
DO YOU MEET AGGRESSION WIT AGGRESSION OR D YOU ALLOW THESE PEOPLE TO TAKE APART EVERYTHIN YOU'VE EVER ACCOMPLISHED?

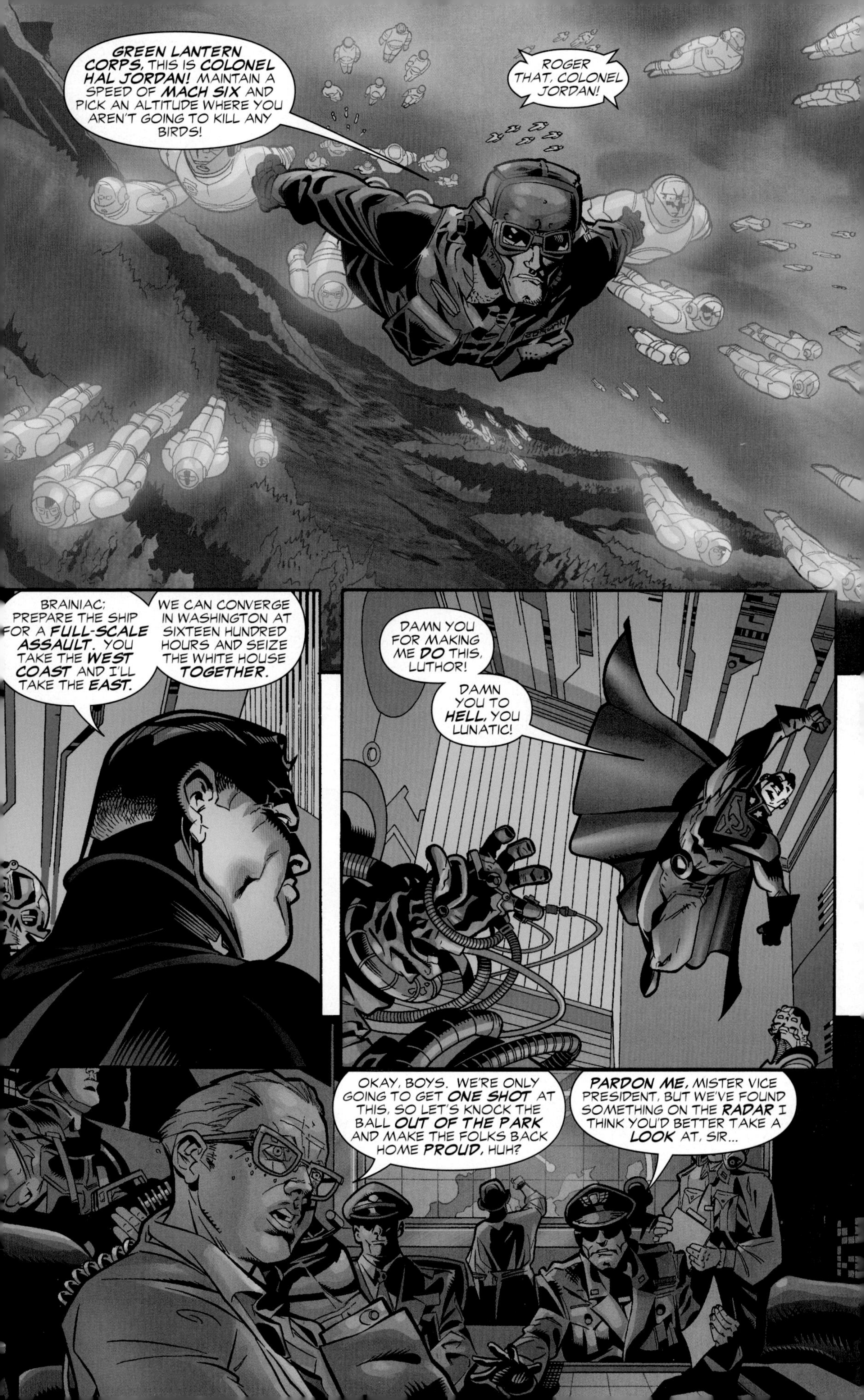
GREEN LANTERN CORPS, THIS IS COLONEL HAL JORDAN! MAINTAIN A SPEED OF MACH SIX AND PICK AN ALTITUDE WHERE YOU AREN'T GOING TO KILL ANY BIRDS!
ROGER THAT, COLONEL JORDAN!
BRAINIAC: PREPARE THE SHIP FOR A FULL-SCALE ASSAULT. YOU TAKE THE WEST COAST AND I'LL TAKE THE EAST.
WE CAN CONVERGE IN WASHINGTON AT SIXTEEN HUNDRED HOURS AND SEIZE THE WHITE HOUSE TOGETHER.
DAMN YOU FOR MAKING ME DO THIS, LUTHOR!
DAMN YOU TO HELL, YOU LUNATIC!
OKAY, BOYS. WE'RE ONLY GOING TO GET ONE SHOT AT THIS, SO LET'S KNOCK THE BALL OUT OF THE PARK AND MAKE THE FOLKS BACK HOME PROUD, HUH?
PARDON ME, MISTER VICE PRESIDENT, BUT WE'VE FOUND SOMETHING ON THE RADAR I THINK YOU'D BETTER TAKE A LOOK AT, SIR...

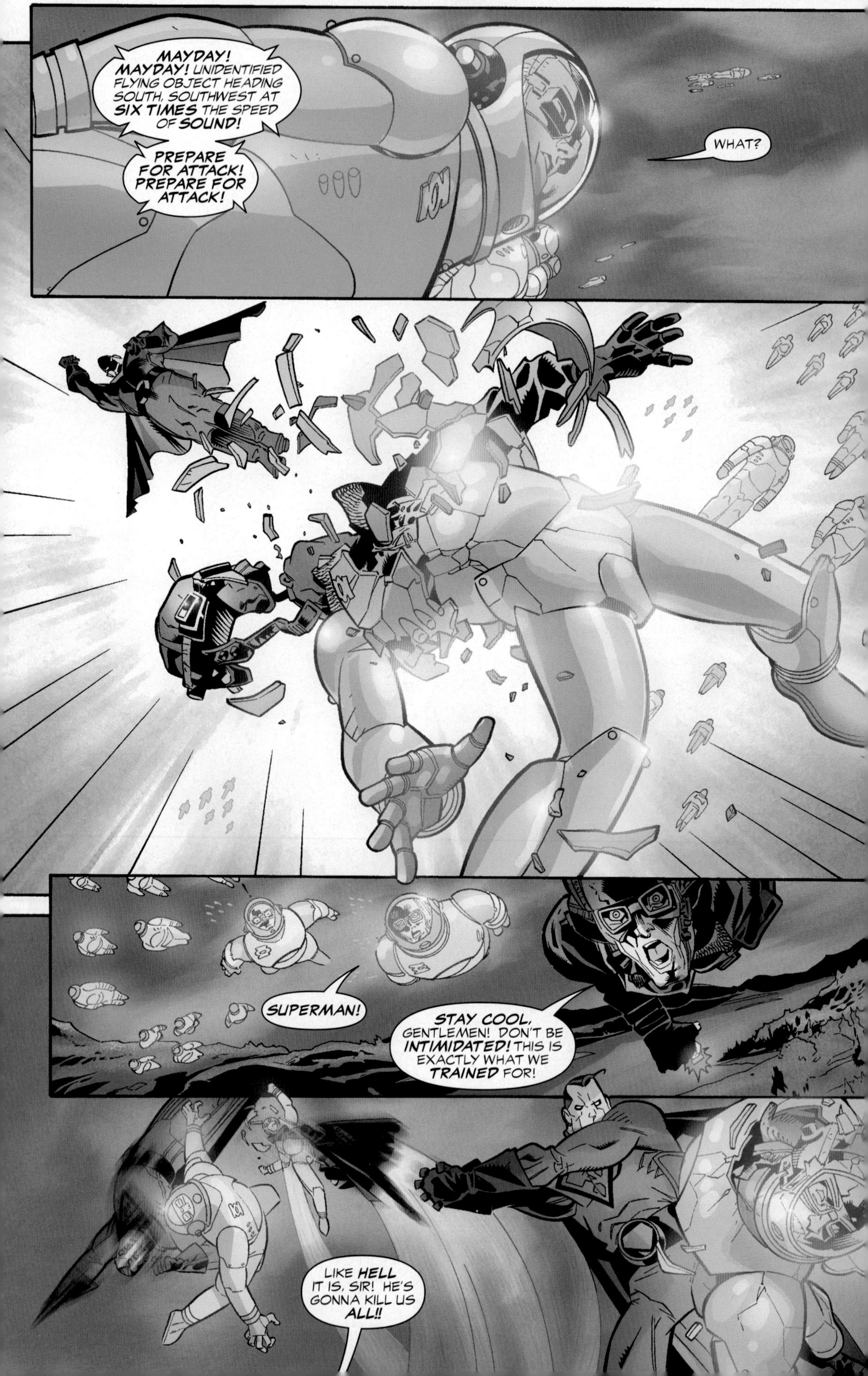
MAYDAY! MAYDAY! UNIDENTIFIED FLYING OBJECT HEADING SOUTH, SOUTHWEST AT SIX TIMES THE SPEED OF SOUND!
PREPARE FOR ATTACK! PREPARE FOR ATTACK!
WHAT?
SUPERMAN!
STAY COOL, GENTLEMEN! DON'T BE INTIMIDATED! THIS IS EXACTLY WHAT WE TRAINED FOR!
LIKE HELL IT IS, SIR! HE'S GONNA KILL US ALL!!

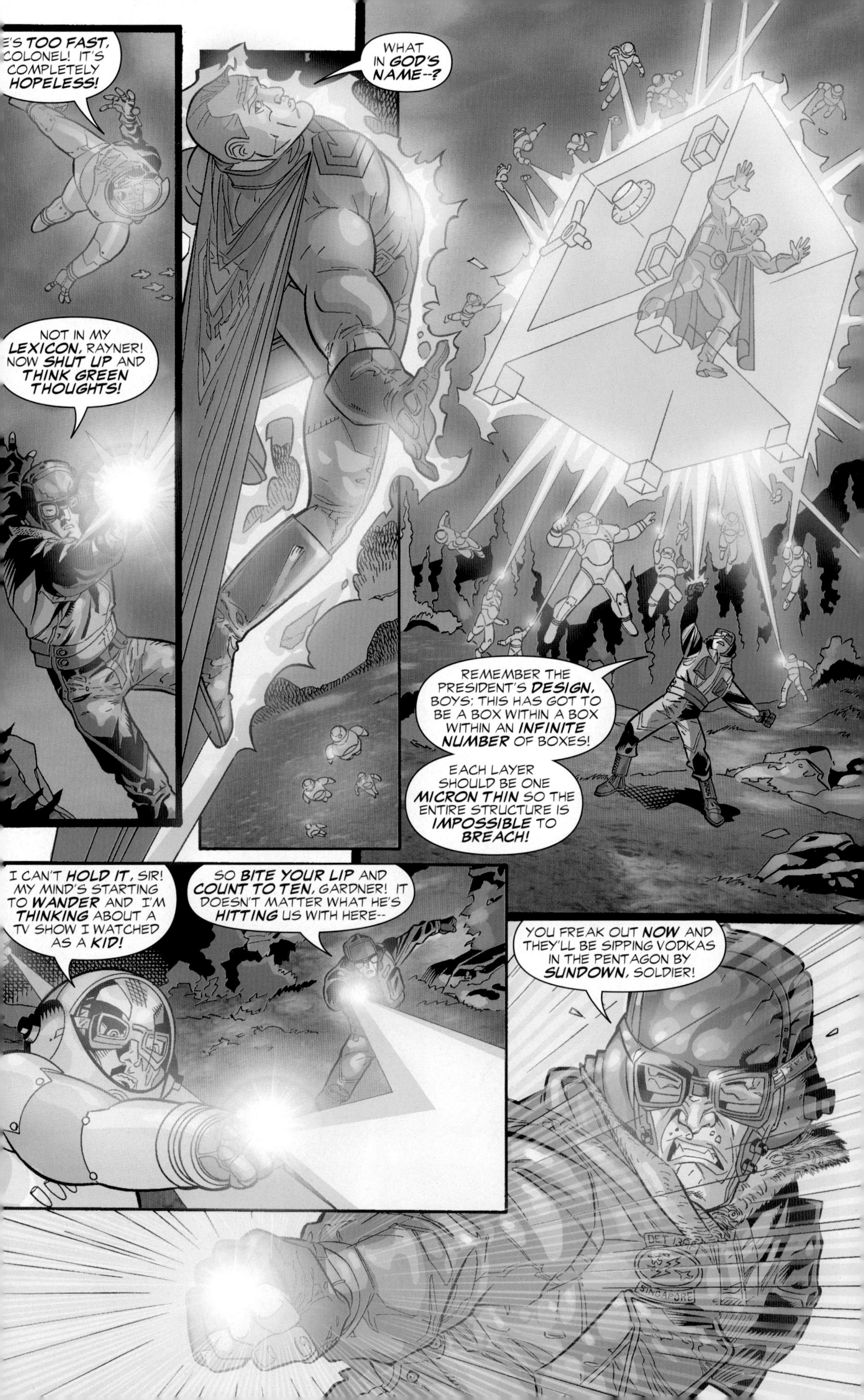

E'S TOO FAST, COLONEL! IT'S COMPLETELY HOPELESS!
WHAT IN GOD'S NAME--?
NOT IN MY LEXICON, RAYNER! NOW SHUT UP AND THINK GREEN THOUGHTS!
REMEMBER THE PRESIDENT'S DESIGN, BOYS; THIS HAS GOT TO BE A BOX WITHIN A BOX WITHIN AN INFINITE NUMBER OF BOXES!
EACH LAYER SHOULD BE ONE MICRON THIN SO THE ENTIRE STRUCTURE IS IMPOSSIBLE TO BREACH!
I CAN'T HOLD IT, SIR! MY MIND'S STARTING TO WANDER AND I'M THINKING ABOUT A TV SHOW I WATCHED AS A KID!
SO BITE YOUR LIP AND COUNT TO TEN, GARDNER! IT DOESN'T MATTER WHAT HE'S HITTING US WITH HERE--
YOU FREAK OUT NOW AND THEY'LL BE SIPPING VODKAS IN THE PENTAGON BY SUNDOWN, SOLDIER!
SINGAPORE

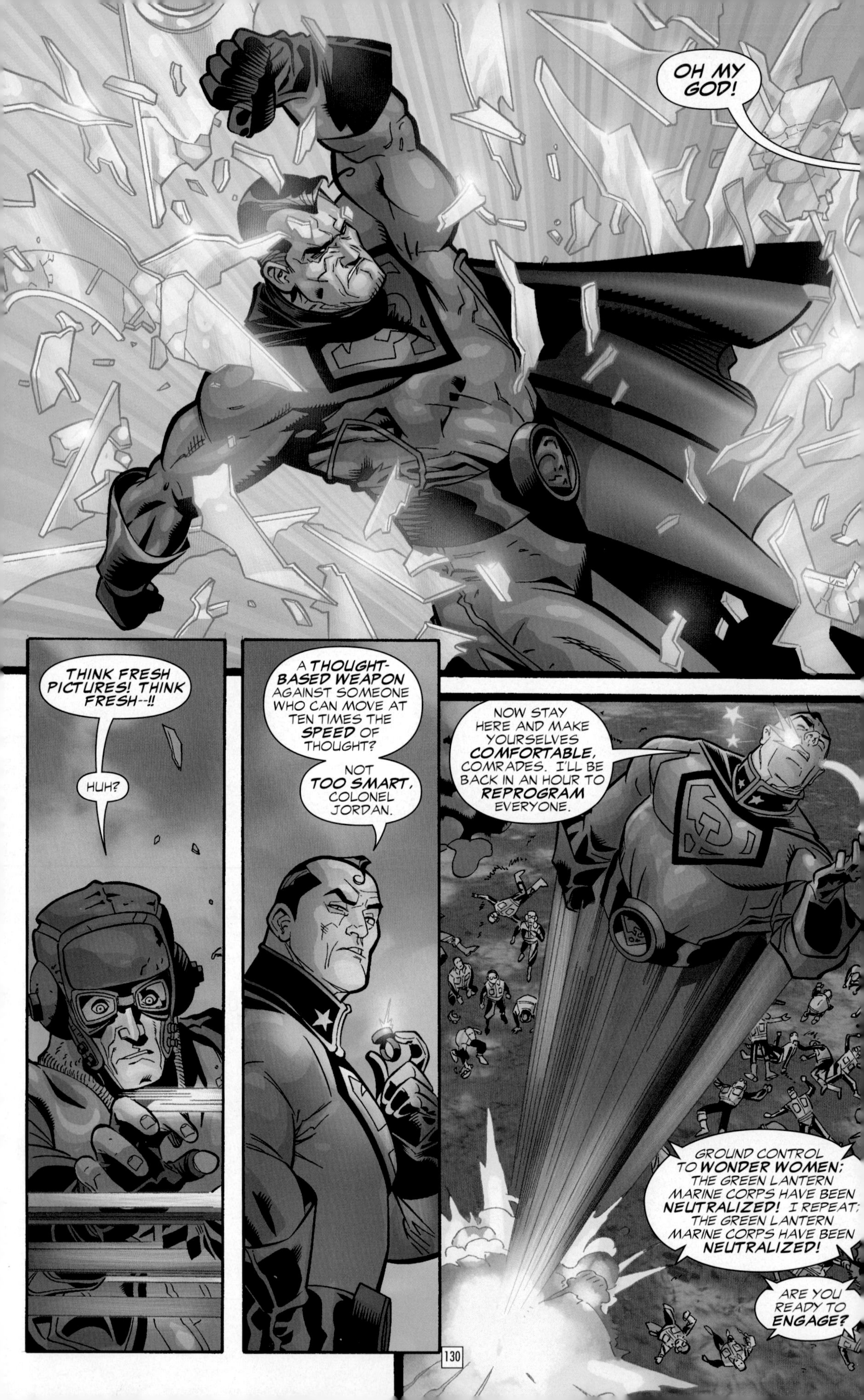
OH MY GOD!
THINK FRESH PICTURES! THINK FRESH--!!
HUH?
A THOUGHT-BASED WEAPON AGAINST SOMEONE WHO CAN MOVE AT TEN TIMES THE SPEED OF THOUGHT?
NOT TOO SMART, COLONEL JORDAN.
NOW STAY HERE AND MAKE YOURSELVES COMFORTABLE, COMRADES. I'LL BE BACK IN AN HOUR TO REPROGRAM EVERYONE.
GROUND CONTROL TO WONDER WOMEN; THE GREEN LANTERN MARINE CORPS HAVE BEEN NEUTRALIZED! I REPEAT; THE GREEN LANTERN MARINE CORPS HAVE BEEN NEUTRALIZED!
ARE YOU READY TO ENGAGE?

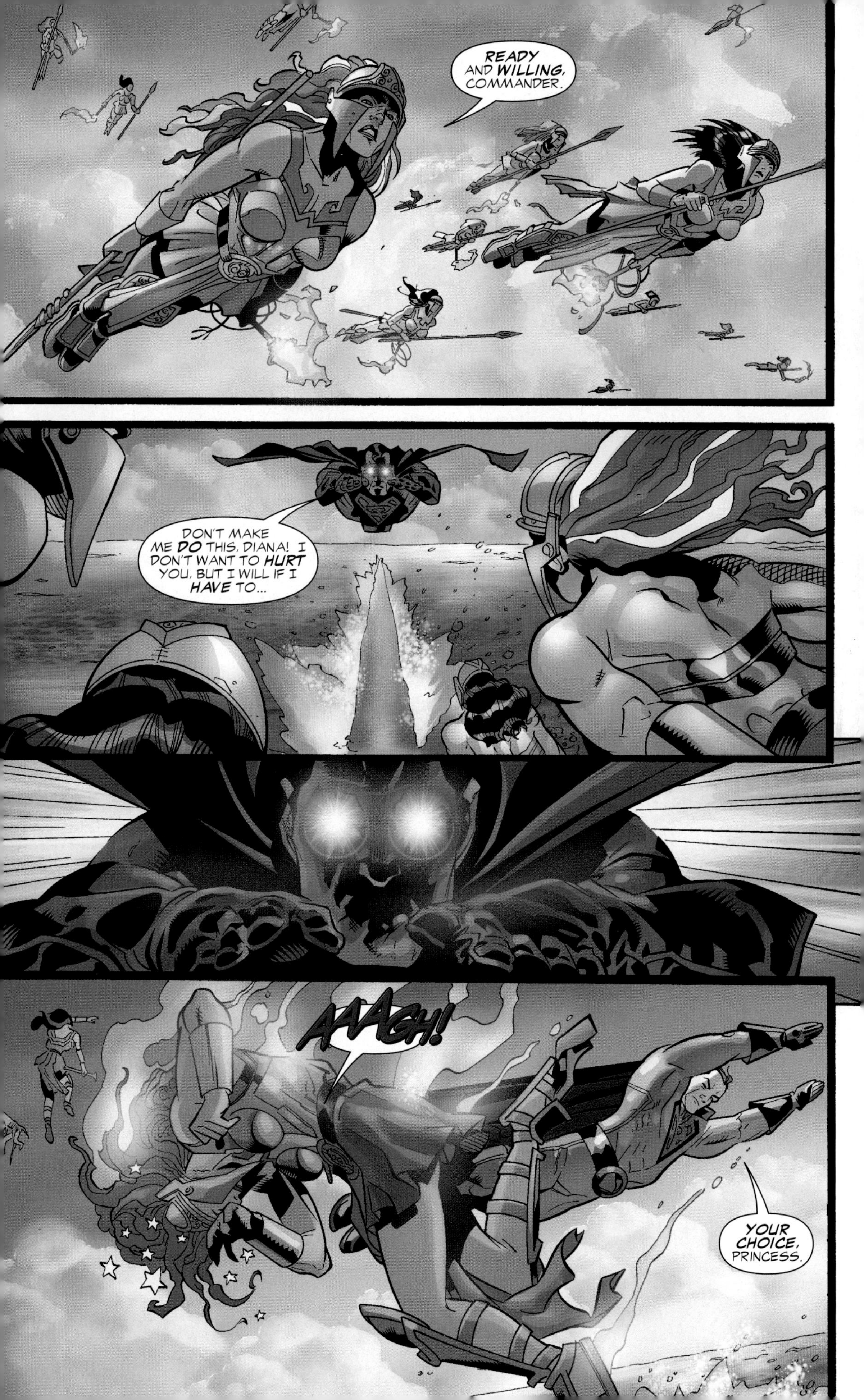
READY AND WILLING, COMMANDER.
DON'T MAKE ME DO THIS, DIANA! I DON'T WANT TO HURT YOU, BUT I WILL IF I HAVE TO...
AAAGH!
YOUR CHOICE, PRINCESS.

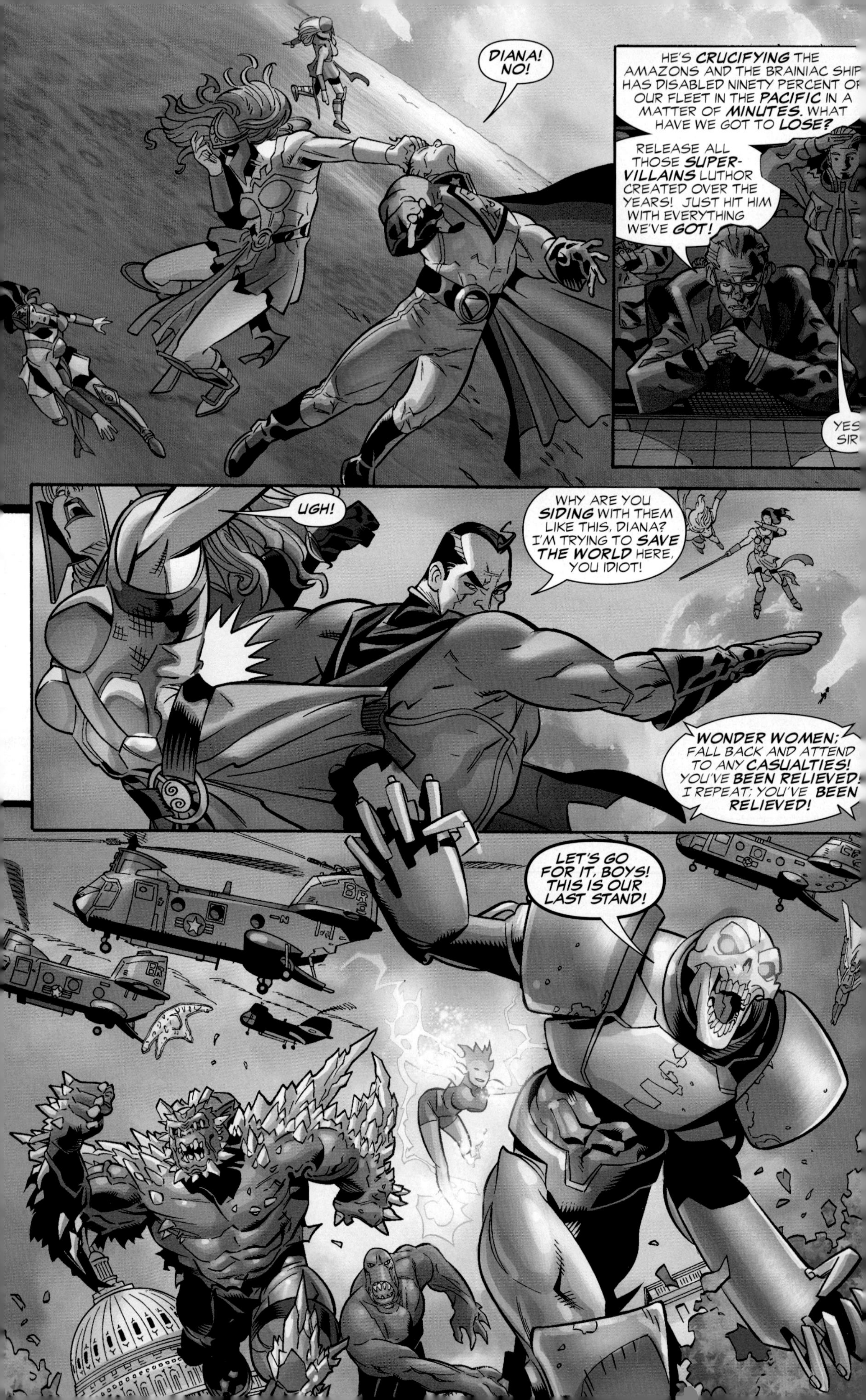
DIANA! NO!
HE'S CRUCIFYING THE AMAZONS AND THE BRAINIAC SHIP HAS DISABLED NINETY PERCENT OF OUR FLEET IN THE PACIFIC IN A MATTER OF MINUTES. WHAT HAVE WE GOT TO LOSE?
RELEASE ALL THOSE SUPER-VILLAINS LUTHOR CREATED OVER THE YEARS! JUST HIT HIM WITH EVERYTHING WE'VE GOT!
YES SIR
UGH!
WHY ARE YOU SIDING WITH THEM LIKE THIS, DIANA? I'M TRYING TO SAVE THE WORLD HERE, YOU IDIOT!
WONDER WOMEN; FALL BACK AND ATTEND TO ANY CASUALTIES! YOU'VE BEEN RELIEVED! I REPEAT; YOU'VE BEEN RELIEVED!
LET'S GO FOR IT, BOYS! THIS IS OUR LAST STAND!

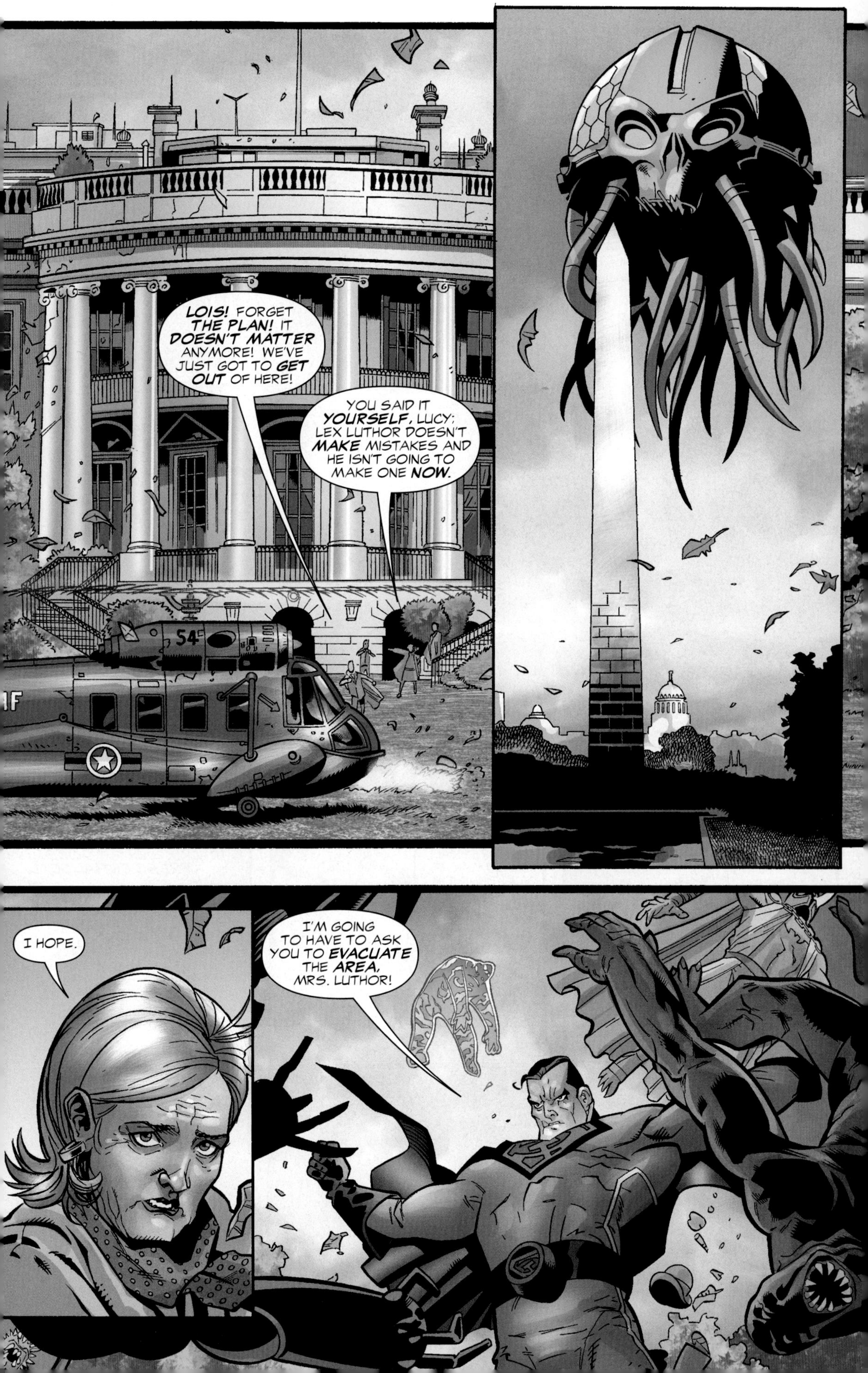
LOIS! FORGET THE PLAN! IT DOESN'T MATTER ANYMORE! WE'VE JUST GOT TO GET OUT OF HERE!
YOU SAID IT YOURSELF, LUCY; LEX LUTHOR DOESN'T MAKE MISTAKES AND HE ISN'T GOING TO MAKE ONE NOW.
I HOPE.
I'M GOING TO HAVE TO ASK YOU TO EVACUATE THE AREA, MRS. LUTHOR!

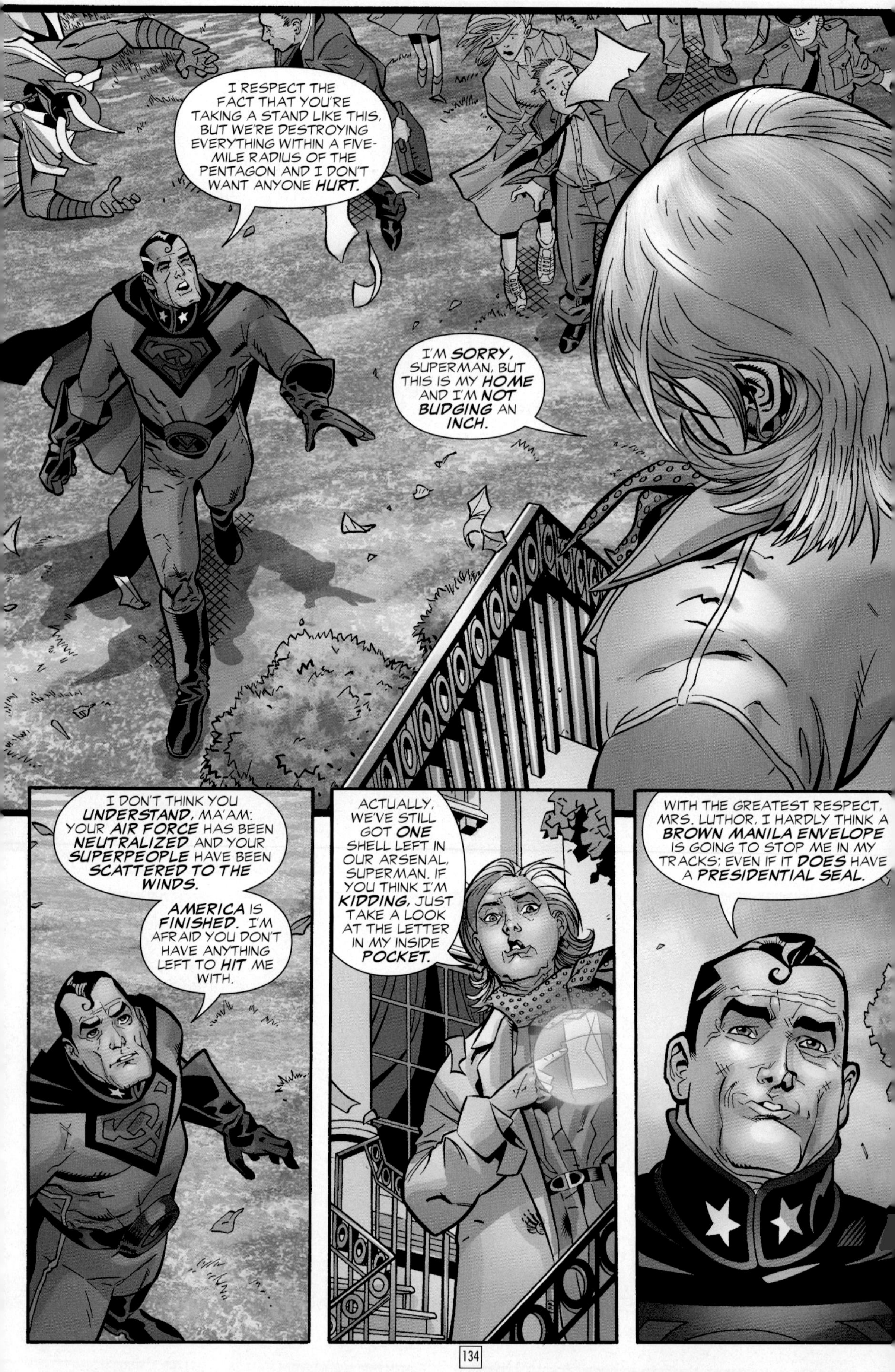

I RESPECT THE FACT THAT YOU'RE TAKING A STAND LIKE THIS, BUT WE'RE DESTROYING EVERYTHING WITHIN A FIVE-MILE RADIUS OF THE PENTAGON AND I DON'T WANT ANYONE HURT.
I'M SORRY, SUPERMAN, BUT THIS IS MY HOME AND I'M NOT BUDGING AN INCH.
I DON'T THINK YOU UNDERSTAND, MA'AM: YOUR AIR FORCE HAS BEEN NEUTRALIZED AND YOUR SUPERPEOPLE HAVE BEEN SCATTERED TO THE WINDS.
AMERICA IS FINISHED. I'M AFRAID YOU DON'T HAVE ANYTHING LEFT TO HIT ME WITH.
ACTUALLY, WE'VE STILL GOT ONE SHELL LEFT IN OUR ARSENAL, SUPERMAN. IF YOU THINK I'M KIDDING, JUST TAKE A LOOK AT THE LETTER IN MY INSIDE POCKET.
WITH THE GREATEST RESPECT, MRS. LUTHOR, I HARDLY THINK A BROWN MANILA ENVELOPE IS GOING TO STOP ME IN MY TRACKS; EVEN IF IT DOES HAVE A PRESIDENTIAL SEAL.

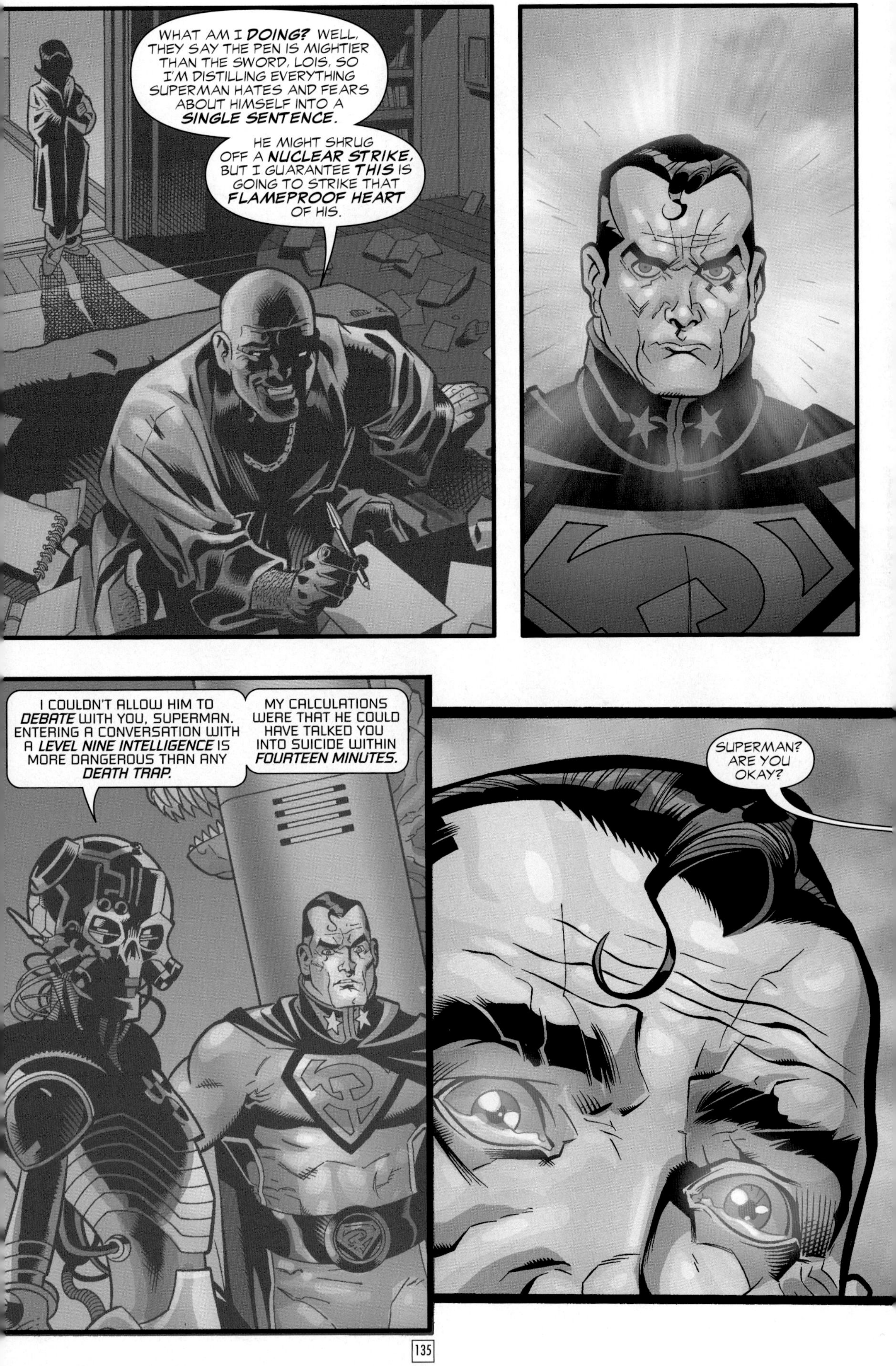
WHAT AM I DOING? WELL, THEY SAY THE PEN IS MIGHTIER THAN THE SWORD, LOIS, SO I'M DISTILLING EVERYTHING SUPERMAN HATES AND FEARS ABOUT HIMSELF INTO A SINGLE SENTENCE.
HE MIGHT SHRUG OFF A NUCLEAR STRIKE, BUT I GUARANTEE THIS IS GOING TO STRIKE THAT FLAMEPROOF HEART OF HIS.
I COULDN'T ALLOW HIM TO DEBATE WITH YOU, SUPERMAN. ENTERING A CONVERSATION WITH A LEVEL NINE INTELLIGENCE IS MORE DANGEROUS THAN ANY DEATH TRAP.
MY CALCULATIONS WERE THAT HE COULD HAVE TALKED YOU INTO SUICIDE WITHIN FOURTEEN MINUTES.
SUPERMAN? ARE YOU OKAY?

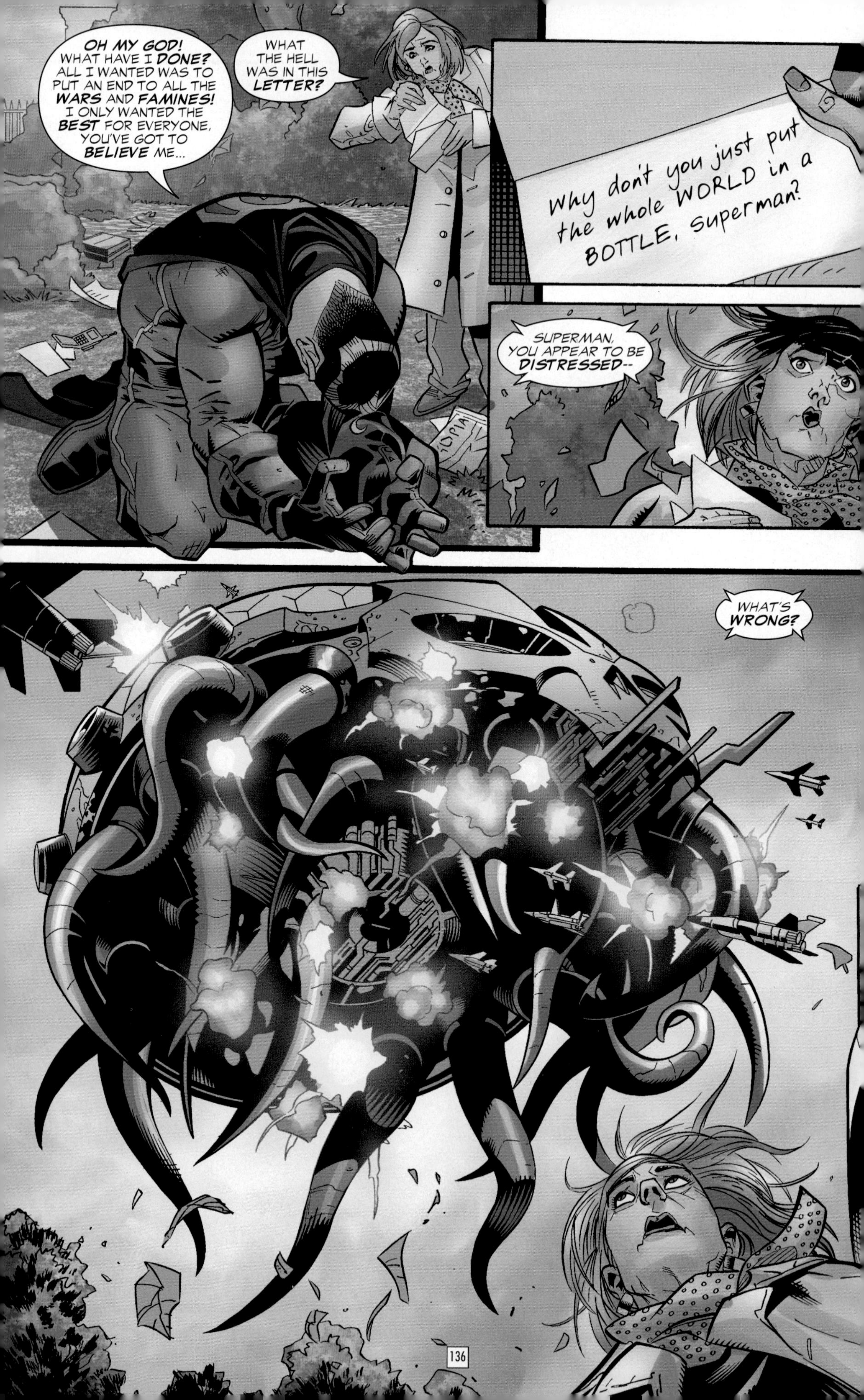
OH MY GOD! WHAT HAVE I DONE? ALL I WANTED WAS TO PUT AN END TO ALL THE WARS AND FAMINES! I ONLY WANTED THE BEST FOR EVERYONE, YOU'VE GOT TO BELIEVE ME...
WHAT THE HELL WAS IN THIS LETTER?
Why don't you just put the whole WORLD in a BOTTLE, Superman?
SUPERMAN, YOU APPEAR TO BE DISTRESSED--
WHAT'S WRONG?

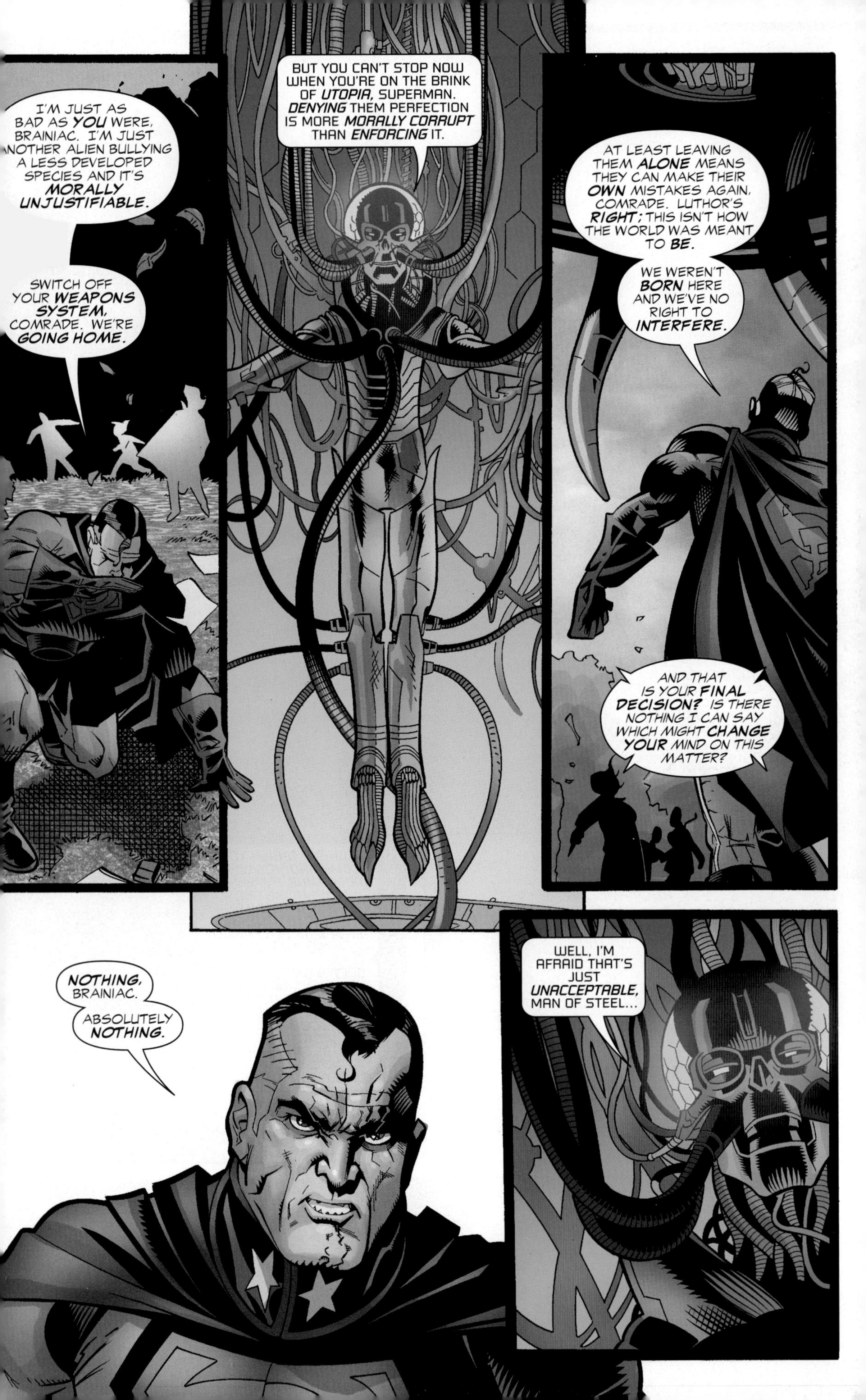

I'M JUST AS BAD AS YOU WERE, BRAINIAC. I'M JUST ANOTHER ALIEN BULLYING A LESS DEVELOPED SPECIES AND IT'S MORALLY UNJUSTIFIABLE.
SWITCH OFF YOUR WEAPONS SYSTEM, COMRADE. WE'RE GOING HOME.
BUT YOU CAN'T STOP NOW WHEN YOU'RE ON THE BRINK OF UTOPIA, SUPERMAN. DENYING THEM PERFECTION IS MORE MORALLY CORRUPT THAN ENFORCING IT.
AT LEAST LEAVING THEM ALONE MEANS THEY CAN MAKE THEIR OWN MISTAKES AGAIN, COMRADE. LUTHOR'S RIGHT; THIS ISN'T HOW THE WORLD WAS MEANT TO BE.
WE WEREN'T BORN HERE AND WE'VE NO RIGHT TO INTERFERE.
AND THAT IS YOUR FINAL DECISION? IS THERE NOTHING I CAN SAY WHICH MIGHT CHANGE YOUR MIND ON THIS MATTER?
NOTHING, BRAINIAC.
ABSOLUTELY NOTHING.
WELL, I'M AFRAID THAT'S JUST UNACCEPTABLE, MAN OF STEEL...

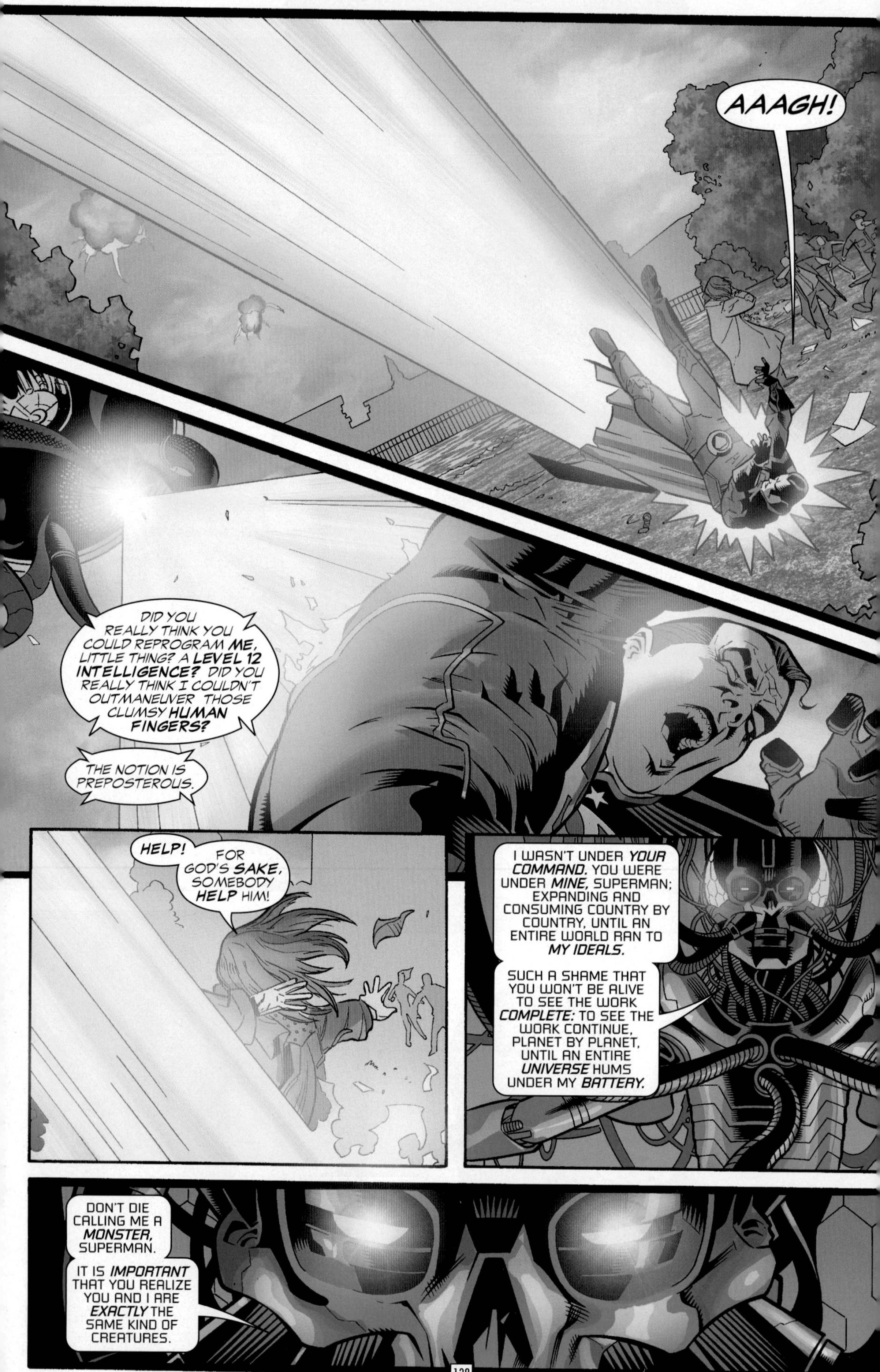
AAAGH!
DID YOU REALLY THINK YOU COULD REPROGRAM ME, LITTLE THING? A LEVEL 12 INTELLIGENCE? DID YOU REALLY THINK I COULDN'T OUTMANEUVER THOSE CLUMSY HUMAN FINGERS?
THE NOTION IS PREPOSTEROUS.
HELP!
FOR GOD'S SAKE, SOMEBODY HELP HIM!
I WASN'T UNDER YOUR COMMAND. YOU WERE UNDER MINE, SUPERMAN; EXPANDING AND CONSUMING COUNTRY BY COUNTRY, UNTIL AN ENTIRE WORLD RAN TO MY IDEALS.
SUCH A SHAME THAT YOU WON'T BE ALIVE TO SEE THE WORK COMPLETE: TO SEE THE WORK CONTINUE, PLANET BY PLANET, UNTIL AN ENTIRE UNIVERSE HUMS UNDER MY BATTERY.
DON'T DIE CALLING ME A MONSTER, SUPERMAN.
IT IS IMPORTANT THAT YOU REALIZE YOU AND I ARE EXACTLY THE SAME KIND OF CREATURES.

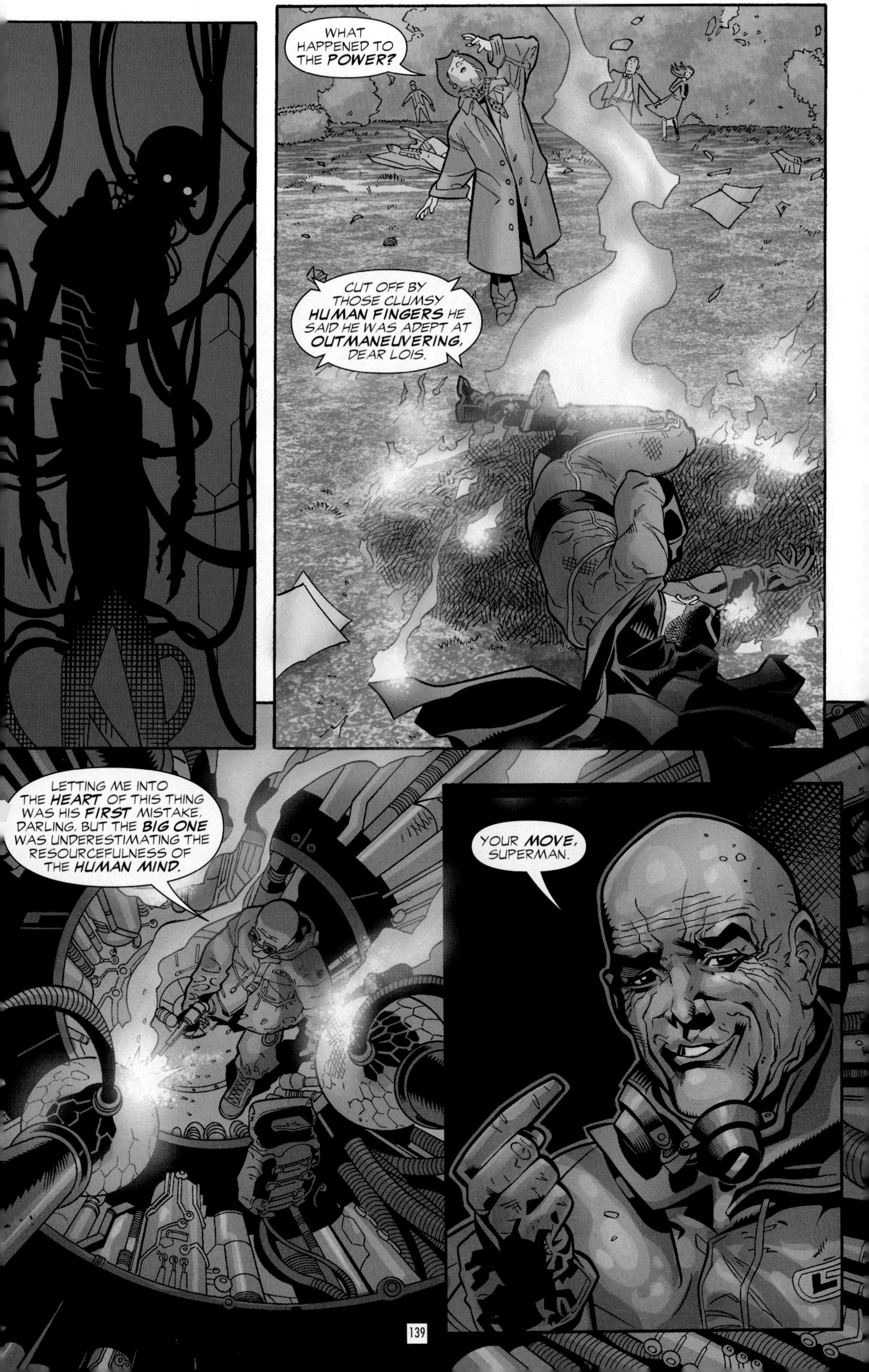
WHAT HAPPENED TO THE POWER?
CUT OFF BY THOSE CLUMSY HUMAN FINGERS HE SAID HE WAS ADEPT AT OUTMANEUVERING, DEAR LOIS.
LETTING ME INTO THE HEART OF THIS THING WAS HIS FIRST MISTAKE, DARLING, BUT THE BIG ONE WAS UNDERESTIMATING THE RESOURCEFULNESS OF THE HUMAN MIND.
YOUR MOVE, SUPERMAN.

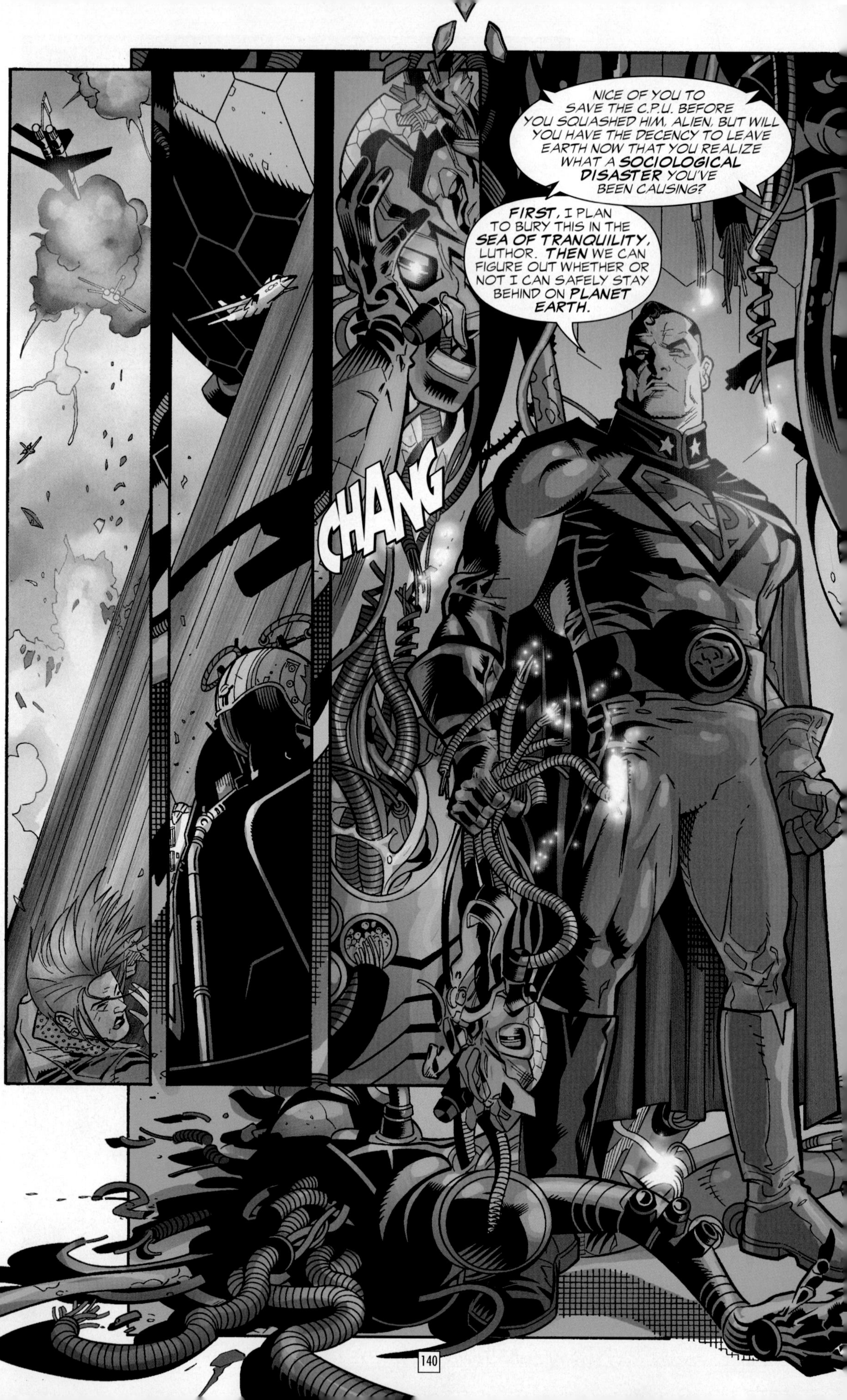
NICE OF YOU TO SAVE THE C.P.U. BEFORE YOU SQUASHED HIM, ALIEN, BUT WILL YOU HAVE THE DECENCY TO LEAVE EARTH NOW THAT YOU REALIZE WHAT A **SOCIOLOGICAL DISASTER** YOU'VE BEEN CAUSING?
FIRST, I PLAN TO BURY THIS IN THE **SEA OF TRANQUILITY,** LUTHOR. **THEN** WE CAN FIGURE OUT WHETHER OR NOT I CAN SAFELY STAY BEHIND ON **PLANET EARTH.**
CHANG

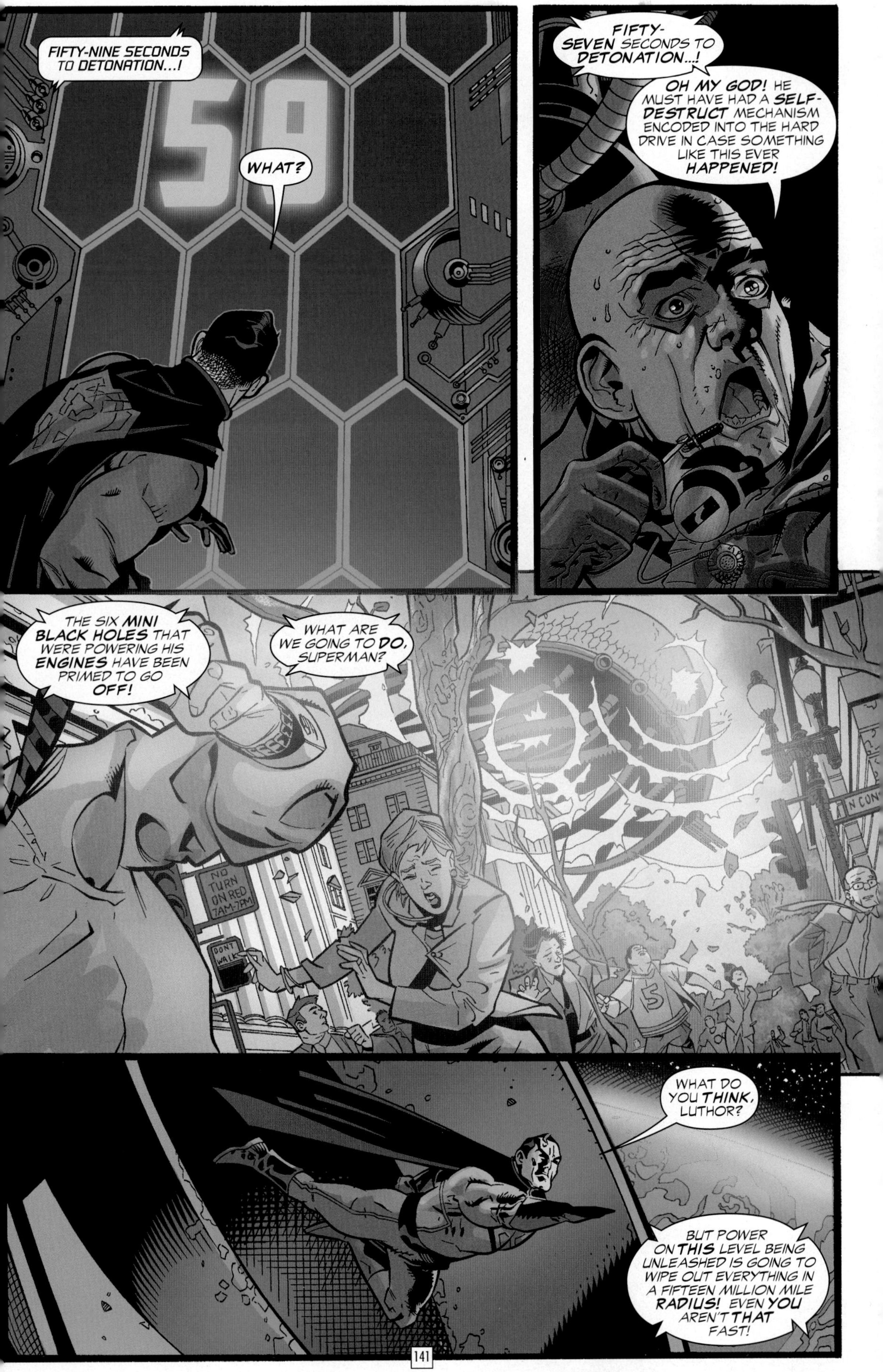
FIFTY-NINE SECONDS TO DETONATION...!
59
WHAT?
FIFTY-SEVEN SECONDS TO DETONATION...!
OH MY GOD! HE MUST HAVE HAD A SELF-DESTRUCT MECHANISM ENCODED INTO THE HARD DRIVE IN CASE SOMETHING LIKE THIS EVER HAPPENED!
THE SIX MINI BLACK HOLES THAT WERE POWERING HIS ENGINES HAVE BEEN PRIMED TO GO OFF!
WHAT ARE WE GOING TO DO, SUPERMAN?
NO TURN ON RED 7AM-7PM
DON'T WALK
WHAT DO YOU THINK, LUTHOR?
BUT POWER ON THIS LEVEL BEING UNLEASHED IS GOING TO WIPE OUT EVERYTHING IN A FIFTEEN MILLION MILE RADIUS! EVEN YOU AREN'T THAT FAST!

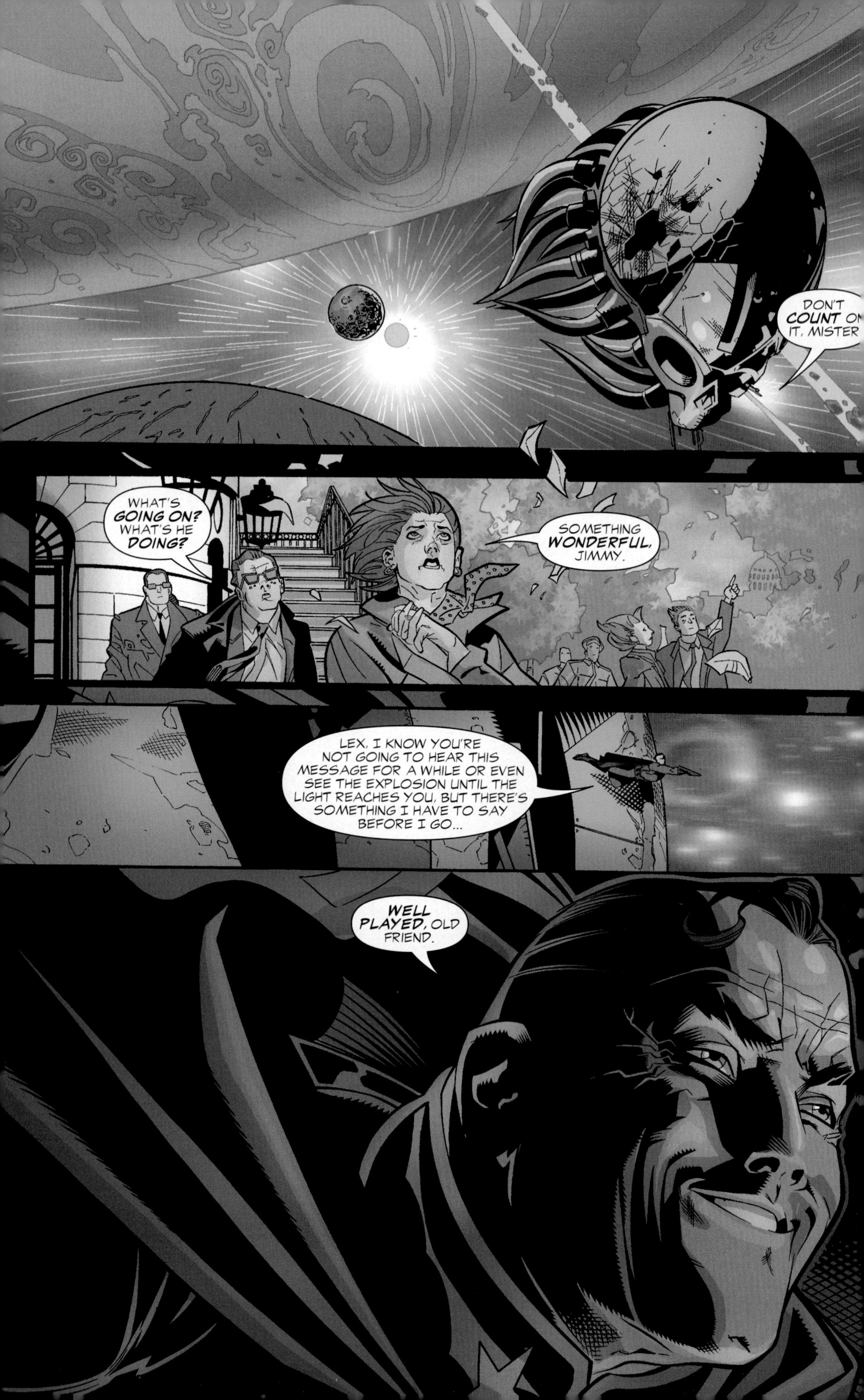

DON'T COUNT ON IT, MISTER
WHAT'S GOING ON? WHAT'S HE DOING?
SOMETHING WONDERFUL, JIMMY.
LEX, I KNOW YOU'RE NOT GOING TO HEAR THIS MESSAGE FOR A WHILE OR EVEN SEE THE EXPLOSION UNTIL THE LIGHT REACHES YOU, BUT THERE'S SOMETHING I HAVE TO SAY BEFORE I GO...
WELL PLAYED, OLD FRIEND.

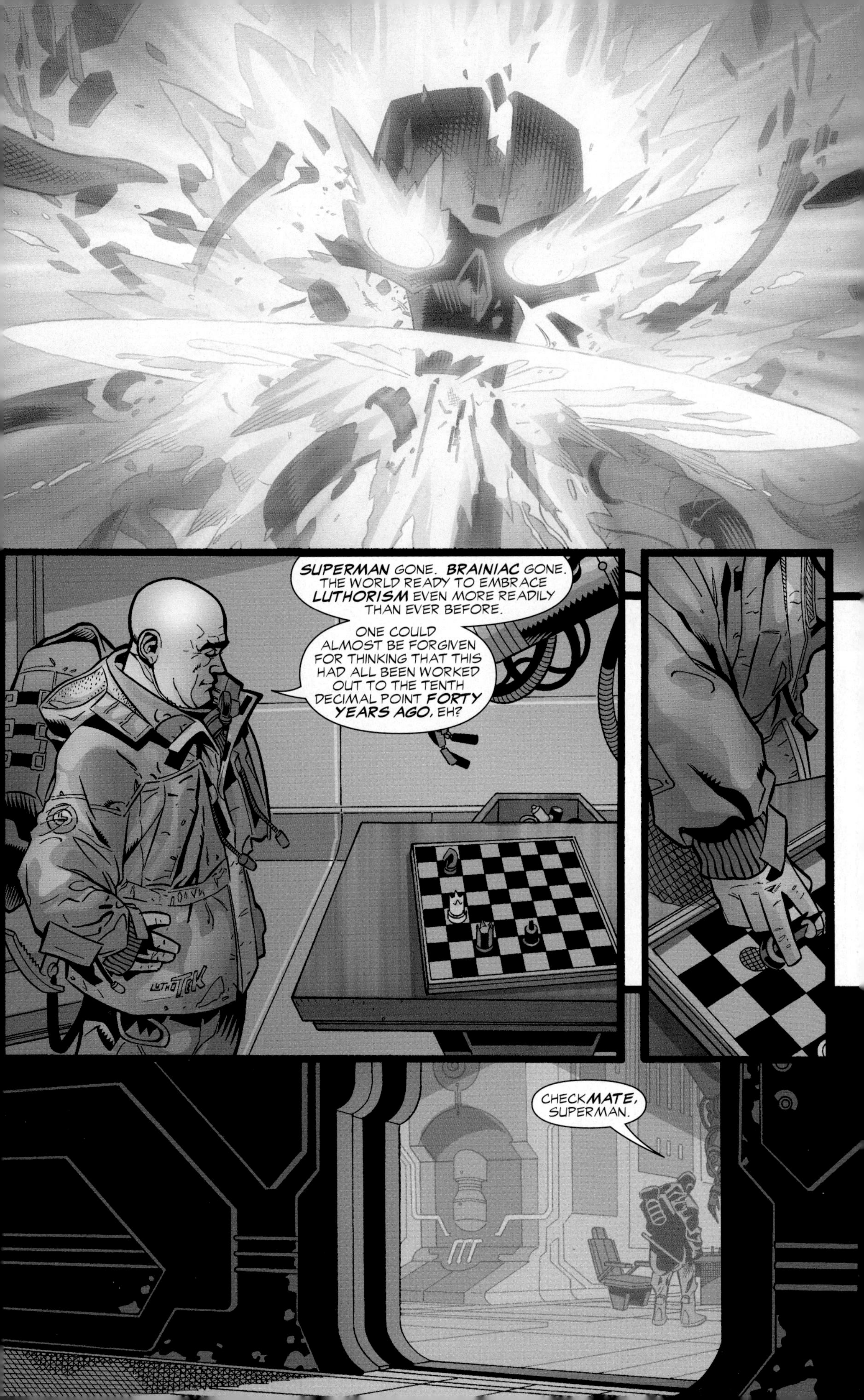

SUPERMAN GONE. BRAINIAC GONE. THE WORLD READY TO EMBRACE LUTHORISM EVEN MORE READILY THAN EVER BEFORE.
ONE COULD ALMOST BE FORGIVEN FOR THINKING THAT THIS HAD ALL BEEN WORKED OUT TO THE TENTH DECIMAL POINT FORTY YEARS AGO, EH?
LUTHOTEK
CHECKMATE, SUPERMAN.

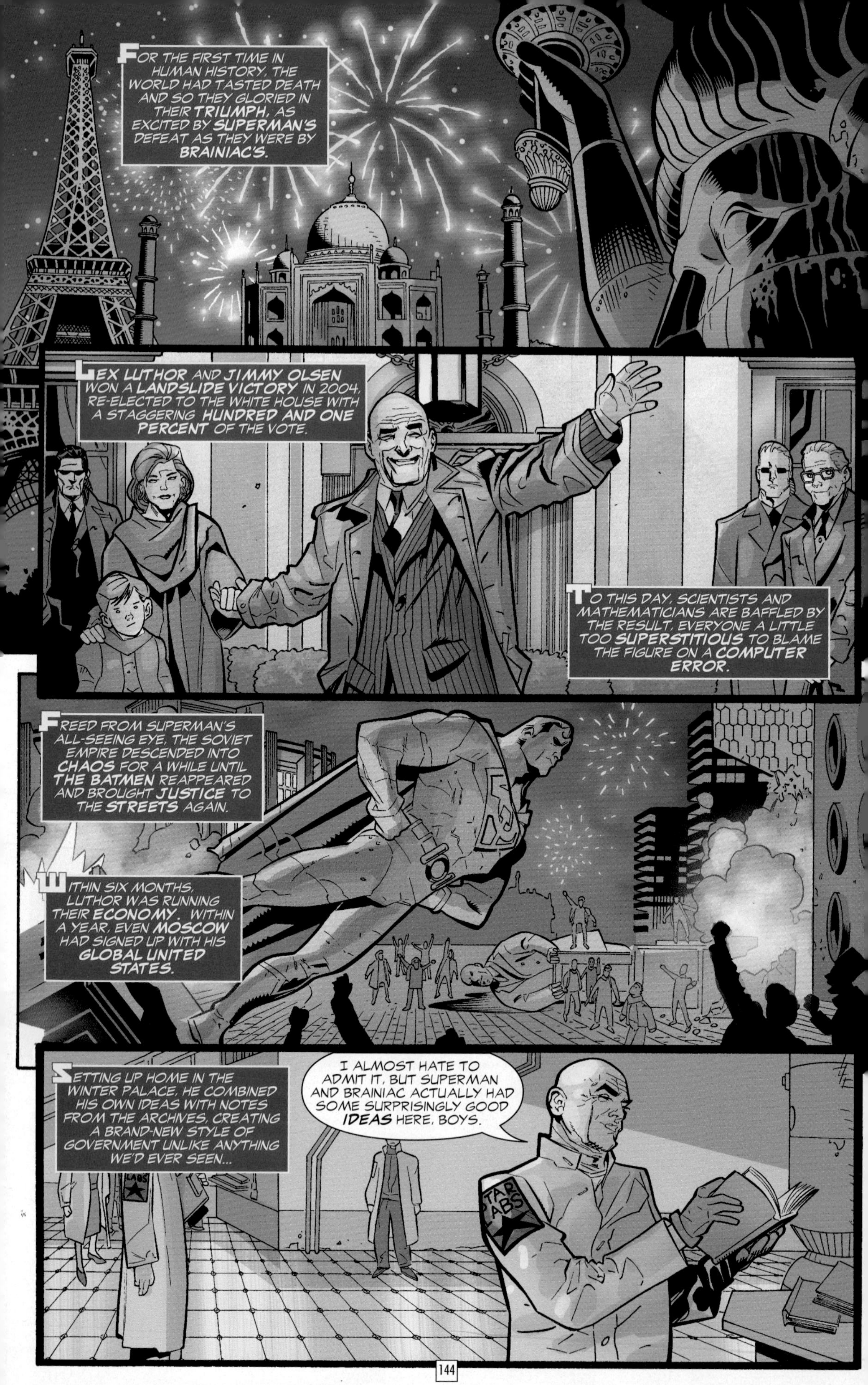
FOR THE FIRST TIME IN HUMAN HISTORY, THE WORLD HAD TASTED DEATH AND SO THEY GLORIED IN THEIR TRIUMPH, AS EXCITED BY SUPERMAN'S DEFEAT AS THEY WERE BY BRAINIAC'S.
LEX LUTHOR AND JIMMY OLSEN WON A LANDSLIDE VICTORY IN 2004, RE-ELECTED TO THE WHITE HOUSE WITH A STAGGERING HUNDRED AND ONE PERCENT OF THE VOTE.
TO THIS DAY, SCIENTISTS AND MATHEMATICIANS ARE BAFFLED BY THE RESULT, EVERYONE A LITTLE TOO SUPERSTITIOUS TO BLAME THE FIGURE ON A COMPUTER ERROR.
FREED FROM SUPERMAN'S ALL-SEEING EYE, THE SOVIET EMPIRE DESCENDED INTO CHAOS FOR A WHILE UNTIL THE BATMEN REAPPEARED AND BROUGHT JUSTICE TO THE STREETS AGAIN.
WITHIN SIX MONTHS, LUTHOR WAS RUNNING THEIR ECONOMY. WITHIN A YEAR, EVEN MOSCOW HAD SIGNED UP WITH HIS GLOBAL UNITED STATES.
SETTING UP HOME IN THE WINTER PALACE, HE COMBINED HIS OWN IDEAS WITH NOTES FROM THE ARCHIVES, CREATING A BRAND-NEW STYLE OF GOVERNMENT UNLIKE ANYTHING WE'D EVER SEEN...
I ALMOST HATE TO ADMIT IT, BUT SUPERMAN AND BRAINIAC ACTUALLY HAD SOME SURPRISINGLY GOOD IDEAS HERE, BOYS.
STAR LABS

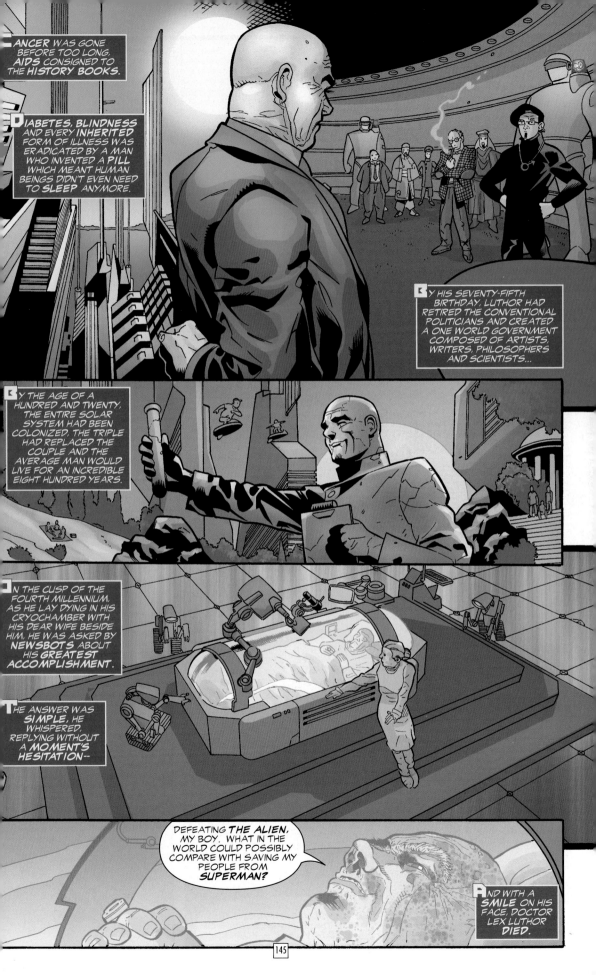

CANCER WAS GONE BEFORE TOO LONG. **AIDS** CONSIGNED TO THE **HISTORY BOOKS.**

DIABETES, BLINDNESS AND EVERY **INHERITED** FORM OF ILLNESS WAS ERADICATED BY A MAN WHO INVENTED A **PILL** WHICH MEANT HUMAN BEINGS DIDN'T EVEN NEED TO **SLEEP** ANYMORE.

BY HIS SEVENTY-FIFTH BIRTHDAY, LUTHOR HAD RETIRED THE CONVENTIONAL POLITICIANS AND CREATED A ONE WORLD GOVERNMENT COMPOSED OF ARTISTS, WRITERS, PHILOSOPHERS AND SCIENTISTS...

BY THE AGE OF A HUNDRED AND TWENTY, THE ENTIRE SOLAR SYSTEM HAD BEEN COLONIZED. THE TRIPLE HAD REPLACED THE COUPLE AND THE AVERAGE MAN WOULD LIVE FOR AN INCREDIBLE EIGHT HUNDRED YEARS.

ON THE CUSP OF THE FOURTH MILLENNIUM, AS HE LAY DYING IN HIS CRYOCHAMBER WITH HIS DEAR WIFE BESIDE HIM, HE WAS ASKED BY **NEWSBOTS** ABOUT HIS **GREATEST** ACCOMPLISHMENT.

THE ANSWER WAS **SIMPLE,** HE WHISPERED, REPLYING WITHOUT A **MOMENT'S** HESITATION--

DEFEATING **THE ALIEN,** MY BOY. WHAT IN THE WORLD COULD POSSIBLY COMPARE WITH SAVING MY PEOPLE FROM **SUPERMAN?**

AND WITH A **SMILE** ON HIS FACE, DOCTOR LEX LUTHOR **DIED.**

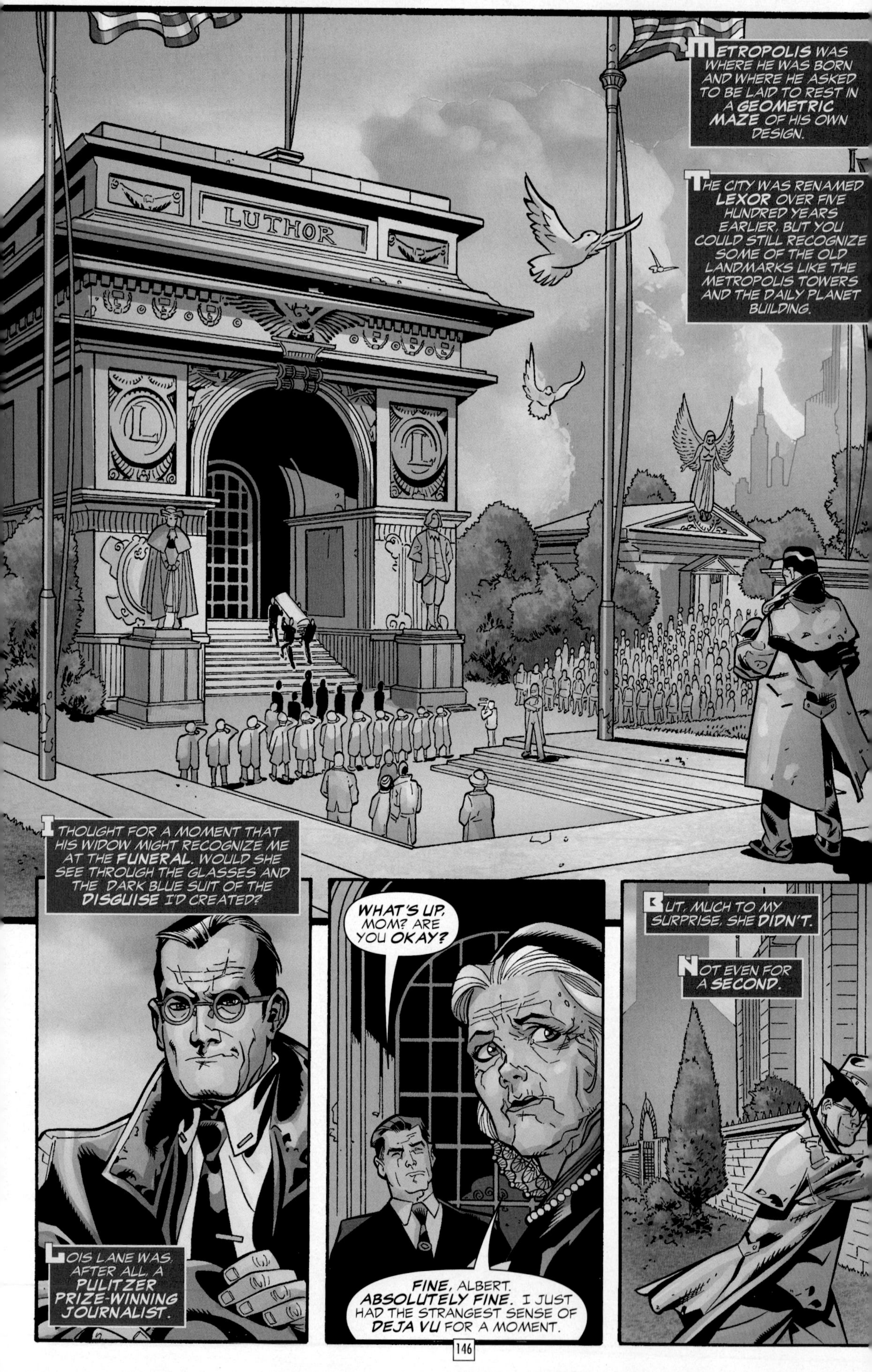
METROPOLIS WAS WHERE HE WAS BORN AND WHERE HE ASKED TO BE LAID TO REST IN A GEOMETRIC MAZE OF HIS OWN DESIGN.
THE CITY WAS RENAMED LEXOR OVER FIVE HUNDRED YEARS EARLIER, BUT YOU COULD STILL RECOGNIZE SOME OF THE OLD LANDMARKS LIKE THE METROPOLIS TOWERS AND THE DAILY PLANET BUILDING.
LUTHOR
I THOUGHT FOR A MOMENT THAT HIS WIDOW MIGHT RECOGNIZE ME AT THE FUNERAL. WOULD SHE SEE THROUGH THE GLASSES AND THE DARK BLUE SUIT OF THE DISGUISE I'D CREATED?
LOIS LANE WAS, AFTER ALL, A PULITZER PRIZE-WINNING JOURNALIST.
WHAT'S UP, MOM? ARE YOU OKAY?
FINE, ALBERT. ABSOLUTELY FINE. I JUST HAD THE STRANGEST SENSE OF DEJA VU FOR A MOMENT.
BUT, MUCH TO MY SURPRISE, SHE DIDN'T.
NOT EVEN FOR A SECOND.

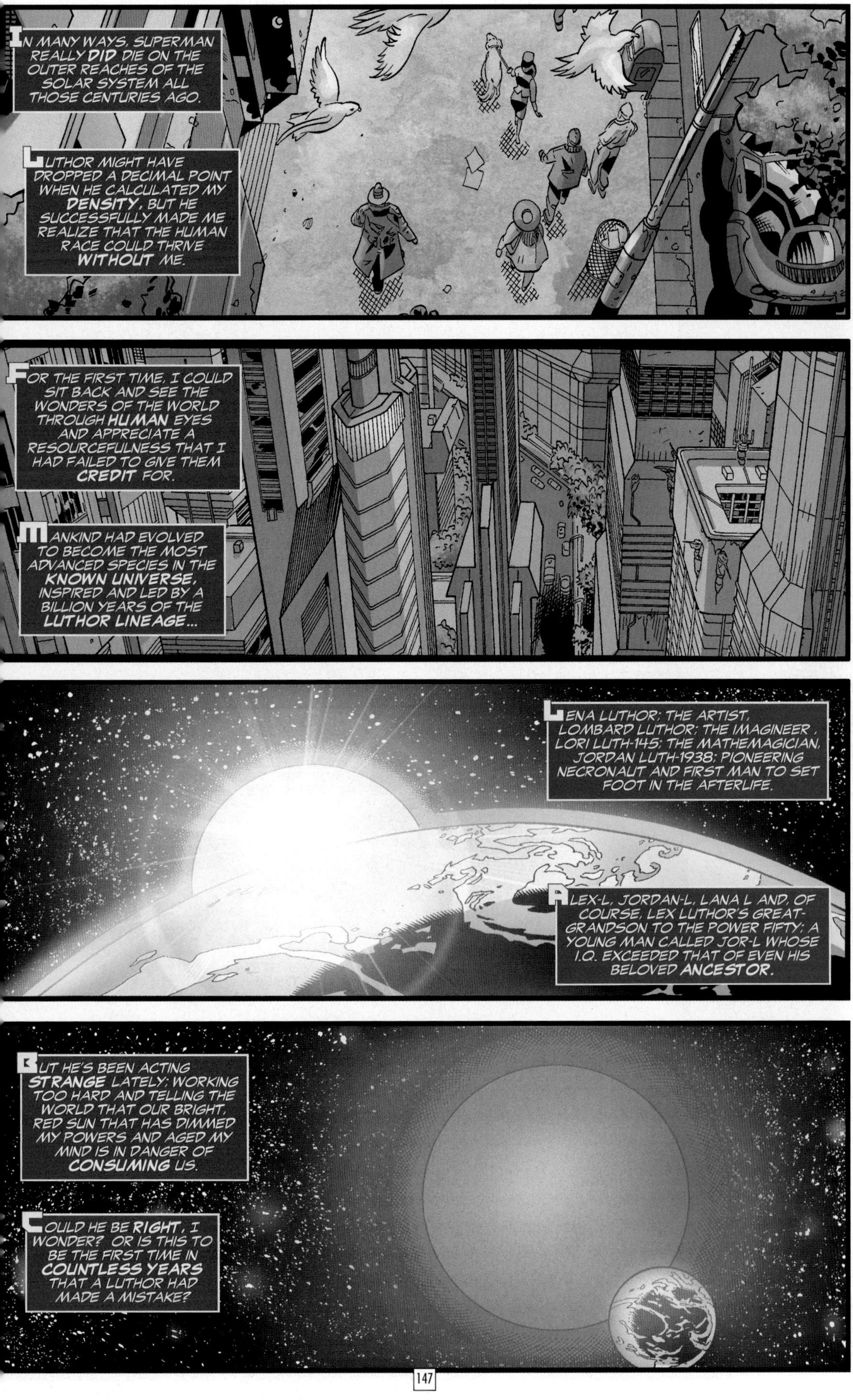
IN MANY WAYS, SUPERMAN REALLY DID DIE ON THE OUTER REACHES OF THE SOLAR SYSTEM ALL THOSE CENTURIES AGO.
LUTHOR MIGHT HAVE DROPPED A DECIMAL POINT WHEN HE CALCULATED MY DENSITY, BUT HE SUCCESSFULLY MADE ME REALIZE THAT THE HUMAN RACE COULD THRIVE WITHOUT ME.
FOR THE FIRST TIME, I COULD SIT BACK AND SEE THE WONDERS OF THE WORLD THROUGH HUMAN EYES AND APPRECIATE A RESOURCEFULNESS THAT I HAD FAILED TO GIVE THEM CREDIT FOR.
MANKIND HAD EVOLVED TO BECOME THE MOST ADVANCED SPECIES IN THE KNOWN UNIVERSE, INSPIRED AND LED BY A BILLION YEARS OF THE LUTHOR LINEAGE...
LENA LUTHOR; THE ARTIST, LOMBARD LUTHOR; THE IMAGINEER , LORI LUTH-145; THE MATHEMAGICIAN, JORDAN LUTH-1938; PIONEERING NECRONAUT AND FIRST MAN TO SET FOOT IN THE AFTERLIFE.
ALEX-L, JORDAN-L, LANA L AND, OF COURSE, LEX LUTHOR'S GREAT-GRANDSON TO THE POWER FIFTY; A YOUNG MAN CALLED JOR-L WHOSE I.Q. EXCEEDED THAT OF EVEN HIS BELOVED ANCESTOR.
BUT HE'S BEEN ACTING STRANGE LATELY; WORKING TOO HARD AND TELLING THE WORLD THAT OUR BRIGHT, RED SUN THAT HAS DIMMED MY POWERS AND AGED MY MIND IS IN DANGER OF CONSUMING US.
COULD HE BE RIGHT, I WONDER? OR IS THIS TO BE THE FIRST TIME IN COUNTLESS YEARS THAT A LUTHOR HAD MADE A MISTAKE?

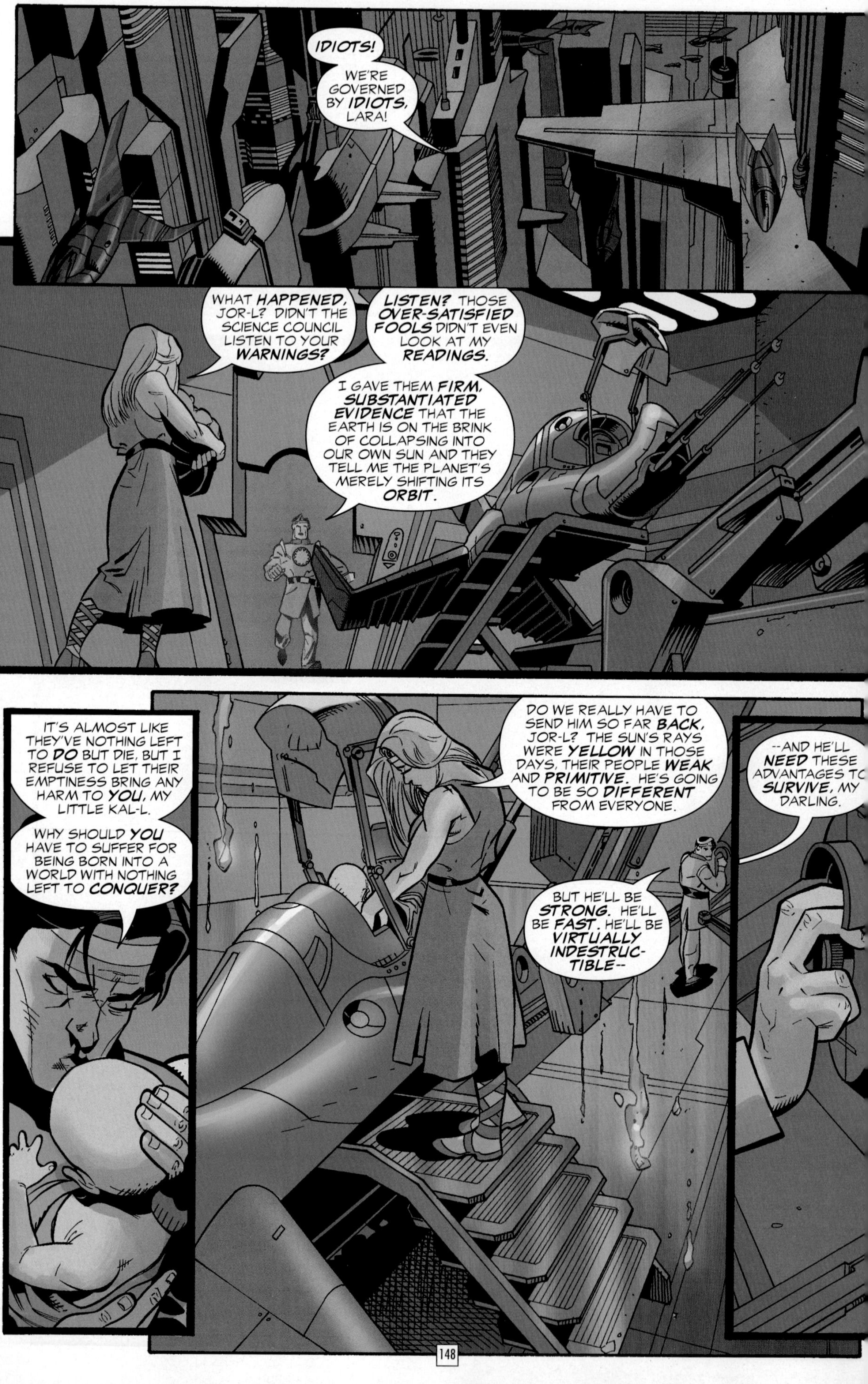
IDIOTS!
WE'RE GOVERNED BY IDIOTS, LARA!
WHAT HAPPENED, JOR-L? DIDN'T THE SCIENCE COUNCIL LISTEN TO YOUR WARNINGS?
LISTEN? THOSE OVER-SATISFIED FOOLS DIDN'T EVEN LOOK AT MY READINGS.
I GAVE THEM FIRM, SUBSTANTIATED EVIDENCE THAT THE EARTH IS ON THE BRINK OF COLLAPSING INTO OUR OWN SUN AND THEY TELL ME THE PLANET'S MERELY SHIFTING ITS ORBIT.
IT'S ALMOST LIKE THEY'VE NOTHING LEFT TO DO BUT DIE, BUT I REFUSE TO LET THEIR EMPTINESS BRING ANY HARM TO YOU, MY LITTLE KAL-L.
WHY SHOULD YOU HAVE TO SUFFER FOR BEING BORN INTO A WORLD WITH NOTHING LEFT TO CONQUER?
DO WE REALLY HAVE TO SEND HIM SO FAR BACK, JOR-L? THE SUN'S RAYS WERE YELLOW IN THOSE DAYS, THEIR PEOPLE WEAK AND PRIMITIVE. HE'S GOING TO BE SO DIFFERENT FROM EVERYONE.
BUT HE'LL BE STRONG. HE'LL BE FAST. HE'LL BE VIRTUALLY INDESTRUC-TIBLE--
--AND HE'LL NEED THESE ADVANTAGES TO SURVIVE, MY DARLING.

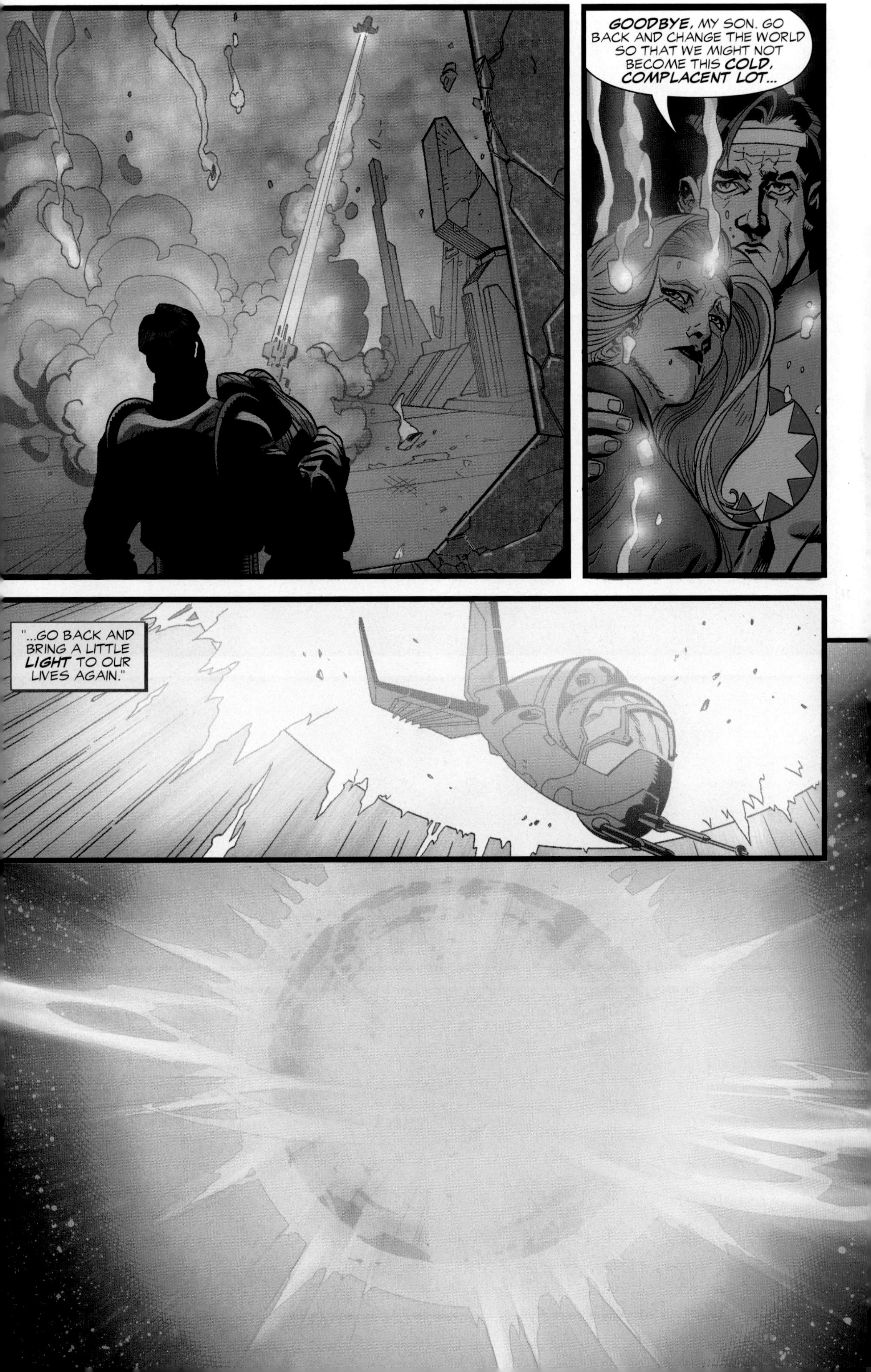
GOODBYE, MY SON. GO BACK AND CHANGE THE WORLD SO THAT WE MIGHT NOT BECOME THIS COLD, COMPLACENT LOT...
"...GO BACK AND BRING A LITTLE LIGHT TO OUR LIVES AGAIN."

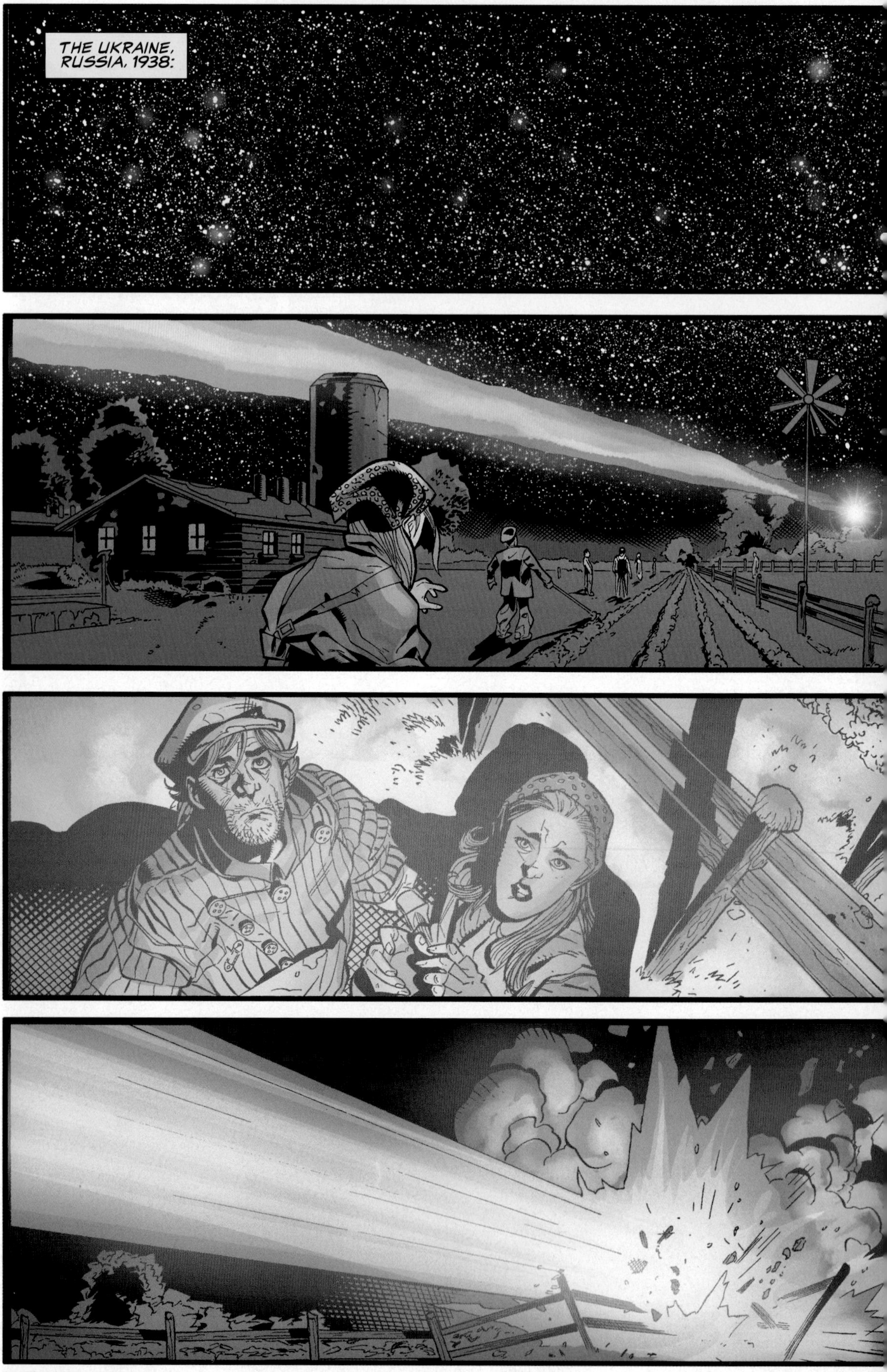
THE UKRAINE, RUSSIA, 1938:

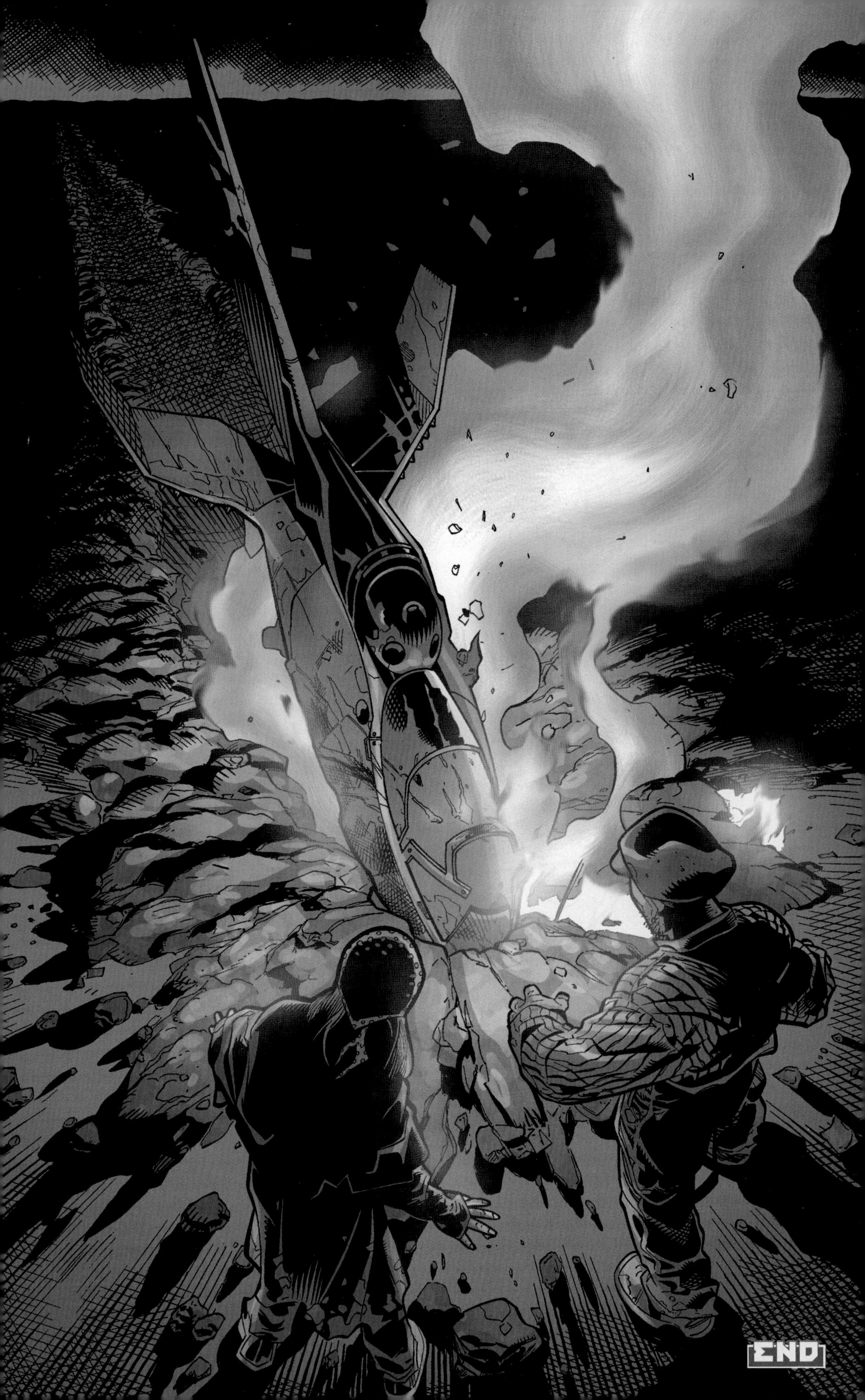
END

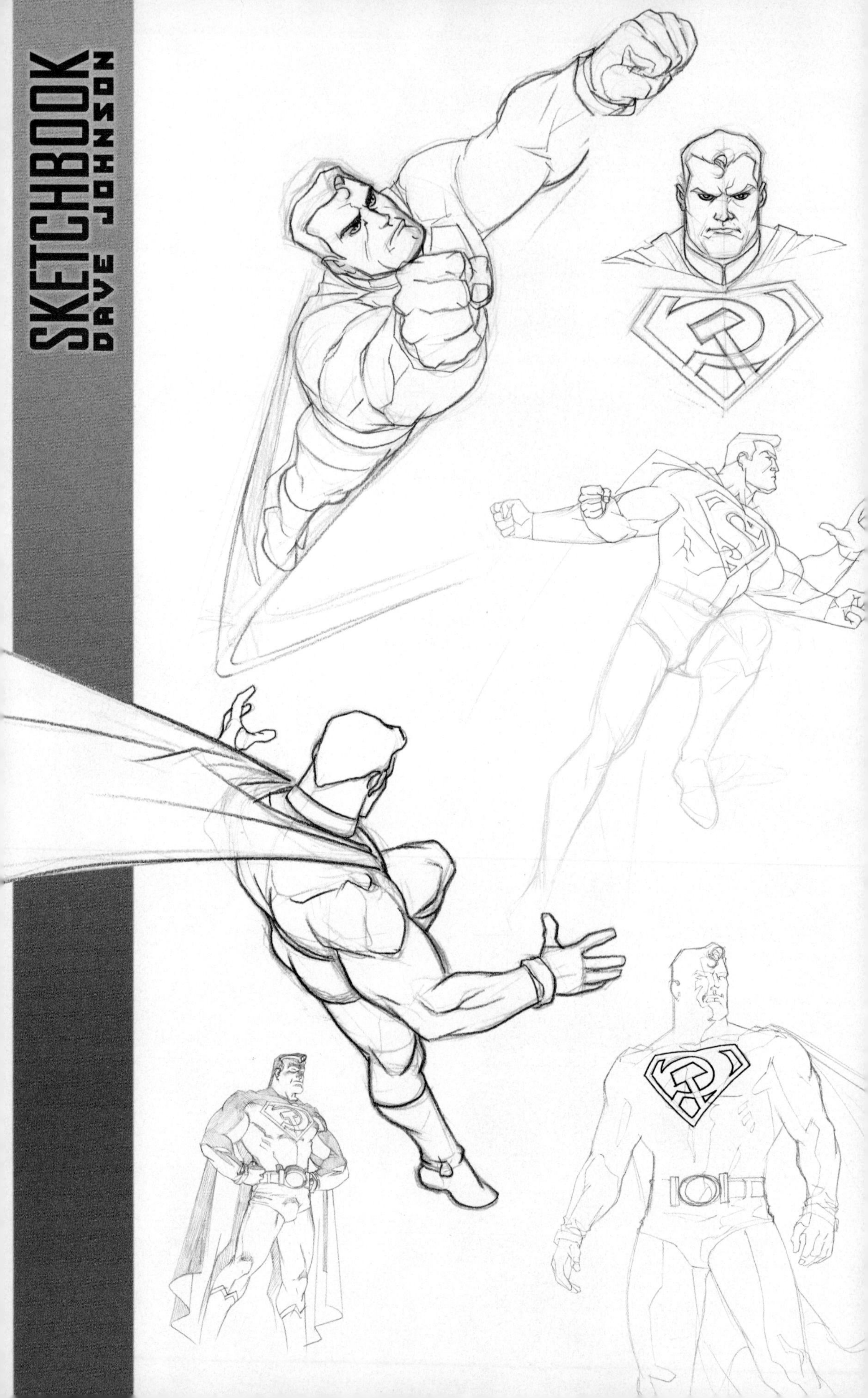

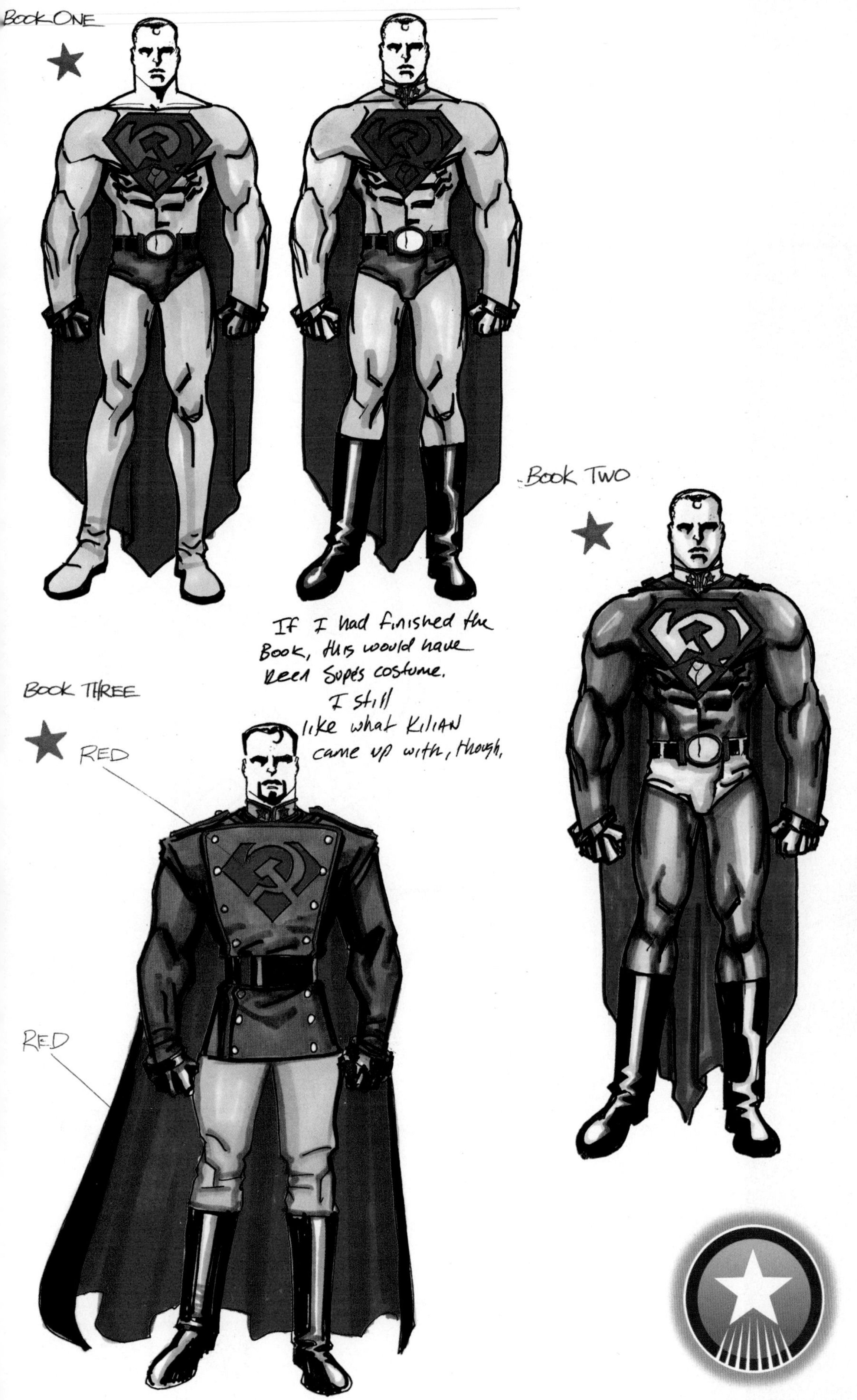

BOOK ONE
BOOK TWO
If I had finished the Book, this would have been Supe's costume. I still like what KILIAN came up with, though.
BOOK THREE
RED
RED

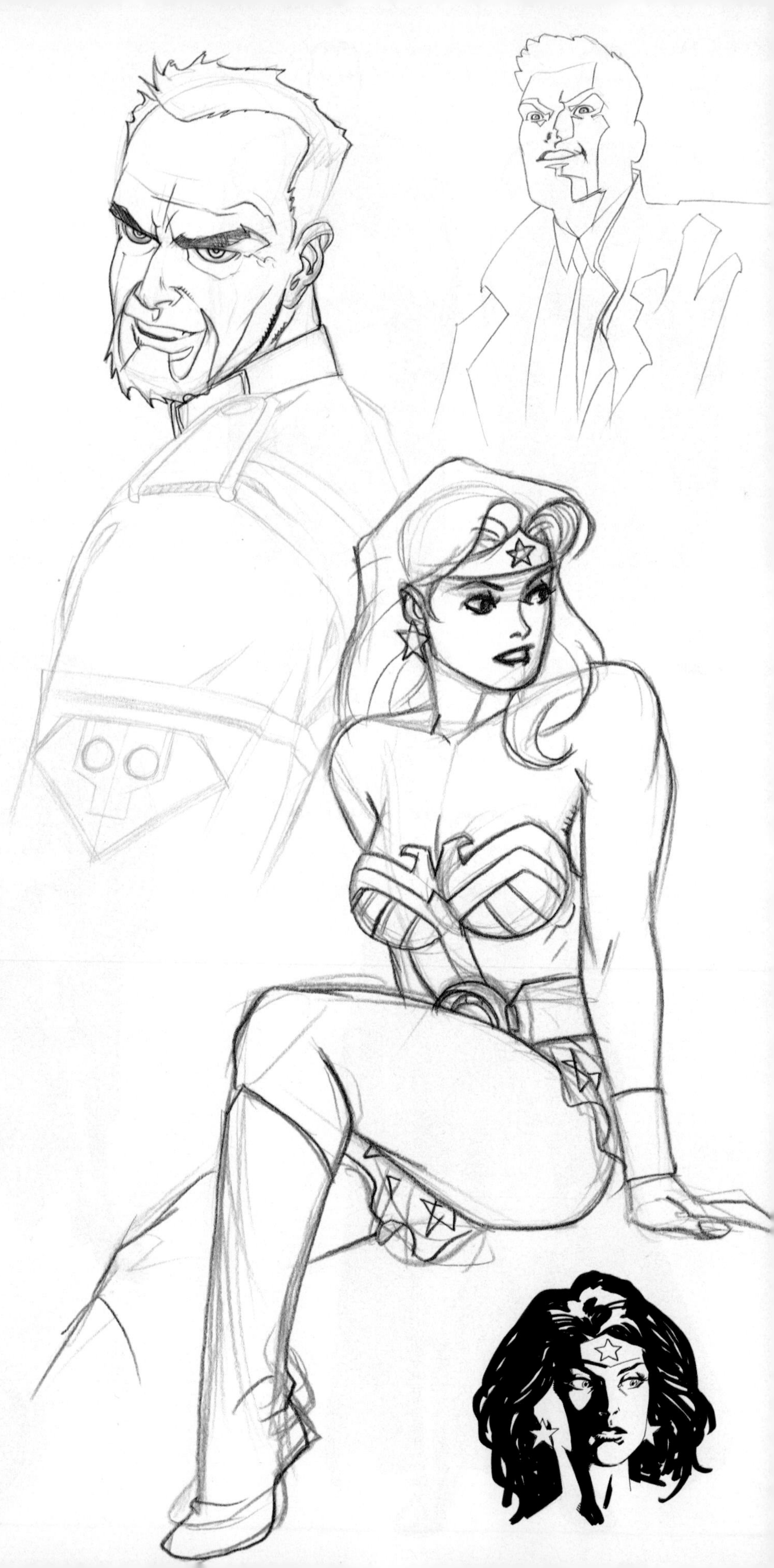

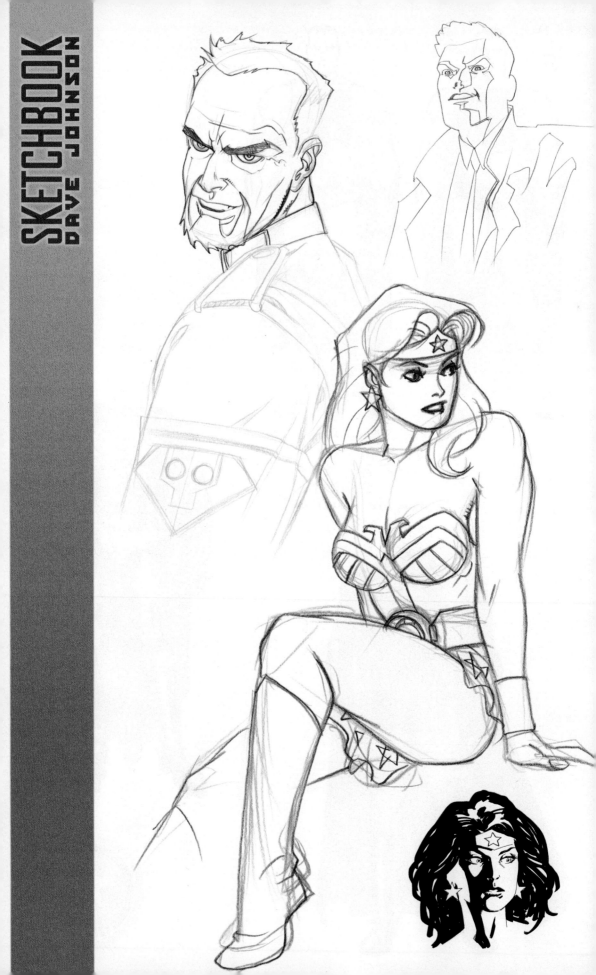

BATMANKOFF

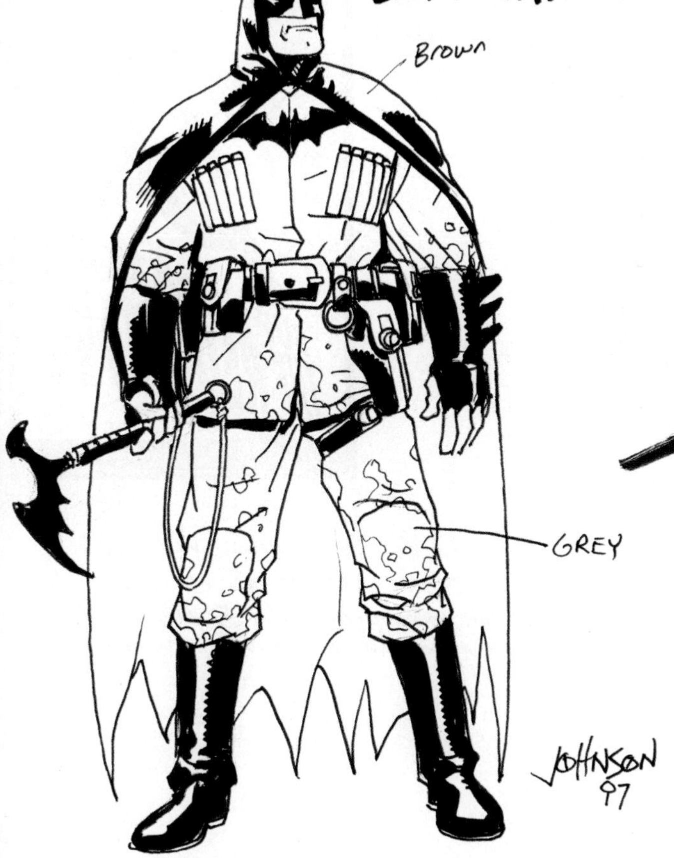

Brown
GREY
JOHNSON 97

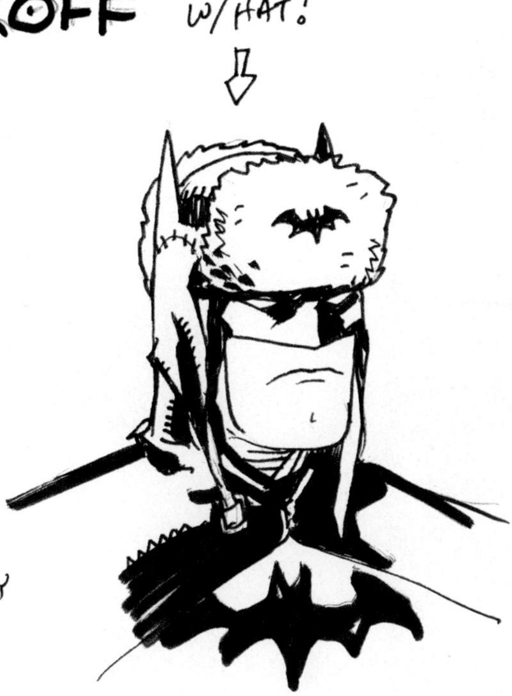

w/HAT!

I took a lot of crap from friends about this Hat. But I still like the design. Russia is cold. Why can't Batman have a warm hat?

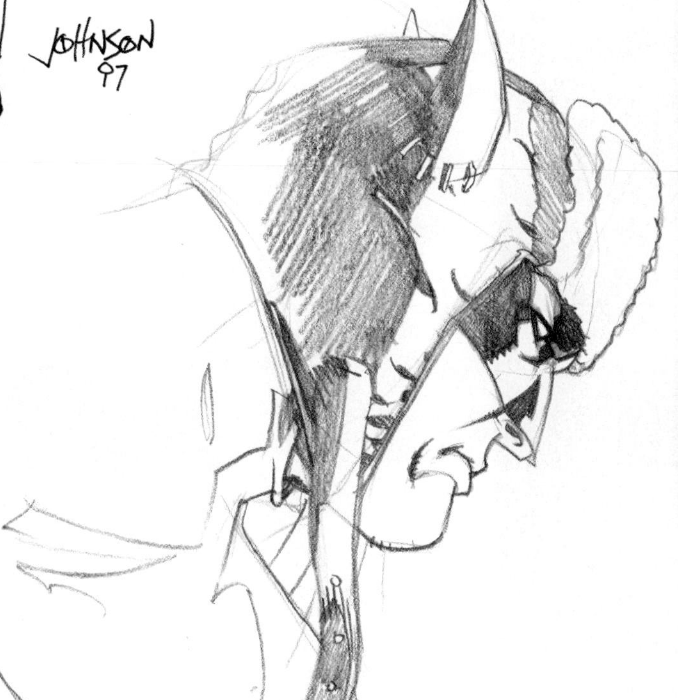

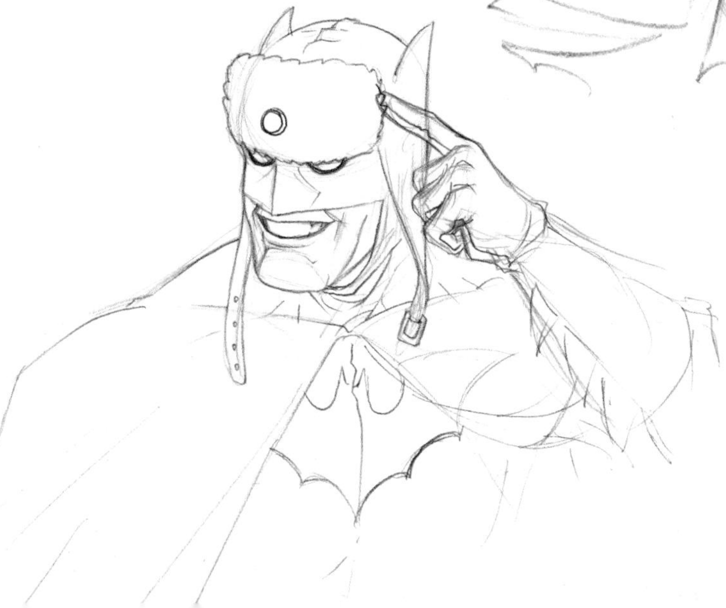

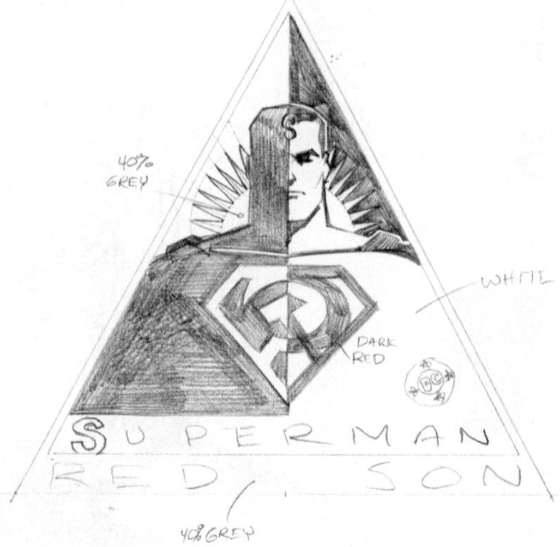
40% GREY
WHITE
DARK RED
SUPERMAN
RED SON
40% GREY

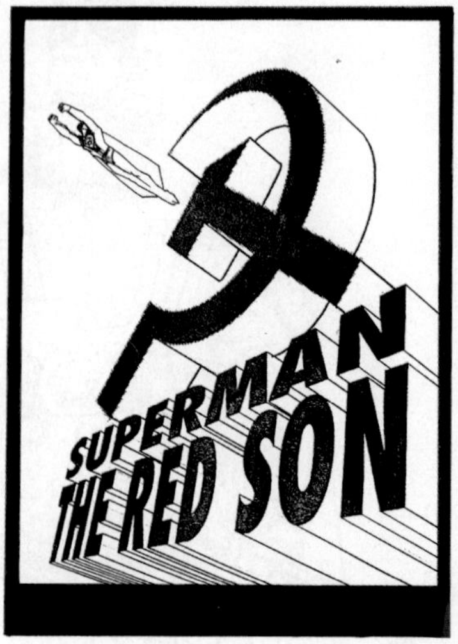
SUPERMAN
THE RED SON

AD LAYOUT FOR PAINTING

Here's two different ways to do the same shot. I think both work but a choice had to be made.
The final version had to be done with 5 point perspective. It's a real pain to do, but worth the effort.

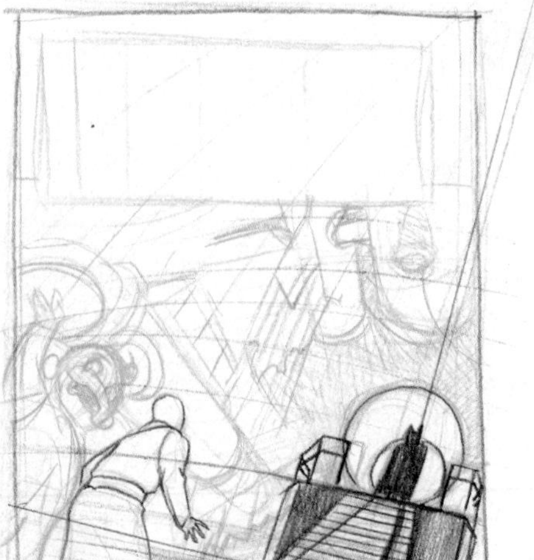

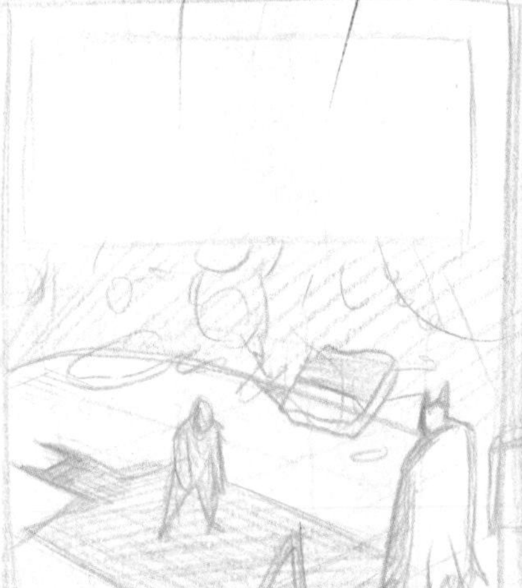

unlike most artists I like to do most of my work on scrap paper then lightbox the final design on the bristol board. Maybe thats why I'm so slow. But it eliminates the pressure of having to get it right on the page the first time.
not to mention I can enlarge or reduce the layout to suit my needs before I commit it to paper.

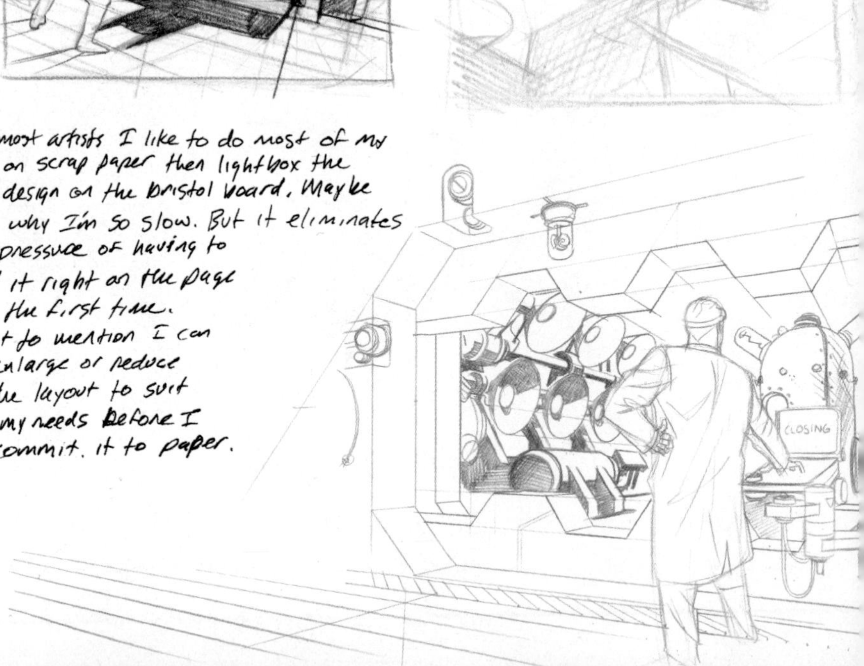
CLOSING

This was the first cover Idea for issue 3. But I felt it didnt fill up the space on the cover. Too much dead area on either side of the figure. Especially after reducing him down to fit under the Title logo. Well, at least it's SEEING the light of day in this book.

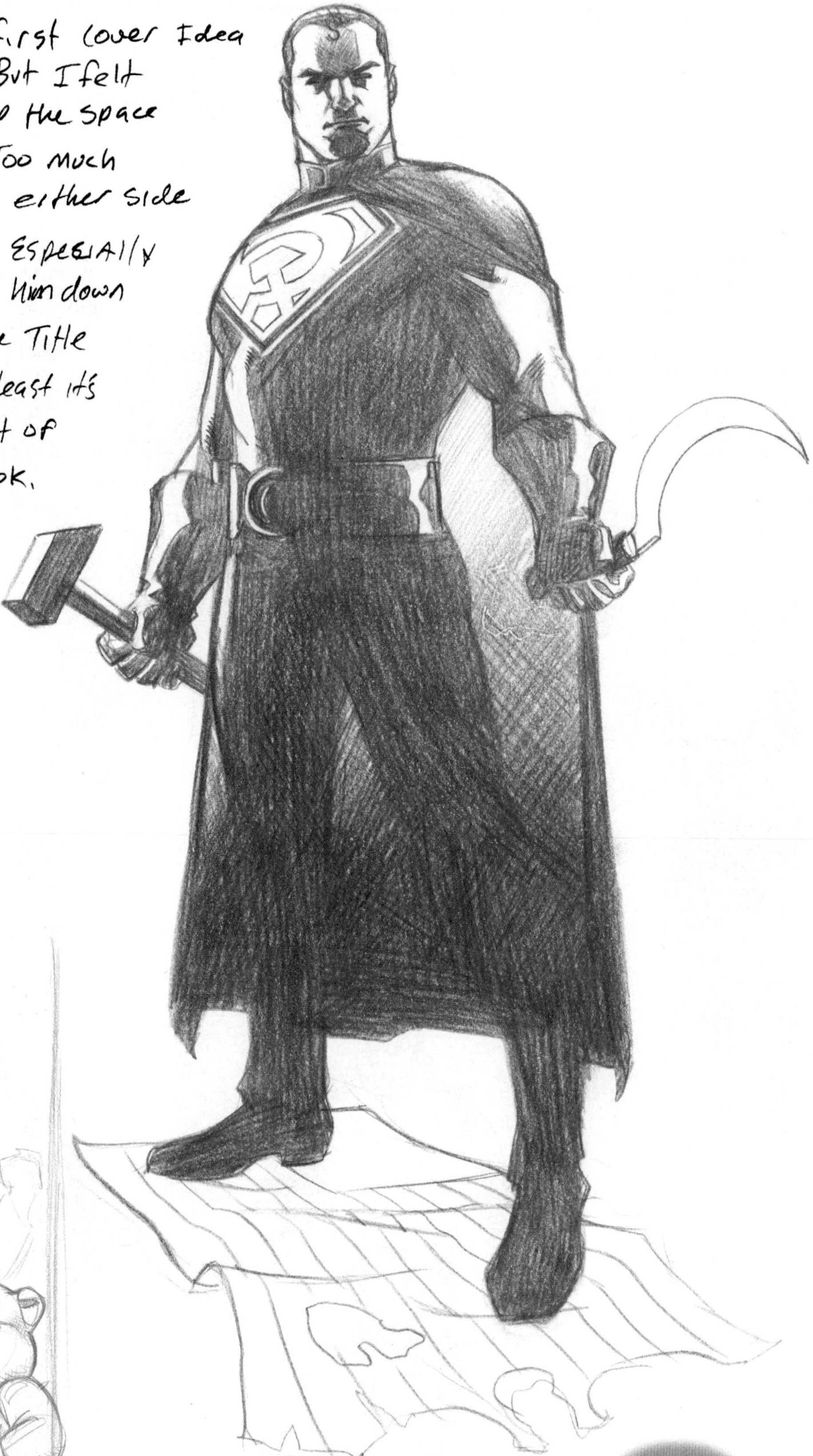

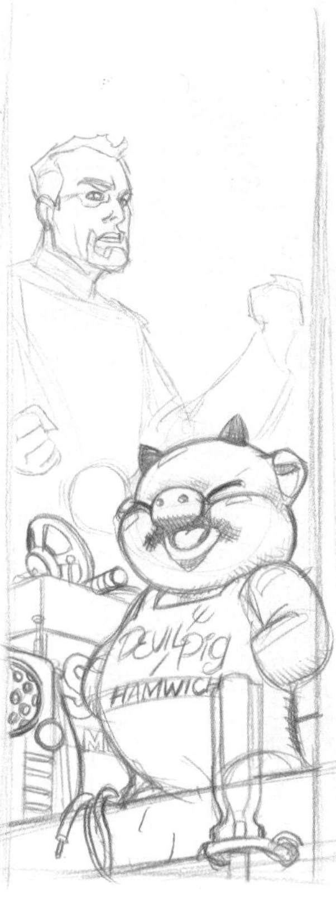
DevilPig
HAMWICH

AHHH, The Devilpig. This little bastard has been showing up Everywhere. Coming to a 100 Bullets cover soon.

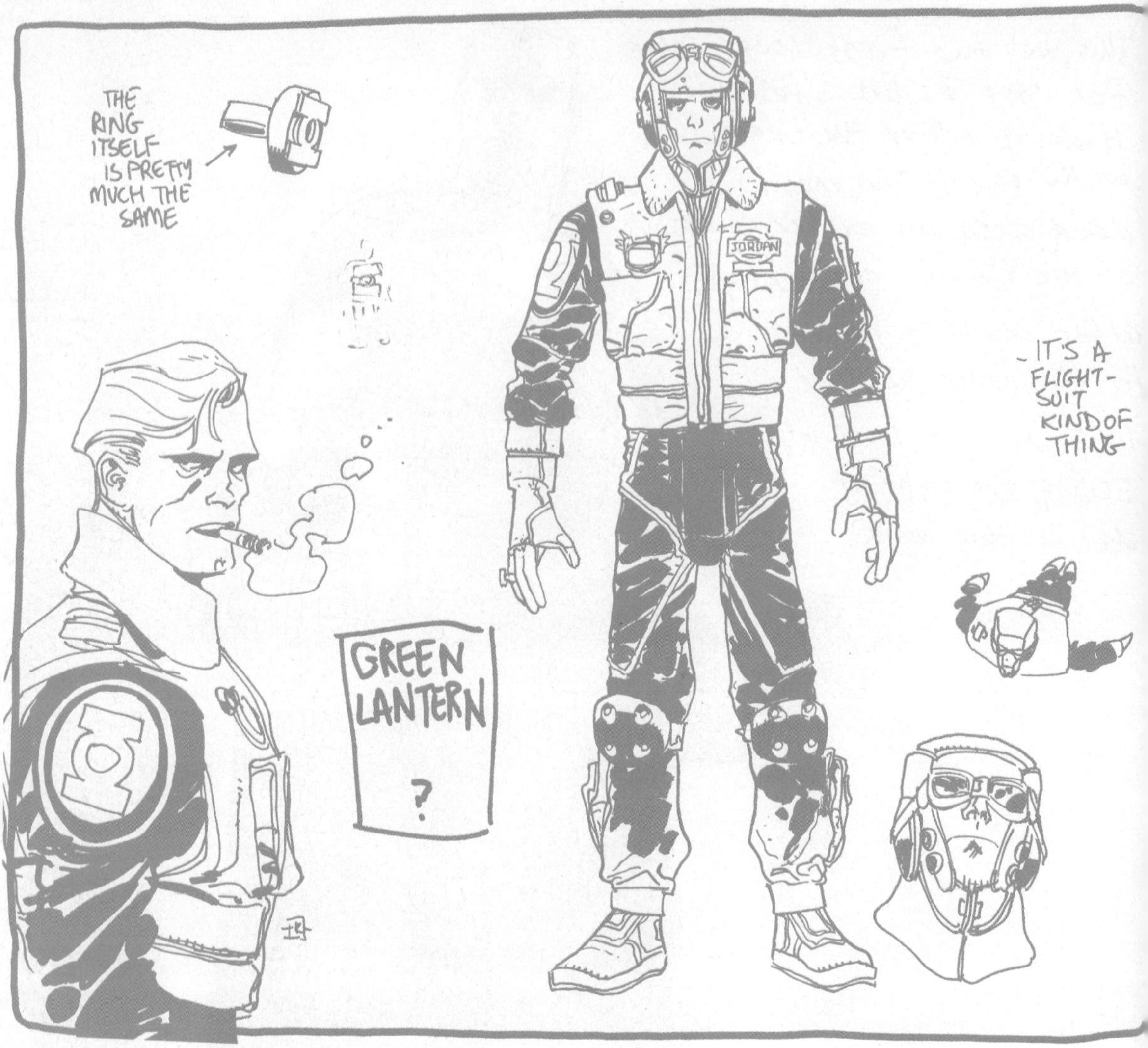
THE RING ITSELF IS PRETTY MUCH THE SAME
JORDAN
IT'S A FLIGHT-SUIT KIND OF THING
GREEN LANTERN
?

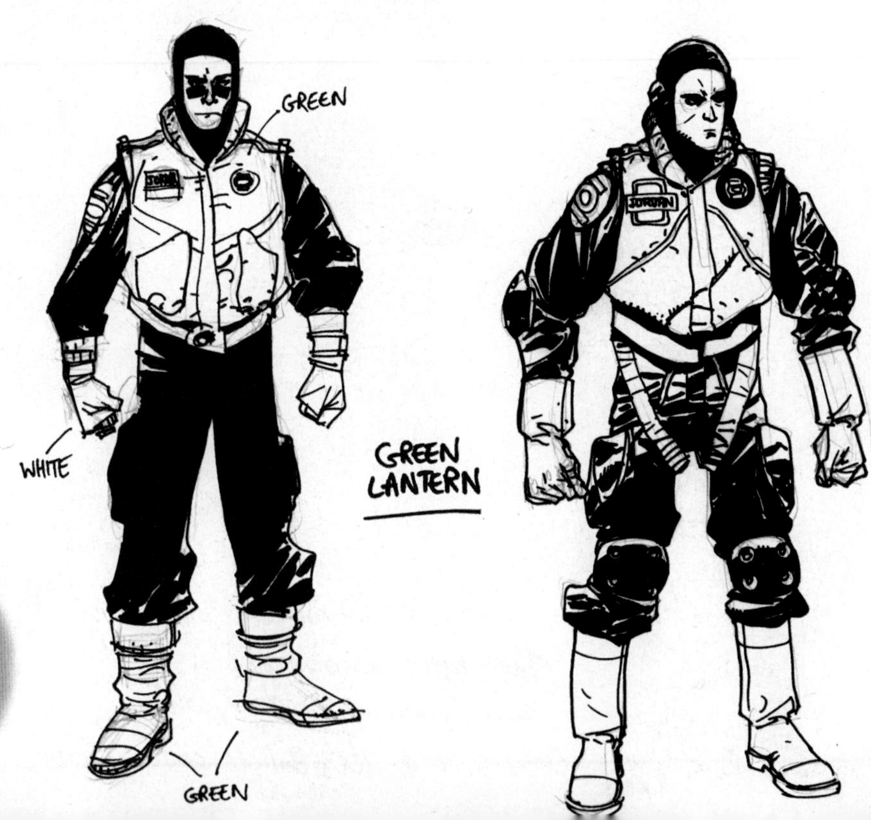
GREEN
JORDAN
WHITE
GREEN LANTERN
JORDAN
GREEN

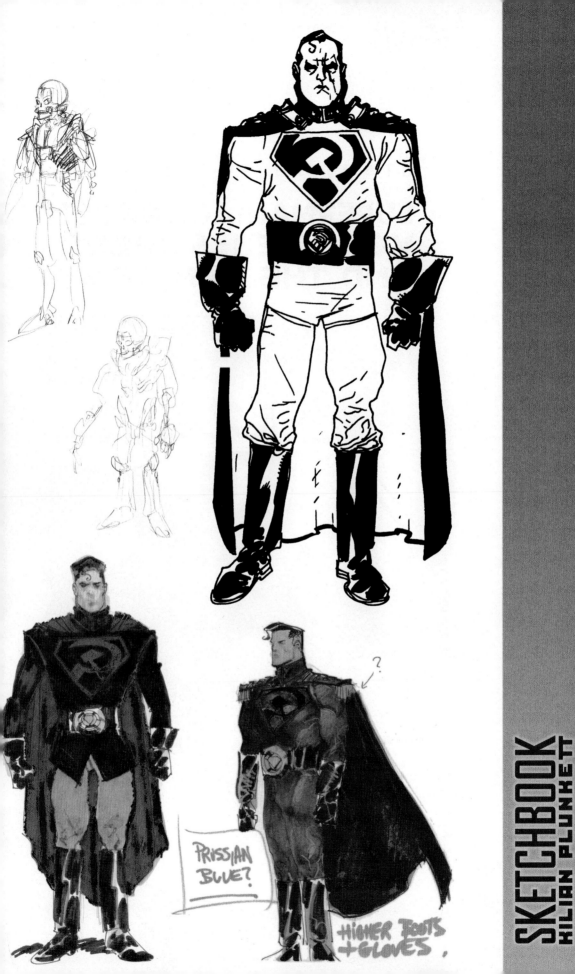

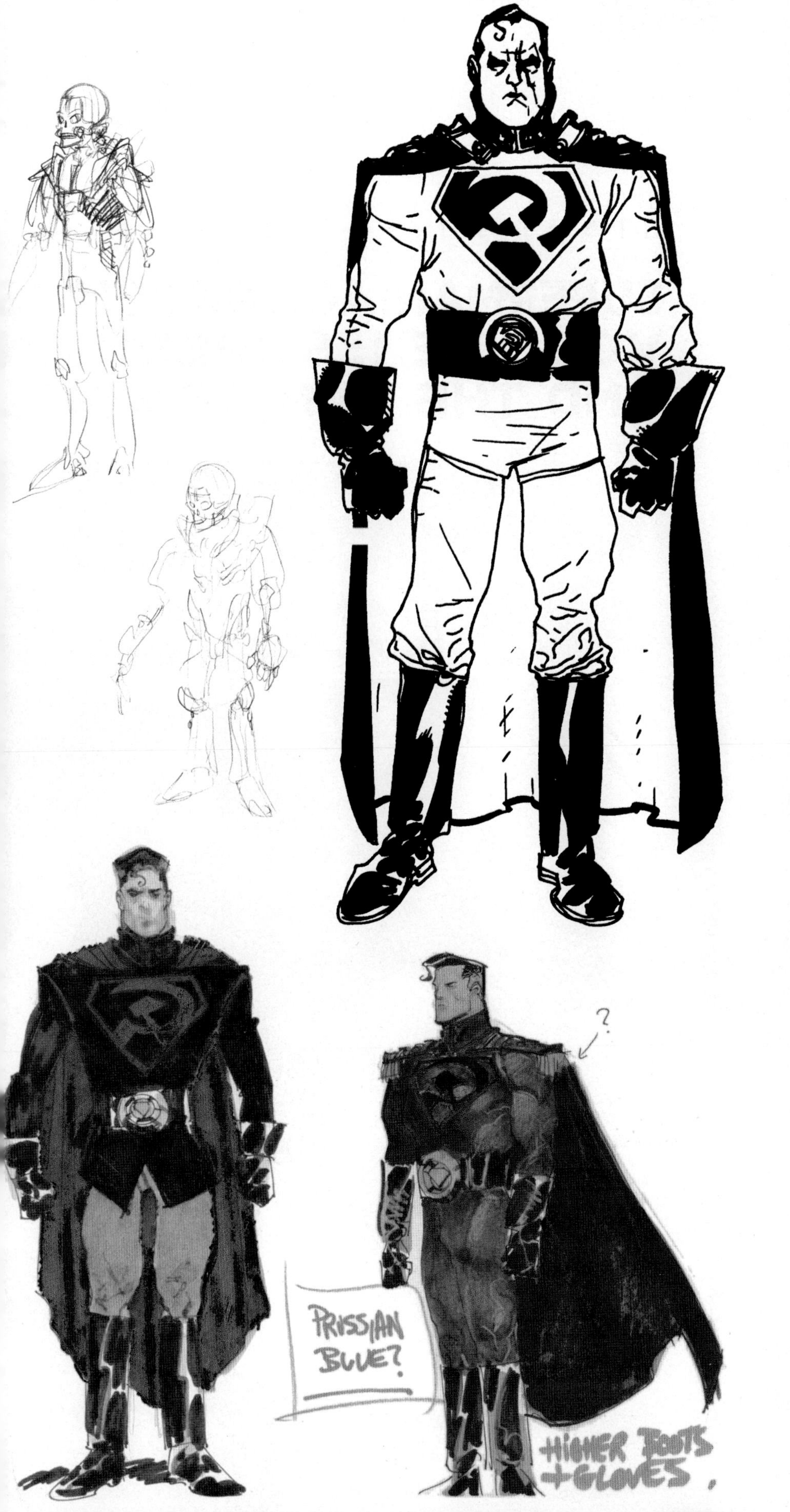
?
PRUSSIAN BLUE?
HIGHER BOOTS
+GLOVES.

*"It's fresh air. I like thi
all-too-human Superman, and I think
lot of you will, too.*
—SCRIPPS HOWARD NEWS SERVIC

START AT THE BEGINNING

SUPERMAN: ACTION COMICS VOLUME 1: SUPERMAN AND THE MEN OF STEEL

SUPERMAN VOLUME 1: WHAT PRICE TOMORROW?

SUPERGIRL VOLUME 1: THE LAST DAUGHTER OF KRYPTON

SUPERBOY VOLUME 1: INCUBATION

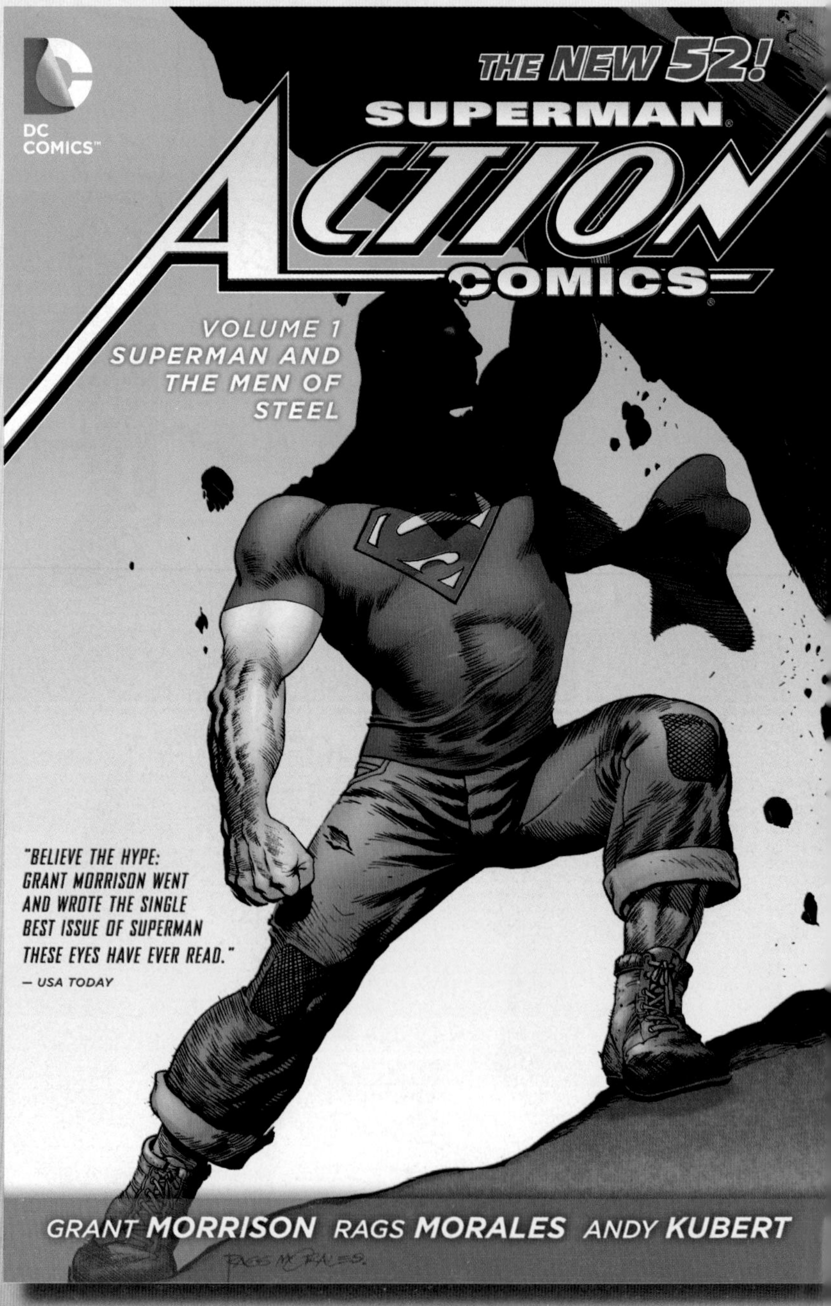

GRANT MORRISON RAGS **MORALES** ANDY **KUBERT**